FAITH & PHILOSOPHY
OF
ZOROASTRIANISM

INDIAN RELIGIONS SERIES: 7

FAITH & PHILOSOPHY OF ZOROASTRIANISM

Meena Iyer

Faith & Philosophy of Zoroastrianism

Rs. 675

ISBN: 978-81-7835-724-9

Published in 2009 in India by
Kalpaz Publications
C - 30, Satyawati Nagar,
Delhi - 110052
E-mail: kalpaz@hotmail.com
Phone: 9212729499

Printed at: Singhal Print Media, Delhi

DEDICATION

This book is dedicated to the loving memory of my late mother S. Thankamani who was a deeply religious and spiritual lady from a conservative and orthodox background. But her modern outlook and faith in the power of the girl child made me what I am today.

Contents

Preface

Zoroastrianism is a monotheistic form of religion. Its founder was Zarathushtra Spitama (Zoroaster, the descendant of Spitama). The religion believes in the existence of one God, whom it knows under the names of Mazda, Ahura and Ahura-Mazda. The religion has undergone more than usual fluctuations and variations.

Zarathushtra was one of the most revolutionary thinkers of his times. His advocacy of salvation and universal compassion and cosmic goodwill has a significant message for the present-day humankind. This book deals with almost every aspect of Zoroastrianism philosophy from personality to doctrine of Zoroaster, fundamental character, nature and spirit of philosophy. The book covers the subject of Zoroastrianism thoroughly in a manner which makes it interesting to read and easy to understand. A special care has been taken to put the principles of Zoroastrianism philosophy in proper order so that the reader finds the book very useful and enjoyable.

A sincere effort has been made to give elaborate details having deep bearing on minute details relevant to the subject. Efforts have been made to mention about the religious customs and ceremonies from birth to death, including religious verses. Indeed the information given in this volume is fairly comprehensive in contents so that all the readers should feel benefited with the text of the religion which they follow, preach, and profess.

A productive bibliography, along with references is provided to prove the authenticity of the work and in order to guide the scholars and readers for further studies. Hopefully, this volume would be able to satisfy the urge of all those who desire to know about Zoroastrianism and also to create a new awareness regarding this religion.

1

Zoroastrianism: An Introduction

Zoroastrianism is a religious belief founded in old times by the prophet Zarathushtra, recognized as Zoroaster. Zoroastrianism is the faith and philosophical system founded on the teachings offered by Prophet Zoroaster (Zarathustra, Zartosht). Mazdaism is the religious belief that acknowledges the heavenly authority of Ahura Mazda, declared by Zoroaster. Zoroastrianism was the main world religion during the Persian times (559 BC. to 330 BC.), and was thus the mightiest world religion at the time of Jesus. It had a great effect on other religious beliefs. It is still followed all over world, particularly in Persia and India.

The Zoroastrian faith, by many perceived to be an old Persian religion only, is as a matter of fact the First Universal and Monotheist religious belief in History. Reestablished Zoroastrianism has brought the benevolent Religion back to the World. It's not an eastern mystical religious sect or religious group, but a global religious faith for all humanity. Subdued and rarely remembered by the World during thousands of years, it is time to remember that God was seen in the basic instructions of Zoroaster, a thousand and more years ahead of any prophet who brought in "heavenly disclosures". Where future prophets described God in rather "humanlike" terms, Zoroaster never did. He understood a God, who's independent of being revered and obeyed and thus God is not about awe, guiltiness, torment, and conviction.

Arising out of the polytheistic customs of historical India and Iran, he was among the first monotheists in human history. Zarathushtra advocated that there was single God, whom he addressed as Ahura Mazda. Ahura means "Lord," and Mazda means "Wise," thus Zoroastrians call God the "judicious Lord." Zarathushtra is known in the West as Zoroaster, from the Greek translation of his name; in Persia and India he's recognized as Zarthosht. No one really knows exactly in which time period Zarathushtra lived. Zoroastrian custom places him at around 600 B.C., but this time is thought by current researchers to be far too late. The approximation of Zarathushtra's date is anyplace from 1500 to 1000 BC.

The fundamental Holy Scripture of Zoroastrianism is a set of five poems addressed as the Gathas, which were compiled by Zarathushtra himself and have been maintained through the millennia by Zoroastrian priests. Over the period many other religious texts have compiled around these Gathas. A great deal of these religious texts were destroyed by the Hellenic, Islamic, and Mongolian encroachments, but a few persist. The Gathas are still the central text of the religion. They are compiled in a very old dialect known as Avestan, which is intimately related to Sanskrit. The proof, researchers use to give a time extension to Zarathushtra is lingual: the dialect of the poems compiled by the Prophet is related to the Sanskrit of the Rig-Veda, an old Hindu text which is dated to the period of 1500-1000 BC.

In the Gathas, Zarathushtra advocated that the single God, Ahura Mazda, is superior, but he's in continuous persuance with humanity and the world God produced by his dimensions. These Characteristics are how God contacts the world, and how the world contacts God. Zarathushtra didn't assign a fixed number of dimensions, but shortly after the Prophet they were set into seven. These properties are called the Amesha Spentas, or "bighearted Immortals." Each one of these personifies a characteristic of God, as well as a human merit. They are also symbolic representations for the various spheres of Creation over which God watches. They are:

Vohu Manah: Good Thought - Connected with Animals

Asha Vahishta: Justice and Truth - Fire and Energy

Kshathra: Dominion - Metals and minerals

Spenta Armaiti: Dedication and Serenity - The earth and land

Haurvatat: Wholeness - Waters

Ameretat: Immortality - Plants

Spenta Mainyu: Creative Energy - Human beings

In the Gathas these are occasionally embodied, and some of the times just thoughts or notions. In future customs, they are embodied, and become like archangels. They are never revered on their own. The "dualism" of Mazdaism is known in the "West," but is mostly misinterpreted. In the Gathas Spenta Mainyu, the "Holy constructive Spirit," is opposed to Angra Mainyu, the unfriendly Spirit. This conflict takes place in the human heart and mind, not in the material World. It is the continuous struggle between good and evil in human beings. This is honourable dualism, the dualism of Good and Evil. In later customs this transferred into a dualism that took in the corporeal world, splitting the World into two camps, each controled by the Good God or the Evil. This is called "celestial" dualism. Some Zoroastrians consider in "celestial" dualism, others in honourable dualism. The commandments of the Gathas, the innovative work of the Prophet, incline towards honourable dualism.

Zoroastrian worship involves prayers and symbolic ceremonies said before a sacred fire. This fire, which was a symbol of God even before Zarathushtra, was employed by the Prophet and by his self controls ever after as the perfect sign of God, who's brightness, warmness and vitality. Zoroastrians do not idolize fire, as some people think. They use Fire as a symbolization, or an image, the focal point of their worship. Zoroastrianism does not teach or believe in rebirth or karma. Zoroastrians believe that hereafter on earth, the human spirit is pronounced by God as to whether it did more good or evil in its life. Those who picked out good over evil go to what Zarathushtra referred to simply as the "most respectable subsistence," or heaven, and those who chose evil go to the "most abominable subsistence," or hell. Zoroastrianism was one of the first religions to give the afterlife an ethical dimension. Zoroastrianism also believes in the progression of sanctified time, and the ultimate end of time. The impression is that the aggregated good acts of human race will slowly metamorphose the defective corporeal world into its heavenly ideal. This is identified as the "frasho-kereti," or "making-fresh," that is, replenishment. At the end of time everything and everybody will be purged, even the spirits in hell, so hell is not endless.

Zoroastrian thoughts of moral dualism, heaven and hell, sanctified time, and angelical beings have influenced Jewish religion and Christian religion, during long centuries of relationship between these religions in the Middle East. If there's anything to remember about Zoroastrianism, it's this multiple path. By conceiving good thoughts, one is moved to speak good language, and that leads to beneficial feats. This is a practical and world-affirming faith that doesn't detest the world nor linger over sin and guilt. Zoroastrians are mostly of Persian origin, though the break down of the Soviet Union has discovered obscure groups of Central Asian and Armenian Zoroastrians as well. In the tenth century AD. groups of Persian Zoroastrians fled an tyrannical Islamic government and settled in Gujarat, in west India. These are the Parsis of India, who are a major influence in Indian society nowadays. From India and Iran Zoroastrians have spread all over the world, and there are communities in England, Australia, Canada, the United States, and other countries. These diaspora communites now face the problems of how to adapt their ancient religious customs to a contemporary world.

MAJOR PRINCIPLES OF ZOROASTRIANISM

God: Ahura Mazda

The God is called Ahura Mazda, implying "Wise Lord." Ahura Mazda is all beneficial, and produced the world and all good things, including people. He is fought by Anghra Mainyu, implying "Destructive Spirit," the incarnation of evil and Maker of all evil t hings. The big celestial battle between good and evil will ultimately guide to the destruction of all evil.

Prophet: Zarathushtra

The religion was established by Zarathushtra. His date of birth is uncertain, but is probably somewhere around 1200 BC. He lived and preached in the Inner Asia. Zarathushtra obtained his revealings directly from Ahura Mazda, and from his Archangels).

Scripture: Avesta

The main Holy Scripture is the Avesta. The most sanctified parts of the Avesta are the Gathas or Hymns of Zarathushtra; they are also the most mysteries. Later sacred literature includes the Pahlavi Texts, which contain all-inclusive citations and paraphrases from missed Avesta texts.

Creed

The religious doctrine is summed up in Yasna 12. It is likely to have been compiled by Zarathushtra himself, and to have been used as an affirmation of religious belief by early converts.

Observances

Two sanctified dresses, the sudreh (shirt) and kusti (cord) are the symbolic representations of the religion. Zoroastrians execute a short ablutionary rite (Padyab), and retie the kusti several times a day with another short rite (Nirang-i Kusti) as a sign of their faith. Other prayers are recited daily from the Khorda Avesta. Supplication is largely done in the Avestan language. The disciple should also take part in seasonal communal festivals ("Gahambars") during the year.

Fire

Fire, as a symbolic representation of "Asha" and the "original light of God," holds a particular place of respect in the religion. Prayer is often done in front of a fire, and sacred fires are kept steadily burning in the major temples. The oldest Zoroastrian Holy Scripture is the Avesta. It is about a thousand pages long. Some parts, including the Gathas, are in an old dialect called 'Old Avestan' or 'Gathic Avestan'. The main surviving parts are:

Yasna: Sanctified Liturgy and Gathas of Zarathushtra

Khorda Avesta: (Text of Common Prayer) having Yashts (hymns to the sacred beings), Niyayeshes (addresses to the sun, Mithra, Water, Fire, and the Moon), Gahs (supplications for the five periods of the day), Afrinagans (ceremony of blessing), and other prayers.

Visperad: Extensions to the Liturgy.

Vendidad: Mainly purity laws, myths, and some medical texts

Fragments: The original Avesta canon contained twenty-two texts, (religious, historical, medical, legal). Its subsistence into the ninth century AD. is well attested. Since then much of the non-religious texts have been missed.

In addition to the Avesta, Zoroastrians have many scriptures from the Sassanian period which are written in a dialect called Pahlavi. Many are exegetic commentaries (called Zand) which interpret, summarise and explain the Avesta. The Pahlavi texts also preserve large summaries and translations of lost Avestan texts. They are believed to be of lesser authority than the Avesta.

Asha

Like 'Dao' in Daoism, Asha is a basic notion in the Gathas and throughout scripture. Also like 'Dao', it is too composite to be translatable by an single term. The more common translations are: trueness, morality ,virtuous, world-order, everlasting law, fitness.

Overview of Zoroastrian Scriptures

Abortion: A child is said to be shaped, and a spirit added to its body, after a woman has been pregnant for four months and ten days. In ancient times, as per the Vendidad, abortion was known to be set up by means of certain plants. It was regarded as murder.

Action: A thousand people cannot satisfy one by words to the extent that one person can satisfy a thousand by action.

Charity: This also is disclosed in the religious belief, that Ohrmazd said to Zartosht, 'He who does charity wittingly and discriminately is like me, I who am Ohrmazd. And he who performs charity obliviously and without understanding and indiscriminately is like Ahriman'. 'Charity is something so worthy, there are thirty-three ways from Garothman (Heaven) to the Chinwad Bridge, and everybody who is blessed on account of meritable action is then able to go on one way, and he who is blessed on account of oblations is able to go on all those ways'. 'Whatever benevolent men give, I give them double in return, and I store it up'.

Education: "It is the hope of Ahura Mazda from persons is this: 'Know me', for he knows: 'If they acknowledge me, everyone will follow me'. The hope of Angra Mainyu is this: 'Do not know me', for he knows: 'If they acknowledge me no one will follow me'."

Evolution: "How is creation brought about? Just as one substance is evolved out of some other concording as per its own laws and in the finite time.

Hell: Hell is just a temporary place, not a permanent place, of suffering for evildoers after demise. When evil is eventually defeated (at Frashegird), the spirits of sinners will be discharged from hell, and will be sanctified by the ordeal of liquified metal. They will then join the fold of God and the saints.

Hope: "There is a cure for everything but demise, a hope for everything but evil, and everything will lapse except virtuousness."

Joy: Angra Mainyu is better fought by joyousness; despondence is a indication of his victory.

Attentiveness: "As the spirit is thus not all, but is in the cosmos for an era of time for asserting the body, it is essential to walk with such circumspection as if one were without shoes, and the whole of this cosmos were full of snakes, scorpions, deadly reptiles, and thorns, and one's fear were: 'Let not the reptiles bite me, or the thorns interpenetrate me.'" In Zoroastrian theological system, paying attention is personified as Sraosha Hearkening.

Prophets: "The Maker Ahura Mazda addressed to Zarathushtra thus: 'O Zarathushtra! I have produced no one better than you in the world, and I shall as well not produce one better after you are gone. You are my chosen one, and I have made this world apparent on account of you. And all these people and monarchs whom I have produced have always asserted the hope that I should produce you in their days, so that they should assume the religion, and their spirits should achieve the supreme heaven.'"

Rebirth: The notion of rebirth is alien to Zoroastrianism. As per Dastur Firoze M. Kotwal, the current head priest of the Wadia fire temple, says "No rebirth as far as our faith is concerned, because if there is rebirth, then there cannot be the idea of resurrection, you see. So these doctrines go counter to one another. Of course, there is a tendency for bringing in rebirth from Hindu philosophies or something, because we are living among the Hindus. But no, this is all recent developments, just to appease the Hindus. But you must be disciple to our religion, because when you wish to bring in something in our religion that is strange, then there is peril of all other philosophies going topsy-turvy."

Obligation: "When Ahura Mazda the Master first produced humanity, He gave the following order: "Be persevering to save your spirits; I shall then provide for your corporeal matters. For it is unimaginable to save your spirits without you." People are deceived in the following manner: they themselves endeavour after material things, and as respect to the things of the spirit, they put their faith in the Yazads."

Suffering: "When someone stands in the faith of the Yazads, the Yazads notice the pain suffered by him in the world — even the fact that he came to pain by foot and that he lives legitimately on the work of his hands; and they carry and keep for him in the Considering of the Spirits (Armageddon) the uncomfortableness, crave, thirst, worry, and illness which affect him."

Truthfulness: "Zartosht asked Ohrmazd, 'Which is the one merit that is most beneficial for humanity?' Ohrmazd said, 'True speech is best, because in true speech there is good esteem in the world and good life and redemption in Heaven; as regards your descendants and progeny, by doing good deeds it will be better for their families, and your spirit will indeed be blessed'. For him who is condemned as regards (material) wealth for the sake of truth, it is better for him than for one who is sentenced as regards the spirit for untruth, because it is possible to collect wealth again, but when people have expired, their spirits pass on. Then there is no cure for it."

RELATIONSHIP WITH OTHER RELIGIONS

Zoroastrianism is unambiguously significant in the history of religious belief because of its possible shaping links to both Western and Eastern spirite customs. As the oldest of the revealed creedal religions, Zoroastrianism probably had more influence on humanity direct or indirectly than any other religion. It has been asserted that key notions of Zoroastrian eschatology and demonology had influence on the Ibrahimic religions. However, scholars also note that Zoroastrianism itself inherited ideas from other belief systems and, like other committed religions, adapts some degree of syncretism. For example, one of the popular strains within Zoroastrianism considers the representation of evil to have been one of God's creations that later on turned from God. This idea of a unity of a creative rationale is a relatively recent evolution and directly assigned characteristic to influence from Christianity, explicitly, the affect of Protestant missionaries on the Indian subcontinent during the 19th century. Many characteristics of Zoroastrianism can be traced back to the culture and notions of the prehistorical Indo-Iranian period, that is, to the time before the movements that led to the Indians and Persian becoming distinguishable peoples. Zoroastrianism consequently shares elements with the historical Vedic religious belief that also has its beginnings in that epoch. However, Zoroastrianism was also strongly affected by the later culture of the Iranian Heroic Age 1500 BC. onwards, an influence that the Indo-Aryan religions were not subject to. Moreover, the other culture groups that the various peoples came to interact with were different, for example in 6th-4th century BC. Western Iran with Geographical region culture, with each side engaging ideas from the other. Such inter-cultural influences nevertheless, Zoroastrian sacred scripture is essentially a product of Indo Iranian culture, and—constituting the oldest and largest corpus pre-Islamic Iranian orientation—is regarded a reflection of that refinement.

Then, together with the Vedas, which present the oldest texts of the Indian offshoot of Indo-Iranian culture, it is possible to reconstruct some facets of prototypical Indo-Iranian beliefs. Since these two groups of sources also represent the oldest non-fragmental evidence of Indo-European languages, the analysis of them also prompted attempts to characterise an even earlier Proto-Indo-European religion, and in turn influenced various uniting theories like those of Carl Gustav Jung or James George Frazer. Although these unifying beliefs deeply influenced the modernists of the late nineteenth- and early twentieth century, they have not fared well under the examination of more recent interdisciplinary peer review. The study of pre-Islamic Iran has itself undergone a revolutionary change in focus since the 1950s, and the field is today indisposed to speculation. Zoroastrianism is often equated with the Manichaeism, which is nominally an Iranian religion but has its beginnings in the Middle-Eastern Gnosticism. Superficially, such a comparing may be apt as both are uncompromising dualistic and Manichaeism nominally borrowed many of the Yazatas for its own memorial. As spirite types they are nevertheless poles apart: Manichaeism compared evil with matter and goodness with spirit, and was therefore especially suitable as a doctrinally base for every form of asceticism and many forms of religious mysticism.

Zoroastrianism then again declines every form of austerity, has no dualism of matter and spirit only of good and evilness, and sees the spritual world as not very different from the natural one and the word heaven applies evenly to both. Manichaeism's fundamental philosophy was that the world and all bodies were manufactured from the content of Devil, an idea that is basically at odds with the Zoroastrian notion of a world that was produced by God and that is all good, and any corruption of it is an consequence of the bad. From what may be deduced from many Manichean texts and a few Zoroastrian originss, the disciples of the two religions or at least their respective priesthoods hated each other intensely. Many aspects of Zoroastrianism are present in the culture and mythologies of the peoples of the Greater Iran, not least because Zoroastrianism was a prevailing influence on the people of the ethnical continent for a thousand years. Even after the rise of Islam and the passing of direct influence, Zoroastrianism remained part of the cultural inheritance of the Iranian language-speaking world, in part as festivals and customs, but also because Ferdowsi integrated a number of the figures and accounts from the Avesta in his epic Shaahnaame, which in turn is crucial to Iranian personity.

THE INDO-IRANIAN MOVEMENT

Several important faiths and movements originated in Greater Persia, that is, among speakers of various Iranian languages and hence with an Iranian ethnical background. The religions of pre-Zoroastrian Iran were polytheism ones, deriving, as Zoroastrianism would also, from the religions of the Indo-Iranian epoch. Famous notions among these was that of the ahuras and daevas, jointly termed the yazatas, suitable of worship, with each person, tribe or clan adopting one or more of these Gods as their patron or guardian entities, but collectively also recognizing and observing the patron divinities of other groups. In later Iran, the term daeva would acquire a negative intension, but this was not yet the case in the Old Iranian religions. Although these pre-Zoroastrian faiths are not directly evidenced, many of these pre-historical notion remain apparent in the texts of the Avesta, and therefore even in the Zoroastrianism of today.

Proto-Indo-Iranian religious belief is the term for the religious belief and notions of the Proto-Indo-Iranians, that is, the common forerunner of the several Indo-Iranian peoples. The Indo-Iranians, i.e. speakers of Indo-Iranian languages, include three different subgroups: speakers of the Indo-Aryan languages that is, the Indic branch including the Dardic languages; speakers of the Iranian languages both east and west and speakers of the Nuristani languages. From the notions of these respective and disseminated cultures, a set that is common to all may be remodelled. This hypothetical set is then what is in academic circles recognized as the beliefs of the Proto-Indo-Iranians, and from which the various religions of the various Indo-Iranian peoples then descended. Deities and heavenly notions that can be remodelled for this conjectural Proto-Indo-Iranian religion include the universal force rta Vedic rta, Avestan asha, the sanctified plant and drink sauma Vedic Soma, Avestan Haoma, and divinities of societal order such as mitra Vedic Mitra, Avestan and Old Persian Mithra, bhaga Vedic Bhaga, Avestan and Old Persian Baga.

Nevertheless, the notions developed in different ways as civilizations came apart and evolved. For example, while in the 'Indo-Aryan' branch Bhaga is a small deity in its own right, in the Iranian branch Baga is a general term for a divinity or group of deities. Likewise, the cosmogonical mythos mythos of the peoples that stayed on the Central Asian fields and the Iranian tableland is to a great degree unlike that of the Indians, perhaps in part because the Indians tended to focus less on the groups of deities daiva and asura and more on the divinities personally, while in Iranian customal knowledge the greater scheme - in which the divinities each play a part - gained attention. By the time of Zoroaster, Iranian culture had also been subject to the turmoils of the Iranian Heroic Age, late Iranian Bronze Age, 1800-800 BC., an influence that the Indians were not subject to. Moreover, the Indians, unlike the more conservative Iranians, were quite originative in their treatment of their Gods. As a result, some divinities were blended with others, or dividing occurred, that is, aspects of a deity grew into divinities in their own right.

Some times certain myths grew into ones completely different from their opposite number: For instance, in the Rig-Vedic Saraswati is lingually and functionally consanguine with Avestan Haraxvaiti Areduui Sura

Anahita. In the Rig-Veda she fights a snake called Vritra, who has amassed all of the earth's water. In contrast, Iranian Harahvati is the world-river that flows down from the central Mount Hara. But Harahvati does no fight - she is barricaded by an obstruction placed there by Angra Mainyu. This story, already attested in early portions of the Avesta, remained in common use as late as the first century AD., for from that century we have a Greek inscription devoted to Great Anaitis of High Hara. In the 1800s, because Vedic texts were until then the most previous lasting evidence of early Indo-European speaking peoples, it was presumed that these texts upheld aspects of Proto-Indo-European culture with special truth. It was thus believed that Indo-Iranian Gods were directly linked to Celtic, Norse, Greek and Roman belief systems.

Many scholars desired to merge these various European accumulations into a Proto-Indo-European belief system. Many a such thinkers, thought that all the Indo-Iranian religions started as forms of sun worship, an idea that has been given up in the early twentieth century. Such ideas shaped the emergence of New Age thinking about myth, and hypotheses such as Jung's belief collective unconscious. More late interpretings include those of G. Dumezil and his following who stress the three-way system of Indo-European religion and society. The system has more recently been expanded to four or even five functions. Although the unification theories of the 19th century no longer merit scholastic attention, contemporary scholarship still considers Proto-Indo-Iranian religion with its constituents of old Indic and old Iranian religion to be an archaic offshoot of a similarly unattested Indo-European religious belief and rite that can be rebuilt in many of their views, but and not unlike learners of Indic and Iranian religion has moved away from considering them near-identical. Rather, since early in the 20th century, the social function of the Indo-Iranian Asura divinities has been emphasized; they are an innovational group not found in Indo-European religion.

REFERENCES

Aerpatastan: Translated from the Avesta-Pahlavi texts by S.J. Bulsara. Bombay, 1915.

Andarz-i Atarpat-i Maraspand: The Pahlavi text, edited and translated by Peshutan Dastur Behramji Sanjana. Bombay, 1885.

Avesta: Translated into English by James Darmesteter and L. H. Mills. In *Sacred Books of the East*, vols, 4, 23, 31.

Balsara, P. P.: Ancient Iran. Its contribution to Human progress. Bombay, 1936.

Bartholomae, Christian: Altiranisches Wörterbuch. Strassburg, 1904.

Cama Memorial Volume: Edited by J. J. Modi. Bombay, 1900.

Carter, G. W.: Zoroastrianism and Judaism. Boston, 1918.

Casartelli, L. C.: The Philosophy of the Mazdayasnian Religion under the Sassanids. Translated from the French by Firoz Jamaspji Jamasp Asa. Bombay, 1889.

Dabistan: Translated from the origina1 Persian by Shea and Troyer. 3 vols. Paris, 1843.

Dadachanji, F. K.: Light of the Avesta and the Gathas. Bombay, 1913.

Encyclopaedia of Religion and Ethics: Edited by James Hastings. 12 vols. Edinburgh, 1908-1921.

Ganj-i Shayigan: The Pahlavi text, edited and translated by Peshutan Dastur Behramji Sanjana, Bombay, 1885.

Gatha: Translated into English by J. M. Chatterjee. Navsari, 1933.

Hadokht Nask: The Pahlavi text, edited and translated by Hoshangji Jamaspji Asa, Martin Haug, and E. W. West. Bombay, 1872.

Harlez, C. de: Les Origines du Zoroastrisme. Paris, 1878, 1879.

Lommel, Hermann: Die Religion Zarathushtras nach dem Avesta dargestellt. Tubingen, 1936.

Lord, Henry: The Religion of the Parsees. London, 1630.

Reitzenstein, R.: Das Iranische Erlösungsmysterium. Bonn, 1921.

Rezwi, T.: Parsis: A People of the Book. Calcutta, 1928.

Rindtortr, E.: Die Religion des Zarathushtra. Weimar, 1897.

2

History

This historical Iranian faith of fire, light, and wiseness still lives today. It is the first monotheistic religion, established by the prophet Zarathushtra. Zarathustra was regarded to have lived during 600 BC. in Persia (the area covered by contemporary Iran and Iraq). Current approximations have revised this date to anywhere between 1500 BC. and 1000 BC. This would make Zoaroastrianism the second oldest Earthly religion, next only to Hinduism. In later times, faith's's priests assumed great power by their mastery of the techniques of cleaning. The priests also had great influence on the regime in the part of Zoroastrianism, that under the Achaemenids, when it was for a time the nation religion. Alexander's subjugation of Persia and the break up of the Achaemenids destroyed the favoured position of Zoroastrianism. Little is known of the religion for the next 500 years, except that a branch, Mithraism (striving from the worship of Mithra), was taking control farther west. Zoroastrianism reappeared under Ardashir I, who established the Sassanian dynasty and fostered a general revival of Achaemenian culture. For four centuries Zoroastrianism was the state religion of the Sassanids, and it successfully met the challenge of emerging Christianity and, later, of dissident Manichaeism. In the mid-seventh century. Persia fell to Islam, and Zoroastrianism almost vanished. Aside from the Parsis of India, fewer than 100,000 persons practice the faith today. Zoroastrianism impacted Judaism (specially during the time of the Captivity) and, through Theological doctrine, Christianity.

ORIGIN

There are many guesses for Zarathustra's date of birth, many deviate by almost 1,000 years. The truth will remain an enigma, but his commandments and his notion in monotheism have continued throughout history. Many scholars believe he was a priest and a prophet. He was associated to the Magi. His spritual influences have always affected human thought and reasoning and his aims, to show human their association a creation and their link to one source. The name Zarathustra is a combination of two words, zarata- "weak", and usatra- "camel", meaning "the one who owns old camels". The first part of the name was at one time commonly interpreted as "yellow" or "golden", from the Avestan "zaray", intending "having yellow camels". The later Zoroastrians said that the name meant "Golden Light," deriving their meaning from the word zara and the word ushas, light or dawn. There is no doubt about Zarathushtra's tribe name, which is Spitama, implying "white." Zarathushtra's father was called Pouruchaspa (many horses) and his mother was called Dughdova (milkmaid). His birthday is observed on March 26, as part of the Iranian New Year Festival.

Some fables place his birth in west Iran, maybe near Tehran; others, which are fairly more likely due to the eastern Iranian language of his versewriter, place his place of birth in the east. As for the date of his birth, it has been since ancient times a subject of argument. Greek sources placed him as early as 6000 BC., a calculation derived from poorly transmitted Zoroastrian fables; few scholars take that date seriously. The traditional Zoroastrian date for Zarathushtra's birth and ministry is around 600 BC. This is derived from a Greek source that places him "300 years before Alexander" which would give that date; other principles for the 600 BC. date identify the King Vishtaspa of Zarathushtra's Gathas with the father of the Persian King Darius, who lived around that time. The enigma of Zarathushtra's time will never be solved. Most historians agree on a time-frame for Zarathushtra which could be between 1700 BC. and 1000 BC.

Zarathushtra encountered his prophetical calling in about his thirtieth year, in which he saw God through Vohu Manah, or "Good Mind." His divinations were not predicting of the future, but radical messages of religious pureness and social justice, speaking out against corrupted priests and dictators. He and his followers roamed until they found a good-hearted friend in King Vishtaspa, who was not the father of King Darius but an earlier sovereign of the same name, who may have lived in eastern Iran or in Bactria, contemporary Afghanistan. There, Zarathushtra won over the King, and his court, and became the court prophet. Zarathushtra is said to have had six children, three boys and three girls. This is not accurate data, since the number and gender equals that of the six Amesha Spentas and may be only symbolic. But the last Gatha is compiled for the marriage of Zarathushtra's daughter Pouruchista (Full of Knowledge) so he is known to have had at least one child. Zarathushtra, in the fables, had three wives of whom the last was Hvovi (Good Cattle) the daughter of King Vishtaspa's chancellor. Hence Zarathushtra wedded into the King's court; Pouruchista, in turn, married the prime minister.

Once again, no one knows how Zarathushtra expired. Many fables, and Zoroastrian custom, say that he was killed, when praying in the sanctuary, by a strange enemy of the King. But there is no holiday remembering the martyrdom of the Prophet, as there would be in other religions (Christianity, for example) and other Zoroastrian customs, and scholars, say that Zarathushtra expired peacefully. He spent years in the wild communicating with God before his first vision, in which Vohu Manah came to him in the form of an immense Angel. All the celestial entities, the Amesha Spentas, taught Zarathushtra in heaven, and he obtained perfect cognition of past, present, and future. Zarathushtra's discourse to King Vishtaspa was raised by miracles, particularly the curing of a paralytic horse that convinced the King to take on the new religion.

Zarathushtra was never a God, not even in the most exuberant legends. He continued as a man like all others, though heavenly empowered with aspiration and intimacy to Ahura Mazda. His life is an inspiration for Zoroastrians of all thoughts, traditionalist and contemporary - in his notion, loving relationship with God, and spritual courageousness he is an example for all his followers. After his demise. Zarathushtra's great spirit attains almost the level of a Bountiful Divinity, but still is not merged in the divinity. Ever since ancient Greek times the name of Zoroaster has stood for mystical Eastern knowledge. In Hellenistic times many secret and occult texts were written using his name and Zoroaster was looked upon as one of the greatest wizards.

Once the Avesta had been brought to the West in the eighteenth century, his name again became celebrated in the West for the humane, monotheistic, ethics found in the Gathas. Enlightenment philosophers mentioned him as a model; the dramatist Voltaire wrote a drama called "Zoroaster." A major celebrity in the history of the religions of the world, Zoroaster has been the aim of much attention for two reasons. On the one hand, he became a fabled figure believed to be associated with occult cognition and magical practices in the Near Eastern and Mediterranean world in the Hellenistic Age (300 BC. 300 AD.).

Then again, his monotheism notion of God has attracted the attention of contemporary historians of religious beliefs, who have mused on the associations between his teaching and Judaism and Christianity. Though extreme claims of pan-Iranianism (i.e., that Zoroastrian or Iranian ideas moulded Greek, Roman, and Jewish thinking) may be dismissed, the permeating influence of Zoroaster's religious thought must all the same be accepted.

EARLY HISTORY

The Median Kingdom

Zarathushtra advocated his religion at the end of the mythical Kyanian dynasty in the sovereignty of King Vistashpa. ModernisticContemporary historians put the date of Zarathushtra around 1200 BC. Shortly after the demise of Vishtaspa the Kyanian Kingdom seems to have decomposed, or even the mythical records are absent. However the faith of Zarathushtra prospered among the Iranian people of north eastern Iran, even without the backing of the Kyanian dynasty. Some of the customs and beliefs of the religions with which the Zoroastrian Iranians came in contact with, were assumed into the religion as well as some of the pre-Zoroastrian customs and beliefs. The first mention of the Iranian people in recorded history is 869 BC., in Assyrian texts . The history of the Iranian people between 1200 and 869 BC. remains an enigma, and we can only estimate what happened. It seems that the Iranians were transmigrating along the mountains of Iran. They started migrating west from Bactria (Afghanistan) towards Mazinderan (Caspian Sea area) along the Elburz Mountains and the south and east along the Zagros chain between the desert of Iran and the Persian Gulf.

Around 850 BC. we know that the Iranians were separated into two big groups. One living in Media and the other in Parsua (Persia). Media is the region southwest of the Caspian Sea and east of the Tigris River, and Parsua is south and east of Media. At this time the Medians and the Parsuans were under the token rule of the Assyrian kingdom and paid safety to the Assyrian kingdom when forced to do so by Assyrian encroachers. Between intrusions they were left very much on their own and even had their own Kings. The first Median King in recorded history is Deioces (known to Assyrians as Daiaukku) who in 670 BC. brought down the Assyrian sovereign of Media and set up a free Median Kingdom. His capital was Ecbatana (Hamadan).

His son was Froartes who governed for twenty years. He tried to take over Assyria but was overcame. He conquered Parsia and made it a vassal state of Media. Fravartish was followed by his son Cyarxes I. In

614 BC. he made a coalition with Babylonia and assaulted Assyria and conquered the capital Nineveh. He then tried to extend his kingdom into Lydia (contemporary Turkey). A long war with Lydia ended when the total solar eclipse of May 28, 585 BC. scared the two forces into burying the hatchet. This exact date of the end of the war is available to us because eclipses of the sun and moon can be computed exactly both backward and forward in time. Astyages was the next King of Media. He governed for a very long time until he was overthrown by Cyrus the Great who founded the first Persian kingdom.

From the time of Fravartish the Parsuans (Persians) were under Median rule but had their own sovereigns. Hakhamanish (700-675 BC.) was the first Persian King. His son was Teispis (also known as Chispish) who governed from 675 to 640 BC. He separated his Kingdom between his two sons and from that time on to 659 BC., there were two Kingdoms in Persia. One of Chispishs' son was Cyrus I (640 to 600 BC.) his rule was succeeded by his son Cambyses I (590-559 BC.), whose son Cyrus II known in history as Cyrus the Great established the Hakhamanian kingdom named after the first Persian King Hakhamanish. The other son of Chispish was Ariamnes (640 to 615 BC.). His son Arsamnes governed about 590 BC. and was succeeded by Hystaspes (Vishtashpa). His son Darius I, became the Persian king after Cambyses II the son of Cyrus the Great.

The Hakhamanian Kingdom

Cyrus the Great: Cyrus II became sovereign of Anshan (one of the two Persian Kingdoms) on the demise of his father Cambyses I (Kambujiyeh). Soon after he became King he captured the other Persian Kingdom of his cousins and founded a single Persian Kingdom. Cyrus was an exceedingly aspirational man. From the beginning he showed signs of independency from the Median King Astyages who was his master. Around 550 BC. Astyages saw the risk from the Persian King and resolved to teach him a lesson. He declared war on Cyrus who met him in battle on the plain of Pasargadae. Cyrus was a natural leader, men looked up to him and he had a personal magnetism about him, such that seeing him, the Median army revolted against their sovereign Astyages and delivered to Cyrus their own King as a captive. Ecbatana (capital of Media) surrendered to Cyrus.

Unlike previous Kings, Cyrus excused both the city of Ecbatana and Astyages, neither were harmed in any way. Median functionaries kept their businesses and their titles, but were monitored by Persians. Cyrus now had at his control the excellent Median army and he turned his attention to Lydia ruled by King Croesus. King Croesus saw the defeat of the Medians by the Persians as a sign helplessness and a chance to capture some Median territory. Cyrus was ready to defend his newly won kingdom. In one month he took his army 1200 miles to Pteria and there the two forces fought. Neither side won, but Croesus decided to pull out, since wintertime was coming. He returned to Sardis his capital and believing that there would be no more fighting until spring, he paid off his soldiers. Cyrus believed in a strategy of surprise, doing things that his opponents never expected. He waited just long enough for Croesus to pay off his troops and then got ahead swiftly to Sardis. Croesus hurriedly called back his troops and the two forces met in battle outside of Sardis. Now Cyrus had another surprise. Recognizing that horses are always afraid of camels, he put his baggage camels bestrode by soldiers out in front and charged the Lydian cavalry.

The smell of the charging camels frightened the Lydian horses and they ran off in every direction. The Lydians lost the battle but were able to retreat into the fort of Sardis. With winter coming Cyrus was in no position to lay siege to the fort. On the thirteenth day he attacked the fort from the most difficult, least defended side. He managed to enter and conquer Sardis. Croesus killed himself by having himself burned at the funeral pyre. The conquest of Lydia brought all of Ionia (contemporary Turkey) under the Persian kingdom.

Cyrus turned east again making a point that the Medians were still under his dominion and then went on north and east, capturing Parthia (old Mazinderan) and Bactria (Afghanistan) and then north to the Oxus river to the Aral sea, throughout the Central Asian plains to the Jaxartes river (Syr Daria). These areas populated by nomadic tribes became part of the kingdom. He declared the Jaxartes river as his north eastern limit. He constructed a series of seven fortresses to guard his north eastern boundary. All these conquests in the north east were done in one year. He had doubled the area of his kingdom and now had the greatest army in the whole world. Cyrus was now ready to take on Babylon, the richest city known to him. Babylon was ruled by Nabonidus, who was not popular with his subjects as he did not take care of the Gods and temple of Babylonia. In 540 BC., Cyrus started his crusade. His army arrived at the Gyndes river and founded it to be not shallow. The Babylonians regarded this river as a limit across which no army could come. Again Cyrus did the unexpected, he told his soldiers to start excavating one hundred eighty channels so as to deviate the water. The water level fell in the river as the water spread out into the diversions and his army crossed the river Gyndes into Babylonia. The Babylonians met his army at Opis and were defeated and sixteen days later Cyrus was at the gates of Babylon. The city wall was unsurmountable and only broken where the river Euphrates entered and left the city. Babylon had food supplies to last twenty years, a siege would not have succeeded. Cyrus used his cleverness once again. He had his soldiers dig ditches round the city wall deep enough to divert much of the rivers water round the city. The waterline of the river fell and Cyrus' army moved into the city using the river bed where the Euphrates entered the city, Babylon fell down to the Persians.

In those times it was customary for the encroachers to kill off the habitants or take them captive as slaves, burn and plunder the city. As soon as the city was securely in his control, he told his soldiers not to harm the citizens. He left their temples alone and went to pay respectfulness to their chief God Marduk. The result was that the Babylonians regarded Cyrus as their own King rather than an encroacher. At this time the Jews were slaves in Babylonia. Cyrus ordered them freed and permitted them to return to Jerusalem to rebuild their temple. He even promised to pay for the rebuilding of the temple. Today, the ruins of the second Jewish temple still stand, known as the Wailing Wall in Jerusalem. It is a holy place for the Jews. In the Old Testament Cyrus is regarded as anointed by the Master for his largesse to the Jews. Cyrus left his son Cambyses and a noble Gobryas to rule Babylon and returned to Ecbatana. He was now the sovereign of the greatest kingdom known to history up to that time. Each captured land became a Satrapy, governed by a Satrap. The military garrison in each Satrapy reported directly to the great King. Often royal inspectors journeyed openly or in camouflage to report circumstances in each Satrapy to Cyrus, King of Kings, King of all Lands, the title that Cyrus most often used.

After his comeback from Babylon Cyrus constructed his new capital Pasargadae, on the plain where he had overcame the Median King Astyages and started his conquerings. In Pasargadae he built his grave. Some years later the tribes north of the Jaxartes river united under a queen Tomyris and intruded on his kingdom. Cyrus led his army to fight the encroachment. In the battle that followed Cyrus was killed. His body was brought back to Pasargadae and buried in the tomb that he had built. At the entrance to the tomb an inscription says: "Adam Kurush Kshayathia Hakhamanish" "I am Kurush the Hakahamanian". As per Plutarch who visited the tomb during the kingdom, there was an inscription on the tomb, now worn away, which read "O man whoever you are and where so ever you come from, I am Kurush who founded the kingdom of the Persians, grudge me not therefore this little earth that covers my body". The proclamation written on a clay cylinder in Akkadian Cuneiform was detected in 1879. The text in English version reads as follows:

"When I entered Babylon without any battle, people welcomed my arrival with rejoicing. In the palace of the Kings of Babylon I sat upon the royal throne. Marduk (the God of the Babylonians) inclined the hearts of the noble people of Babylon favourably towards me because I looked upon Him with respect and love. My large army entered Babylon comfortably. I did not allow any calamity to befall the people of this city and this country. "The internal conditions of Babylon and its sacred places touched my heart. I ordered that all the people were free to worship their God—and irreligious persons should not harm them.

"I ordered that none of the houses should be ruined. I ordered that none of the citizens should be put to demise. The great God (Ahura Mazda) was pleased with me and bestowed upon me Cyrus and upon my son Cambujiyeh and upon all my soldiers the gifts of his blessings. "Kings who are sitting in their palaces in all the countries of the world, Kings from across the seas and the Kings of the west, all of them brought rich tributes and in Babylon they kissed my feet. I ordered that all the temples of Babylon, Sussa, Akkad and in the territory beyond the Euphrates which were built in ancient times and were closed should be reopened.

"I restored all the Gods of this temple to their places so that they may remain there for ever. I gathered together the people of the areas and rebuilt their houses which had been demolished, the Gods of Sumer and Akkad safely restored to their palaces known as "Delight of the Heart'. I bestowed upon all the people peace and happiness"

This was the human behaviour of Cyrus. Previous sovereigns at their time of victory killed and destroyed the conquered cities, while Cyrus declared his pride in the freedom and pleasure of his people. The declaration lays down the freedom of rights and worship of conquered people for the first time in history.

Now compare this with the behaviour of Ashur Banipal (who existed only a hundred years ahead of Cyrus) when he captured Susa. In his own words: "I conquered Susa, I removed the seals from the treasuries and stores, accumulated by the Kings from olden times. All the silver, gold, jewels cloaks and furniture of the palaces, statutes of Kings made from gold and silver and precious stones were sent to Assyria. Then I rooted out the temples of Susa and reduced their Gods to sand and rubble.

The territory which was within the marching distance of one month and twenty days I made barren from end to end, loaded thorns into it and converted it into a marshy land. The sons and daughters of Kings and all the members of the royal family, governors, officers, weapon makers, artisans, men or women and all the cattle were taken to Assyria. I crushed the head of Elam and removed the cries of joy and rejoicing from that territory. I converted the country into the dwelling of wild donkeys, wild boars, devils and wild beasts."

Likewise Nebuchadnezar who govern Babylon a few years earlier to Cyrus' intrusion of Babylon writes"I ordered that a hundred thousand eyes may be brought before me and a hundred thousand shanks of the legs may be broken. With my own hands I gorged out the eyeballs of the commander of the enemy from the sockets. Thousands of boys and girls were burnt alive. I battered the houses in such a way that the sound of living persons may not come out of them again."

Cambysis II: Cambyses, Cyrus' first born son became sovereign of the kingdom in 529 BC. He put into process the plan that Cyrus had depicted out for the conquering of Egypt. Five years afterward Cambyses captured Egypt and Pharaoh Psammenitos was taken captive. From that time forward for 124 years the Persian Kings made up the 27th dynasty of Egyptian Pharaohs. While Cambyses was still in Egypt, a man named Gaumata (also known as Bardya or Smerdis) and as per some historiographers a half brother of Cambyses, assumed power in Media and announced himself king. On hearing the news Cambysys hastened towards Pasargadae but died on the way. One account has it that he fell off his horse onto his own spear and was killed. Disarray followed the rebellion of Gaumata and the inadvertent demise of Cambyses. Inside eight months the kingdom started to fall apart and the captured states rebelled and announced their independency.

Darius from the other royal Persian family, had came with Cambyses to Egypt and was his spear carrier (a high military rank). Seeing the decomposition of the family kingdom Darius returned to Pasargadae and planned with seven other Persian nobles and wiped out Gaumata. He announced himself King of Kings, King of all Lands.

Darius I

Darius became King of Kings in 522 BC. At that time it was a hollow title. The kingdom that Cyrus had built was in revolt, small Kings declared their independency in Media and even in Persia. Babylon was in uprising as was Egypt, Parthia and the Scythian territories in the north. In fourteen months of hard struggling from one end of the kingdom to another Darius retrieved most of the kingdom putting down one rebellion after another with his small army and a few Persian nobles. In two years he had brought back all the territories that Cyrus had conquered back under the Persian kingdom. Darius now had time to reflect. He realized the failings of Cyrus' kingdom. Nothing bound the kingdom together other than the military mightiness of the Persian army. Darius set about to compensate this by passing a set of reforms that applied to all the kingdom and bonded it into an economical and administrative body.

Darius' first plan was to have a consistent set of laws for the whole kingdom. A law text was rapidly prepared based on the former laws of Hamurabi an old King of Babylon. Darius named his laws (Persian Dat) The Ordinance of Good Regulation. Its presentation read " a great God is Ahura Mazda, who produced earth, who produced the sky, who produced man, who produced all good things for man, who made Darius, King, one King of many, one Master of many, a great God is Ahura Mazda, who gave this beautiful work, who gave favour to man, who gave knowledge and friendliness to Darius the King." The King's laws were implemented with great equality through out the kingdom, a Persian nobleman or a Babylonian slave both had to obey and abide by the same laws. The punishments for breaking the laws was applied evenly to all rich or poor and the laws remained unaltered throughout the three hundred years of rule by the Hakhamanian family. So noteworthy was the incorrupt use of these laws that the words "The Laws of the Medes and Persians" became a by-word of juridical sincerity and harshness.

A Uniform Set of Weights, Measures and Currency: Darius also brought in a single set of weights and measures all over the kingdom. Using these weights and measures, permitted commerce to proceed without disarray and time consuming translation of one countries weights and measures to another. A new currency to be used through out the kingdom was introduced in which the highest denomination was a gold coin called the Daric. Again business could continue without the demand for conversion of one currency to some other.

Darius also brought in uniform tax revenue throughout the kingdom. All nationals paid the same taxations with the exclusion of the Persians and Medes who paid none. The taxes were moderate and permitted Darius a steady income to use for the governance of kingdom and to build his capital cities, without destructing the economy. Under the peace established by Persia, trade between nations of the kingdom grew tremendously and a general increase in the living standard of all the people was seen. Darius also built roads throughout the kingdom and introduced a system of King's messengers (the world's first postal system). The couriers called Angarum rode day and night in a relay arrangement, a fixed distance each, communicating the message from one to the next. By this system a message could be sent from Susa to Sardis a length of 1500 miles in a week and Darius could know all that passed off in his kingdom within a week of its happening.

Satrapies: In the administration of his kingdom he kept to the arrangement of Satrapies and Satraps that Cyrus had used. The armed forces garrison in each Satrapy reported straight to the King of Kings, and imperial inspectors made declared and unannounced visits to the Satrapies to describe circumstances to Darius.

Cities of the Kingdom: There were five significant cities of the kingdom. Susa and Babylon cities older than the kingdom were administration centers. Pasargadae constructed by Cyrus was the place of the coronation of all Hakhamanian Kings a symbolization of the memory of Cyrus, founding father of the kingdom. Ecbatana the old Median capital, 6000 feet above sea level was used as the summer capital. The gem of the kingdom, the pride of Darius and the following Kings was Persepolis or Parsua as the Persians called it. It was started by Darius and it reflected the ability and riches of the kingdom. Here every Jamshedi Nowrooz the Persian King received tribute of jewelry, horses, cattle, silk etc. from the subjects of every satrapy. It was here that special envoys from the kingdom were received in great pomp and glory. Great fetes and festivals were held here on main occasions. At Persepolis were stored all the treasures of the kingdom. A great library of texts on Zoroastrianism, written in golden ink on hides also existed.

After a long sovereignty of 38 years during which he brought the Persian Kingdom to the height of its glory, Darius died at the age of 65. He was a soldier, a statesman, an economic expert, a great benefactor of his people. He brought peace and success to the world which he ruled. The laws and institution he produced became the base of the Hakahamanian dynasty so that even though the sovereigns who followed him were not as good as he was, the kingdom survived for nearly 300 years. He governed most of the known world with justice and morality as a true Zoroastrian. He was one of the greatest sovereigns of the world. He was certainly one of the greatest personalities of human history. He was buried in a cave on a cliffside near Persepolis.

The Inscriptions of Darius I: During his farsighted, prosperous rule of the Persian Kingdom, Darius left many inscriptions on rocks and buildings, to leave behind for human race an idea of what kind of person he was and his accomplishments. The inscriptions can be found at Persepolis, at Naksh-I-Rustom, where his tomb is and most importantly on the rock face at Bisitun (Behistun, Bagastana). On the main caravan route between Ecbatana and Babylon, where the road enters Iran, the mountains on the side of the road have many rocky cliffs. One of these permitted Darius with just the right place to have his life history inscribed for all descendants to see. The inscription itself can not be seen from the road. After it was made, the cliff itself was chiseled smooth so that no one could climb to it easily. Darius had this done purposely so that the inscription would not be vandalised. It took Henry Rawlinson twelve years, from 1835 to 1847 to make a full copy of the inscription. Often he worked dangerously perched on ladders, or hanging from a rope.

The writing describes how he assumed power, how he overcame Gaumata, the pretender on the Persian throne, how he rebuilt the kingdom and gives the names of the states that were part of the kingdom. Here he even left some blank spaces to be filled in as his conquests increased. A forty foot carving showing Darius victorious over Gaumata and the other rebellion leaders, as prisoners accompany the inscription. Over this scene looms the sculpture of the Farohar symbol. Copies of this symbol are worn by many Zoroastrians today. The inscription is written in three languages, Old Persian, the language of Darius, Elamite and Akkadian, using the cuneiform script used in those days. This inscription was used as a stele to decode Elamite and Akkadian.

In Darius' own words:

"A great God is Ahura Mazda, who produced the earth, who produced yonder sky, who produced man, who produced pleasure for man, who made Darius King, one King over many, one master over many—. Ahura Mazda, when he saw this earth in trouble, he bestowed it upon me, he made me King. I am King. By the grace of Ahura Mazda I set the earth in place—. This which has been done, all that by the will of Ahura Mazda I did. Ahura Mazda bore me aid, until I finished the work."

"Ahura Mazda bore me aid because I was not hostile, I was not deceitful, I did not act falsely, neither I nor my family. I conducted myself as per justice. Neither to the weak nor to the powerful did I do wrong. The man who was excellent, him I rewarded well; him who was evil, I punished well. By the grace of Ahura Mazda I am of such a sort that I am a friend to right, I am not a friend to wrong. It is not my desire that the weak man should have wrong done to him by the mighty; nor is it my desire that the mighty should have wrong done to him by the weak. What is right, that is my desire——— It is not my desire that a man should do harm; nor is it my desire that if he should do harm, he should not be punished."

On his conviction in Ahura Mazda:

"Who so shall worship Ahura Mazda as long as his strength shall be, for him both while living and in demise there is happiness."

On his notion that Drauga (deceit, falsehood) as being the biggest evil:

"Thou who shall be King hereafter, protect thyself from Drauga. May Ahura Mazda protect this land from a hostile army, from famine, from Drauga."

Xerxes I

The great King Darius I expired in November of 486 BC. Four years before his demise the Persian army had attempted to conquer Athens and Sparta. It was defeated at the battle of Marathon by the Greeks. Some historians consider this battle one of the most significant in the history of the western world, because had the Persians won, Persian culture and language instead of Greek culture and language may well have become the origin of western culture. Actually, the loss did not change much except the mental balance. It was the first victory of any state over the Persians and it surprised both parties. Before Darius could avenge the defeat, he died in Persepolis at the age of 64 having ruled for 36 years. His son Xerxes, became sovereign. In the first year of Xerxes' sovereignty Egypt revolted, four years later Babylon also revolted. Both rebellions were vigorously put down and the two countries were dealt with harshly. The autonomy that Cyrus had granted to Babylon was taken away. As a matter of fact the Satrapy of Babylon was united with that of Assyria so that Babylon lost its personality. Xerxes had been the Satrap of Babylon for 12 years during his fathers sovereignty and the rebellion of Babylon was a personal insult to him. After the seventh year of his sovereignty he did not use the title King of Babylon among his other titles.

Xerxes now focused his attention on to Greece. With a vast army of 200,000 and 1200 ships he crossed the Hellespont, like his father on a bridge of boats. His first bridge was broken up by a storm. His second bridge was successful and the huge army crossed over into Europe. It had taken Xerxes four years to get his armed forces and naval forces ready. The Greeks had time to prepare themselves. They united under the leadership of Sparta and chose the battles carefully. At Thermopylae, a constrict pass in the mountains the two forces clashed. In the narrow confines of the pass, the huge Persian army was ineffective and the Greeks were able to block the Persians and inflicted huge losses on the Persian army until the Persians were able to find a way around the mountain pass to Athens. Athens was easily taken and the city was burned and looted. Xerxes did not behave like his forefathers and did not spare the city and its habitants. One hundred and fifty years later Alexander would avenge this act by burning Persepolis. Further conquest of Greece was given up when the Persian navy was badly defeated at Salamis. As at Thermopylae, the Greeks selected to fight in a constricted watercourse which was to their advantage, since their ships were smaller and more manoeuvrable. Xerxes retreated back across the Hellespont leaving behind his general Mardonius to continue to conquer the Greek states. Mardonius was defeated in 479 BC. and Greece did not become a part of Xerxes' kingdom.

After the loss of Greece, Xerxes abandoned ideas of more conquest and focused in governing the kingdom and completing the work his father had initiated at Persepolis. Xerxes was not quite the man his father was. He had lived too long in the shadow of his illustrious and powerful father and was no longer a young man when he became King of Kings. Instead of innovating and thinking ahead he was satisfied in doing things his father's way. Even the writings he left behind look like imitations of his father's inscriptions. His harshness in handling the rebellions of Egypt and Babylon, and his destruction of Athens were unlike the behavior of Cyrus and Darius. Unlike them he failed to win over the hearts of the conquered people. Above all Xerxes seems not to have checked his own household and his court. There was corruption and intrigue at home. The Persian King in the Biblical story of Esther is believed to be Xerxes I, known by the name Ahasuerus. Xerxes was assassinated by the captain of his own escort, Artabanus, in conspiracy with the Kings personal attender Mithridates.

The Selucid Rule of Iran

The subjugation of Iran by Alexander saw the end of the Hakhamanian Kingdom. Alexander died in 323 BC. and Iran was governed by one of his generals Seleucus Nicator, who founded the Seleucid Dynasty. From 312 BC. to 250 BC. Iran was part of the Seleucid Kingdom.

During this time considerable Greek influence entered into Iran's culture, religion and language. Simultaneously Iranian culture also shaped the Greeks. Many Zoroastrian texts were taken away to Greece and they influenced Greek doctrine, science and culture and through the Greeks all Western culture.

The Parthian Kingdom

In 250 BC. in Parthia a man of Iranian ancestry named Arsaces (Arshak) arose against the Seleucid Greeks and started his own Kingdom in Parthia. He initiated a long line of Iranian Kings who built an kingdom almost as large as the Hakhamanian kingdom. This was known as the Parthian or Arshakian kingdom. Originally the Parthians were a warlike people. During the first 123 years the Parthian Kings Arsaces (250-247 BC.), Tridates (247-211 BC.), Artabanus (211-191 BC.), Priapatus (191-176 BC.) and Phrates I (176-171 BC.), little by little beat back the Greeks out of Iran. The next King Mithradates I (171- 138 BC.) really established the Parthian kingdom, he conquered Babylonia and Mesopotamia and then entered Persia. Mithradates I issued his own coinage. The next King Phrates II (138-128 BC.) completed the task of throwing the Seleucid Greeks out of Iran. He was succeeded by Artabanus II (128-123 BC.) and then Mithradates II (123-87 BC.). Mithradates II brought the Parthian kingdom to its height extending it from the Indus river in the east through Afghanistan and Iran to the Oxus river in the north and south to the Persian gulf. In the west it reached contemporary day Turkey. At this time in the west Greece had been replaced by Rome as the super power. Mithradates II was the first Parthian King to come into contact with the Romans. Ambassadors were exchanged between the two countries.

After Mithradates II the Kings who succeded were Sinaturkes (80-69 BC.), Phrates III (69-57 BC.) and Orodes II (57-37 BC.). During the sovereignty of Orodes II, the Roman governor of the east, Crassus decided to conquer the Parthian kingdom. He crossed the Euphrates and entered Parthian territory and defeated the army of the Parthian Satrap (governor). The key Parthian army under General Suren assaulted the Romans and in the battle of Carrhae (53 BC.) the Roman army was smashed. The Parthians refrained from chasing the Romans beyond the Euphrates. This began an era of conflict with Rome that would last beyond the Parthian kingdom into the Sassanian period of Iranian history. In 37 BC. Mark Anthony, general of Julius Caesar assaulted Parthia and like Crassus endured a big defeat from the Parthian army. Again the Parthians remained east of the Euphrates. During the sovereignty of Phrates IV (38-2 BC.) Rome and

Parthia were friends again during the time when Augustus was consul of Rome. Phrates V was sovereign of Parthia at the time of Jesus' birth in Palestine which was under the dominion of the Roman kingdom.

During the sovereignty of Vologese I, Nero was Roman Kingking, they fought a bitter battle over Armenia and after various Parthian victories, Rome concurred to Vologeses' brother Tridates to be King of Armenia. Tridates was a adherent Zoroastrian and during his time Zoroastrianism became the official religion of Armenia. Vologeses I ordered the compilation of all the unwritten and written texts of the Zoroastrian faith, which had been dispersed since the time of Alexander's invasion. The Roman king Trajan attacked Iran and came across the Euphrates and Tigris rivers and captured the Parthian capital of Ctesiphon. The Parthian king fled to the east, raised an army and drove the Romans back across the Euphrates. The Roman king Hadrian signed a peace treaty with Parthia, which survived only a short while. During the time of Parthian king Vologeses II (148-192 AD.) war broke out again. Ctesiphon was again captured by the Romans under king Severus in 198 AD., when Vologeses IV was king of Parthia.

In 218 AD. Artabanus V conquered king Macrinus of Rome. He was the last Parthian king. He was defeated by the King of Persia Ardeshir Papakian who founded the Sasanian Dynasty. Zarathushtra brought his religion to the Iranian people around 1200 BC., in the time of the Kyanian King Vishtaspa. Ahead of his time the Iranians revered a large number of Gods related with different facets of world, such as the sea, moon, water, fire, wind, rain etc. The form of worship involved oblation sacrifices to these Gods, who in return would be pleased and prize the worshipper with good fortune. The priests of that time performed these sacrifices and sang hymns of praise to the Gods.

Zarathushtra preached a totally new way of viewing life. He was the first to teach that there was only one powerful, almighty, wise God, who was the creator, the law-giver and the final judge. Zarathushtra called him Ahura-Mazda, the wise lord. Ahura Mazda did not want sacrifices of animals or food made to him. He called for humanity for its own happiness, live a life of virtuous and actively battle for the good and fight against evilness. If man chose to do only that, he would be happy and bring about the perfection of God's creation. By this act he would become a co-worker with God. Zarathushtra brought in the notion of the six Amesha Spenta, the embodied dimensions of Ahura Mazda, which are: Asha-morality, Vohu Mano-wiseness, Kshathra Variya- the good power,

Aramaity- benefaction or right mindedness, Houravat- perfection and Ameretat- immortality. He also introduced the notion of Spenta Mainyu the spirit of goodness and Angre Mainyu the spirit of evil. These are two opposing forces that pull creation towards perfection or away from it.

Zarathushtra was the first to instruct that man's spirit survives after demise and that man is accountable for his activities while living. After demise, man will be judged for his actions while living. He also taught that there would be a final judgment at the end, before which a savior would appear and would bring about the total triumph of good over evil. Shortly after the demise of Zarathushtra and King Vishtaspa, the Kyanian family line ended. The special safety granted to Zoroastrianism as a state religion also came to an end. The new ideas of Zarathushtra were accepted by the people of north eastern Iran, but the older Iranian custom of multiple Gods could not be drawn out of their culture. The priests who became Zoroastrian priests integrated the older Gods into Zoroastrianism creating them the Yazatas or Endearing ones, aspects of God related with various facets of nature such as wind, fire water etc. or characters such as justice, victory etc. The hymns that used to be sung to the older Gods were modified to fit Zoroastrian doctrine and these became our prayers that are called Niyayeshs and Yasht. This was the state of Zoroastrianism when the Hakhamanian dynasty came to power in 559 BC.

During the time period of the Hakhamanian Kings, Zoroastrians expanded to many different parts of the kingdom and came into contact with other civilizations and faiths which were often older than theirs. Hakhamanian Kings respected the religions of the territories they conquered. There is no evidence that Zoroastrianism was forced upon the subjects of any conquered lands. To the contrary we know that Cyrus the Great paid his regards to the God Marduk of Babylon, shortly after he conquered the city. Because, the Hakhamanian Kings, who were Zoroastrians (we know that from the inscriptions of Darius, Xerxes and the later Kings) were open minded about the religion of their subjects, many Zoroastrians started to respect the Gods of other religions. There appears to be a considerable mixing of religious beliefs. The Yazata, Anahaita, the female deity Yazata related with water, became similar to the Greek Goddess Artemis and the Babylonian God Ishtar. Similarly, the Yazata, Mehr, and the God Mithra became synonymous. The later Hakhamanian Kings regarded Anahaita and Mithra almost as important as Ahura-Mazda.

Just as Zoroastrianism was influenced by other faiths, it influenced the other faiths of the kingdom. Cyrus had liberated the Jews from Babylon and permitted them to rebuild their Temple in Jerusalem. The Jewish scholars studied the religion of their new sovereigns, a religion which like theirs believed in one God. They were deeply influenced by the ideas brought in by Zarathushtra. It is after this period that we see, in Judaism the idea of a universal God, as opposed to a tribal God, the spirit existing after demise, the idea of a judgment after demise, the coming of a savior (Zoroastrian Soshyant) and the final judgment of creation. Through Judaism these ideas were introduced into Christianity and into Islam. These ideas are the basic principles of all three faiths. When Alexander conquered the Hakhamanian kingdom, the central library at Persepolis was destroyed, the religious texts were scattered and many were taken away to Greece. Aristotle who was the tutor of Alexander and had accompanied him on his conquests is said to have gathered up most of the Zoroastrian texts and was influenced by Zoroastrian doctrine. Though Aristotle and other Greek scholarly persons who examined these religious texts, Zoroastrian thoughts spread into Western civilization.

The attack on Iran by Alexander was a huge set back to Zoroastrianism. Many temples were demolished and learned priests who had learned the religious literature were killed and both the written and the oral custom suffered a great loss. Under these circumstances, the tendency of Zoroastrians believing in different Gods seems to have increased. One of the religions that became very powerful, was Mithraism. It believed in a war-like God Mithra (in Zoroastrianism the Yazata Mehr) related with the sun and triumph in combat. Mithraism spread in Iran and spread to Greece and then to Rome. It contained many of the ideas of Zoroastrianism. It believed in the thoughts of a sovereign creator, an immortal spirit, which is judged after demise, a concluding victory of good over evilness, and a Redeemer at the end of time who is the God Mithra himself. In Mithraism, Ahura-Mazda is still respected but not as the supreme God. In Mithraism, time (Zurvan) is the supreme creator, Mithra acts as mediator between God and humanity. The solstice, after which the daytimes become longer again, when the sun seems to grow stronger again, was observed as a great Mithraic festival by the Romans. When Christianity became the state religion of the Roman kingdom, this same festival was observed as the birthday of Christ.

Despite these numerous influences, Zoroastrianism did not die off. In eastern Iran and in Paras it was still the prevailing religion. The Parthian Kings, at least the later ones were staunch Zoroastrians. Like the Hakhamanian Kings they were tolerant not only of other religions but also different forms of Zoroastrianism. At this point in time there were two varieties of Zoroastrian temples. One kind had a consecrated fire which was worshipped as a symbol of Ahura-Mazda, this kind of temples were started in Hakhamanian rule around 400 BC. The other kind of temples had statues of the Yazatas and Ahura-Mazda as the central focus of worship. The Parthian sovereign Vologeses I, ordained the compilation and bringing together for safe-keeping every existent unwritten and written pieces of the Avesta. The Parthian dynasty kept the Greeks and Romans out of Iran and prevented these western influences from spreading in Iran. In this way it permitted Zoroastrianism to flourish again. Since the Parthian sovereigns did not intervene in the religious practices of their people, Zoroastrianism survived in many different forms of practice and notion from place to place in the kingdom. This was the state of this religion at the end of the Parthian rule in 226 AD., when Ardeshir Papakian overthrew the Parthian king and started the Sasanian dynasty which was to change Zoroastrianism profoundly.

MEDIEVAL HISTORY

The Sasanian Empire

The dynasty of Papak were the dominating princes in Paras under the Parthian kings. To this family was born prince Ardashir (old Persian name Artakshir, Artaxerxes). His father's name was Sasan. Ardashir grew up in the courtroom of the Parthian king Ardavan but he arose against Ardavan. He fled to Paras and raised an army and challenged Ardavan to battle. After some reluctance Ardavan decided to suppress this rebellious prince and in the battle that followed Ardavan was killed. Ardashir declared himself king of all Iran. His army captured all the parts of the Parthian kingdom inside a few years and he began the Sasanian dynasty.

Ardashir was a adherent person and likely came from a priestly family, he was also ambitious and a firm administrator. He was determined to make Zoroastrianism the state religion of Iran. Since there were many forms of Zoroastrian beliefs and practice at this time in Iran, he chose the practice and beliefs that were followed in his home province Pars as the standard form of Zoroastrianism. In this job he was assisted by a bright priest, Tansar, who he made the high-priest of the kingdom. Tansar and his successor high-priests were comparable in authority and power to the Christian popes. Ardashir and Tansar gathered all the scattered teachings of the religion, all the texts, the oral customs, the different practices and ceremonies. From these Tansar picked out one custom and one set of sacred scripture as the true one and this Ardashir attempted to enforce all over Iran. This was not well accepted by the Zoroastrians of other provinces who had their own old customs and practices. Ardashir, even ordered the destruction of Zoroastrian temples which did not confirm to the version that Tansar had decided on. Fresh temples were constructed in their place. History records considerable fighting between Zoroastrians of other areas and the forces of Ardashir. In the end Ardashir and Tansar prevailed, partly by force and partly by Tansar's power of persuasion and an uniform Zoroastrianism became the state religion of the land. Ardashir brought in a new 365 days day calendar in place of the old 360 day calendar adding the five Gatha days at the closing of the calendar year. This also caused great confusion and anger amongst Zoroastrians.

Ardashir's sovereignty of 15 years appears to have been really busy. He had not only to bring about the unification of Iran under his rule but also simultaneously fight the Romans. He sent a delegation of Persian nobles to Rome to demand the return of all Iranian territory and the withdrawal of Romans back to Europe. The Romans viewed this as a proclamation of war. The Roman king Alexander Servus prepared for battle. The years of fighting that followed changed the boundary between Rome and Iran very little and both sides gave up on the fighting for the time being.

Ardashir formed the kingdom along conventional lines adopting the Hakhamanian and Parthian custom of organizing Satrapies governed by a Satrap, who now was a Persian nobleman. There was also a military governor in each Satrapy directly accountable to Ardashir. He tried his best to claim descent from the Hakhamanian Kings who were also Persian (i.e. from Pars). Not far from Persepolis, close to the tombs of the Hakhamanian Kings at a place that is at present called Naksh-i-Rustom, Ardashir had an immense sculpture made. Here he is shown receiving the heavenly glory (Khwaraneh) from Ahura-Mazda. He is also shown stepping on the dead body of Ardavan, the last Parthian King, while Ahura-Mazda is shown stepping on Ahriman. This sculpture has a big similarity to that of Darius the Great at Behistun. On Ardashir's carving the three languages used are Middle Persian, Parthian and Greek. These were the common languages of the kingdom. Ardashir died in 241 AD.

Shapur I

On the demise of Ardashir his son Shahpur became King. His sovereignty was marked by uninterrupted campaign against Rome.. From 235 AD. to 254 AD., seven Roman kings were declared and murdered.

Shapur took advantage of the instability in Rome and drove the Romans from the Tigris to the Euphrates. He also squashed the revolt in Armenia and Asia Minor and captured Syria. Valerian became Roman king in 254 AD. and tried to regain territory lost to the Iranians. In the battle with Shahpur, Valerian and much of his army was captured at Edessa. This outstanding triumph of Shahpur is recorded in a shrine near Persepolis. In honour of this victory, Shahpur built many Atash Behrams all over Iran.

Shapur's high priest was Kirder (Kartir), plausibly the most influential priest in Zoroastrian history. He was permitted to have his own inscriptions like royalty and after Shapur's demise was also King-maker. In his inscription at Sar Mashed he says" Through my actions, religious activities were increased, many Vahram fires (Atash Behrams) were founded and many priests became happy and prosperous, much benefit accrued to Hormazd and the Yazads and there was much harm to Ahriman and the Devs and the doctrine of Ahriman and the Devs departed the land and was no more believed. And Jews, Buddhists, Brahmans, Mandeans, Christians and Manichaeans are being defeated in the land." At this moment in time there seems to have been contentions between Zoroastrianism and the minor religions of the land and Kirder played a significant role in guarding the philosophies and practices of Zoroastrianism against the priests and missionaries of other faiths.

One particular derivative of Zoroastrianism was Manichaeism which was initiated by an Iranian prophet Mani. He kept some of the fundamental teachings of Zoroastrianism, such as belief in one God, the devil, subsistence of the spirit after demise, the person judgment after demise and the final victory of good over evil. However instead of teaching men to fight evil and work for the good he taught that humanity would be best off, if they gave up earthly duties and became hermits. Much to the pleasure of Kirder, Shahpur asked Mani to come to his court, where he was present for many years. Shapur had a great religious curiosity and liked to hear about the different religions of his kingdom. He died in 271 AD.

Kings After Shahpur I

After Shahpur I's demise, there was a speedy succession of Kings, Hormazd I (271-272 AD.), Bahram (Vahram) I (272-275 AD.), Bahram II (275-292 AD.) and Bahram III (292-293 AD.). During this time, the Romans took advantage of the imbalance in Iran and won back some of the territories that Shapur had won from them. On the religious front,

Kirder was still in charge. He was at the pinnacle of his might and was able to play a significant role in selecting the succession of Kings. He managed to have Mani tried and killed in the sovereignty of Bahram I. After these Kings, Narseh the youngest son of Shapur became King and ruled from 292-302 AD. During his sovereignty the Romans were able to push the their borders to the Tigris river. Narseh abdicated the throne in shame and Hormazd II became King, ruling from 302-309 AD. He died in 309 AD. His queen was expecting and the nobles chose this unborn child as the next sovereign.

Shapur II

Shahpur II was coronated when he was just forty days old. A wise counselor ran the country for 16 years until Shapur took the responsibility of power at the age of 16. The early part of his long sovereignty was spent in fighting the Romans who had again occupied some territories east of the Tigris. In a war of twenty-seven years Shahpur II was able to force back the Romans back to the Euphrates. He also won back Armenia from the Romans. It was during Shapur II's sovereignty that the Roman king Steadyine became a Christian and Christianity became the state religion of the Roman kingdom. In these times to be a Christian in the country of Iran or to be a Zoroastrian in Rome was nearly like being a traitor since it was like following the religious belief of the enemy.

Although both faiths worshipped one God, their method of approach was rather different. Zoroastrians showed great respect for nature and worshipped Ahura Mazda through the worship of his creations. Corporeal cleanliness and maintaining the purity of the elements was of great importance to them. At that time, Christians paid no care to their person hygiene and did not revere natural world. Zoroastrians regarded life to be a blessing to be enjoyed while one performed good deeds and fought evil. Many Christians believed asceticism and a life of poverty and suffering insured them a place in heaven. Many a Christians believed in chastity. These conflicting views and the fact that the Christians were always trying to convert people to their religion, caused considerable enmity between the two and Christians were often persecuted in Iran. During the sovereignty of Shapur II, a wise Zoroastrian High cleric by the name of Adurbad Marespand, re-explained the historical Avestan prayers and made many free translations from Avestan into the common language, Pahlavi. Avesta, by now was a dead language, understood only by a few learned priests. Zoroastrians could now pray in a language they could understand. To demonstrate to the world that his versions were reliable,

Adurbad Marespand underwent and came through the primeval trial by ordeal of having molten metal poured on his chest. To this day, we honour this great priest by remembering his name in our prayers of remembrance for the dead.

Despite the struggle with Rome and the interior differences with Christians (mostly in western Iran), Shapur's long sovereignty was a flourishing and happy time for Zoroastrian Iran. The initial conflicts produced by the unification of the Zoroastrian church were in the past. A great rejuvenation and understanding of the faith among its followers was taking place. The power of the church was supreme but not yet oppressive. Shahpur II expired in 379 AD.

Yazdegard I

Shahpur II's offspring, Yazdegard became sovereign in 399 AD. and reigned for twenty-one years. Initially he was kind to the Christians and Jews in Iran. He even permitted them to bury their dead (pollute the earth, from the Zoroastrian point of view). For this, he is notorious in Zoroastrian literature as Yazdegard the offender. Because of his leniency towards the Christians, the Christians became quite bold. There are records of Christians in Iran destroying fire-temples, extinguishing sacred fires and celebrating mass in those temples. Occurrences like these changed Yazdegard against the Christians and finally he took strict actions against them. Around this time two great national fires were started. Adur Faranbag in Pars was the special fire of the priestly class and Adur Gushnasp in Media was the special fire of the Kings and warrior class. These two fires now rivaled the ancient fire Burzin-Mihr, which had been started by the Parthian Kings in eastern Iran and which had been their Kingly fire. Adur Burzin-Mihr at that time became the special fire of the farmers.

The remnants of Adur Gushnasp can even be found in Azerbaijan region of Iran. Adur Gushnasp was built on a very beautiful location. It was on the top of a flat mountain, where there was a natural lake. The temple was constructed alongside the lake and was bordered by brick ramparts on three sides. From the gates of this wall a magnificent roadway took the pilgrims to the entrance of the temple. The Sasanian Kings made pilgrimages to this temple on many important occasions and sent large gifts to the temple on the birth of royal children, on the occasion of a great victory, etc. These three fires are still thought of at the end of the Atash-Ni-Niyaesh.

Bahram V

Yazdegard's offspring Bahram V became emperor on his demise. It seems that the imperial assembly wanted Khusrow, another noble family member, to become King. There was danger of a war between the two factions. Rather, it was decided that the imperial crown be placed on the throne, to which two barbaric lions were bound and whoever was able to overcome the lions and sit on the throne would be coronated as King. Bahram V, won this contest. Bahram V was also known as Bahramgur, because he was fond of hunting wild asses (onagers). This King was religious minded but he loved riding, hunting and wrote poetry. His dominion seems to have been genial and good-hearted, he cut down taxes and reigned rightly and he was a very well-liked King. During his sovereignty the Romans again started a war, Bahramgur successfully fought them and in the end signed a treaty which granted religious freedom for Zoroastrians in Rome and Christians in Iran. Bahramgur is said to have travelled to India, masquerading as his own envoy to the court of King Vasudeva of Kanoj in western India.

Yazdegard II

During the sovereignty of Yazdegard II, there was a risk to Iran from wandering tribes from the north east and Yazdegard had to move his royal court to the north east part of Iran for seven years, to be closer to the place of trouble. He was influenced during this time by the more ancient customs and names of the north east and these were introduced into the Iranian court.

Kobad I

For a time period of hundred years, from Shahpur II's demise to the sovereignty of Kobad I, the Zoroastrian institute developed progressively in magnitude and in influence. Iranian Zoroastrian society became a feudal system in which most of the land was owned by the church or the nobility and the common man was left to pay the taxes. Neither the priesthood nor the nobility was subjected to taxes. The judicial organization was also in the hands of the clerics, so that in struggles with the religious institute, justice favoured the religious institute. The same combination of church and state which had worked to unify and rejuvenate Zoroastrianism was now functioning to oppress the masses, often in the name of religion.

During Kobad I's sovereignty a new religion, an off shoot of Zoroastrianism was started by Mazdak. He instructed that men should not slay animals and consume flesh. He taught that asceticism and withdrawal from worldly attachments was a good thing because it reduced greed. He taught that all men should share everything equally, food and property. He was the first to teach a communistic way of life, where no one owned anything. To the oppressed masses whose share in the riches of Iran was negligible, Mazdakism made sense and he had many followers.

Kobad began liking his preachings and backed Mazdak. The noble and priests opposed this movement and after a few years Kobad was deposed and his brother Zamasp became King. Kobad fled to the nomads of the north east and with their help he regained his throne. Nevertheless, he discontinued his support for Mazdak. His eldest son had become a Mazdakite and he made his third son Khusrow heir to the throne. In 528 AD., Khusrow invited all the Mazdakites to a royal banquet and while they were there he had them massacred, including Mazdak their leader. That was the last of the Mazdakite religious movement. Kobad died soon after and Khusrow became King.

Khusrow I

Khusrow reigned for fifty years. He was a firm King and his dominion is well documented and historically he is one of the better known Sasanian Kings. Having destroyed the Mazdakite movement, he introduced far reaching reforms that benefited the common man and the farmers. He lowered the tax on the common man, including the land tax on farmers and reformed the judicial system. He made improvements that profited the farmers and augmented the agricultural production, which added affluence to Iran. He was a religious King and worked closely with the priests. In a text called the Karnamag-I-Anoshirvan, he says, " I give thanks to Ahura Mazda for the favours he has shown me. These favours require in return a deep sense of obligation on my part, which I express in both words and deeds. I, therefore, select a course of action, which will support the Law of Asha, which is the great celestial moral principle that governs life and sustains all the good creation of Ahura Mazda." Led by these beliefs Khusrow gained the title Anoshirwan (of immortal spirit) by his people for his just rule.

He had to battle the Romans and also wandering tribes in the north. After subjugating the nomads he made them defenders of his northern borders. He sent priests to teach them Zoroastrianism and built fire-temples in these areas. A main happening that took place during Khosrow I's sovereignty or some time before that, was the creation of the new Avestan alphabet. Up to this time there always had been a difficulty in the writing of the Avestan language. There was no alphabet available that would guarantee the correct pronunciation of the words. The Avesta thus depended upon an oral transmission from generation to generation, with the written word used only as a irregular guide. An unknown genius priest, invented the Avestan alphabet by expanding the 20 letter Pahlavi alphabet to a forty-six letter completely phonetic alphabet. With this tool the priests started to write down the entire Avesta, the twenty-four Nasks. Along with this, the Pahlavi explanations was also written down using this alphabet. This written Avesta and the commentary, which is called the Zand is still available to us in part. Much of it was destroyed or lost, after the Arab invasion of Iran. One more chief event was the birth of the prophet Mohammed in Arabia, who founded Islam, which was in future to intrude on and destruct Zoroastrian Iran.

Hormazd IV

Hormazd followed his father in 579 AD. He was kind to Christians and to other faiths in Iran. In a war with Rome, the Iranian army under the general Bahram Chobin, was defeated. Hormazd heaped insults on the general. In resentment against his unjust treatment, Bahram assaulted the capital Ctesiphon, defeated Hormazd and put him to death. However, the Persian nobles did not regard Bahram to be the rightful heir and supported Hormazd's son Khusrow. The new Roman king Maurice also supported Khusrow and with his help, Khusrow was able to regain the throne. Bahram took flight to east and expired soon after.

Khusrow II

Khusrow II's sovereignty was the last long sovereignty of a Zoroastrian King in Iran. The beginning of his sovereignty saw his forces conquering Palestine and Egypt from the Romans. The Iranian army was at the gates of Steadyinople, the capital of Byzantine Rome. The fortune of the Roman king was captured by the Iranians and with it the Cross of Jesus, on which he was crucified. These early victories earned Khusrow II the title "Pervez" (the victorious). His victories were short lived. The Romans mobilized and attacked Iran, caught Ctesiphon and also demolished the great fire temple, Adur-Gushnasp. Now the Iranians fought back and recaptured their capital and the Romans were driven out of Iran and Adur Gushnasp was rebuilt. In all this fighting, Khusrow II ignored the danger in the south. The Arab clans were merging under the standard of Islam and beginning to conquer the world.

Khusrow II lived in great splendor and made large gifts to various fire-temples. Near Hamadan in a grotto called Taq-I-Bastan, in today's Iran, Khusrow had a huge carving made which depicted his coming to the throne of Iran. During his sovereignty the Zoroastrian institute became very influential, controlling the lives of the ordinary Zoroastrian. Zoroastrians were expected to have large number of ceremonies performed on every occasion and observe the strict reigns of cleanliness and rite purity. Like his father Khusrow blamed his generals for the defeats he suffered against Rome. They were affronted and rose in rebellion and killed him. His son Kobad became King in 628 AD.

End of the Sasanian Dynasty and Zoroastrian Iran

Exactly when Iran needed a firm King to keep it united and stand up against the Arab forces which were moving to north, there was none. The Sasanian royal family was divided and struggling for power amongst themselves. The royal council and the generals could not agree on who should be King. Iran now had a series of eight Kings and two queens within a span of five years. Their names were: Kobad, Ardashir III, Shahrbaraz, Queen Purandokht, Zurvanshah Gushnabad, Queen Azarmidokht, Farrokhzad, Peroz II, Khurzad Khusrow and Hormazd V. After five disastrous years in which the affairs of the country were neglected and the confidence of the Iranians in the Sasanian royal family destroyed, the last Sasanian King Yazdegard III came to the throne at the age of 21, in 632 AD. As this was the last Zoroastrian King, Parsis still abide by the calendar which starts with the first year of his sovereignty as year one. Thus 632 AD. is year one in the Zoroastrian calendar, whether it is Shanshahi, Kadimi or Fasli. The prophet Mohammed expired in the same year.

Four years after the demise of their prophet, the Arab forces having captured Egypt, and Syria, were at the gates of the Iranian kingdom. Yazdegard now had to protect Iran, his force under Rustom Farrokhzad met the Arab army under Saad-ibn-Waqqas at Qadisiyya and after a ferocious encounter the Iranians were defeated. The Arabs entered Ctesiphon and plundered it. Yazdegard retreated east and in 641AD. with another army fought the Arabs at Nihavand. The Iranians, even though they defended their country ferociously, were defeated again. Yazdegard fled further east. He moved from place to place trying unsuccessfully to raise another army while being pursued by the Arabs. In 652 AD., he was betrayed and executed by a miller named Khusrow, at whose home he had taken sanctuary, in the city of Merv. This was the end of the Sasanian dynasty. The Arabs continued their conquest of Iran eastward. Person provinces and cities held out against the Arabs, for a while. Many small Zoroastrian princes reigned for a significant time, particularly in the mountainous regions of Iran and it was almost three hundred years before all of Iran came under Muslim rule. For a time there were small Zoroastrian Kingdoms in western China, Tabaristan, Mazendaran, Khurasan and Kerman. The Sassanian period of Zoroastrianism is unparalleled in history. It was the only time in period that a major union of the religion took place. Sometimes it was bloody and politically motivated, yet it was an honest attempt to rid the faith of heresies, new modes of worship and differences in religious practice that had accumulated over nearly 2000 years. It was also the only time that the rites and religious practices underwent an ascertained changes leading to a faith that all of a sudden became alive, as its ritesrite, ceremonials and prayers became apprehensible in the language of the day. Under the Sassanians the literature of the faith was written down in an alphabet that did not require oral transmission. Finally it was Sassanian Zoroastrianism that stood up to the missionary zeal of Christianity and Buddhism and later was able to survive the holocaust of the Islamic invasion. Possibly without the merger enforced on it by Sassanian monarchs, Zoroastrianism may well have vanished under the attack of Christianity, and Islam.

MODERN HISTORY

History Of Zoroastrians In Iran Under The Caliphs

The Arab intrusion of Iran was somewhat different from that of Alexander, the Greek many a centuries before. The purpose of the Arabs was not only to conquer but to spread Islam. Unlike the Greeks, the Arabs set out to destroy Zoroastrianism in Iran. This was accomplished not by wiping out Zoroastrians but by creating laws and reigns which made life difficult for Zoroastrians. All non-Muslims were made to pay an extra tax called the Jizya. The penalty for not paying, was demise, captivity or imprisonment. Even when the Zoroastrians paid the tax, they were subjected to insults by the tax-collectors. Zoroastrian temples were systematically destroyed and mosques built in their place. Zoroastrians who were caught as slaves in wars were given their liberty if they changed to Islam. Because of these many difficulties Zoroastrians started to convert to Islam. Many who converted just for the convenience were unable to return to their faith, even if they wanted to, because the penalty for re-conversion was demise. Once a Zoroastrian household changed to Islam, the children had to go to Muslim religious school and study Arabic and the commandments of the Quran. These children lost their Zoroastrian identity.

Many Zoroastrians found similarity between the two religions. These similarities were the thoughts of heaven and hell, the last judgement, supplications five times a day (similar to the five Zoroastrian Gehs). These similarities made it easy to convert. Early Islam was free of rites and ceremonies and this was an attraction to some Zoroastrians who were tired of the multitude of rites and ceremonies in Sasanian Zoroastrianism. Once a Zoroastrian changed over to Islam, he did not have to abide by the rigid laws of personal and rite purity and cleanliness that were so much a part of religion at that time.

Though many Zoroastrians changed over to Islam, many could not give up their old religion for a new one, whose religious text was written in a different language of the vanquishers. They could not give up the worship of Ahura Mazda through the Holy Fires, for the veneration of a distant stone, the Kaaba in Mecca, of which they had no idea. They could not bring themselves to kneel in prayer before a blank wall facing towards Mecca, instead of standing before a bright fire. Generally they could not conceive that the supreme God, Allah could be both the origin of evil and good and therefore a Deity you could not comprehend. In contrast, in this religion, Ahura Mazda is the source of all that was good, and evil comes from a separate force that has to be battled against, with the help of Ahura Mazda and the Yazatas. They could not understand the new customs of not eating certain meats such as pork and not drinking wine. Under the first four Caliphs (632-661 AD.), the direct line of the prophet Mohammed, Iran stayed mainly Zoroastrian and the high priest of the Zoroastrians still made his home in Ctesiphon, the Sasanian capital.

The first four Caliphs were succeded by the Umayads (661-750 AD.), who governed from Syria. They seemed to have left the Zoroastrians alone as long as they paid the Jizya tax. During this time, the official language of Iran became Arabic instead of Persian. While Muslim Iranians promptly learned the new language, the Zoroastrians despised it, and tried to avoid it as the language of Muslims. Thus they were left out of all government positions. The Iranian Muslims at this time started a new custom, which made Islam appear as a partly Iranian religion. They commented that Iranian Zoroastrian, Salaman -I-Farsi had a big influence on Mohammed, the prophet. They also made the myth that Husayn, the offspring of the fourth Caliph had married a Sasanian princess, named Shahr-Banu, whose son became the fourth Shia Imam (and initiated the Shia branch of Islam). These two notions made it easier for Zoroastrians to convert to Islam.

The Umayads were succeded by the Abbasid family which came to power with the help of Iranian Muslims. They respected not only the Iranian Muslims but also the Zoroastrians. Iranian Muslims were welcomed to the court, but not Zoroastrians and some Zoroastrians found it advantageous to convert to Islam. Hence even the benignity of the Abbassids seemed to have worked to change over more Zoroastrians to Islam. The Abbasids were followed by the Saffavids (869-903 AD.). During their sovereignty the Zoroastrians, for the first time became a minority in Iran. The Zoroastrians existed under the guidance of their High Priest, since they had no sovereign. The great fire temple of Adar Gushnasp was still functioning up to the middle of the 10th century. Zoroastrian priests and even some lay persons wrote texts on our religion. It was during this time that the Dinkard was written down. This text which is still available to us has many discussions on religion. Most especially it sums up the contents of the nineteen of the twenty-one Nasks (the religious literature written in twenty-one texts). By this time one of the Nasks was entirely lost and another only existed in its Avesta form, its Zand (the Phalevi commentary) was lost.

At the commencing of the tenth century a small group of Zoroastrians residing in the region of the town of Sanjan in the state of Khorasan, decided that Iran was no more safe for Zoroastrians and their faith. They resolved to migrate to India. They travelled to the port of Hormazd on the Persian Gulf and sailed for India. They landed on a small Island called Div on the coast of Gujarat in the year 936 AD. There they lived for about twenty years in great difficulty. They acquired the local language and introduced their subject to Jadi Rana, the sovereign of that area. Jadi Rana in return for some promises of behavior, permitted them to settle in his Kingdom. The Zoroastrians founded a settlement, which they called Sanjan, after the town they had left behind in Iran nearly 30 years ago. They devoted their first Atash Behram fire inside five years of coming to Sanjan. This attracted other Zoroastrians from Iran and also some Zoroastrians who had personly come over the years and settled in various parts of western India. This was the start of the Parsis in India.

It is told that on their travel by sea from Div to Jadi Rana's Kingdom, their ships were battered by a fierce storm. The Zoroastrians made a pledge to Ahura Mazda that if they survived, they would consecrate an Atash Behram fire. They fulfilled this pledge in five years. This first fire consecrated in Sanjan by Parsi founders even burns today. It is called the Iran Shah fire and is kept in a temple in Udvada, a small town hundred miles north of Bombay.

Zoroastrians in Iran from Tenth to Twentieth Century

The tenth century BC. was an era of peace for the Zoroastrians in which they could follow their faith, compose religious texts and make a calendar alteration to bring Noruz back to the March equinox. This was the peace before the storm. Early in the eleventh century the Seljuk Turks swept into Iran killing Muslims and Zoroastrians alike as they conquered Iran. Once established they persecuted the Zoroastrian Iranians like the regimes before them. As though this was not enough the thirteenth century brought the Mongol intrusion of Iran under Chengiz Khan. The Mongols were fierce barbarians, who killed Muslims, Christians, Jews and Zoroastrians without discrimination. They destroyed all kinds of texts and killed all those who professed learning. It was likely in this devastation that the last great collected works of Zoroastrian texts was lost. The last of the great fire temples was also destroyed.

Within fifty years of their conquering of Iran the Mongols, themselves were changed to Islam. Islam revived in Iran but for Zoroastrians, persecution continued, now by these new converts to Islam. For the Zoroastrians, now, the best way to survive was to be as inconspicuous as possible. The clerics of the Zoroastrians went to a small village called Turkabad, near Yazd, in the early fourteenth century. The fires from the two great temples Adur Faranbagh and Adur Anahid were brought and placed in an obscure mud brick building, in the village of Sharifabad. These two villages became the religious centers for the Zoroastrians. A cleric school was retained there to train new priests. A pilgrimage to the province of Yazd became an obligation for all Iranian Zoroastrians. Kerman also became a center of Zoroastrianism.

From 1502 to 1747, the Saffavid dynasty assumed control in Iran. Shah Abbas the great who ruled from 1587 to 1628, was the most famous King. The Saffavids made Isfahan the capital of Iran. Because of the constancy and affluence brought about by the Saffavids, Zoroastrians came to settle down in Isfahan. They worked here as labourers, carpet weavers, nurserymen and farmhands. There was a large society of Zoroastrians, about 3000 families who lived in a suburb of Isfahan, which was called Gabr-Mahal, Gabristan or Gabrabad. The word Gabr was an insulting term that the Muslims used for Zoroastrians.

Many western travellers visited the royal court at Isfahan and accounted the Zoroastrian society in Gabrabad. They reported the Zoroastrians as modest, gentle people who lived under the guidance of their elders. The women, unlike the Muslim women wore no veils and talked readily to strangers. Both men and women were modestly dressed but the Zoroastrian men were not permitted to wear clothes which were dyed. Zoroastrians could always be recognised by their clothes. The western travellers found the Zoroastrians were not willing to talk about their religion and their customs because they did not want the Muslims to learn about them. By now the Zoroastrians had invented a new dialect, which only they could understand, which they called Dari. The Zoroastrians established a mental barrier between themselves and the Muslims in order to stay alive. Even the sacred fires were now hidden away in the fire temple. A false fire would be kept in the open, so that any marauding Muslim who came to defile the temple would most likely destroy or pollute the false fire. Existing in this oppressive atmosphere, the Zoroastrians still managed to savour life as far as possible, observing their festivals with jovial atmosphere.

Although under Shah Abbas the Great, the Zoroastrians were permitted to live near Isfahan and left somewhat alone, the later Saffavid Kings were not so tolerant. Shah Abbas II, through them out of Gabrabad, because he wanted to build a place there. The last Saffavid King, Sultan Hossayn decreed that all Zoroastrians in Isfahan should convert to Islam. The Zoroastrians fire temple was destructed and many Zoroastrians were coerced to convert at sword point. Those that refused were killed. A few escaped tom Yazd. Nowadays there are households in Yazd who retrace their ancestry from these refugees from Isfahan. In 1821 a western traveller, Ker Porter, visiting Isfahan described that there were hardly any Zoroastrians in Isfahan and Gabrabad was in ruins.

In 1719 the Afghans rebelled against Iran and invaded it by way of Sistan and Kerman, both Zoroastrian centers. In Kerman, the Zoroastrians were not permitted to reside in the walled city. They lived in an area called Gabar Mohalla, outside the fortified city. When the Afghans attacked they first killed all the defenseless Zoroastrian men, women and children in Gabar Mohalla. A couple of rich and influential Zoroastrians such as the high priest of Kerman who resided in the city got away. So many Zoroastrians were killed that there was no way to place them in the Dokhma. The bodies were collected together on the plain and a wall was built around them to produce a make-shift Dokhma. This improvised Dokhma can be seen nowadays some distance from the ruinations of Gabar Mohalla, in Kerman.

The Afghans ruled Iran for 7 years and were driven out by the Qajars, a Turkish tribe of northern Iran. The first sovereign was Nadir Shah who invaded India and sacked Delhi. Amongst the booty he took back was the Peacock Throne of the Mughal Kings of India. Nadir Shah was killed in 1747. One of his captains Karim Khan Zaid, started the Zaid dynasty. During the rule of Karim Khan, a Parsi, Mulla Kaus, visited Kerman, with the last of the Rivayet questions. He found the Zoroastrians devastated, and still paying the same amount of Jizya tax, they had been paying before, in spite of their far smaller numbers. Mulla Kaus took their cause to Karim Khan and received relief from the exuberant tax.

The Zaid dynasty was brought down by the Qajar, Aga Mohamed and this dynasty ruled Iran until 1925. Under the early Qajar dynasty the Iranian Zoroastrians saw the worst time of their subsistence. They were not permitted to ride horses or to tie their turbans neatly or to wear socks. Frequently they were threatened, beaten up and fleeced and their religious texts ruined. The news of their plight reached the Parsis who by this time had become quite prosperous. Parsi funds were set up to help the Iranian Zoroastrians. A Parsi, Manekji Hataria, was sent to help them. He discovered only 7000 Zoroastrians in Kerman, Yazd and Tehran (now the capital of Iran). Using his influence with the British government he managed to get some of the repression against Zoroastrians removed. He also founded western style schools for Zoroastrians.

As soon as the Zoroastrians got some exemption from oppressiveness, their natural power to work hard and wisely, expressed itself. Some Zoroastrians became quite prosperous, helped by the fact that they were the only society in Iran to get a western education, at the beginning of the 20th century. Jamshid Bahman started the first bank in Iran and became a very influential man in Iran. He headed the social movement for constitutional reform. A parliament was set up in 1906 and he was one of its first members. In 1909 when it was decided that each minority send one spokesperson to the Iranian parliament (Majlis), Kaykhosrow Shahrokh became the first Zoroastrian representative. In 1925 the Majlis forced out the last Qajar sovereign and placed Reza Shah Pahlevi on the throne. Reza Shah set out to modernize Iran. Iranian Zoroastrians who were already educated in the western style, started to play important roles in his government. Reza Shah brought in a new solar calendar, eliminating the Islamic calendar. It was essentially the Zoroastrian calendar, with dates one to thirty instead of the names of the days. The months had the same Zoroastrian names.

A movement of Zoroastrians from Yazd and Kerman to Tehran took place. Although the society flourished financially, it failed to keep up some of the customs that existed in Yazd and Kerman. The priestly schools were not maintained. The number of priests decreased rapidly so that the society had to depend on priests from India or Iranian Zoroastrian priests trained in India. Under the rule of Reza Shah Pahlevi and his son Mohamed Reza Pahlevi, the Zoroastrians were once again able to play constructive roles in Iranian civilization. They became flourishing business men such as Arbab Rostom Guiv and Meherban Zarthoshti. Zoroastrians became doctors, engineers and served in the Iranian armed forces earning the respect of non-Zoroastrian Iranians. Dr. Farang Mehr assisted the last Shah as a deputy prime-minister. The Islamic revolution in 1979, set the Zoroastrians back some what and led to a migration of Zoroastrians from Iran to the countries of the West.

HISTORY OF THE PARSIS IN INDIA

Early History

The Parsis first settled down in Sanjan on the west coast of India in the empire of Jadi Rana. The account of their arrival in India is to be found in a poem written in Sanskrit by a Parsi priest Bohman Kaikobad in 1600 AD. English translations of the poem are available. The first three hundred years after their appearance in India, is cloaked in mystery. However by the tenth century they had spread out from Sanjan into the cities and villages of Gujarat north and south of Sanjan. Parsi settlements could be found in Anklesahvar, Bharuch, Khambat, Navsari, Surat, Vankaner and Variav. About the year 1290 the Parsis were under five different groups of priests based on the geographical location in Gujarat. These hieratical factions were: The Bhagarias (Navsari), Bharucha, Godavra (Surat), Khambatta and Sanjanas.

One of the first accounts of the Parsis is a few letterings in the Kanheri caves near Bombay written in Pahlevi on October ten,1009 and November twenty-four, 1009. Towards the end of the eleventh century the Parsi settlement at Variav had become prosperous and strong and they refused to pay the Rajput prince of the area the excessive tribute he demanded. When the prince sent in troops to enforce the payment the Parsis fought them and defeated them. A bit later the prince sent out a fresh force that arrived while the Parsi men were at a marriage party out of town. The Parsi women put on armour and opposed the Rajput force and were about to succeed when one of the ladies lost their armour plate and Rajputs seeing that they were fighting women mustered. The Parsi women were about to be defeated and instead of surrendering, drowned themselves in the sea along whose shore the battle had been fought. This early tragedy is still remembered by a special ceremony performed in Surat every year.

IranShah Fire

About the year 1400 the Hindu empire of Sanjan was intruded on by the Muslims who prevailed in north Gujarat, the Hindu sovereign asked the Parsis for assistance and the Parsis raised an army of 1400 men under their chief Ardeshir. Fighting alongside the Hindus they defeated the invading Muslims. The Muslims returned with a larger force and this time the Hindus and Parsis were defeated and Sanjan was destroyed, but not before the Parsis were able to take their holy fire IranShah to a nearby mountain forest called Bahrot. The fire was maintained there for twelve years and then taken to a close hamlet called Bansda, where it remained for another fourteen years. Then at the invitation of the Navsari Parsis the IranShah fire was brought to Navsari. The Sanjana priests who came with the fire from Bansda and the Bhagaria priests of Navsari had an agreement that the Sanjana priests would only take care of the IranShah fire and not perform priestly services for the Navsari Parsis. Services such as the functioning of Navjote, Jashans etc. in Navsari were the privilage of the Bhagaria priests.

Iran Shah stayed in Navsari for 320 years except for an era of three years (1733-1736) when it was shifted to Surat because of political unstableness in Navsari. In 1740 IranShah was moved into Bulsar and then in 1742 to Udvada, back in the dominion of the Sanjana priests and there it continues to this day. IranShah was not the only fire temple of the Parsis. As early as the tenth century one knows of the subsistence of a fire temple in Bharuch.

Rivayets

The Parsis had come to India to maintain the pureness of their religion. In the fifteenth century they became conscious of the fact that they were losing their religious knowledge. They decided to send messengers to Iran to see how much the observance of their religion differed from that of the Zoroastrians of Iran. They also wanted to attempt and settle some of the spirite controversies brewing in India by getting guidance from the Zoroastrian priests in Iran. Over an era of almost 300 years, from 1478 to 1773, twenty-six messengers took questions to Iran and brought back answers from the Zoroastrian priests in Iran. This discourse between the twenty-six messengers from India and the Zoroastrian priests in Iran, are known as the Revayats. In addition, manuscripts of Avesta and Pahelvi texts as well as data about the state of the two communities were interchanged. Many of the Revayat questions originated in Navsari and were answered by Iranian priests of Kerman, Isfahan, Sharafabad,

Turkabad, and Yazd. Nariman Hoshang brought back to India the first Revayat. The voyage expenses for Nariman Hoshang were paid up by Changa Asha a celebrated leader of the Navsari Parsis who lived from 1450 to 1512.

Start of Sucess

By the 11th century, Parsis were well based in Gujarat and are frequently cited in the travel accounts of Arab, Portuguese, French and English travellers to India. These aliens recognized the Parsis as a separate group of Indians who originated from Iran. The Parsis were traders, farmers, merchants, brokers, doctors (vaids), weavers, and performed all kinds of trades except ironsmiths. This final trade called for functioning with fire and demanded snuffing out it with water and they felt it was not a religious thing to do.

In the sovereignty of the great Mughul king of India, Akbar, Parsis priests were invited to the Delhi court to explain their religion to Akbar. Dastur Meherji Rana led the delegation and so impressed the Mughul king, that he instructed that a holy fire be kept in the court at all times. He even substituted the Muslim calendar and followed the Parsi calendar. Akbar also observed Zoroastrian feasts as per the calendar. Other Parsis honoured by Akbar were Meherji Vacha and Mehervaid, a great Parsi doctor of that time. Parsis continued to be in frequent attendance at the court of the Mughul kings after Akbar. Meherji Kamdina and Hoshang Ranji received grants of land from King Jehangir. Rustom Maneck Seth of Surat visited the royal court of Aurangzeb. Rustom Maneck Seth, was a dominant Parsi who lived from 1635-1721 in Surat. He was a broker by trade hired by English and Portuguese. He helped them to set up trading manufacturing plants in Surat which at that time was under the Mughul kings of Delhi.

Bombay Parsis

The first Parsi to make it to Bombay was Dorabji Nanabhoy in 1640, shortly after the Portuguese founded the township of Bombay. He worked as a manager for the Portuguese. In 1668 when Bombay was given to the British, Dorabji became the tax collector and his family held the position through 1834. Later on, after 1668, more and more Parsis came to Bombay from Gujarat and finally it became the heart and spirit of the Parsis in the nineteenth and twentieth centuries. The arrival of the Parsis in Bombay coincided with the rule of the British over most of India, and a golden period for the Parsis started. Lowji Nasserwanji Wadia built the first dry dock in India at Bombay. He began constructing ships, many of which were ordered by the Royal British Navy. The Ship Foudroyant built in 1817 at the Wadia docks is still in service and served in World War II.

The Parsis after coming to Bombay keenly studied western knowledge, medicine, engineering and other professings and became skilled in the English language ahead of the rest of the people in India. With their advanced Western learning, they led the Indians in starting almost every industry in India. Many Parsis involved in trade within India and with the outside world made large fortunes. Kavasji Davar started the first textile mill in 1851. The Jeejeebhoy, Petit, Tatas and Cowasji Jehangir kins and their descendents played a significant role in the growth of the Parsis in India and especially of Bombay.

Jamsedjee Jeejeebhoy made his fate by trading with China. He used his immense wealth to found the Parsi Benevolent Institution which runs schools for the poor of all communities and religious backgrounds. He also constructed fire temples and towers of silence for the Parsis and paid for the Poona waterworks, the first of its type in India. During the potato famine in Ireland Jamsedjee Jeejeebhoy donated large amounts of money to feed the Irish. Dinshaw Petit made his fate trading in cotton. He also started the Bombay Stock Exchange. He used his wealth to build the first engineering school in Bombay. His charities helped less fortunate Zoroastrians in India and Iran.

Jamsedjee Tata was born in a poor hieratical family. He somehow managed to educate himself in engineering and started the first steel works in India. His family has become a great industrial power in India by carrying on the custom and pioneering new industries in India. Nowadays the Tata name is well acknowledged for being the first to start industries like chemicals, locomotives, truck and car manufacturing. The Tatas were the first to start an airline business in India out of which both Air India and Indian Airlines developed. In more recent years they were the first in India to start computer consulting services. Jamsedjee Tata was also responsible for building hydroelectric works at Lonavla to supply Bombay with electricity. The Tatas built the first school of Social Sciences in India. The family also founded the Tata Institute of Basic Research, where research in nuclear sciences and mathematics is carried out. It was started at the advice of Dr. Homi Bhabha, the founder of Indian atomic industry who was functioning at this institution until his sad demise. In ensuing years the Tata family has bifurcated into the manufacture of health and beauty aids, and food products. The Godrej family is another significant industrial family involved in the manufacture of electrical appliances (refrigerators, washing machines, fans etc.) and items such as office equipment, locks and safes, soaps. In recent years they fabricate several other items and are direct competitor with Procter and Gamble. Another personality, Sorabji Pochkhanawalla founded the Central bank of India.

REFERENCES

Avesta: The Sacred Books of the Parsis. Edited by Karl F. Geldner. Stuttgart, 1885-1896. (For Yt. 22-24 and the Avestan Fragments see N. L. Westergaard's Zendavesta, Copenhagen, 1852-1854.).

Benveniste, Emile: the Persian Religion according to the chief Greek Texts. Paris, 1929.

Bharucha, Sheriarji D: A Brief Sketch of the Zoroastrian Religion and Customs. Bombay, 1893.

Bilimoria, N. F.: Zoroastrianism in the Light of Theosophy. Bombay, 1896.

Clemen, C.: Die Griechischen und Lateinischen Nachrichten über die Persische Religion. Giessen, 1920.

Collected Sanskrit Writings of the Parsis: Part 1. Khorda-Avesta. Part 2. Ijisni. Part 3. Mainyoi Khard. Part 4. Skanda Gumani Gujara. Edited by Sheriarji D. Bharucha. Bombay, 1906-1913.

Desatir: Published by Mulla Firuz Bin Kaus. Persian and English. 2 vols. Bombay, 1818.

Dhalla, M. N.: Zoroastrian Theology. New York, 1914.

Gathas: Translated into English by K. E. Punegar. In *the Journal of the K. R. Cama Oriental Institute*, No. 12. Bombay, 1928.

Geiger, Bernhard: Die Amesha Spentas. Wien, 1916.

Hodivala, S. K.: Indo-Iranian Religion with parallelisms in the Hindu and Zoroastrian Scriptures. Bombay, 1925.

Hoshang Memorial Volume: Bombay, 1918.

Kapadia, S. A.: The Teachings of Zoroaster and the Philosophy of the Parsi Religion. London, 1905.

Karaka, Dosabhai F.: History of the Parsis. 2 vols. London, 1884.

Modi, J. J.: The Religious Ceremonies and Customs of the Parsees. Bombay, 1922.

Modi Memorial Volume: Bombay, 1930.

3

Philosophy

In Persian chronicles, the most noteworthy contribution to religious doctrine is made by Zoroastrianism. As per this doctrine, not only are truth and goodness eternal, but falsehood and evil also share eternity with them. Both have separate Gods who have their own independent orders of management. There is a God of goodness, Ahura Mazda, alias the God of light and there is a God of evil, Ahraman, also known as the God of dark; each has his own well-defined role to play. All action within the cosmos results from the confrontation and interaction of these two opponent Gods, who are forever locked in a forbidding battle of endurance and supremacy.

The powers of the God of goodness are steadily striving to prevail those of the God of evil. Like a see-saw, the outcome of this struggle is always changing sides sometimes in favour of goodness and sometimes in favour of evil. Thus Zoroastrian doctrine presents a simple explanation for the cosubsistence of evil and suffering, goodness and happiness, by attributing their origin to two different sources. All the ailment s in the grief, suffering, ignorance and agony, are believed to result when the God of evil gains the upper hand.

BASIC PHILOSOPHY

Zoroastrianism deserted the accepted notion of many Gods and founded one of the first monotheistic (one God) religions. It is based on two predominant spirits: Ahura-Mazda (also known as Ormazd), the spirit of light and good, the true God, the Wise Lord; and Ahrulman, the spirit of evil and darkness, the Evil. Each side has forces of warriors, angels on the good and monsters on the bad. Eventually, the Zoroastrian prophesies contend, Good will triumph over Evil on Judgment Day. Two principles form the base of Zoroastrian morality: preserve a good life and fight against evil. Included is the belief that prize or punishment are earned after demise as per one's deeds in life. The fundamental doctrine is 'Good Thoughts, Good Works, and Good Deeds.' Contained is an acceptance of all faiths and races as well as respect for the earthly environment.

A basic characteristic of Zoroastrianism is the sacred fire. It is kept burning in the temples, and often the homes, fed with fragrant sandalwood and cedar. Fire is regarded the great purifier, the sustainer of life, and the nature of the sun. Another characteristic is the needful dressing (sudreh-kusti, a white shirt and woolen sash or cord). Tightening of the kusti is part of the basic daily prayers.

DIVINE LAWS

Asha

Subsistence upon the earth unveils to man that an even and elegant and consistent movement goes on all-round him in world. Spring and summer, autumn and winter, with their ceaseless seasonal succession of changes, take their unvarying course. The tides rise and fan punctually. The daybreak and morning and noon and evening and night do their continuous daily round. The dying day gives birth to the night. The night hangs its myriad of silvery lamps to lighten the darkness. The dawning breaks to revive the day and the day goes the repeated round of its birth. The heavens and their glittering hosts, the sun and the moon and the stars and the planets march at a regulated space. Despite the casual freaks and caprices, the laws governing the movements of nature seem to be changeless.

This trustworthy regularity of nature led the Indo-Iranians to recognize the fact that a stable order persisted in the world which assured its subsistence. They callled it rta (order or course of things). They emulated this universal order and introduced it in all their human activities. They proffered prayers to Gods, they sacrificed to them seasonal offers oblation. All this was to be done at fixed times, reciting specific formulas, chanted in a prescribed manner and with regulated movements of sacred implements. The ceremonials were thus to be per formed in accordance with the established reigns and under a fixed order. This order was rta in rites or rite, a word derived from the same origin.

Thus bit-by-bit they progressed higher and saw that human life can best be lived when man's relations with his neighbours, his obligation towards his fellowmen and towards the heavenly beings were governed as per fixed laws. Thus they came to recognition of a fundamental moral order regulating human affairs and understood by rta employed in ethical matters as right or virtuousness, word, of the same significance. Varuna, Mitra, and the Adityas, as also Agni and Soma, came to be looked upon the sustainers of the moral order.

The Variant of RTA: A key figure most conspicuous outstanding in the Gathas is Asha. Its familiar and widely known Iranian variant is arta, areta, equivalent to the Vedic rta (order or course of things). Words derived from this stem must been freely used in Western Asia and surrounding countries about four thousand years ago. Scholars gather from the clay bearing wedge-shaped inscriptions detected at Tell-el-Amarna in Middle Egypt and the great find of tablets at Boghaz-Keui in Asia Minor that Dushratta, a Mitanni King, was reigning in Syria about 1600 BC. In his letter to his brother-in-law Amenhetep III of Egypt he mentions his brothers who bear the names Artashumara and Artatama. His grandfather also was named Artatama. Zarathushtra thus finds the stem arta or areta in vogue, but we do not find him employing it in the Gathas. He uses its variation asha instead and makes it the basic base for the structure of his moral doctrine. The Later Avestan works follow him in their general use of the word. It is in the Old Persian inscriptions, however, that we find the use of arta as an element of proper names. The Pahlavi writers make a more frequent use of the arta form than of asha.

Asha Stands for Morality: Ahura Mazda is the father of Asha, says Zarathushtra. He formed Asha through his knowledge. Asha is of one will with Ahura Mazda. He is the teacher of Ahura Mazda, and lives in one dwelling with Ahura Mazda and Vohu Manah. He is given the characteristic Vahishta, 'best'. It is not used in the Gathas as his fixed title, as it becomes in the later Avesta where Asha Vahishta is used as a combined word.

The Vedic writer asks why does not the sun come down t from the sky, why do waters of the all rivers running into the ocean not fill it, where do the stars go throughout the day and related questions concerning the functioning of the celestial order in nature. Zarathushtra, in similar manner, asks Ahura Mazda to tell him who is the father of Asha, the incarnation of the order ruling the world, who has influenced the way of the sun and the stars, and by whom does the moon wax and wane, who preserves the earth and the celestial sphere from falling, who has made waters and plants and who has given speed to winds and clouds, who has made light and darkness, and morning and noon and night. In one place we discover him telling Ahura Mazda that the sun and the daybreak take their course for his glory through Asha. Asha's one name is the shining one.

A few passages guide us to delineate some connection between Asha and the rite. Zarathushtra speaks of himself as a zaotar, Vedic hotar, sacrificing priest, and says that he learns the straight or orderly way through Asha. Ceremonial oblations are made unto Ahura Mazda and Asha. Ahura Mazda knows those who are better in the remembrance of the Yasna sacrifice as per Asha. The adherent make ceremonial oblations to Asha along with Ahura Mazda.

Zarathushtra is virginal in body, mind, and heart. He is the incarnation of good sentiments, good words, and good deeds. He thinks, speaks, and acts virtuously. He lives in the atmosphere of virtuousness and spread it all around him. He is the very virtuousness itself living in flesh for the good of humanity. Virtuousness sustains him in his hardships and trials. When his outstanding prophetic work is beset with much difficulties; when the prophet of Ahura faces resistance from all sides; when friends forsake his company and relatives abandon his campaign; when the sovereigns of the land look upon him with distrust and the evil seek to compass his ruin; when, friendless and forsaken, booed and hooted, ridiculed and persecuted, he roams about the villages and towns of Iran, he turns his eager eyes to Mazda and Asha in search of inbound peace, and obtains it. Cut down to the brink of the direst poverty, Zarathushtra does not seek temporal riches, but the enduring wealth of the spirit, that is, virtuousness.

Asha is the highest word in the Zoroastrian language, and its offshoot ashavan forms the name of the man who is most angelic and owns the noblest character. The term is applied to Ahura Mazda, Zarathushtra, and to all who are religious. Virtuousness is the will of Ahura Mazda; it is the rule of man's obligation, and to be virtuous is synonymous with being religious. The law of morality is the norm to which the disciple has to adapt his life in this world. Good thoughts, good words, and good deeds form the ethical base upon which virtuousness rests and the basis upon which the entire structure of the system of the Mazdayasnian doctrine is reared. This noble truth, at once so pithy and simple, is accessible to all. It does not attract the intellectual few and leave aside the uninformed many; nor does it become the privilage of a few thinkers and persons; but it can reach all and become the precious possession of the prince and peasant alike. Every Zoroastrian child absorbs the triad of good thinkings, good words, and good acts at its mother's breast.

Zarathushtra longs to make Asha his own all along with Ahura Mazda and Vohu Manah. He yearns to see Asha and his celestial associates. He is eager to behold him coming with the dedication of Armaiti. Through the deeds prompted by the good thoughts of Vohu Manah he aspires to reach Asha. He begs Asha to come unto him along with Ahura Mazda and Vohu Manah. He advises his daughter Pouruchisti to seek companionship with Asha. He prays that Hvogva may make Asha her own. He longs for the day when Asha will come among the Fryan nobility through Armaiti. He advises marrying couples that as husbands and wives they should endeavour to excel one another in their pursual of Asha. Asha is approached through the practice of noble deeds as per the primeval laws ordained by Ahura Mazda. Zarathushtra looks for dedication to come with Asha among his followers. Those who live in communion with Asha reap the best reward. Zarathushtra prays for the benedictions of Asha. Asha is asked to grant that benediction which forms the honour of Vohu Manah. Zarathushtra, says Ahura Mazda, is the one man who has heard the heavenly commandments and undertaken to live and work for the furtherance of Asha's virtuousness. The prophet of Ahura Mazda declares that as long as he shall have vigour and strength he will urge all to yearn for Asha, and work for the spread of Asha's precepts. He further says that he shall protect Asha's morality all his life. The devout everywhere welcome Asha's manifestation, and the wise uphold him through their words and deeds. Who so ever spreads Asha's morality in the house and district is like unto Ahura Mazda. Those that are best unto the virtuous ones shall be in the pastures of Asha and Vohu Manah.

Zarathushtra knows Ahura Mazda through Asha. He prays for the good acts of the Holy Spirit and the knowledge of Vohu Manah. He asks Ahura Mazda to give help through Asha, and beseeches him to cede the desires of those who are devoted to Asha. Ahura Mazda gives wealth of Vohu Manah through Asha, and Zarathushtra seeks to discover how the riches can be obtained. Those who put down violence and discord gain Vohu Manah's prize through Asha. He is implored to come through Asha and Vohu Manah, and asked to give mighty power through Asha. Those who practise morality win power as prize from Ahura Mazda through Vohu Manah. Zarathushtra asks Ahura Mazda what prize will be given him through Asha and Vohu Manah.

These honours are the benedictions of both worlds given by Ahura Mazda through Asha. Zarathushtra asks Asha together with Vohu Manah about the reigns of life that guide to happiness. Ahura Mazda sees exposed and hidden faults of men through Asha Kinship with Vohu Manah is sought through Asha. Ahura Mazda wields power between the rival factions of morality and evil through Asha. Through Asha and Vohu Manah Ahura Mazda apportions vigour and durability, weal and immortality unto those who practise morality and good thinking. Through Asha's morality does the world flourish by deeds prompted by Vohu Manah's good thoughts. Through Asha again is Ahura Mazda's help sought that Vohu Manah may come. Ahura Mazda is implored to reveal knowledge of the way of Vohu Manah through Asha.

The Maker of the world consults Asha to know about a master who can cure the sufferings of the human kind. Zarathushtra seeks to know through Vohu Manah what Asha said to the creator. Ahura Mazda is asked to give long life which is Asha's gift. The virtuous declare that they will never arouse the wrath of Asha.

Ahura Mazda asks Zarathushtra to seek knowledge from Asha. Asha gives guidance to those who listen to him. Knowledge exalts communities through Asha's morality. Ahura Mazda knows what is best for man in this life through Asha. He teaches his best philosophies through Asha. Armaiti is asked to clear the conscience of men through Asha. Men of good understanding know Armaiti's dedication as the source of Asha's morality. Asha and Armaiti are combined in the heavenly lands. Ahura Mazda has prepared his creed with Asha that Vishtaspa embraces.

Asha gives authority to his avid disciples. He furthers men's possessions. Men make the pastures prosper through the practice of Asha's morality. The sinful endeavour to hinder the good work of those who further Asha's morality by prospering the cattle by their diligence. Ahura Mazda produced plants for the cattle. Diligent persons gain cattle through Asha. The prophet is awarded precious animals and weal and immortality by Ahura Mazda through Asha.

The Way of Morality: The Rig Veda refers to the way of rta. The Gathas similarly address the way of Asha, morality, and the idea, is formulated in the Later Avesta. The way of morality leads to heaven and the evil spirits, we are told, shake at the Bridge of Judgment because they have diverted from the way of Asha through their words and deeds. Ahura Mazda dwells in the straight paths and Zarathushtra seeks their knowledge through Asha. Deviation from the way of morality spells man's destruction. Zarathushtra exhorts his hearers that every man and woman is free to select for himself or herself the way of morality or the way of evil. The decision between the two ways of life rests with the person. Man is the arbiter of his destiny. He has the power and freedom to select between truth and falsehood, morality and evil, good and evil. He is accountable for the moral choice he makes and is consequently accountable for his actions. If he makes the right choice and embraces morality, he will harvest its reward, but if, as a free agent, he chooses evil, the answerability will be his and his own daena or self will guide him to retribution.

Self Control in Morality: The prophet inculcates morality in his teachings, and strictly enjoins his followers to combat evil. By his birthright man belongs to the world of morality and is sent into this world for its furtherance and for the destruction of the world of evil. He is a friend of the virtuous and their morality, but a foe of the evil and their evil. It is expressly said that he alone is virtuous who is a friend to the virtuous; but he who, through maudlin sentimentality, is good unto the evil and palliates his evil is to be regarded evil, for by failing to do his obligation he puts a premium on evil. To condone evil in a evil person is a surrender to evil. Before the person sets out to fight evil in the outer world, he has first to establish order in his inner world. Concord and not discord, order and not disorder, morality, and not evil, should be his steady inward experience.

With strict self control he has to work for the spritual development of his self. He is taught to subjugate his passions, eradicate evil thoughts from his mind, and conquer the animal in him by an incessant warfare with the forces of evil. The way of morality leads to the dwelling of Ahura Mazda. But the way is not without its difficulties and trials. Firm resolution, strong will, and sustained effort are required before one can successfully tread it and reach the final aim. It needs no effort to be evil and be a passive victim of the flesh, but it does take a hero to be virtuous and live for the spirit. There are tempting pitfalls and alluring snares that beguile the devotee and guide him astray to the way of evil. The quest is fraught with great difficulties. But then the prize it brings is also matchless. The aim is not easy to reach. Many more are the chances of misses than of hits, and the aspirant has to try again and again before he can successfully strike the mark. Our attempt may prove fruitless for the time being, but there is merit in having aimed at realizing the ideal. If we win, it is good.

If we lose, it is also good. Man has to keep himself pure and clean bodily, mentally, and spritually. Purity of body and mind is the best thing for man in life. It strengthens morality and sanctity. The blending of the virtues of Vohu Manah and Armaiti in the life of man makes him virtuous. The fusion of the noble qualities both of the head and heart make the person virtuous. Vohu Manah purifies the mind, Armaiti sanctifies the heart. Vohu Manah's knowledge enlightens the world, Armaiti's dedication ennobles it. Without knowledge man is poor indeed, but without dedication he courts demise in spirit. Knowledge teaches the spirit the doctrine of life, dedication lends to the spirit the zest to act it, and the true religion begins with this acting. The philosopher may think of Ahura Mazda, the metaphysician may speculate about his origin, but the adherent actually imitates him in action. Knowledge gives a right view of life, teaches man about his relations to his Heavenly Father and the world, and creates ideals for him; but dedication strives to realize these. Knowledge is good, knowledge is better; but knowledge tinged with dedication is best.

The wise knows Mazda, the adherent owns Mazda; and the blending of the virtues of both makes man the consummate one, the saint, the ashavan or virtuous one.

The creed of Asha leads to felicity, whereas the opposite way of evil brings destruction. Those who follow the ways of evil destroy the world of Asha's morality. Zarathushtra seeks from Asha and his heavenly associates power with which he and his followers may smite evil. Asha's morality leaves evil doers who embrace not dedication and good thinking, just as wild beasts flee from men. Vohu Manah leaves those who think not of Asha. Ahura Mazda is invoked to teach how the disciple can drive away the Druj and those persons who, in defiance of the heavenly precepts, follow not Asha. The prophet asks Ahura Mazda how best he can put evil in the hands of morality and bring punishment unto those who embrace evil. Vohu Manah will establish the heavenly Kingdom of Ahura Mazda for those who vanquish evil and deliver it into the hands of Asha. The world will ultimately embrace morality through the effective teachings of the Saviours of the world and Ahura Mazda is asked to announce when that happy day will come to the world. Zarathushtra tells Ahura Mazda that his heavenly purpose will be accomplished and his name will be glorified when as ordained by him both men and demons will see at the end of the world that Asha triumphs and his morality smites evil and the world will be blessed with the happy tidings.

He eagerly hopes for the period when every person in his or her own capacity will embrace and act morality and will thus make the entire world of compassion gravitate towards Asha. In this consists the final victory of good over evil, and the Heavenly Kingdom of Ahura Mazda will come when morality wholly permeates the world. All, therefore, have to supply to this mighty work. The virtuous ones living in different ages and at different places form the members of one virtuous group, inasmuch as they are all motivated by one and the same motive and work for the common cause. Though separated by time and place, as also by their respective tenements of clay, they are one in spirit, and work for the inauguration of the Kingdom of Morality.

Fire: Zarathushtra says that the best oblations that the self-righteous can make to the fire of Ahura Mazda are the virtuous deeds inspired by Asha and declares that as long as he has energy left in him he will think of Asha whenever he will carry his gift of adoration unto fire. Through the fire and the thought of Ahura Mazda, he says, he will find safety against the Evil and his evil machinations and it is through them that Asha's morality will thrive.

Corporeal impurity is removed by fire and Zarathushtra applies this symbol of cleaning in the eschatological sense to burn and destroy spritual uncleanliness or sin. Thus will the fire be the great purifier of spirits steeped in evil. Through Asha and fire will Ahura Mazda give his final award unto the good and the evil. Asha and Armaiti will help Ahura Mazda when he will split the virtuous from the evil through his fire. The fire of Ahura Mazda is mighty through Asha and will bring apparent joy unto the virtuous but a visible harm unto the evil. Ahura Mazda's power and holiness, says Zarathushtra, will be apparent when he will deal out the destinies unto the virtuous and the evil through the glow of fire reinforced by Asha.

Khshathra

One of the first characteristics that man learns to distinguish in the heavenly beings is their power or power. It is apparent in their actions as creatures, sustainers, and sovereigns. The ancestors of the Indo-Iranians called it kshatra, and employed it to Mitra, Varuna, Indra, and the Adityas. Zarathushtra, we find, adopts it in its Iranian form khshathra and uses it in its ordinary meaning, power, or applies it explicitly to heavenly power, symbolized in the Kingdom of Ahura Mazda. He gives it the name vohu and calls it vohu khshathra, 'the Good Kingdom, or call it as khshathra ishtoish, 'the Kingdom of Desire,' or names it Khshathra vairya, 'the Wished for Kingdom.' Ahura Mazda has produced Khshathra. In the post-Gathic period of time the compound Khshathra Vairya gains ground and is always used as the name of the archangel symbolizing Ahura Mazda's heavenly majesty.

The creator, sovereign, and master of both the worlds is Ahura Mazda. The devout appeal to him to guide them to work in his Kingdom upon earth for the sucess of men and their cattle. They pray that they may get happy homes, rich in pastures, attended by Khshathra. All creatures prosper in Mazda's Kingdom through Vohu Manah, and through him again Ahura Mazda gives Khshathra's power to the good. Nobler than the sphere of earthly riches is Khshathra's domain of spritual riches. Ahura Mazda reigns over his earthly Kingdom and prepare humanity for his heavenly Kingdom of perfection and goodness that is yet to be. Despite its much good, this world harbours in its midst much that is evil. Man's work in this life is to fight and rout the forces of evil. Zarathushtra had laid the base of the Heavenly Kingdom and has allotted to man the collosal task of building and founding the ideal Kingdom in which good alone will exist. Evil lurks in man and through man bestrides the world. It is his obligation to clean his inner nature of all impureness and extinguish evil from the world without. Zarathushtra is optimistic and convinced that one day evil will not be.

It is left to man to bring that day close or keep it at length. It is in his hands to achieve it now or keep it long in the coming. The prophet of Ahura Mazda is serious and eager to hasten its advent. He asserts, with repeated emphasis, that the Kingdom is near at hand, if only humanity sets about zealously and strenuously to inaugrate it. He passionately exhorts his hearers not to waver, not to be staggered by the formidable nature of the task, but to aim for and work and struggle and fight for it with body and mind, heart and spirit. With deep religious fervour he sings that he is ready to lay down the life of his body to guide humanity to work for the advancement of the Kingdom in obedience to the commandments of Ahura Mazda. With Ahura Mazda on his side, he makes the good thoughts of Vohu Manah and morality of Asha his own and, with the burning dedication of Armaiti, he works for the advent of the imperishable Kingdom. Triumph of morality over evil will usher in the Kingdom and he prays for strength for himself and his followers so that they may wage a successful war against evil.

The devout pray that they may participate in the inauguration of the Kingdom of Mazda. Vohu Manah, the guardian of good thoughts, furthers the Kingdom. As right thinking is the source of good conduct and try to work for the advent of the Heavenly Kingdom, it is sometimes spoken of as belonging to Vohu Manah. The Kingdom, it is said, is in the possession of Vohu Manah and Ahura Mazda and Asha and Armaiti live in it. The Kingdom of Vohu Manah is furthered by Asha's morality. To be worthy of entering the Heavenly Kingdom and living in it is man's highest aspiration. Asha assures the life in the Kingdom to those who work zealously for the furtherance of morality. Through morality is the heavenly help gained in Mazda's Kingdom. Zarathushtra is eager to enter the blessed Kingdom, and a long life of felicitous subsistence in it, and to share its splendours. Wise Jamaspa courts the life of morality and longs for the Kingdom as the gift of Vohu Manah. Zarathushtra prays that Frashaoshtra may win the Kingdom of Ahura Mazda for all time; He asks Ahura Mazda to apparent unto him the incomparable things that humanity will witness in the Heavenly Kingdom as the prize of Vohu Manah. Ahura Mazda is asked to give the Kingdom through Vohu Manah as prize to those whom he knows to be doing what is best in life.

Vohu Manah will declare the advent of the Kingdom. Ahura Mazda has ordained through Vohu Manah and Asha to give unto the good paragon and immortality in his Kingdom. Through Khshathra he allocates the destinies unto the good and the evil as per their deserts. The devout yearn for the presence of Ahura Mazda with Vohu Manah, Asha, and Khshathra when they enter the paradisiacal Dwelling of Song. Ahura Mazda will come at the last aim accompanied by his Holy Spirit, Vohu Manah, Asha, Khshathra, and Armaiti. With evil uprooted and imperfectness at an end, the world that will emerge on the occasion of the settlement of the Heavenly Kingdom will be altogether a new world, a perfect world.

Ahura Mazda has produced the earth rich in soil and has filled its bowels with much mineral wealth and has desired that humanity should prosper and flourish through the riches obtained by their thoroughness and labour. Wealth is the natural concomitant of all earthly Kingdoms. All earthly and spritual riches therefore are embodied in Khshathra. The later Avestan texts attribute the charge of metals, the visible token of wealth, to Khshathra. The Gathas are silent over the association of Khshathra with metals. The ordeal of molten metal does however play an outstanding part in cleaning the world of all moral impurities to make way for the coming of Khshathra's Kingdom. Ahura Mazda knows best the retributions that will take place through the molten metal. The virtuous will reap their final prize and the evil will meet with their retribution when Ahura Mazda will judge them through the molten metal.

PRIMARY BELIEFS

Zoroastrians are taught that there is one God who is all good and whose notion is visible in the natural cosmos around. The order and regularity of the orbiting planets, the moon, the tides, and the seasons all testify to a higher-ranking organizing mind – all the work of Ahura Mazda.

Within this natural world, just as there are corporeal opposites such as dark and light, night and day or positive or negative energies in magnets, so too in the moral sphere diametrically opposed forces are at work.

Zoroastrians are therefore alerted to the subsistence of the negative forces which live within nature but also within the human mind and about which they need to be consciously wakeful. Zoroastrians are therefore instructed to fight against being drawn in by the negative forces which are manifested in dissincerity and sinceritytreachery. For this reason Zoroastrians encapsulate their ideal aspirations in the motto Good Thoughts, Good Words and Good Deeds and are presumed to be honest, straightforward and benevolent.

Zoroastrians are encouraged to base their lives on the rationale of Asha or Right Behaviour which can be accomplished by right thinking or Vohu Manah. This state of thinking can be accomplished through functioning within or reflection of nature, or through chanting songs of praise, both a form of meditation.

Zoroaster makes it clear that each human is able of making choices and thus obligation for any action comes down to the person. There is no compulsion to have the message that Zoroaster has received and gives expression to in the Gathas, but he states that every Zoroastrian should share this doctrine of truth and morality with others and give them the opportunity to join the society of the Good Religion.

In the Heavenly Songs, Zoroaster addresses both men and women and makes it clear that his admiration for humans extends to both sexes equally. Thus throughout the social history of the society, women have always enjoyed an raised status and have been able to take part in all activities that men power undertake.

While there are some beliefs of what happens at demise, the main concern of a Zoroastrian is with life on this earth rather than with the hereafter. The most basic prayer known as Ashem Vohu, makes it clear that it is on this earth that pleasure is bestowed upon the person who does good for its own sake, rather than in the hope of reward. It is therefore clear that doing good brings pleasure which is the ultimate benediction upon every person. It is the Zoroastrian's obligation to leave the earth a better place through the efforts and results of each person throughout his/her lifetime.

In terms of death, it is thought that the spirit leaves the body and crosses a bridge where one's good deeds are weighed against one's bad deeds. If the balance of good is greater, the spirit will begin its journey to the dwelling of everlasting light and bliss and be reunited with the celestial energy. Beyond this, there is no elaboration. If good does not prevail, then the spirit is left lingering in limbo. In traditional practice, the dead body is not left to pollute the earth which supports life.

Instead it serves the living by furnishing nourishment to the carrion birds that visit the final resting place of the bodies on high unaccessible mountain plateaux surrounded by man-built walls. Nowadays many prefer cremation although in Iran this is not permitted by the present authorities so burial is the only possibility, however distatsteful it may be to orthodox Zoroastrians. Later Zoroastrianism has developed more elaborate notions of hell, and a final day of judgement when a Saviour will appear and Good will triumph ultimately over Evil.

Ahura Mazda

Literally interpreted, Ahura means The Master Creator, and Mazda means Supremely Wise. This was the name by which Zarathushtra addressed his God. He declared that there is only one God, who is the singular originative and nourishing force of the World. Zarathushtra was the first Prophet who brought a monotheistic religion.

Dualism

As humans we are given the right to choose. However, because of the law of cause and effect, we are also accountable for our choices, and must face their consequences.

Despite the fact that there is only one God, our world works on the basis of ethical dualism. There is Spenta Mainyu (progressive mentality) and Angra Mainyu (evil or regressive mentality). Zarathushtra pleaded with us to think clearly before we select, and asked us to select the progressive choices to bring about good consequences. He said that Ahura Mazda would not order us to select either this or that.

In other words, having given us the power to choose, Ahura Mazda leaves us alone and permits us to make our choices. And if we select good, we will bring about good, and if we select evil, we will cause evil. This is how the moral world operates.

Ahriman

Based on the above principle, we are the causes of all the good and all the wickedness that happens in our moral world. Or plainly stated, as per Zarathushtra, there is no Devil. However, some of the Post-

Zarathushtra sacred scripture introduced the notion of the Devil, or Ahriman, which was effectively a personification of Angra Mainyu.

Purpose in Life

To be amongst those who renew the world, to make the world growth towards perfection.

Pleasure is a by-product of a way of living. And pleasure is for those who work for the pleasure of others.

Amesha Spentas

Zarathushtra tells us that Ahura Mazda produced everything based on the six Amesha Spentas, which are in fact heavenly aspects of the creator. These are:

Vohu Mano:The spirit of the Good Mind

Asha:The spirit of Truth and Right

Khshatra:The spirit of Holy sovereignty

Spenta Armaiti:The spirit of Benevolent Dedication and Love

Haurvatat:The spirit of Perfection and Well-Being

Ameretat:The spirit of Immortality.

As per Zarathushtra not only the world was produced on the basis of these six, but also they infuse every aspect of creation including ourselves.

Angels

Later on, Post-Zarathushtra Zoroastrianism mythicized the Amesha Spentas into angelical hierarchies, and brought back some of the Pre-Zarathushtra Gods into the holy scripture as angels.

Cosmology

Ahura Mazda first produced Vohu Mano or the Spirit of the Good Mind, through which God produced a plan or blueprint for the world. Part of this blueprint was to incorporate an operating mode and operating laws. This was Asha or the spirit of Truth and Right (the software of the world).

Then comes the actual act corporeal creation, which involved certain actions and manifestations. This is Khshatra or the spirit of Holy Sovereignty. These manifestions are actualized through Spenta Armaiti, with much dedication, faith and love.

And finally that the world is produced in the spirit of Perfection (Haurvatat) and is timeless and immortal (Ameretat).

Microcosm

Each one of us carries the heavenly essence within ourselves. It is our obligation to recognize this and act accordingly. Based on Zarathushtra's teachings, we can and should act like Ahura Mazda. We should think about every choice that we wish to make and in the spirit of our good mind select wisely. We should respect the natural and moral laws and operating mode of the world. We should act diligently, with love and faith. And we will then make ideal and timeless choices, and accomplish our purpose of regenerating the world.

Co-workers

We are co-workers and co-creators of God. We are here to accomplish the heavenly plan, not to become dutiful slaves of God, nor to be helpless children of God. And this is why we are given the choice. Even the choice not to co-operate with God's design and go against it, and that is why we find evil in the world. Because there are some who select not to work as per God's plan.

Heaven and Hell

As per Zarathushtra after we leave this life, our spirit leaves the body, and depending upon the choices that it has made, either it will go to the House of Songs or Kingdom of light (if he has made good choices) or to the Kingdom of Darkness and Separation (if evil choices).

Heaven and Hell are not corporeal places, but are depicted as timeless states of awareness: either state of oneness with or separation from Ahura Mazda.

Post-Zarathushtra Zoroastrianism mythologized these timeless states of consciousness into everlasting corporeal locations and descriptive places. This later notion permeated into Judeo-Christian religions.

Inferences

Since we are all empowered with the heavenly essence, we are all good and heavenly. Therefore it is not the humans who are evil, but their selections, activities and deeds that could be good or evil.

There is only one way to battle evil, and that is by spreading out goodness, just as there is only one way to fight the wickedness, and that is by spreading light. Similarly, only by spreading out love can we annihilate hatred and enmity, and not by fighting and opposing each other.

Canonical Maxims: Humata, Hukhta, Huvarshta, which mean: Good Thoughts, Good Words, Good Deeds.

There is only one way and that is the way of Truth.

Do the right thing because it is the right thing to do, and then all beneficial rewards will come to you also.

ETHICS

The Zoroastrian faith lays enormous emphasis on morals and ethics. A Zoroastrian is expected to make a conscious effort every moment of his life, to reject all forms of evil and the lie - in thought, word and deed and try at all times to walk on the way of Asha.

Asha is the Law Immutable, the Law Eternal, the Celestial Law of Order and Harmony on which the entire World is based. It is through Asha that Ahura Mazda produced the world and it is through Asha that humanity will attain perfection and be one with Ahura Mazda. In the Hoshbam prayer we aim for, "Through the best Asha, through the highest Asha, may we catch sight of Thee (Ahura Mazda), may we approach Thee, pay we be in perfect union with Thee".

It is only by taking the way of Asha that man can attain unification with his maker. The colophon to the Yasna is quite clear on this point, "There is but one path, that of Asha, all other paths are false paths".

As per Zoroastrianism, it is the sum total of a man's thoughts, words and deeds which will determine the fate of his spirit in the other world - it is these thoughts, words and deeds, good or bad, which will guide his spirit either to he gates of heaven or to the pathway of hell.

The Zoroastrian holy scriptures specify a number of virtues, which a Zoroastrian should aim for and try to cultivate and imbibe, and a number of vices from which he should guard himself and struggle to keep away.

Some of the virtues are as follows:

- Unwavering faith, dedication and love for Ahura Mazda and His prophet, Zarathushtra;
- Offering the Faraziyat (obligatory) prayers and giving thanks to Ahura Mazda, the Amesha Spentas and Yazatas for Their Grace and Bounty;

- Celebrating and preserving all the principles and customs of the religion and society, particularly with regard to respect and reverence for fire and' oblation worship through the medium of Atash Behram, Atash Adaran and Atash Dadgah, to the one and only God, rite purity in day-to-day life and observing privacy during menses and forty days after child birth, mental and corporeal hygiene with the performance of padyab-kusti and a rite or ordinary bath on contact with certain forms of druj. For example, a nahn or rite bath forty days after child birth and an ordinary but complete head bath after a hair-cut, shave, paring of nails or going to a paidust (funeral), wearing the sudreh kusti at all times of the day and night, apart from when having a bath, BunakPasbani or "Preservation of the seed", of the Mazdayasni Zarathushti society, by marrying only within the society, Dokmahnashini as the only legitimate method for the disposal of the dead, Performing and participating in all the necessary high and holy religious ceremonies and rites, Oblation the manthravani prayers only in the original language of the divine revelation or composition, for its full, potent and rich effect, Observing the Zoroastrian calendar and remembering the Amesha Spentas and Yazatas commanding over the thirty days and twelve months, Remembering the holy fravashis of the dead and celebrating all the parabhs, gahambars and other feasts and festivals;
- Speaking the Truth always. As per Herodotus, the Persians laid great stress on speaking the truth, riding a horse and archery and this formed the fundamental education for all Persian children. As per Yasna "A truth-speaker receives honour and is a master without fear", while as per the Sarosh Yasht Hadokht, "By speaking true words we receive many victories;
- Moderation in affairs of food, drink and other worldly delights. Neither fasting nor overeating and neither celibacy nor lechery is desirable;
- Charity and love for all humans. Zoroastrianism does not look down upon acquisition of wealth. In fact, wealth is seen to be basicly positive, provided it is put to judicious use and used for the well being of others. As per Yasna "He is a good man through whom goodness reaches other persons in all places. God gives such persons greatness;

- Industry and honest labour. As per Yasna 46.12 "those who make the world prosperous through good thoughts and honest endeavours are those who live a virtuous life in good thoughts. The Visperad (7.1) also praises, "industry and courage." Conversely as per the Visperad (18.2), "a man who is idle is worthy of hell";
- Keep a promise at all cost. In fact Yasna 61.3 strongly advises, "keep away from a covenant breaker and from one who tampers,"
- Aim for for higher knowledge and acquire knowledge under a proficient teacher;
- Honour ones elders and superiors. "He who does not show respect to an elder will never receive honour" (Yasna 29.6);
- Sincerity and integrity in ones dealings in this world;
- Forgiveness, mercy and tolerance- As per the Denkard, a good Zoroastrian must endeavour to make enemies his friends; purify the sinful and make the ignorant well-informed;
- Sincerely repent for ones sins (committed knowingly or unknowingly) by doing patet.

In Zoroastrianism, there are vices from which a Zoroastrian should guard himself and fight to keep away:

- Anger and envy- As per the Yasna "Those who promote wrath and jealousy are of evil intellect."
- Avarice and idleness- Yasna warns "Keep away from the greed of a wicked man", while the Visperad states, "a man who is idle is worthy of hell."
- Haughtiness-Little knowledge, power and wealth often makes a man arrogant. Arrogance leads to other vices and the road of ruin. The Ardibehest Yasht warns us to "keep away from these who have arrogant thoughts";
- Apostasy - As per Vendidad "if a person, being a member of the good religion, willingly accepts the commandments of another religion and speaks negatively of our religion, he becomes a sinner";
- infidelity - Zarathushtra asks God: "0 Ohrmazd, who is vengeful, toward you and who harms you most among those who cause harm?" Ohrmazd replied: "An adulteress";

METAPHYSICS

The contemporary world has lifted the cult of the personal to an art; so much is this the persisting ideal that in dealing with old world texts texts up-to-date savants forget that spritual teachers of yore laboured for the impersonal; they not only preached for their pupils, and themselves practised, the demolition of the sense of separateness, which is the spirit of that cult, but also applied the principle in and to their own public and exoteric work.

In every case we find the character of the teacher almost lost in the mass of teachings and customs which have gathered round his name. The name itself becomes the mask that hides more than one personality. It was an universal custom in the ancient world for the Teacher to assume a Name-Title occultly indicative of his mission and those who continued His work adopted it; thus the teacher's name invariably became a generic denomination of the School he founded, e.g., the name-title of the Iranian Reformer Zorathushtra — the star who ponders and sacrifices to the Living sun.

Of course, in the advancement of time with the rise of aspirational and unprincipled persons within the fold, came the faithlessness to the cause for which the School itself was founded. For Instance, the name-title of one of the greatest of Adepts, Shankar-Acharya, has been used in India these many centuries, by the Schools (Mathams) which came into being under His influence. The official manager-expounder in each of such schools called himself Shankar-Acharya, in conformity with the practice of the old occult customs; their obligation was to preserve intact and prevent any violation of the teachings of the Adept in their respective schools. To this day, in India several Shankar-acharyas have spritual sway over large masses of Hindus, but they are more rivals than co-operators, and hardly any impart the pure and genuine doctrines of the original Reformer. The form has survived, but the Spirit is absent.

Like all other custom-institutions this is rooted in truth. The teaching about the Guruparampara Chain which has degenerated into the gross and immoral doctrine of Apostolic Succession has an mystical aspect, viz. that the office of the Teacher is never empty and that orphan humanity is never without its Guides and Gurus. The highest title of the Buddha — and there are as many Buddhas as there are Sankaras — is Tathagata, he who is like his predecessors and heirs. And what is true of Buddha, the Enlightened One, is equally true of Christ, the Anointed One.

In studying ancient Systems this is a factor the student has to keep well in head. Thus in the consideration of Zoroastrian System we have to remember that the School represented by Zoroaster is very old.

If we had to illustrate broadly the origin of this religion from the viewpoint, and upon the authority of the Occult teachings, we would call it by its original, archaic name, that of Magianism. Locating its first improvement in those vast regions which would have to be described as the whole area between the Persian Gulf and the Sea of Okhotsk in its length, and that which stretches through the undiscovered deserts between the Altai and the Himalayan mountains in its breadth, we would place it back at an epoch, undreamt of by contemporary science and, therefore, declined by all but the most inquisitive and daring anthropologists.

We have no right to give out the correct number of years or rather of ages upon ages, since — as per the philosophies of the Secret Science — the first seeds of Magianism were sown in by the hand of the being to whose obligation it falls to rear, nurse and guide the tottering steps of the resurgent human races, that awake anew to life on every planet in its turn, after its periodical "obscuration." It goes as far back as the days of our local Manvantara, so that the seeds sown among the first "root-race" began germinating in its infant brain, grew up, and commencing to bear fruit toward the latter part of the second race, formulated fully during the third, into what is known among Occultists as the "Tree of Knowledge," and the "Tree of Life" — the real meaning of both having been, later on, so sadly blemished and misunderstood by both Zoroastrians and Christians.

Now, Occult accounts claim to have the correct dates of each of the thirteen Zoroasters. As per the said Records, Zoroastrianism as a distinct religio-philosophic school is of early Atlantean origin, i.e., before spritual sinfulness overtook that race. The establishing of this School concurs with the commencing of the cycle of the Iranian branch of the Aryan stock; this event is marked by the corporeal incarnation of the first Zoroaster from whose psycho-spritual seed sprang the builders of Iranian Mysteries and culture. In the narratives of his life-labours, mythical and astronomical events were incorporated, as said in the previous article of this series.

In the beginning the Vendidad was pre-eminently an Occult treatise; it has passed through innumerous vicissitudes and deformations during these thousands of years, as through scores of editions in the course of the evolution of languages; in its present form it is but a fragment, and a patched-up one at that — put together mostly from retention and surviving texts, some of doubtful legitimacy from the occult point of view, after the feats of the vandal Iskander, whom the West knows as Alexander.

From the days of the first Zoroaster this School (like the Sister Schools in other lands) has bent to the blows of cyclic law; it became greatly spoilt in its public ranks at times and became only a lasting esoteric centre; prospered through its benevolent and authoritative works at others. During this ebb and flow Adept-Teachers of different ranks restored the teachings and resuscitated the work; all of Them were reformers and protestants against anti-Theosophic philosophies and practices; one of them protested and led a revolt against the Vaidic corruptnesses when cultured relations between India and Persia was close and friendly; another reformed the magic-practices of Egyptians and Chaldeans in their sub-cycles of degradation.

In doing all this they always used the name-title of the Original Founder and with good reason; for they were, one and all, but Incarnations, however limited, of the Original Influence. The last one to do this was the constructor of the Temple of Azareksh, many ages before the historical era; he was the Mage who instructed the doctrines of Heavenly Magic which spread from Bactris to Medes and thence under the name of Magism were used by the Adept-astronomers in Chaldea which shaped substantially the Mosaic doctrines; he was the author of the Zend-Avesta which, as Darmesteter explains, is "a commentary or explanation of the Law", i.e., he was the transcriber and annotator of the works on the primeval sacred Magian religion. The original Zend is a secret code of certain words and formulas agreed upon by the original compilers, and the key to which is but with the Initiates. Neither was The Avesta of Ardeshir identical with that which was brought out and given to Gushtasp, by Zara-Ishter the thirteenth prophet of the Desatir; nor that of the second quite the same as the original Zend, although even this one was the public version of the Zen-Zara. While certain Persian texts repeating the Occult education speak of thirteen Zoroasters, we must not forget that there were other persons associated with the exoteric side of the School who also claimed from time to time the name-title of Zoroaster for themselves. Such applicants deformed and disfigured the pure teachings and have left their mark and impress on the outer story of the School. Naturally, these unauthentic claimants do not form part of the Occult Records about the true Zoroasters.

The original writings, codes of law like the Vendidad, or hymns like the five Gathas, or speeches like the Yasna are almost all destroyed. The sparse fragments we now possess are worse than fragmentary, for interpolations have taken place. All the same they are full of high doctrine, noble ethics, and not altogether devoid of occult lore and esoteric teachings, though they are rightly called "the ruins of a religion".

The extant Zoroastrian texts and texts will not be treasured till all this is kept in mind. What we now own is the residue of centuries of trials and visitations through which Iranian culture came to birth, culminated, declined and from all appearances is becoming extinct, this last is one phase of the communal karma which the contemporary Parsis, only some 95,000 strong, are facing today.

Highly mixed as this balance is, there is enough of Theosophy not only to interest but also instruct our readers. We will here examine some of its metaphysical propositions, then turn to its cosmo- and anthropogenesis, and finally to its psychology, and gain inspiration from its noble ethics.

Magianism, in the days of its full development and practice, and long ages before the first of the twelve great religions, its direct branches, mentioned and lightly described by Mohsan Fani in the Dabistan, ever saw light; and even much prior to the appearance of the first devotees of the religion of Hush-ang was long anterior to that of Zeratusht, the prophet of the contemporary Parsis, that religion, as we can undeniably prove was atheism. At any rate, it would be so regarded now, by those who call Kapila and Spinoza, Buddha and our Mahatmas, Brihaspati of the Charvack and the contemporary Adwaitees, all alike, nastikas or atheists. Assuredly no doctrine about a personal God, a gigantic man and no more, was ever taught by the true Magi. Hence Zoroaster, the seventh prophet (as per the Desatir, whose compilers mixed up and confused the Zaro-Ishtars, the high priests and initiates of the Chaldean worship or Magian Hierophants would be regarded as an atheist in the contemporary sense of the word.

The corporeal and visible Nature is energised by the psychical and both are ensouled and enclosed by the spritual. Ahura Mazda, the Sovereign Spirit, is the Universal Power, one with his manifestation. Of course he is personified and the latter has become an object of prayer and worship with the ignorant. The Ahura Mazda Yasht is highly reminiscent of the ninth, tenth, and eleventh preachings of the Bhagavad Gita. Like Shri Krishna, Ahura Mazda in reply to his preferred adherent, Zoroaster, describes his own nature. He gives his own many names, feature of that Nature and starts with "Ahmi—I am." The original construction (no doubt purposely employed just as Krishna plays on the word Atma in the sixth Gita) also leads to the transformation: "I am that about which every one enquires and questions."

The second name which has mystified Orientalists and even Parsi philologists is rendered "Herd-giver" by Darmesteter among the former, and as "protector and nourishers of the Herd" by Ervad Kanga among the latter. It really pertains to the character of Ahura Mazda as forming the hierarchy of beings which is immanent in the manifested world; in his transcendent nature he is the energising enspiriting Power who, like Krishna, having established this whole World with a fragment of himself, remains separate. The very third name, "I am the one strength in everybody," and those which follow, are clearly indicative of the all-pervasive nature of Ahura Mazda-Knowledge Incarnate.

Zoroastrianism is not a monotheistic religion, however much some of its Anglicized disciples of today make that claim, copying the unphilosophical churches of Christendom; nor is it polytheistic, though among the irrational of the society there prevails ceremonial and other worship of the elemental, psychic and spritual forces, personified in the Zend Avesta; nor is it even pantheistic as pantheism is conceived by the contemporary West. It is a philosophic hylo-zoism in which matter and life are inseparate and inseparable, the Unit made up of numberless units, each a manifestation of Knowledge Heavenly which is the container and common link of its two aspects.

On the subjective side Zoroastrianism teaches the doctrine of emanations, on the objective that of evolution. These Emanations (like the Syzigies of Simon Magus) are always in pairs, one of the pair itself an emanation of the other. Thus Ahura-Subsistence-Beness, and Mazda are a pair; Mazda the coeval and coeternal emanation or inherent radiation of Ahura. Then Ahura Mazda emanates Vohu Mano, the Good Mind, and these two labour for the spritual unfoldment of the manifested world. For this purpose is begotten Asha Vahishta, Heavenly Harmony the third of the Amesha Spentas; thus the first and the second, the second and the third, the third and the fourth, the fourth and the fifth, the fifth and the sixth, the sixth and the seventh, and the last Ameretat, Immortality and the first Ahura Mazda, work for the preservation and regeneration of all. The last pair represents the end of toil Immortal Repose, Equipoise, Nirvana. Thus the Seven Primal Builders give forth one from the other and form the Great Circle, the Circle of Everlasting Divinity knowing Its own immortal nature. The Great Dragon of Knowledge, Ahura Mazda, biting his own tail, Immortality-Ameretat, remains always and ever in limitless Duration, Zrvan Akarana, and sporadically casts its shadow, Zrvan Daregho-Khaodata, the Circle of Time, the Chakra-Wheel of Periodicity. Zrvan Daregho-Khaodata is the infinity of the world in toto as a boundless plane periodically the playground of numberless worlds; Zrvan Akarana is the Vibrant Sphere of Duration, boundless and limitless, of which sphere the Zrvan Daregho-Khaodata is the plane-circle. The Cycle in motion is the emanation of the Sphere which is Motionlessness, such is the Zoroastrian mode of expression about the Absolute and the Great Breath.

Thus we have the root of cycles of differing periods in the notion of Zrvan Daregho-Khaodata-Circles of Manifested Time, each of which has a origin and thus an end; this latter is the second of the pair, the first being Zrvan Akarana, "Limitless Time", which is Duration beginningless and endless. Every traditional Parsi in reciting his matin prayers repeats: Zrvan Akarana yazmaidae, Zrvan Daregho-Khaodata yazmaidae- "Sacrifice of praise unto the Boundless Duration, sacrifice of praise unto the sovereign Time of the Great Period."

Unfortunately, however, this primal metaphysical duality in time notion is not given (by contemporary students of Zoroastrianism) the consideration it deserves. There is another pair which meets with a similar fate, Ahura Mazda, Absolute Knowledge which apparents itself as Ahuna Vairya the Veracious Word. The abstraction Mazda Ahura, the Knowledge which is becomes incarnate, expresses itself as the Word, as Brahman becomes Pranava.

This Word, Ahuna Vairya or Honover, is compiled of three couplets and twenty-one words. From Pahlavi and Persian texts we learn that these twenty-one words are the names of the twenty-one Sacred Texts of the Holy Law which are mostly ruined; remains of fragments only are available at present. This Right Word is like the sacred formula of the Buddhists or like the Brahmanical Gayatri. It is at once a mantra with tone effects, a colorful ideograph, an occult cipher to be deciphered as per the true science of Numbers. Metaphysically speaking, it unveils the nature of Deity and Cosmos, and from the psychological viewpoint is the Spirit-Power which all true men and good use to destroy the mighty magic of Ahriman, following the example of Zoroaster himself. It is called the "axe of victory" by which man cut down the Tree of Evil.

This Word was the main manifestation and came into being before the World, hence, as Darmesteter points out "in the boundless Time"; i.e., the Word and the Cycle or Period of Time are coeval and coeternal two aspects of the one. This manifestation of the Word is described in some detail in Yasna XIX. The chanting of this Word has several meanings, celestial and human; it contains the three stages, like the Three Steps of Vishnu and Jehovah Elohim by which Ahura Mazda accomplished his task of creation; it is the Note struck for his people by the first Zoroaster, a cyclic avatara; it is the knowledge about twentyone natures of man; seven Spritual-monadic, seven Intellectual-person, and seven Formal-personal, so that every one can employ the Word in pursuance of the injunction-Man know thyself.

REFERENCES

Aogemadaecha: Translated into English by James Darmesteter. In Sacred Books of the East, Vol. 4, second edition.

Aogemadaecha: The Pahlavi Texts of, Edited by B. N. Dhabhar in *Indo-Iranian Studies in honour of Dastur D. P. Sanjana*, p.117-130. London, 1925.

Bundahishn: Translated from the Pahlavi text by E. W. West. In *Sacred Books of the East*, vol. 5.

Bundahishn: An Untranslated Chapter of the Bundehesh. Edited and translated by Jivanji Jamshedji Modi, in Journal of the Bombay Branch of the Royal Asiatic Society. Bombay, 1902.

Cumont, Franz: Texts et monuments relatifs au culte de Mithra. 2 vols. Paris, 1893.

Cumont, Franz: The Mysteries of Mithra. Translated from the French by T. J. McCormack. Chicago, 1903.

Dastur, M. N.: The Moral and Ethical Teachings of Zarathushtra. Bombay, 1928.

Dawson, M. M.: The Ethical Religion of Zoroaster. New York, 1931.

Fox, W. S., and Pemberton, R. E. K.: Passages in Greek and Latin Literature relating to Zoroaster and Zoroastrianism translated into English in *the Journal of the K. R. Cama Oriental Institute*, No.14. Bombay, 1929.

Gray, L. H.: The Foundations of the Iranian Religions. Bombay, 1929.

Lazarus, M. E.: The Zend-Avesta and Solar Religions. New York, 1852.

Lehmann, Edvard: Zarathushtra. Kobenhavn, 1899.

Modi, Jivanji J.: The Parsis at the court of Akbat and Dastur Meherjee Rana. Bombay, 1903.

Modi, Jivanji J.: A few events in the early history of the Parsis and their dates. Bombay, 1905.

Moffatt, J.: Zoroastrianism and Primitive Christianity. In *Hibbert Journal*, 1903, p. 763-780; *ibid*, 1904, p. 347-359.

4

Concept of God

Zarathushtra's is a message about a spirituality that progresses towards self-realization, fulfillment and completeness, as a good creation of a totally good God. It is a message of freedom - freedom to choose, freedom from fear, freedom from guilt, freedom from sin, freedom from stultifying rituals, superstitious practices, fake spirituality and ceremonials. The God of Zarathustra, is not a God of "Thou shalt" and "Thou shall not". God in Zoroastrianism does not care what you wear, what and when you eat or where and when you worship. God instead cares how righteous, progressive and good you are.

DEFINING GOD

The Iranians had brought to their new homeland several gods of the Indo-Iranian pantheon. Zarathushtra does not mention them by name in his hymns. This omission is not accidental; it is deliberate. His is altogether a new religion. No wonder he tells his hearers that he speaks to them words that are unheard of before. All thinking and doing, whether human or divine, is done through the mind. It is knowledge or wisdom which creates, moulds, and guides anything and everything. He, therefore, clothes the idea of godhead with wisdom and names him 'Ahura Mazda.' This collocation means literally, 'The Lord Wisdom' or 'The Wise Lord.' The first element of this compound, Ahura, 'Lord,' is one of the Indo-Iranian generic forms of godhead and Zarathushtra confers upon it the Iranian epithet Mazda, 'Wise.' The Aryan and Semitic gods that preceded Ahura Mazda were nature gods. Some of them later rose to a higher spiritual level and acquired spiritual epithets. Ahura Mazda was never a nature-god.

He was what he ever is, the highly spiritual being. Apart from its use in the Gathas, the term Mazda is found in its derivative form Mazdaka, used as a Median proper name in 715 BC. in the Assyrian inscriptions of Sargon. Moreover, the compound Ahura Mazda itself is found in its Assyrian equivalent Assara Mazas in an inscription of Assurbanipal. Though the inscription bears the date of the sovereignty of King Assurbanipal, it records the use of this Assyrian form of Ahura Maida in the latter part of the second millennium.

Zarathushtra uses the divine name variously as the metrical composition of the hymns requires. He employs the combinations Ahura Mazda and Mazda Ahura or the forms Ahura or Mazda respectively, designating God in all cases. In many instances the terms Ahura and Mazda are used separately in a single strophe, the one at the opening and the other at the close with different exhortations and prayers to each, yet in both cases as applied to the Supreme Being Ahura Mazda.

DIMENSIONS OF GOD

Ahura Mazda sits at the apex among the celestial beings of Garonmana (Heaven). He is not begotten, nor is there one like unto him. Beyond him, apart from him, and without him nothing exists. He is the Supreme Being through whom everything exists. He is brighter than the brightest of creation, higher than the highest heavens, older than the oldest in the universe. He is the best one. He knows no elder, he has no equal. There is none to dispute his supremacy and contest his place. Nor is there one to struggle successfully with him for the mastery of the heavens. He is the first and foremost. He is the most perfect being. He is almighty. He is the absolute sovereignty. He is beneficent. He is changeless. He is the same now and for ever. He was, he is, and he will be the same transcendent being, moving all, yet moved by none. In the midst of the manifold changes wrought by him in the universe, the Lord God remains changeless and unaffected, for he is mighty. He will decide victory between the rival hosts of good and evil. He is the most worthy of invocation, and the first possessor of felicity and joy. There is none before him. He is the greatest of all. He is the only God proper, than whom there is none higher. Everything comes from him and through him. He is the lord of all. Many are his attributes.

Nature of Ahura Mazda

Ahura Mazda is spirit in his being. The cardinal attribute Spirit or Beneficent Spirit or Most Beneficent Spirit is his very essence. Zarathushtra acquaints mankind for the first time in the history of religions with the concept of the godhead that is most incomparable in sublimity and unprecedented in the grandeur of nobility. He is higher than the highest being worshipped by mankind before his day. He is devoid of all anthropomorphic traits which characterized the Aryan and Semitic gods. Man, however, can comprehend abstract ideas and spiritual conceptions when they are put before him in words and expressions clothed in the garb of earthly imagery and compassed in human language. Zarathushtra, therefore, speaks of Ahura Mazda in human analogy. He conceives of Ahura Mazda in thought and apprehends him with his eye.

He asks him to teach by the word of his mouth and to tell him with the very tongue of his mouth. He is also spoken of as distributing good and evil to men by his own hands, and as observing with his eyes all things hidden and open. He lives in the empyrean enthroned in his majesty. He is ever present in the straight paths that lead mankind to righteousness. In his resplendence he lives in the heavenly realms and wears the firmament as his garment. Yahweh, likewise, covers himself with light as with a garment. Expressions like these are symbolical and they are not to be taken literally, since Ahura Mazda, as the whole tone of the Gathas proves, is to be seen or conceived only through the mind's eye. The finite can describe the infinite through finite analogies and similes alone.

The Otherworldly Immanency of Ahura Mazda

Ahura Mazda has his celestial mansions in the highest heavens, upon the vast expanse of the earth and in the hearts of the righteous persons. He is transcendent in as much as he is infinitely more sublime and greater than his creatures. Yet he is not so remote and ineffable as not to be approached and addressed and greeted by his ardent worshippers. He is immanent in the sense that man can enter into close and loving relations with him, and own him as his father and brother and friend. He befriends those who seek his friendship and loves those who long for his love. Zarathushtra addresses Ahura Mazda as his friend. He is life's safest anchorage and Zarathushtra, in his misfortunes, pours out his heart in his divine friend's bosom and cries unto him for help and protection as a friend helps a friend.

He lovingly helps those who flee unto him in their distress and betake themselves to his protection. There is none other than he who shields men against harm and they invoke his protection through Asha. We sleep secure because he guards us lovingly and we live in safety because he stands by our side when we awake out of sleep. His goodness towards us knows no bounds. Immortality, holiness, power, and perfection are his gifts to those who deserve them through their deeds and words and prayers. Man can become his friend and companion through his words and deeds of righteousness. He is invoked to bestow upon the pious the good things of life for his love of them. With his good understanding, man can imitate him and be like unto him by promoting the welfare of all around him through righteousness.

The prophet prays for his vision and communion with him. He strives to approach him through Good Mind, and through his devoted supplications. With outstretched hands he aspires to reach him with songs of praise on his lips. Thus will he continue his praise, he says, as long as he has strength and vigour, and adds that the stars and the sun and the dawn all unite in singing praise unto him. Consumed with the fervour of religious emotion, he implores Ahura Mazda to rise up for him, and to come to him and manifest himself to him in his own person. Sraosha comes with Vohu Manah unto him whom Ahura Mazda desires.

The Creator

Creation is a free act of the divine goodness of Ahura Mazda. In the beginning when he lived in his supreme self-sufficiency, he conceived the thought to clothe the heavenly realm with light. He created light, and darkness was there, for darkness shadows light. He is the father and creator of Vohu Manah, of Asha, of Khshathra, of Armaiti, of Haurvatat and Ameretat, and of Geush Tashan. The joy-giving cattle and this universe are his creations. He upholds the earth and firmament from falling. He made the moon wax and wane, and determined the path of the sun and stars. He yoked swiftness to wind and clouds. He clothed the heavenly realms with light. He it was who made morning and noon and night. He created kine, waters and plants. He created human beings and their spirits, breathed life in their bodies and endowed them with the freedom of will. He inspired love between the son and father. He made sleep and wakefulness. He is the beneficent dispenser of blessings to mankind. Weal and woe are ordained by him.

The Lord of Wisdom

The very name of the godhead embodies in itself great wisdom. Ahura Mazda is the wise lord. He has created the universe through his wisdom and rules it through wisdom. He is the most knowing one. He is the far-seeing one, and so is he the all-seeing one. He knows all that is done in the past and all that will be done in the future, and judges through his omniscience. Zarathushtra seeks knowledge from him of what will be and what will not be. Through his Best Mind he knows man's desert at the reckoning. Human beings have their masks drawn on their faces and none can see what is hidden within. But Ahura Mazda has an eye over them all and with penetrating eyes he sees their open and secret faults. None can deceive his wisdom, for he is undeceivable. He is the consummate teacher of those who believingly hear him and become of one mind with him and who, inspired by Asha and Vohu Manah, exalt him by their words and deeds.

The Law-giver and Judge

With the creation of man Ahura Mazda has ordained laws for the rightful conduct of his life. The great mission of the prophet is to acquaint mankind with these and to lead all to see for themselves with their intelligence that their welfare depends on the faithful adherence to them. He exhorts his hearers to give a careful hearing to his words, understand with clear discernment what he tells them, and, with the discreet exercise of the freedom of the will, with which Ahura Mazda has endowed them, make their own choice of conduct. The divine law-giver has established the moral order in the beginning of the world. He has ordained the commandments of reward and retribution to the righteous and the wicked, and Zarathushtra asks his followers to keep them in mind and live lawful lives so that they may thereby win felicity for themselves.

Every man and every woman that lives this earthly life will have to stand at the reckoning one day to receive his or her own desert, and Zarathushtra teaches them all the laws of the requitals of human conduct in which Ahura Mazda himself has instructed him. Ahura Mazda is the lord who knows and watches and judges the deeds of mortals. He holds the destinies of mankind in his hands and apportions reward and retribution unto the righteous and the wicked. The righteous souls will live in the abode of Ahura Mazda. He punishes the wrong-doers just as he rewards the righteous, but he shows compassion also and forgives when the penitent sinner casts himself on his mercy.

DEITIES

Vohu manah

When Ahura Mazda was with none beside him, in his supreme isolation, he evolved in his mind the thought of creating the universe. He named his first creation after his mind and called him Vohu Manah, Good Mind. Zarathushtra fondly speaks of him as Ahura Mazda's son. He is often addressed in the Gathas in the superlative as Vahishta Manah, Best Mind. Occasionally, Vohu Manah is converted into Vohu Mainyu, Good Spirit or Vahishta Mainyu, Best Spirit. It has to be noted that Vohu Mainyu or Vahishta Mainyu has nothing in common with Spenta Mainyu or the Holy Spirit, the first of the two Primeval Spirits of Ahura Mazda.

The ethical system of Zarathushtra has the triad of good thoughts, good words and good deeds as its basis. Good words and good deeds proceed from good thoughts and good thoughts are inspired in man by Vohu Manah. In all his waking hours man thinks and thinks incessantly. He thinks useful thoughts and wise thoughts and great thoughts and wholesome thoughts and kindly thoughts and virtuous thoughts and good thoughts. But he thinks also idle thoughts and foolish thoughts and mean thoughts and malicious thoughts and cruel thoughts and vicious thoughts and evil thoughts. The mind soars high and wings its way in the realm of righteousness or it sinks low and grovels in the mire of wickedness. Man thinks thoughts, but thoughts make man. Thoughts make him a human being, a saint, and an angel; and thoughts make him an animal, a sinner, and a demon. Man is thought materialized in word and deed. Vohu Manah is the ideal that man as a thinking being has to realize.

Armaiti

Armaiti is cognate with Vedic Aramati, who is a shadowy personification of piety or devotion, She retains the same meaning in the Gathas and is emblematic of Ahura Mazda's love or devotion. Ahura Mazda created her, and she is lovingly called his daughter, or again, his own. Holy or spenta, which is her standing epithet in the later period, is applied to her sometimes in the Gathas.

Through fervent meditation on his own inner nature and patient study of Ahura' Mazda's marvellous work in creation, Zarathushtra understands the ways of Ahura Mazda. He knows the wise lord through the enlightenment of his mind. His heart yearns to own Ahura Mazda. From the depth of his heart, he prays unto him, invokes him in silence and with the pronounced words of his mouth. He burns incense of devotion unto his maker upon the fire burning on the altar in the holy temple of his heart. The fire first flares and flickers, then blazes and burns, and illumines the sublime path that leads to Ahura Mazda. He dedicates his will and his desire and his heart and his life and himself unto him. He loses himself in devoted love for him.

He sees with Ahura Mazda's eyes and hears with Ahura Mazda's ears. He communes with him and he becomes one with him. He is eager that his hearers should share the incomparable gift of Armaiti with him. With earnest longing he asks Ahura Mazda when Armaiti's devotion will ennoble the lives of those to whom he proclaims his faith. The members of different ranks of Iranian society that have embraced his religion fervently pray that the good and holy Armaiti may be theirs. Those who have devoutly accepted the commandments of Ahura Mazda are eager to devote their hearts unto him.

Armaiti teaches the ordinances of Ahura Mazda. She furthers the imperishable Kingdom of Ahura Mazda. Those who make Armaiti's devotion their own, becomes holy. Armaiti blesses them with plenty and prosperity. Ahura Mazda is asked to give vigour through her. Zarathushtra asks the faithful to exalt Ahura Mazda with devotional prayers. His religion inspires truthful deeds through the words of Armaiti. In the Vedas we find Aramati linked with rta, that is, devotion in connection with the moral order. So we are told in the Gathas that Asha's righteousness is furthered by Armaiti. As righteousness is the outcome of the life of Armaiti's devotion, the wise one bases his conduct upon her inspiration. The prophet asks Frashaoshtra to lead the faithful to the life of communion with Asha's righteousness and

For the union of both furthers the Kingdom of Vohu Manah The coming of Asha and Armaiti to inspire their lives is eagerly sought by the pious. Armaiti inquires after the misdeeds and shortcomings of the true speaker and the false speaker, the wise and the ignorant. The wicked Bendva, the inveterate foe of the prophet, does not follow Armaiti. Righteousness deserts those who know Armaiti as the beloved of Ahura Mazda, and yet estrange themselves from her devotion. Zarathushtra asks her to give him and Vishtaspa their heart's desire. He implores her to teach men's consciences through righteousness. She is besought to grant as a gift the riches of the life of Vohu Manah's good thoughts. One serves the Most Holy Spirit the best by the performance of the deeds inspired by Armaiti's devotion. Armaiti is invoked to send righteous and not wicked ones to rule over the world. Armaiti will co-operate with Ahura Mazda at the final dispensation.

Sayana glosses Aramati by bhûmi, 'earth'. Armaiti plays a prominent part as the genius of earth in the later Avestan period. Though the Gathas do not clearly emphasize this aspect of her work, we can trace in them the belief in Armaiti's connection with the earth. Zarathushtra preaches the usefulness of settled agricultural life as opposed to the nomadic life prevailing in his days. He says that Ahura Mazda has laid out the beneficent path of agriculture and asks men to choose it. Armaiti is here conjointly mentioned with Geush Tashan. The noble descendants of the Turanian Fryana, prompted by righteousness, further the settlements of Armaiti through their diligence. The Maker has, in consultation with Vohu Manah, the genius of cattle, created Armaiti or earth and replenished it with pastures.

Haurvatat and Ameretat

Haurvatat and Ameretat form an indissoluble spiritual pair and are always celebrated together in the Gathas. No single hymn is addressed to Haurvatat or to Ameretat alone. Haurvata means or perfection, and Ameretat is emblematic of immortality. The dual earthly gift of endurance and vigour of body is paralleled with the heavenly blessings of perfection and immortality. Ahura Mazda bestows through Vohu Manah and Asha endurance and vigour of body in this world and Haurvatat's perfection and Ameretat's immortality in the next, upon those who offer him the sacrifice of devotion. The earthly boons are the gifts of Haurvatat and Ameretat. Whoso piously pronounces the sacred formulas dedicated to Haurvatat and Ameretat receives the best reward. Through the recital of these holy words and basing their lives upon righteousness, do the faithful win for themselves the blessings of Haurvatat and Ameretat. Zarathushtra fervently prays for the participation in these blessings. Those who offer willing obedience unto the teachings of the prophet will attain unto Haurvatat and Ameretat. He who befriends Ahura Mazda with his thoughts and words and deeds wins them for himself. Man comes by them in Ahura Mazda's Kingdom through his good thoughts, words, and deeds, and his life of righteousness and devotion. It is the wicked who defraud mankind of happy life and immortality by means of evil thoughts, evil words, and evil deeds.

The Gathas hint at the connection of Haurvatat and Ameretat with water and plants, over whom they preside in the Later Avesta. Ahura Mazda who has created water and plants is invoked to give Haurvatat's perfection and Ameretat's immortality. On the eschatological side Haurvatat figuratively represents ambrosia and Ameretat stands for nectar that the pious souls receive in heaven.

Sraosha

In the later period, Sraosha rises to great prominence as the divine teacher of Mazda's religion. Zarathushtra longs to see Sraosha", and prays that he may come unto every man whom Mazda Wills. The prophet teaches the new faith to the world of humanity. He exhorts mankind to pay heed to the words that are best for the mortals to hear and tells them that Ahura Mazda will give them perfection and immortality if they will bring Sraosha's obedience unto him. By teaching mankind to obey the ordinances of Ahura Mazda, and inspiring them to work according to them, through good thoughts, words, and deeds for the furtherance of righteousness in the world, Zarathushtra helps in the inauguration of the Divine Kingdom of Ahura Mazda. In the later period Sraosha acts as a co-assessor with Mithra and Rashnu, who all combine to make up a heavenly tribunal for the judgment of the dead. Mithra and Rashnu, the two brother judges, seated with Sraosha, do not appear in the Gathas, but a passage speaks of Sraosha's coming as a judge with the reward unto the good and evil contending parties. Zarathushtra invokes Sraosha as the greatest of the heavenly beings to appear at the final consummation of the world.

The word sraosha occurs also in several Gathic passages in its ordinary meaning of obedience, and not as the personified spirit of this abstract virtue.

Atar

Atar or fire corresponds to the Vedic Agni Atar's functions are elaborately delineated in the Later Avesta. We shall therefore leave the discussion of the resemblance between them for subsequent pages. The early Aryan settlers of Iran had brought the cult to their new home as their cherished heritage bequeathed to them by their Indo-Iranian ancestors. Tradition speaks of several great sacred Iranian fires consecrated by the pre-Zoroastrian Kings. The Pahlavi Bundahishn says that Yima and Kavi Haosrava established the fires Froba and Goshasp; and that Vishtaspa, the royal patron of Zarathushtra, consecrated the fire Burzin Mihr. The Mohammedan writers of the tenth century speak of some ten such places dedicated to fire before Zoroaster's time. The prophet of Iran thus found the cult of fire already established in Iran when he entered upon his divine mission on earth. He purified its archaic form and incorporated it into his new system. Of all the elements, he raised fire, or light, to a place of the highest distinction in his faith.

Ahura Mazda is eternal light, his very nature is light. He lives in the everlasting lights of the highest heaven. Light in its various manifestations, whether as the fire of the hearth on earth, or the fiery substance in the bowels of the earth, or as the genial glow of the sun in the azure vault of heaven, or the silvery sheen of the crescent moon in the sky, or the flickering brilliancy of the stars in the firmament, or even in the form of the life-giving energy distributed in the entire creation, is emblematic of Mazda. No wonder, then, if the prophet of Ancient Iran made fire the consecrated symbol of his religion, a symbol which in point of sublimity, grandeur, and purity, or in its being the nearest earthly image of the heavenly lord, is unequalled by any of its kind in the world.

When Vohu Manah approaches Zarąthushtra, and enquires of him what is his most ardent desire, the prophet replies that his inmost yearning is to think of righteousness through the devotional gifts of his homage to Atar's fire. When the chosen of the Lord is thwarted at times in his great mission by the Druj or Lie, he turns to Atar as one of the protectors that will best help him in the furtherance of the mighty cause of righteousness. The fire of Mazda plays an important part in the work of the last judgment at the final Renovation of the world. Mazda has promised through Asha that he will give award unto the contesting parties of good and evil through fire. The Heavenly Father will deliver his final judgment upon the righteous and the wicked through fire together with the Holy Spirit. It is through fire that the creator will bestow profit upon the righteous and bring harm unto the wicked. Mazda will apportion reward and retribution to both the good and the evil through the glow of fire, which is emblematic of righteousness. The believers therefore pray that fire, which is mighty through righteousness, may be a manifest help unto the faithful, but a veritable harm unto the foe. The noble truth of the prophetic words of Zarathushtra will, in this manner, be vindicated when, at the final Dispensation, divine judgment shall be meted out to man through the red fire of Mazda.

Ashi

Ashi represents sanctity and destiny, or reward. In one passage she is given the epithet vanghuhi, 'good', which in the Later Avesta is inseparably associated with her name. She represents the life of piety and its concomitant result. Zarathushtra invokes Asha to come with Ashi. She apportions Mazda's ordinances, about which the prophet desires to learn. He invokes her in his crusade against Druj, or the Lie. Whoso, through the power that Ashi confers upon him, deprives the wicked of his possessions, reaps the rewards that Mazda has promised.

In an eschatological sense, she forms the reward assured in heaven to those who have led a life of sanctity upon earth. It is with the accompaniment of Ashi's recompense that Sraosha approaches the seat of judgment to reward the righteous and wicked souls Zarathushtra asks Ahura Mazda to manifest unto him the incomparable things of his Divine Kingdom which are rewards of Vohu Manah, and seeks to know the reward that will be his in the Good Kingdom.

Ashi's sphere of activity grows in the later development of her cult and, in addition to representing the reward of the pious in heaven, she stands also for the earthly prize of those who are diligent. She becomes the genius of fortune, and the eager eyes of her numerous votaries are always turned to her for her favour. This new phase of her activity will receive attention in the place assigned to her in our treatment of the Later Avestan period.

Geush Tashan and Geush Urvan

The Gathas speak of three beings, Geush Tashan, 'the Creater of the Bull or Cow,' Geush Urvan, 'the Soul of the Bull or Cow,' and Gav Azi, 'the Bull or Cow Azi.' Av. gav, and Skt. go, both mean bull or cow. The Vedic divinities Dyaus, 'the Heaven,' and Prithivi, 'the Earth,' have the epithets bull and cow applied to them from their physical characteristics. After the analogy of the Skt. go, 'bull or cow,' which also means earth, some are led to think that the above expressions are used with reference to the earth. The Pahlavi, Sanskrit, Persian, and early Gujarati versionists, it may be noted, adhere to the original meaning and explain the words with reference to the bull or cow.

Some creation-myths of the world relate that the earthly creatures have sprung from the bodies of the primeval man or of the cosmic cow killed by the gods or, as in the case of the later Zoroastrianism, by the Evil Spirit. In Babylonian mythology it is Marduk who killed Tiamat and the creatures came into existence from his body. According to the Vedic texts the gods sacrificed Purusha and brought the earthly and aerial creatures into being from his body. Ahriman, say the Pahlavi works, killed Gaya Maretan, the Primeval Man and Gavyokdat, the Primeval Bull, and men and animals and plants came into being from the various parts of their slaughtered bodies.

Cattle were the source of all wealth and the ox who drew the plough and enabled man to cultivate his field was held in religious veneration among the pastoral and agricultural Aryans and Semites from early times. Mithra was the most powerful Indo-Iranian divinity when Zarathushtra preached his new religion. The Iranians worshipped Mithra as 'the lord of wide pastures,' which is his standing epithet in the Younger Avesta.

According to the ancient myth Mithra killed the Primeval Bull and thereby became the creator and fashioner of the earthly beings. The Mithraic sculptures represent him sitting on the bull's back, seizing it by the nostrils with one hand and plunging his hunting knife deep into its back. Zarathushtra did not include him in the heavenly hierarchy, but adapted the legend of the immolation of the Primeval Bull by Mithra to ethical ends.

Geush Tashan stands in the Gathas for the creative activity of Ahura Mazda. He is said to be Ahura Mazda's own, and Mazda is spoken of as his lord. Geush Urvan is the spirit of the animal Kingdom, and the obscure Gav Azi, who is spoken of in the Gathas as the giver of joy and prosperity, represents the animal creation. Tradition explains Gav Azi as 'the three years old cow.' It is evidently gav aevodâta, 'the sole created bull or cow,' of the Later Avesta, and Gavyokdât, 'the Sole Created Bull' of the Pahlavi and subsequent Sanskrit, Persian, and Gujarati versionists.

Geush Urvan complains in a bewailing tone before Ahura Mazda that anger, rapine, plunder, and wickedness are harassing its very existence and therefore its soul sighs for a deliverer. Ahura Mazda holds a celestial conference to redress the grievances of the Soul of the Kine. After patient deliberations, in which Vohu Manah, the genius of cattle, Asha, the guardian of peaceful, settled life, and Geush Tashan take part, Vohu Manah, as the premier councillor, declares that Zarathushtra is the only mortal who has heard the divine commands, and he is the one person suited to be sent to the world as the spiritual and temporal lord who could remove the grievances of Geush Urvan. The Soul of the Kine is disconsolate and cries in despair that its sufferings are so great that it would be beyond the power of the prophet to assuage them. Further pleadings soften its despair and Zarathushtra is chosen for the mighty work.

We can see in this account an attempt to convince the waverers, disbelievers, and heretics of the true mission of the prophet. The later texts resort to miracles of various sorts to fulfil the same purpose. Those who have not yet come, in Gathic times, to any definite conclusion as to the choice of their faith, and are still hesitating before embracing the new creed, are shown how preparations were made in heaven for Zarathushtra's mission, and how it is with the divine approval that the new prophet comes to them for their good.

Zarathushtra preaches the advantages of a settled life, and persuades his hearers to emerge from the pastoral life and embrace agricultural habits. He exhorts them to work diligently for the kine's welfare, grow fodder for their nurture, and lead an active and an industrious life. This is a stage of transition, and all could not easily give up the unsettled habits of life in which they were brought up. Naturally, therefore, there is much disorder in the land and Zarathushtra enters upon his mission to establish ordered social life.

Geush Tashan is mentioned along with Armaiti's earth and Ahura Mazda shows the advantageous path of the industrious agriculturist who tills the earth by his diligence and prospers Vohu Manah's cattle, whereas the indolent persons who do not practise husbandry fail to reap the fruits of life. Ahura Mazda has created cattle that give the good things of life to men. Moreover, he has created Armaiti's earth for the pasture of Geush Tashan. Whoso wishes pasture of cattle reaps the reward for his labour. Ahura Mazda fulfils the desire of the bodily life of those who, inspired by Vohu Manạh, work for the welfare of the cattle. Unto those who lead righteous lives and work the will of Zarathushtra, will be given in the next world happiness such as the possession of cattle gives.

PHILOSOPHY OF GOD

Spenta Mainyu

The supreme godhead, we have seen, is immutable, perfect, spiritual unity. Zarathushtra solves the problem of reconciling the unchangeable nature of Ahura Mazda with the world of change by postulating a principle that intervenes between the unmoved mover and the moved. This working medium of Ahura Mazda spans the chasm between the supersensuous and the sensuous. He brings the transcendence and immanence of Ahura Mazda into a synthesis. Ahura Mazda is neither completely separated nor completely merged in the world. He is the primordial, self-existing being. In his infinite goodness he wills the creation of the universe. Both heavenly and earthly existence lived with him and in him as idealized contents of his being.

The projection or manifestation of his creative will and thought is his active working principle Spenta Mainyu, Holy Spirit. Spenta Mainyu is as old as Ahura Mazda, for be ever was in Ahura Mazda and with Ahura Mazda. Though he is thus part of Ahura Mazda, in his manifestation as the working self of Ahura Mazda he is different from Ahura Mazda. He is not an entity or personality. Ahura Mazda is the greatest spiritual personality. Spenta Mainyu is his image, his replica. He represents the creative attribute of Ahura Mazda in his relation to the created world.

Spenta Mainyu symbolizes the ideal or perfect existence as conceived in thought by Ahura Mazda. The materialization of the divine thought in creation spells imperfection and Spenta Mainyu is shadowed by his inseparable opposite. These two primeval spirits, who are spoken of as twins, emerged from the divine bosom and by their innate choice appeared as the better and the bad in thought, word, and deed, He, the Most Holy

Spirit, chose righteousness and he who is called the Evil Spirit wooed the worst as his sphere of action. The better one of the two spirits told the evil one that they were by nature opposed to each other in their thoughts and teachings, understandings and beliefs, words, and deeds, selves and souls — in nothing could they twain ever meet. When the two first came together in the world, they created life and non-life and established the law of reward and retribution for mankind, that the righteous will reap at the end of existence the weal of Best Thought and the wicked the woe of the Worst Existence.

The Gathas variously speak of Spenta Mainyu either as the attribute of Ahura Mazda or as his vicegerent, or as his co-worker, or as identified with him or as distinct from him. It is Spenta Mainyu that Ahura Mazda creates cattle and water and plants and all that exist. Ahura Mazda is asked to give ear to man's invocation through Spenta Mainyu, and to strength through him. Through him does Ahura Mazda give Perfection and Immortality unto the pious that live a righteous and devoted life of best thoughts, words, and deeds. Ahura Mazda is implored to teach by his own mouth, on behalf of his Spirit, how the world first came into being.

It is through his Spirit that Ahura Mazda furthers his blessed realms He gives the best unto the righteous through Spenta Mainyu. Zarathushtra asks Ahura Mazda what award he will make unto the believers and the non-believers through his Spirit. Mazda will come at the final dispensation with Spenta Mainyu. Through him does one win the felicity of paradise. The devout seek to be acquainted with the works of Spenta Mainyu. The Spirit knows the attitude of the false speaker and the true speaker, the wise and the unwise as they are led by the promptings of their hearts and minds. Spenta Mainyu is the friend of all and he protects them through Righteousness in both the worlds from transgression. It is the wicked that are hurt by him.

Spenta Mainyu or the Holy Spirit is sometimes spoken of as the Good Spirit, or the Best Spirit, or the Most Holy Spirit. This superlative title, the Most Holy Spirit, is sometimes applied to Ahura Mazda himself. It is also used for Spenta Mainyu as apart from Ahura Mazda. For example, Zarathushtra tells Ahura Mazda that he chooses his Most Holy Spirit for himself. The Most Holy Spirit, the one who stands in opposition to his evil twin brother, dons the massive heavens for his garment.

Amesha Spentas

Zarathushtra holds before mankind six cardinal virtues of Ahura Mazda for emulation. Primarily, they are pure abstractions, etherealized moral concepts, symbolic ideals, abstract figures. They have no individuality, no characteristics, no mythology as the Indo-Iranian divinities have. Zarathushtra aims at replacing the divine beings that owe their origin to some natural phenomena and later rise to moral stature, by spiritual ideals. The heavenly beings that he finds honoured among his people are such ancient beings that have evolved from the various aspects of nature. Such are Mithra and his associates that hold spiritual sway over the hearts of the Iranian peoples. The prophet substitutes for these august concrete beings his worshipful attributes of Ahura Mazda. In the heavenly hierarchy they represent altogether a novel feature.

They are entirely unlike the gods whom mankind had been accustomed to worship under various names before his advent. He names these divine qualifications Vohu Manah, 'Good Mind,' Asha, 'Righteousness,' Khshathra, 'Divine Kingdom,' Armaiti, 'Devotion,' Haurvatat, 'Perfection,' and Ameretat, 'Immortality.' They form Ahura Mazda's being. That is, Vohu Manah is Ahura Mazda's Good Mind or Good Thought, Asha is his Righteousness and so are others his different virtues. This idealistic phase that Zarathushtra puts before man does not long retain its character. The abstract virtues soon get detached from Ahura Mazda and assume thin personification. In two instances we meet with the appellative terms Mazdâo (schâ) Ahurâonghô 'Ahura Mazda and his associates,' like the Vedic plural expressions Varunas and Rudras. Here we witness the Amesha Spentas or the Holy Immortals of the post-Gathic period in the making.

These six divine attributes which we have said tend towards forming the heavenly host of Ahura Mazda, it is suggested, have originated under the influence of the Vedic Adityas. Unlike the seven Gathic divine appellations, the Adityas, however, are variously spoken of as six or seven or eight or even twelve in number. They include great Vedic divinities like Varuna, Mitra, Aryaman, Indra, and others and even sun and moon and fire. Zarathushtra has set his face against them. His spiritual impersonations of the godhead are, it seems to us, a class by themselves and are particular to him.

Vohu Manah, Asha, and Khshathra are neuter nouns taken in the later Avestan as male members of the divine hierarchy and Armaiti, Haurvatat, and Ameretat are feminine names. They occur in the different

Gathic stanzas individually or two or three or four or more together indefinitely. The hexad, or taken along with Ahura Mazda, the heptad, is not fixed in the Gathas as we find it in the later Avesta, where it is expressly said that the Holy Immortals are seven. Yet we have instances where Ahura Mazda and his six epithets are mentioned together. Asha stands first in the number of times he is mentioned and Vohu Manah, though first of the heavenly host, comes second. They are followed by Khshathra and Armaiti respectively.

Haurvatat and Ameretat, who invariably occur together, make up the rear. With the exception of Vohu Manah, whose name is always a fixed compound with Vohu, 'Good,' qualifying Manah, 'Mind,' all the others have not the stereotyped epithets that the four of them are given at the later period. At times Vohu Manah's epithet designating his goodness is transferred to Khshathra. As the process towards the personification of Ahura Mazda's attributes has already begun, it is often extremely difficult to decide whether the qualitative divine expressions stand for personified beings or as abstract nouns designating certain virtues in application to Ahura Mazda himself or to man.

The prominent feature of these six abstract attributes when they have fully grown into Ahura Mazda's ministering angels is the twofold character of work they are assigned to perform. In addition to a specific virtue that each represents on the spiritual side, a material object is put under his or her direct guardianship on the physical side. This physical aspect of their functions is most marked in the later period. Its origin, however, can be traced in the Gathas where we find a beginning already made of associating some one material creation with every one of them. We shall now deal with them individually.

Symbol of Ahura Mazda's Wisdom

Man thinks but he reasons besides, and his reasoning raises him above the level of the animal world. The Gathas employ khratu and chisti to designate wisdom. They do not, however, classify wisdom as the later Avesta distinguishes the innate wisdom from the acquired wisdom. The loftiest ideal for man upon earth is to be like unto Ahura Mazda and it is through the wisdom of Vohu Manah that man can realize it. Zarathushtra invokes Ahura Mazda to grant him the wisdom of Vohu Manah, and longs to be acquainted with the decrees of Vohu Manah. He desires to know to whom among his followers will the wisdom of Vohu Manah descend. The wise man of good understanding performs deeds that are pleasing to Vohu Manah. The enlightenment that Vohu Manah gives enables the devout to practise the doctrines of weal and woe. They pray for thoughts to turn where wisdom abides. Mazda is implored to fulfil the desires of the wise who are devoted to Vohu Manah

Zarathushtra adores Vohu Manah with songs of praise, and teaches his followers to offer him praise. He asks Ahura Mazda to teach him how best he could inspire men to the deeds of Vohu Manah. He tells his heavenly father that he will always work for the furtherance of the domain of Vohu Manah, and adds that as long as he has strength left in him he will, in union with Vohu Manah, lead mankind on the path of righteousness. He implores Ahura Mazda to come down to him through Vohu Manah. Through Vohu Manah does the prophet long to reach Ahura Mazda, and through the performance of the deeds pleasing unto Vohu Manah does he long to glorify and reach his maker. Pouruchisti is advised to seek Vohu Manah's fellowship. The devout seek to propitiate Vohu Manah to win his kinship. Ahura Mazda is besought by them to be the revealer of Vohu Manah unto them. When enlightenment descends upon Zarathushtra, he longs to see Vohu Manah, and prays that he may come to help him. His yearning to have a glimpse of the divine mind is satisfied. Vohu Manah comes to him and illumines his mind. The prophet seeks to know from him the rules of life that lead to happiness. Vohu Manah teaches him the working of Ahura Mazda. He asks Mazda to teach him through Vohu Manah his secret doctrines.

Life led according to the promptings of Vohu Manah is life lived well and Zarathushtra prays for the life, of Good Mind. The blessings of Vohu Manah form the precious reward for man and are gained through the performance of good deeds inspired by righteousness. Zarathushtra longs to know through Vohu Manah the straight paths of life. There are the paths of Vohu Manah and Mazda is invoked to reveal them, Ahura Mazda grants the prayer and speaks about the paths of Vohu Manah to Zarathushtra. Wicked persons mislead men who strive to live an upright life and follow the paths of Vohu Manah. The prophet warns his followers against the evil teachers who keep them back from appreciating the worth of acquisition of Vohu Manah. The evil-minded Bendva defies the counsel of Vohu Manah. The faithful are eager to learn how they could keep far from those that do not seek Vohu Manah's counsel. The evil doers are separated from Vohu Manah. Vohu Manah leaves those who do not practise righteousness, and righteousness flees from those who follow not Vohu Manah, in the same manner as noxious creatures fly from men, The pious therefore declare that they will not annoy Vohu Manah. Vohu

Manah is dispenser of the riches of the well disciplined mind and Zarathushtra longs to win it through righteousness.

The pious invoke Mazda to reward their efforts to lead righteous lives by bestowing upon them the riches of Vohu Manah. It is the teachers of evil that prevent men from valuing these riches. The prophet prays for the gifts of Vohu Manah for himself and his associates. Vohu Manah's reward is an incomparable blessing. Ahura Mazda is asked to grant the wishes of those who are worthy of Vohu Manah's reward owing to their righteousness. Those that are good unto men who endeavour to lead righteous lives will share the blessings of Vohu Manah. They are religious in truth who embrace the good thoughts of Vohu Manah and base their actions of life upon them; such persons win prosperity and happiness. The prophet prays for chieftainship through Vohu Manah. Man obtains power through goodness of his mind and he invokes Ahura Mazda to grant him that power through Vohu Manah. Zarathushtra asks Vohu Manah to bestow power upon his disciples. Girt with such power, man can wage a successful war against wickedness, therefore do the votaries beseech Vohu Manah to endow them with it. Mazda gives power unto the righteous as reward through Vohu Manah. He is invoked to give endurance and durability through Vohu Manah.

These he gives and in addition he bequeaths upon the good, perfection and immortality. Those who in obedience to the teachings of the prophet do the deeds of Vohu Manah are given good abodes and joy in life, and perfection and immortality. Whoso befriends Mazda through thoughts and deeds will be given steadfastness of Vohu Manah. Vohu Manah protects the poor. Through him does Ahura Mazda know the deserts of mankind. Zarathushtra asks Mazda to let him know the award he will give him through Vohu Manah. Those in whose life righteousness and devotion are blended, further the dominion of Vohu Manah. The righteous bring prosperity to the World through the deeds of Vohu Manah Mazda awards his bounty to those who through deeds of Vohu Manah work for the world. He promotes the best wishes of the truthful workers through Vohu Manah. The prophet promises to give through Vohu Manah the best that is in his power to those who rejoice him by their goodness. One acquires the best of the Holy Spirit through the words of Vohu Manah and the devotion of Armaiti. Vohu Manah furthers the Kingdom of Ahura Mazda. He prospers the possessions of those that rejoice Zarathushtra. He welcomes the Turanian Fryans to the joy of Mazda. Vohu Manah will announce the advent of the Kingdom of Ahura Mazda. He will establish it at the end of time for those who have helped righteousness to rout wickedness. He will come to the help of the Saoshyants at the Renovation.

This becomes most marked in the later period. The beginning towards this phase is already to be noted in the Gathas. Vahishta Manah or Best Thought is spoken of as the paradise itself where the righteous will go after demise. Vohu Manah dwells in the heavenly home along with Mazda and Asha. Paradise is said to be the heritage of Vohu Manah. Zarathushtra knows the rewards of deeds done for Ahura Mazda and desires to lead his soul to paradise through Vohu Manah. Those who oppose the evil deeds of the wicked who are wilfully blind and deaf to the teachings of the prophet, will go to the heavenly abode of Vohu Manah. The mighty power of Vohu Manah will be manifested when Mazda will deal out justice to the righteous, and the wicked through his fire Through the words of Vohu Manah the prophet honours those who have worked for the divine purpose and whom Mazda will therefore gather in his abode. The pious pray for long life of felicity in the paradisiac domain of Vohu Manah.

Vohu Manah's connection with animal life is hinted in the Gathas. This trait becomes much emphasized in the later period when he becomes the genius of cattle and takes the animal world under his protection, as a secondary part of his function as the premier angel of Ahura Mazda. When Geush Urvan, as the genius of the sentient beings, living upon earth, complains of the wrath and rapine to which the animal Kingdom is subjected, Vohu Manah consoles her with the gladsome news that the creator of the world was sending Zarathushtra, his messenger, to teach mankind to protect the cattle and kine. In consultation with Vohu Manah, it is said, Ahura Mazda created cattle and pastures to feed them. Vohu Manah is the protector of cattle. They are a precious asset of Vohu Manah and give durability and endurance to mankind. It is through the good understanding of Vohu Manah, that men are inspired to work for cattle.

MESSENGERS OF GOD

Zarathushtra

Prophets are gods in the flesh, and Zarathushtra, the prophet of Iran, was such a man-god. His date of birth is placed anywhere between 600 BC. and 6000 BC. It is an uncontested fact that there is a marked closeness between the grammar, metre, and style of the Rig Veda and the Gathas. The Gathic inflexions are more primitive than the Vedic. The period of the position of the Gathas, therefore, cannot be separated from the Vedas by any considerable distance of time. Zarathushtra's place of birth is of equal uncertainty. His earliest appearance in the Gathas is at the period of his life when he has left his pupilage behind. He has evidently learnt all he could from what the teachers of his days could give him. He has conversed with the wise men of his country. He has often visited the central places where trade routes from distant lands converged and has gathered information and experience from the worldly-wise travellers, merchants, and pilgrims. But the more he has learnt, the more eager his desire to learn further has grown. His teachers had instructed him in knowledge based on tradition. But tradition is stagnant, and knowledge is ever on the onward move. Besides, tradition is wedded to the time that is dead, and knowledge looks to the time to be born without end. Moreover, tradition demands its instruction to be taken on trust, and knowledge is based on inquiry and discussion.

Reason is shadowed by doubt and doubt is the parent of knowledge. Zarathushtra, a paragon of reason, doubts the wisdom of his teachers. Zarathushtra resolves to be his own teacher, and to learn by observation and thinking. He thinks and thinks deeply and comprehensively on the conditions prevailing around him. He considers that life is not woven of the tissues of joy and happiness alone, but of considerable sorrow and misery also. Injustice and inequity, strife and oppression, poverty and destitution, greed and avarice, wrath and rapine, falsehood and deceit, envy and malice, hatred and jealousy, crime and vice, sorrow and suffering, filth and disease confront him everywhere. He is keenly responsive to human sufferings and the groans and sighs of the agonized hearts. The misery of the multitude touches his heart. His flesh creeps, his heart is heavily oppressed, and his spirit is depressed at the sight of this dark side of human life. He suffers at the sight of suffering and, with eyes suffused with tears, he lives from day unto day thinking and brooding over the woes of the world. Zarathushtra doubts the goodness of gods.

He is religious at heart, but his daily experience of the religion practised and lived around him tends to estrange him from the faith of his forefathers. He sees with horror temples reeking with the blood of sacrifical animals. He finds that barren formalism, sanctimonious scrupulosity, meticulous ablutions, superstitious fear, and display of external holiness pass for religion. Zarathushtra doubts the religion of his birth.

Solitude is nature's sublime temple where spirit can commune with spirit in the surrounding silence and unruffled calm. Mountains lift their heads majestically on the Iranian plateau, and Zarathushtra retreated into the mountain fastness. Here, far removed from the stress and strife of life, and with no human sound to distract his thoughts, he made his home. He breathed the refreshing air. The twittering and chirping and whistling and singing of birds filled the air. Here the earth and waters, birds and beasts, sun and moon, stars and planets worked as his teachers. He read some lesson, some message written by the hand of the maker of all on every pebble and every leaf, every dewdrop and every sunbeam, in every star and every planet. Here he plunged into a reverie or gazed into vacancy.

The calm atmosphere is conducive to communion, and here, in the monastic void; he communed with nature which inspired solemn thoughts in him. He communed with his mind and he communed with his inner self. He thought and he reasoned, he cogitated and he contemplated, he mused and he dreamed. He meditated upon the essence of divinity, the anomalies of life, and the human destiny after demise. Here in this great and glorious temple of nature, built by divine hands, his eyes of spirit saw what the eyes of flesh could not see. Here in the sublime sanctuary spoke the solemn voice of the divine vicar and he heard it. Zarathushtra's creative mind evolved the highest conception of godhead, whom he named Ahura Mazda or the Wise Lord.

Zarathushtra has prepared himself through the wise discipline of mind and heart and through the life of piety to receive his message from Mazda. He longs for the moment when, being enlightened in mind, he shall visualize Vohu Manah or Good Mind, Asha or Righteousness, Sraosha, the embodiment of Obedience to divine commandments, and the sublime seat of beneficent Ahura. Mind alone can understand and realize the supreme mind and Zarathushtra longs to approach Mazda through Vohu Manah. Mind is the repository both of knowledge upon which rests the enlightenment of life, and pure thoughts which form the basis of good conduct.

He developed this dual aspect of mind to a prominent degree and prayed that Vohu Manah might bless him with his presence. He had not long to wait, for Vohu Manah, he who impersonates the divine mind, one day came to him and inquired who he was and to whom he belonged and what he wished for. Seeing Vohu Manah, Zarathushtra got a glimpse of Ahura Mazda, whom he now conceived as holy, and for the first time felt himself acquainted with the words of wisdom. When his ardent desire to meet Vohu Manah is fulfilled he now aspires through him to greet Ahura Mazda himself. His one consuming passion now is to see Mazda face to face and hold communion with him, so that he may have the most comprehensive understanding of the divinity. He desires and yearns and prays that Mazda may vouchsafe unto him his heart's longing. Devotion for Mazda wells up in his heart, and he is filled with the divine spirit. He feels himself lifted above the earth, and in his supreme moments of transcendent ecstasy he has the beatific vision of Mazda. He has now found Mazda and he pours out his devout heart at his feet. He longs to be alone with him, belong wholly to him, and live in his love and attachment. He praises him, worships him, makes songs of devotion to him, he yearns to weave his personality with Mazda like the warp and woof, and he longs to lose himself in the divine bosom. His whole life is bound up in one idea: Ahura Mazda.

Zarathushtra has thought out many problems of life but he is still unsatisfied with his discoveries. He has doubts on many points, and who but Mazda can solve them satisfactorily? He asks Mazda for whom has he created the weal-dispensing cattle, who has marked out the path of the sun and the stars, by whom does the moon wax and wane, who has yoked swiftness to winds and clouds, who withholds the earth and the sky from falling down, who made the waters and the trees, what artificer made light and darkness and wakefulness and sleep, who made the dawn and the day and the night that remind man of the intelligence of his duty, who is the creator of Good Mind, who formed the blessed devotion in the divine Kingdom and who with wisdom made the son dutiful to his father, how should devotion embrace those to whom his religion is proclaimed, whether devotion furthered righteousness through deeds, how was the prayer to be addressed to him, who was righteous and who was wicked, with whom did the enemy of all side and who was like unto him, was not the person that repudiated Mazda's beneficence himself the enemy, how was the wickedness of those who ran counter to the rules of righteousness and good thought to be put down, how was wickedness to be brought into the hands of righteousness, who would gain victory when the powers of righteousness and wickedness came to grips, who would smite victoriously the enemy with the mighty words of Mazda, how would recompense to the righteous and retribution to the wicked be accorded at the reckoning, how the best existence was to be won, would the divine Kingdom be made known to God's faithful through Good Mind, what were the ordinances of Mazda, how should he, Zarathushtra, approach Mazda with love, with what goodness would his soul win felicity, and many such questions pertaining to the way of life. He felt Mazda's inspiring presence within him, he heard his whispers. Mazda spoke through his mind and he was enlightened. He sought instruction from Mazda and had now acquired it.

The work of prophetic preparation was now completed. Zarathushtra was girt with wisdom and righteousness. He had heard, comprehended, and made his own the message of Mazda and was now ready to convey it to mankind. One phase of his life had now ended. He was now ready to leave the life of seclusion and turn towards the clamour and clatter of town traffic and live in the midst of the sight and sound of throbbing human life. He had a new mission, a new hope, a new way of life to regenerate the world. Mankind was steeped in the slough of despair and despondency, helplessness and hopelessness. He was to be the bearer of the message of hope to mankind and salvage it. He was to wean the hearts of men and women from wickedness, to lead them on the path of righteousness, to assuage the sufferings of humanity, to establish a new social order, and to found a new moral world.

He was burning with zeal to embark upon his great mission. He was the chosen of Mazda, who now speaks with sublime satisfaction that Zarathushtra alone among mankind had heard his divine commands and having heard them was now going to make them heard among all mankind, therefore he was bestowing on him elegance of speech. The great work that he had now to undertake of propagating his new religion and winning people for it would be beset with untold obstacles and hardships and Zarathushtra realizes it. But the messenger of Mazda is determined to face them and overcome them and emerge triumphant in the end. He tells Mazda that he will lead mankind on the path of righteousness and sing untiringly his praise all around as long as his life is blessed with power and strength. He speaks of his faith in terms of a universal religion. He is convinced that the religion that Ahura Mazda has commissioned him to preach is the best for all mankind. He looks forward to winning all living men for the faith of Ahura Mazda.

But the ardent desire of the prophet was not to be fulfilled at the moment, nor to be accomplished in full measure in after ages. Though possessed of all the best elements that fitted it to be a world creed, Zoroastrianism has never shown any signs of becoming a universal religion. In the midst of the vicissitudes of fortune, it has been a national religion at best. Little short of a miracle has saved it from total extinction, and various causes have combined to reduce it to the narrowest limits today as the communal religion of a hundred and twenty-five thousand souls. This fact will be brought out more prominently in the treatment of the religious development during the subsequent periods.

Zarathushtra turned his steps to his place of birth and childhood. His kinsfolk and friends recognized him and yet they were bewildered to witness a marvellous change in him. He was of course grown in years and stature.

But there was something indescribable that those who saw him could not realize. His face had grown sweet and serene. It breathed ineffable kindness and bore shining reflection of his pure inner life. It wore the expression of gentleness and cheerfulness, hope and confidence. A resplendent halo of righteousness encircled his magnetic face. He moved among people with a friendly look and a kindly word to all. His moral grandeur struck awe unto those who came near him. The sublimity of his serene behaviour, the childlike simplicity of his speech, the unassuming attitude of his movements, the imperturbable calm and passive countenance aroused feelings of reverence in those who met him. They greeted him with salutations and adoration. His advent soon became the event of surrounding villages. All eagerly pointed to him and talked abour him. In dumb veneration people gazed at him, admired him, adored him, and marvelled at him. He was Zarathushtra of the Spitamas, they said, yet he was altogether a novel personality. He was of them and yet above them, he was akin to them and yet unlike them. He spoke unheard of words, he talked of unknown things. He was what they were not. They were but men, he was greater than man, he was an angel, he was a godling.

Zarathushtra has seen by this time that there were some people who were anxious to hear what he had to say. He now began to give lengthy talks on subjects of great importance to his eager listeners. He saw that he could sway and draw the hearts of his hearers to himself. He gave forth publicly that he came from his maker Ahura Mazda, whom he declared to be incomparably greater than the gods they had so far known. This great God had sent him as his chosen prophet to preach a nobler religion than the one they followed. Their priests had laid great emphasis on outward observances and carried rules for rituals to meticulous casuistry.

Their gods were fond of sacrificial offerings of animals and birds. Religion, preached Zatathushtra, did not consist in a scrupulous observance of outward forms, but was based mainly upon the heart. A broken heart and a contrite spirit were the choicest sacrifices that the faithful could offer to their creator. Burning tears of a penitent heart were better than a cupful of oblations. The aim and object and end of the religion that Mazda had commissioned him to teach was righteous conduct. His worship was founded on righteousness. Genuine piety is of the heart and its outward expressions are good thoughts, good words, and good deeds. The beliefs and practices of his hearers were irreconcilably alien from what he taught. His outspoken utterances created diverse effects upon those who flocked to hear him daily. Some felt themselves moved and influenced by them.

There were others among his hearers who had approached him specially with the intention of finding out his views without rousing his attention to their ill-will. They took alarming reports to their associates. They saw danger ahead of them. They waited and watched, suspected and spied. They were adroitly prepared themselves to face the ominous situation; and they had not to be long in waiting. Signs of disapprobation, whispers of disapproval, murmurs of indignation now appeared in various threatened to break out in open revolt.

The priests of the ancient faith were now alarmed. They attempted to dissuade the prophet from disturbing the peace of the people. They met often to argue with him on the questions he was raising, but were foiled in the controversies. They felt themselves humiliated before the people and gave up meeting the prophet. They began to work against him and tried in all possible manners to frustrate the effect he was daily producing upon his hearers. They were accustomer to fatten upon the profits of the elaborate ceremonials and rich sacrifices that people offered under their guidance. They were renowned as exorcists who cast out demons, who read dreams, prognosticated the future, warded off the effect of the evil eye and, with ingenious charlatanism, had prospered among the credulous and superstitious. Zarathushtra reproved their greed and avarice. He exhorted the people to give up these superstitious practices and warned them that they were causing great harm by following such false teachers. His denunciation of their practices made them furious and now they sought his ruin. They accused him of preaching doctrines that were subversive of the religion of their forefathers and the established form of worship, and of blaspheming their gods. They incited the people to oppose him and made frantic appeals to the rulers of the land to drive him out from their midst.

Zarathushtra's heart was burning with indignation against these hypocrisies. With his holy spirit aglow with righteous wrath, he called these Pharisees and Scribes of Iran, Kavis and Karapans or seeingly blind and hearingly deaf. These terms belong to the Indo-Iranian period and were evidently used in a good sense, before the Aryan groups separated. They share the fate of the cardinal word daeva and are assigned derogatory meaning in the Gathas. The Vedic hymns use the word kavi in the sense of a sage. It is freely applied to the seers and to Soma priests. It is further used as an epithet of gods. Agni, in particular, bears this honoured title. In the Gathas the word is curiously used with a double meaning. It is given a bad connotation whenever it is applied to the priests of the Daeva-worshippers. But the second Iranian dynasty is known as the Kavi or Kianian [Kayanian]. Its renowned Kings who lived before the coming of Zarathushtra were Kavi Kavata, Kavi Usa, and Kavi Haosrava. Even Vishtaspa, who later became the royal patron of the new religion, retains this title and Zarathushtra speaks of him as Kavi Vishtaspa. It is significant, however, that Vishtaspa is the last King who shares this epithet with his royal predecessors. The Kings who succeed him and with whom the dynasty dies out do not share the title. To the class of the Kavi belong the Karapan, corresponding to Skt. kalpa, 'ritual,' and the Usij, Skt. ushijah.

These heretical priests give the cattle to violence, they mislead mankind by their evil teachings and bring destruction to them and their cattle, but the prophet knows that they will face ruin, and in the end their own corrupt consciences will condemn them to eternal damnation. Through the drunken orgies they and the wicked lords of the land who follow them cause misery to all around them, and Zarathushtra implores Ahura Mazda to put down their evil. The bitterest foe of Zarathushtra who opposes him and thwarts his work is Bendva, who does not himself embrace righteousness and incites others to follow his lead. Zarathushtra invokes Mazda to overthrow this chieftain from power. Grehma is another powerful Kavi who always intrigues for Zarathushtra's undoing. Mazda denounces him and his evil associates, for their teachings lead to the destruction of the life of cattle and they lead others to wickedness. This wicked leader will bewail his evil fate and repent that he did not accept Zarathushtra's message, when at the end of his wicked life his soul will be consigned to the worst abode of woe. Usij is yet another class of the false priests who work violence to cattle and husbandry.

These evil teachers, complains Zarathushtra, misinterpret the doctrines that he preaches and deceive people. They are devoid of goodness of mind and heart and are the beloved of the Daevas. They defraud mankind of the happiness of both the worlds. Like the Daevas whom they follow, they are known throughout the seven regions of the earth as the offspring of Evil Thought, Lie, and Arrogance. They persecute the righteous and desolate their pastures. Those who strengthen the hands of such false leaders given over to wickedness incur Ahura's displeasure. Zarathushtra exhorts all not to listen to the words and commands of the liars who bring misery and destruction to the house and clan, district and country, but to resist them with all their might. These persons who do not embrace Righteousness and Good Thought are Zarathushtra's enemies. They are powerful and they strive to frighten Zarathushtra who is weak. He looks to Ahura Mazda for protection against them and prays that instead of causing him harm, their hostile actions may recoil upon themselves. The enmity and hatred towards the prophet, however, increase day by day and he is now aware that the opponents are bent upon doing him the utmost harm that they can, that is, they conspire to kill him.

REFERENCES

Arda Viraf: The Pahlavi text, edited and translated by Hoshangji Jamaspji Asa, Martin Hang, and E. W. West. Bombay, 1872.

Arda Viraf Nameh: The Original Pahlavi Text with Persian version of Zartosht Behrain in verse, edited by Kaikhusru J. Jamasp Asa. Bombay, 1902.

Brodbeck, A.: Zoroaster. Leipzig, 1893.

Cheyne, T. K.: Book of Psalms, its origin, and its relation to Zoroastrianism. In Semitic Studies in Memory of Rev. Dr. A. Kohut. Berlin, 1897.

Dinkard: Books 7-9. Translated from the Pahlavi text by E. W. West. In *Sacred Books of the East*, vols. 37, 47.

Dinkard [Denkard]: The Complete Text. Edited by D. M. Madan. 2 vols. Bombay, 1911.

Geiger, Wilhelm: Civilization of the Eastern Iranians in Ancient Times. Translated from the German by Darab Dastur Peshutan Sanjana. 2 vols. London, 1885, 1886.

Geiger, W., and Windischmann, Fr.: Zarathushtra in the Gathas and in the Greek and Roman Classics. Translated by Darab P. Sanjana. Leipzig, 1897.

Inostranzev, M.: Iranian Influence on Moslem Literature. Translated by G. K. Nariman with Supplementary Appendices from Arabic Sources. Bombay, 1918.

Jackson, A. V. Williams: Zoroaster, the Prophet of Ancient Iran. New York, 1899.

Jackson, A. V, Williams: Die Iranische Religion. In *Grundriss der Iranischen Philologie, vol. 2, p. 612-708. Strassburg, 1896-1904.*

Jackson, A. V. Williams: Zoroastrian Studies. New York, 1928.

Mills, L. H.: Zarathushtra and the Greeks. Leipzig. 1903. 1904.

Mills, L. H.: Zarathushtra, Philo, the Achaemenids and Israel. Leipzip, 1905, 1906.

Mills, L. H.: Avesta Eschatology compared with the Books of Daniel and Revelations. Chicago, 1908.

Spiegel Memorial Volume: Edited by Jivanji Jamshedji Modi. Bombay, 1908.

Vendidad, Vispered, Yasna, Pahlavi Texts: Edited by F. Spiegel in Avesta Die Heiligen Schriften der Parsen. Wien, 1853.

5

Main Figures

MAIN FIGURES IN EARLY PERIOD

Zoroaster

It is a well-known fact that very little evidence about the times and life of Zarathushtra has reached our times. In fact the major piece of evidence that has reached us is the text of his Divine Songs, the Gathas. Historians have tried to reconstruct Zarathushtra's life mainly with this one piece. However, they face a very challenging task, since this is not meant to be a biographical account, nor even a historical account of his times, but poetry describing Zarathushtra's spiritual philosophy and worldview. Trying to reconstruct his life from this text is like trying to discover about Shakespeare through his works; not his entire works, but only one of his plays.

Nevertheless, there are sufficient indications to be able to piece together some basic background information. However, this has left ample room for various mythologies to evolve around his life. This text will discuss both documentary aspects of his life, as well as mythical stories. Not much is known about his youth except that he was very curious and wanted to find out about things. He spend a long time outdoors, contemplating nature and the questions of life.

Zarathushtra encountered many difficulties and challenges imposed on him through the opposition of the established priests and local ruling princes. He tries to promulgate his teachings, but every time, the established traditions, what people were used to, manage to stop him. Eventually he and his followers leave their homeland for other lands. Still anywhere they go, they meet similar opposition from both rulers and priests.

Finally, in the land of King (Kavi) Vishtaspa, he manages to get an audience with the King. During this encounter, many of the leading priests and wise men were present, to quiz Zarathushtra and test his new philosophy.

Zarathushtra manages to answer all questions to the satisfaction of the King, who after a few days of pondering the situation, embraces this new religion and urges his subjects to do the same. This was the major breakthrough in Zarathushtra's propagation of his message. Two of the noted disciples of Zarathushtra, as mentioned in the Gathas, are Frashaoshtra and Jamaspa of the Hvogva family. Later on, Zarathushtra's daughter, Pouruchista gets married. In the Gathas, Zarathushtra advises his daughter as well as all brides and grooms-to-be, but does not name the bridegroom. However, later tradition says that she marries Jamaspa. Zarathushtra lived a healthy life to old age. According to later tradition, Zarathushtra passes away at the age of 77, of natural causes.

Cyrus the Great

Cyrus (580-529 BC.) was the first Achaemenian King. He founded Persia by uniting the two original Iranian Tribes- the Medes and the Persians. Although he was known to be a great conqueror, who at one point controlled one of the greatest Kingdoms ever seen, he is best remembered for his unprecedented tolerance and magnanimous attitude towards those he defeated.

Upon his victory over the Medes, he founded a government for his new Kingdom, incorporating both Median and Persian nobles as civilian officials. The conquest of Asia Minor completed, he led his armies to the eastern frontiers. Hyrcania and Parthia were already part of the Median Kingdom. Further east, he conquered Drangiana, Arachosia, Margiana and Bactria. After crossing the Oxus, he reached the Jaxartes, where he built fortified towns with the object of defending the farthest frontier of his Kingdom against nomadic tribes of Central Asia. The victories to the east led him again to the west and sounded the hour for attack on Babylon and Egypt. When he conquered Babylon, he did so to cheers from the Jewish Community, who welcomed him as a liberator- he allowed the Jews to return to the promised Land. He showed great forbearance and respect towards the religious beliefs and cultural traditions of other races. These qualities earned him the respect and homage of all the people over whom he ruled.

The victory over Babylonia expressed all the facets of the policy of conciliation which Cyrus had followed until then. He presented himself not as a conqueror, but a liberator and the legitimate successor to the crown. He took the title of "King of Babylon King of the Land". Cyrus had no thought of forcing conquered people into a single mould, and had the wisdom to leave unchanged the institution of each Kingdom he attached to the Persian Crown. In 537 BC. he allowed more than 40,000 Jews to leave Babylon and return to Palestine. This step was in line with his policy to bring peace to Mankind. A new wind was blowing from the east, carrying away the cries and humility of defeated and murdered victims, extinguishing the fires of sacked cities, and liberating nations from slavery.

Cyrus was upright, a great leader of men, generous and benelovent. The Hellenes, whom he conquered, regarded him as 'Law-giver' and the Jews as 'the annointed of the Lord'.

Prior to his demise, he founded a new capital city at Pasargade in Fars. And had established a government for his Kingdom. He appointed a governor (satrap) to represent him in each province, however the administration, legistlation, and cultural activities of each province was the responsibility of the Satraps. Accoding to Xenophon Cyrus is also reputed to have devised the first postal system, (Achaemenide achievements).

His doctrines were adopted by the future kings of the Achaemenian dynasty. Darius I (521-486 BC.) brought together skills and craftsmen from all over the kingdom in building the city of Persepolis.

Darius the Great

Enthroned in Peresepolis, the magnificent city that he built, Darius I firmly grasps the royal scepter in his right hand. In the left, he is holding a lotus blossom with two buds, the symbol of royalty.

Darius, a member of the Achemenides family, rose to the throne of the Kingdom of Persia by taking part, in 522, in a plot to assassinate Smerdis, who had assumed the Kingship that same year at the demise of his brother Cambyses on his way back from Egypt. Both Cambyses and Smerdis were sons of Cyrus the Great, the founder of the Persian Kingdom. Darius, on the other hand, was a remote cousin of them. The story of the plot of Darius and six other high-ranking Persians to assassinate Smerdis, who, they pretended, was not the son of Cyrus by that name, but an impostor, a Medean magus posing for Cyrus' son, who, by their account, had been murdered earlier at the request of his own brother Cambyses, is told by Herodotus in his Histories. It offers him an opportunity to put in the mouth of three of the conspirators, when time comes to decide how tu rule the kingdom, three speeches, one in favour of democracy, one in favour of aristocratic oligarchy, the rule by a small group of persons chosen among the best citizens, and the last one, by Darius himself, who eventually prevails, in favour of monarchy, supposed to be the very best of all three regimes, each taken at its best.

If Cyrus and Cambyses built the Persian kingdom by conquering a terrritory spanning from the Ionian coast west to India east, and from Scythia, Caucasus and the southern shores of the Black and Caspian Seas north to Lybia, Egypt and the shores of the Persian Gulf south, it is Darius who organized its administration. He moved his residence to the Elamite city of Susa, which became the administrative capital of his kingdom and where he had a gigantic palace built for himself. He divided his vast kingdom into satrapies headed by Satraps and submitted to an annual tribute, and built roads across the kingdom to ease the communications required to administer such a huge territory (Herodotus in his Histories gives a description of the road leading from Sardis, the capital of Lydia, along the Ionian coast, which had become the siege of a satrapy, to Susa). He also directed the building, in his native country of Persia, of another palace at Persepolis.

But Darius was not merely an administrator and, after curbing several rebellions in various parts of the kingdom during his first year in power, he also continued the politic of expansion of his ancestors, toward the east in India, as well as toward the west and Europe, starting with Thracia. In 499, some Ionian Greek cities of the satrapy of Lydia, under the leadership of Aristagoras of Miletus, rebelled against the Persians and set fire to Sardis. It was not until 494, with the naval victory of the Persian fleet at Lade, off the shores of Miletus, and the recapture of Miletus, that the rebellion was completely curbed. Having thus subdued the Ionian Greeks, Darius set out to conquer the rest of Greece, which led to the first Persian War. But his troops were stopped by the Athenians at the battle of Marathon in 490. It was left to his son Xerxes to lead a second attempt in 480, with no more success.

Darius' sovereignty marks the apogee of the Persian Kingdom, which started to crumble by the mere fact of its size after his demise, until it was conquered by Alexander the Great.

The sovereignty of Darius spans most of the period covered by Herodotus' Histories, a part going from the middle of book III to the beginning of book VII. In the Phædrus, Plato cites Darius at the side of Solon and Lycurgus, the half legendary lawgiver of Sparta, as examples of successfull lawmakers. And in the Laws, the Athenian stranger praises

Darius for the way he ruled his country, but reproaches him not to have learned from Cyrus' mistakes in raising his children, and to have done the same mistakes with his son Xerxes, that is, to let him have a pampered childhood he himself didn't have, not being the son of a King. In the Menexenus, faithful to the rules of the funeral oration he is caricaturing, he exalts the power of Darius only to give more lusters to the Athenian victory at Marathon.

MAIN FIGURES IN MEDIEVAL PERIOD

Xerxes

Xerxes became King of Persia at the demise of his father Darius the Great in 485, at a time when his father was preparing a new expedition against Greece and had to face an uprising in Egypt. According to Herodotus, the transition was peaceful this time. Because he was about to leave for Egypt, Darius, following the law of his country had been requested to name his successor and to choose between the elder of his sons, born from a first wife before he was in power, and the first of his sons born after he became King, from a second wife, Atossa, Cyrus' daughter, who had earlier been successively wed to her brothers Cambyses and Smerdis, and which he had married soon after reaching power in order to confirm his legitimacy. Atossa was said to have much power on Darius and he chosed her son Xerxes for successor.

After quelling the revolt of Egypt, Xerxes finally decided to pursue the project of his father to subdue Greece, but made lengthy preparations for that. Among other things, remembering what had happened to Mardonius' expedition a few years earlier (his fleet had been destroyed by a tempest in 492 while trying to round Mount Athos), he ordered a channel to be opened for his fleet north of Mount Athos in Chalcidice. He also had two boat bridges built over the Hellespont near Abydus for his troop to cross the straits.

The expedition was ready to move in the spring of 480 and Xerxes himself took the lead. Herodotus gives us a colorful description of the Persian army that he evaluates at close to two million men and about twelve hundred ships. Modern historians find these figures irrealistic, if only for logistical reasons, and suppose the army was at most two hundred thousand men and the fleet no more than a thousand ships, but this still makes an impressive body for the time.

Xerxes' expedition moved by land and sea through Thracia, the fleet following the army along the coast. It didn't meet resistance until it reached Thessalia, where the Persian army defeated the Spartans and their allies at the pass of Thermopylæ while, on sea, neither the Persian nor the Athenian fleet could win the decision in the battle that took place near Cape Artemisium, along the northern coast of the island of Euboea. Because of Themistocles' decision to evacuate Athens, Xerxes managed to take the city and set fire to the temples of the Acropolis, but his fleet was soon after destroyed by the Athenian fleet of Themistocles at the battle of Salamis.

After this defeat, Xerxes returned to Asia via the Hellespont, leaving part of his army in Greece under the command of Mardonius. But the following year, after having taken Athens a second time, the Persian army was defeated, in September of 479, at Platæa, near Thebes in Boeotia, in a battle that lasted 13 days, in which Mardonius was killed while, at about the same time, what remained of the Persian fleeı was destroyed by a Greek fleet under the command of the Spartan general Leutychides off Cape Mycale, a promontory of the Ionian coast, north of Miletus, facing the island of Samos. This was not the end of the war between Persia and Greece, but it was the end of the incursions of the Persian army on mainland Greece. And without a fleet, Persia had to abandon control of the sea to Athens. Xerxes died in 465, assassinated probably upon order by one of his sons, Artaxerxes, who succeeded him.

In the Laws, Plato compares Xerxes to Cambyses in that, as him, he was victim of his education at the court, unlike his father Darius, who was not a son of King. And he goes on to say that it is almost impossible for someone raised in an extremely rich family to become virtuous, and to explain thus why there was no other great King of Persia after Darius. But it is Xerxes who serves as an example to Callicles in the Gorgias to show that the stronger should have a greater share.

Kartir

Kartir Hangirpe was a highly influential Zoroastrian high-priest of the late 3rd century AD. and served as advisor to at least three Sassanid kings. Kartir was probably instrumental in promoting the cause of Mazdaism (as opposed to Zurvanism, the other - now extinct - branch of Zoroastrianism), for in his inscription at Naqsh-e Rajab, Kartir makes plain that he has decided that there is a heaven and there is a hell, thus putting himself at odds with the principles of (fatalistic) Zurvanism. Nonetheless, it was during the sovereignty of Shapur I to whom Kartir was first appointed advisor - that Zurvanism appears to have developed as a cult, and this contradiction remains an issue of scholastic dispute.

Simultaneously, Kartir is also considered to have been a significant force in an iconoclastic movement that would result in the loss of favour of the shrine cults, an alien (to Indo-Iranian religious tradition) form of worship inherited from the Babylonians and instituted six centuries earlier by Artaxerxes II as an instrument for tax collection. It was during Kartir's time as high-priest that the shrines were - by law - stripped of their statues, and then either abandoned or converted into fire temples.

According to his own inscriptions, Kartir rose to power during the sovereignty of Shapur I, to whom he served as advisor and accompanied on travels. Shapur's son Hormizd I appointed Kartir Moabadan-Moabad, 'priest of priests', a position Kartir ruthlessly used to promote his own position and to punish lower-ranking priests whose opinions he considered contrary to his own. Under subsequent kings, Kartir called for the persecution of adherents of other religions, in particular Manichaeans, whose prophet Mani was sentenced to demise by Bahram I, very likely on the instigation of Kartir and even though Shapur I had previously been a patron of the prophet. The persecution ceased during the sovereignty of Narseh, probably after the demise of the high-priest. Kartir is not well attested in sources other than his own inscriptions on the Ka'ba-i Zartosht (at Naqsh-e Rustam) and at Naqsh-e Rajab.

Azar Kayvan

Azar Kayvan was a Zoroastrian high priest of Istakhr and native of Fars who emigrated to the Gujarat in Mughal India during the sovereignty of the King Akbar and became the founder of a Zoroastrian school of ishraqiyyun or Illuminationists. Exhibiting features of a Zoroastrianized Sufi order, this school became known as the Sepassian.

Details regarding Azar Kayvan's life are scanty and are mainly culled from the hagiographical literature of the school. This hagiography places Azar Kayvan, son of Azar Gashasb, and his ancestry back to Sasan the Fifth then through Sasan the First to the Kayanids, Gayomart, and finally to Mahabad, the figure who appeared at the very beginning of the great cycle of prophecy, according to the "Bible of the Prophets of Ancient Iran," and who seems to be none other than the primordial Adam. His mother was named Shirin; her ancestry goes back to Khosrow I Anushiravan. According to the Dabestan-i-Mazahib, as a young boy Azar Kayvan showed signs of his calling to the contemplative life.

Through dreams and visions he received the teaching of the ancient sages of Iran, which allowed him to give extraordinary replies to questions which were asked of him at the madrasa where he was a student, and which won him the nickname Zu'l-'Olum (master of the sciences). Internal references in the biography by his devotees allow us to determine that his residence was at Estakhr (about a hundred kilometers north of Shiraz), where he spent the first thirty or forty years of his life in contemplation and where he assembled his first assembly of disciples.

Around 1570, drawn by the religious revival which was taking place in India around the King Akbar, he left with them to settle down in the town of Patna in the Gujarat, where he lived until he died at around eighty-five years of age. Amongst his students, certain of these hagiographical sources place key Shi'ite Muslim theosophical figures of the Safavid philosophical revival at Isfahan within his circle. Notably among these figures was Shaykh Baha' al-Din Amili and Mir Findiriski, on whose behest the latter seems to have translated a major Tantric yogic text from Sanskrit into Persian. According to some scholars, Dastur Meherji Rana, who had influenced Akbar and founded the famous lineage of Parsi high priests at Navsari, was a disciple of Azar Kayvan.

MAIN FIGURES IN MODERN PERIOD

Maneckji Nusserwanji Dhalla

Maneckji Nusserwanji Dhalla also abbreviated M. N. Dhalla, was a Zoroastrian priest and religious scholar.Dhalla is best known for his criticism of the orthodox factions within the Parsi community. In particular, he was stringently opposed to the excessive ritualization of religious practice, including that of the use of the Towers of Silence. In his autobiography, he was also critical of the orthodox refusal to accept converts, noting that "the permanent blockade to an influx from outside, the abandoning of the fold by an increasing number of both men and women, and the ever-falling birth-rate of the community.

Maneckji Dhalla was born on September 22, 1875 in Surat, India into a family of Godavara priests. At age 3, he was sent with his father Nusserwanji Dhalla to Karachi (then a city in the Sindh province of British India, and today lies in Pakistan), where his father had subsequently employed.

In 1890, at the age of 15, Dhalla began his training for the priesthood. Shortly thereafter he interrupted his studies in order to work and so augment the family's meagre income. In 1894, Dhalla became editor of a monthly magazine Goolshan-e-Danesh. Two years later, Dhalla acquired ownership of the magazine but was forced to shut it down when funds ran out a few months later. The debt incurred would remain with him for many years.

Dhalla completed his clerical training on March 21, 1895 at the age of 20 and his first lecture as a full-fledged priest was on atash, fire. In the next three years, he published six booklets (in the Gujarati language) on various aspects of the Zoroastrian religion. On September 21, 1900, just shy of his 25th birthday, Dhalla delivered his first public lecture in Bombay (present day Mumbai), the first of what would become a lecture tour of the Indian subcontinent.

The lecture series made him famous among the Parsi community, and in August 1901 Dhalla was accepted at the postgraduate degree program in Avestan and Pahlavi studies at the Sir Jamsetjee Jejeebhoy Madressa in Bombay. He graduated in 1904, having completed the five-year course in just over three.

In May 1905 and with the financial support of Parsi, Dhalla continued his studies at Columbia University in New York City, where he studied under the personal tutelage of A. V. Williams Jackson, an authority on the Avestan language. Even with the preparatory assistance of Shapurji Saklatvala and Jivanji Jamshedji Modi, New York was initially quite a culture shock for Dhalla, who until his arrival in the United States had never even worn fosovereignty attire.

Nonetheless, and with great pecuniary discipline, for the next three years Dhalla studied Iranian languages and Sanskrit as majors with minors in philology and philosophy. He received a Master's degree in 1906. Following the publication of his thesis on The Nyaishes or Zoroastrian Litanies, Dhalla was awarded a Ph.D. in May 1908.

The experience at Columbia University gave Dhalla a new outlook on life and he began observing religious literature from a new angle. He renounced conventional religion and his fascination for ritualistic religion faded. He now considered ethics as the highest form of religion and embraced the path of devotion. His antagonism for western culture turned to amity. Although it would be later said that his time at Columbia had made him felt attracted to mysticism, Dhalla unambiguously says the opposite in his own autobiography.

On April 22, 1914 Dhalla and his wife again sailed again for the United States, where Dhalla was to have his book Zoroastrian Theology published. While there, Dhalla delivered a series of lectures on 'The Culture of the East' under the chairmanship of Williams Jackson.

In September 1921 Dhalla, accompanied by his wife and son (Nariman, who would eventually also study at Columbia), again proceeded to New York, this time to have his book Zoroastrian Civilization published. On the way, the family also spent four months in Iran and Iraq, where Dhalla again gave a series of lectures. Although Dhalla was appalled at the living conditions (not just of Zoroastrians), he found that the still-medieval infrastructure afforded him with opportunities for closer contacts with the people that he would have had with more modern forms of transportation. In New York, Dhalla delivered lectures whenever the opportunity arose. Following the publication of his book, Dhalla and family returned to Karachi via London, Paris, Berlin, Vienna, Milan, Rome, and Naples, and felt the effects of the war that had ended only three years previously. Following a five-week layover in Bombay, they returned to Karachi in July 1922.

In 1929, Dhalla journeyed again to New York to attend Columbia University's 175th anniversary celebrations, and at which he received an honorary Doctor of Letters (Litt.D.). His book Our Perfecting World: Zarathushtra's Way of Life was subsequently published there and he again delivered lectures. On his return journey – this time eastwards – he was surprised to discover that he was known in Japan. It turned out that a newspaper article on him had recently been published. Dhalla was upgraded to a first class cabin for the onward journey to Karachi.

In June 1935, Dhalla was awarded the title of Shams-ul Ulema by the British colonial government. In January 1938, Dhalla again travelled to New York, where his magnum opus The History of Zoroastrianism was then published.

On June 24, 1942 his wife Cooverbai died of a stomach affliction. She was 65. Dhalla continued to write and give lectures until 1954. He died in 1956, aged 79. He was succeeded as High Priest of Karachi by Godrej Sidhwa.

Godrej Sidhwa

Ervad Godrej Sidhwa was born in Karachi, Pakistan, in 1925, and studied Avesta, Pahalvi, Persian & Pazend languages, plus Ancient Iranian literature at M.F. Cama Athornan Institute, Andheri, Mumbai, for 6 years. He got initiated into the Zoroastrian priesthood by going through the Navar and Maratab initiation ceremony from Iranshah Atash Behram, Udvada, India. His initiation as a priest accounts for the "Ervad" ('Reverend') title.

Godrej has been the instructor of Zoroastrianism and Ancient Iranian History at the B.V.S. Parsi High School and Mama Parsi Secondary School, Karachi, for the last 45 years. He was appointed as the Honorary Lecturer in Zoroastrian Theology at colleges in Karachi for the Zoroastrian students. He was also appointed as Examiner in Zoroastrian Theology by the University of Karachi, Pakistan, for the Bachelor's degree program. After the demise of Dasturji Dr. M. N. Dhalla he took up all the duties of the late Dasturji, in the religious as well as the social areas.

Ervad Sidhwa has lectured on Zoroastrian Theology in India, Pakistan, Iran, Canada, UK, USA and UAE. He has also lectured on Zoroastrianism at University of California, Berkeley. On several occasions he has been invited by the Government of Pakistan to discuss the Human Rights and problems faced by religious minorities in Pakistan.

He is the Honorary Secretary of The Karachi Parsi Anjuman Trust Fund, Karachi Athornan Mandal, and Joint Honorary Secretary of Dr. Dhalla Memorial Institute since its inception in 1965. He is also a jury delegate of Karachi Parsi Matrimonial Court, Government of Sindh, Pakistan, since 1960.

REFERENCES

Avesta: The Sacred Books of the Parsis. Edited by Karl F. Geldner. Stuttgart, 1885-1896. (For Yt. 22-24 and the Avestan Fragments see N. L. Westergaard's Zendavesta, Copenhagen, 1852-1854.).

Bundahishn: Edited by T. D. and B. T. Anklesaria. Bombay, 1908.

Dadistan-i Dinik: Translated from the Pahlavi text by E. W. West. In Sacred Books of the East, vol. 18.

Henry, Victor: Le Parsisme. Paris, 1905.

Hodivala, S. K.: Zarathushtra and His Contemporaries in the Rig Veda. Bombay, 1913.

Meillet, A.: Trois Conferences sur les Gathas de l'Avesta. Paris, 1925.

Menant, D.: Les Parsis. Paris, 1898; tr. in English by M. M. Murzban, The Parsis of India. 2 vols. Bombay. 1917.

Pazend Texts: Collected and Collated by E. K. Antia. Bombay, 1909. Two Afrins, three Patits tr. into Eng. from Spiegel's German translation by A. H. Bleeck in *Khordah Avesta* Hertford, 1864. Seven Afrins, Sitayishes, and other Pazend prayers tr. into Gujarati by Phiroze E. Masani in *Pazend Prayers Series* Nos. 1, 2, 3. Bombay, 1916, 1920, 1931.

Ragozin, Z. A.: Media. New York, 1888.

Rapp, A.: The Religion and Customs of the Persians and other Iranians as described by the Grecian and Roman Authors. Translated from the German by K. R. Cama. Bombay, 1876-1879.

6

Scriptures

The Yasna and the Visparad are the holy books of Zoroastrianism. The first part of Yasna comprises of Gathas or verses which came from the mouth of the prophet. The Gathas are five in number. The Gathas are written in metres which correspond to the metres of the Sama Veda. The second part of Yasna contains prayers addressed to the Supreme Master and other deities who form the spritual hierarchy.

Visparad is a aggregationcompilation of invocations or speeches which are recited before other prayers and holy scriptures. The twenty-one Nasks cover all kinds of Sciences, such as medicine, astronomy, agriculture, botany, etc. They correspond to the Vedangas of Hinduism. Then there is the Khordah Avesta or little Avesta which contains Yashts (invocations) and prayers for the use of lay persons. The contemporary Parsis recite these prayers daily.

Zoroastrian holy scriptures are called Zend Avesta. They contain three parts. The first is Vendidad. This comprises of spiritual laws and ancient mythological tales. The second is Visparad. The third is Yasna. The Avesta contains direct speeches between Zoroaster and Ahura Mazda, the Supreme Lord.

RELIGIOUS SCRIPTURES

Avesta

The Avesta is the main compilation of sacred texts of Zoroastrianism, compiled in the Avestan language.

The texts of the Avesta, which are all in the Avestan language, were collected over several hundred years. The most significant portion, the

Gathas, in Gathic Avestan, are the hymns thought to have been compiled by Zarathushtra (Zoroaster) himself, and date linguistically to around 1000 BC. The religious texts of the Yasna, which includes the Gathas, is partially in Older and partially in Younger Avestan. The oldest parts may be older than the Gathas, later adjusted to more closely follow the philosophy of Zoroaster. The various Yashts are in Younger Avestan and thought to date to the Achaemenid era (559–330 BC.). The Visperad and Vendidad, which are also in Younger Avestan, were in all probability compiled even later but this is not certain.

The various texts are thought to have been carried by word of mouth for centuries before they were penned. The Text of Arda Viraf, a work compiled in the third or fourth century, suggests that the Gathas and some other texts that were integrated into the Avesta had previously existed in the royal library of the Achaemenid Kings (559–330 BC.). As per Arda Viraf 1.4-7 and Denkard 3.420 the royal library was lost in a fire caused by the troops of Alexander the Great. However, neither assertion can be confirmed since the texts, if they existed, have been lost.

Nevertheless, Rasmus Christian Rask resolved that the texts must indeed be the leftovers of a much larger literature, as Pliny the Elder had hinted in his Naturalis Historiae, where he depicts one Hermippus of Smyrna having "interpreted two million verses of Zoroaster" in the 3rd century BC. An Introduction to an Ancient Faith proposes the Gathas and older Yasna texts would not have retained their old-language qualities if they had only been orally transmitted.

As per the Denkard, a semi-religious work written in the ninth century, the King Volgash undertook to have the religious texts collected and compared. The results of this project, if it occurred, have not survived.

In the third century, the Sassanian king Ardashir I (226-241 AD.) ordered his high priest Tonsar (or Tansar) to compile the religious texts. As per the Denkard, the Tonsar effort ensued in the reproduction of twenty-one volumes, called nasks, subdivided into 348 sections, with about 3.5 million words in total. One final editing took place under Shapur II (309-379).

The Avesta, as known nowadays, represents only those parts of the text that are used religiously, and therefore lived in the memory of the priests; and, as it now consists of all lasting religious texts in the Avestan language, it may include material that never formed part of the twenty-one nasks at all. In that sense, the current Avesta is a "prayer book" rather than a "Bible". The remainder of the twenty-one nasks has been lost since then, especially after the fall of the Sassanid Kingdom, after which Zoroastrianism was supplanted by Islam. Nevertheless, some secondary literature in Pahlavi purports to contain paraphrases or lists of subjects of the lost texts.

The Zend

The word Zend or Zand, literally implying "interpretation", refers to late middle Persian language rephrases of commentaries on theindividual Avestan texts: they could be equated with the Jewish Targums. These commentaries - which date from the third to tenth centuries - were not meant for use as religious texts by themselves but for religious instruction of the (by then) non-Avestan-speaking public. In contrast, the texts of the Avesta proper remained inviolate and continued to be recounted in Avestan, which was regarded a holy language.

Manuscripts of the Avesta exist in two forms. One is the Avesta-o-Zand (or Zand-i-Avesta), in which the individual texts are written together with their Zand. The other is the Vendidad Sadeh, in which the Yasna, Vispered and Vendidad are set out in alternate sections, in the order used in the Vendidad ceremony, with no comment at all.

The use of the phrase Zend-Avesta to refer to the Avesta in general is a misinterpretation of the phrase Zand-i-Avesta (which literally means "interpreting of the Avesta").

An associated mistake is the use of Zend as the name of a language or book. In 1759, Anquetil-Duperron reported having been told that Zend was the name of the language of the more ancient texts. In his third discourse, published in 1798, Sir William Jones mentions a conversation with a Hindu priest who told him that the script was called Zend, and the language Avesta. This error results from a misinterpretation of the term pazend, which in reality refers to the use of the Avestan alphabet in writing the Zand and other Middle Persian religious texts, as an expression meaning "in Zend".

The misunderstanding then became too universal in Western scholarship to be repealed, and Zend-Avesta, although a misnomer, is still from time to time used to denote the older texts. Rask's seminal work, A Dissertation on the Authenticity of the Zend Language, may have added to the confusion. N. L. Westergaard's Zendavesta, or the religious texts of the Zoroastrians only spread the error.

Structure and Content: In its contemporary form, the Avesta is a compilation from various sources, and its different parts date from different periods of time and deviate widely in character. Only texts in the Avestan language are regarded part of the Avesta.

There are solid lingual and cultural similarities between the texts of the Avesta and those of the early Indian Rigveda; the similarities are presumed to reveal the common beliefs of Proto-Indo-Iranian times, with the deviations then assumed to reflect autonomous development that occurred after the pre-historical split of the two cultures.

According the Denkard, the twenty-one nasks mirror the structure of the twenty-one-word-long Ahuna Vairya prayer: each of the three lines of the prayer consists of seven words. Correspondingly, the nasks are divided into three groups, of seven volumes per group. In the first place, each volume had a word of the prayer as its name, which so marked a volume's place relative to the other volumes. Only about a one-fourth of the text from the nasks has lasted until today.

The subjects of the Avesta are separated topically (even though the organization of the nasks is not), but these are not determined or canonical. Some scholars prefer to place the categories in two groups, the one religious, and the other general.

The Yasna

Yasna is the name of the main religious compilation of texts of the Avesta as well as the name of the main Zoroastrian act of worship at which those verses are recited.

A well-schooled priest is able to recount the entire Yasna in about two hours. With extensions, it takes about an hour longer. Yasna section and verse pointers are traditionally abbreviated with Y.

The text of the Yasna is organized into seventy-two sections also known as hads or has (from Avestan ha'iti, 'cut'). The seventy-two threads of the Zoroastrian Kusti - the sanctified girdle worn around the waist - represent the seventy-two sections of the Yasna. The compilation includes the seventeen sections of the Gathas, the oldest and most sacred texts of the Zoroastrian tenet.

Some divisions of the Yasna occur more than once. For example, Yasna five is repeated as Yasna thirty-seven, and Yasna sixty-three consists of passages from Yasna 15.2, 66.2 and 38.3. The capacity to recite the Yasna from memory is one of the requirements for Zoroastrian priesthood.

Content and Organisation: Yasna one opens with the extolment of Ahura Mazda, numerating his heavenly titles as the Creator, "radiant, glorious, the greatest, the best, the most beautiful, the most firm, the most wise, of the most perfect form, the highest in morality, possessed of great joy, Maker, fashioner, provider, and the Most Holy Spirit." Yasna one then numerates the divinities, inviting them to the service.

Yasna two, the Barsom Yasht, introduces libation and the barsom (a bundle of twenty-three twigs bound together, symbolizing sanctity) to the invited divinities. Yasna two-four complement Yasna one. Most verses in Yasna two-three begin with the formula ayese yeshti ..., "by means of this sacrifice, I call ...", followed by the name of the divinity being invoked.

Yasna three-8 known conjointly as the Sarosh dron, introduces other oblations (zaothra). Yasna three draws the attention of the divinities invoked in Yasna one, and in Yasna four, the oblations are consecrated to the divinities.

Yasna five is repeated in Yasna thirty-seven. Yasna six is almost identical to the first ten verses of Yasna seventeen.

Yasna nine-eleven is the Hom Yasht, a compilation of eulogies to the Haoma plant and its divinity.

Yasna twelve constitutes the Fravarane, the Zoroastrian religious doctrine and declaration of faith. It is in "Artificial" Gathic Avestan, that is, it is stylistically and linguistically aligned with the language of the Gathas, but imperfectly. The last stanza of verse seven as well as all of verses eight and nine are incorporated into the Kusti rite.

Yasna thirteen-eighteen are comparable to Yasna one-eight in that they too are a compilation of invocations to the divinities.

Sections fourteen-eighteen serve as an introduction to the Staota Yesniia of Yasna nineteen-fifty-nine. The first ten verses of Yasna seventeen, "to the fires, waters, plants", is almost identical to Yasna six.

Yasna nineteen-twenty-one, the Bhagan Yasht, are commentaries on the three 'high prayers' of Yasna twenty-eight-fifty-three.

Yasna twenty-two-twenty-six is another set of invocations to the divinities.

Yasna twenty-seven has the prayers referred to by Yasna nineteen-twenty-one. These are:

The Ahuna Vairya invocation (also known as the Yatha Ahu Vairyo) is the most sacred of all Zoroastrian prayers.

Yasna twenty-eight-fifty-three include the (linguistically) oldest texts of the Zoroastrian canon. seventeen of the twenty-six sections make up the Gathas, the most sacred hymns of Zoroastrianism and thought to have been composed by Zoroaster himself. The Gathas are in verse. These are structurally interrupted by a) the Yasna Haptanghaiti ("seven-section Yasna",thirty-five-forty-one), which is as old as the Gathas but in prose, b) two short sections (forty-two and fifty-two) that are not as old as the Gathas and Yasna Haptanghaiti.

Yasna twenty-eight-thirty-four: Ahunavaiti Gatha

Yasna thirty-five-forty-one: Yasna Haptanghaiti, the "seven-section Yasna", also in Gathic Avestan but in prose.

Yasna forty-two: a four verse section invoking the elements.

Yasna forty-three-forty-six: Ushtavait Gatha

Yasna forty-seven-fifty: Spenta Mainyu Gatha

Yasna fifty-one: Vohu Khshathra Gatha

Yasna fifty-two: an eight verse hymn to Ashi. Verses 52.5 - 52.8, in Younger Avestan, are a duplicate of Yasna 8.5 - 8.8.

Yasna fifty-three: Vahishto Ishti Gatha

Yasna fifty-four has the text of the a airiiema ishiio, a prayer referred to in Yasna 27.

Yasna fifty-five is a praise to the Gathas and the Staota Yesniia.

Yasna fifty-six is again an invocation to the divinities, appealing for their attention.

Yasna fifty-seven is the Sarosh Yasht, the hymn to the divinity of religious self control. It is closely related to, and appears to have sections borrowed from Yasht 10, the hymn to Mithra.

Yasna fifty-eight is again a "hidden" Yasht, here to the genius of prayer.

Yasna fifty-nine is a repetition of the sections from Yasna seventeen and twenty-six.

Yasna sixty is benediction upon the house of the ashavan ('just' or 'true' man). Yasna 60.2-7 constitute the Dahma Afriti invocation, also known as the Afrinagan Dahman.

Yasna sixty-one praises the anti-demonic powers imbued in the Afrinagan Dahman, Yenghe hatam and the three principal prayers of Yasna twenty-seven.

Yasna sixty-two constitutes the Ataksh Nyashes, prayers to fire and its divinity.

Yasna sixty-three-sixty-nine constitute the prayers that accompany the Ab-Zohr, "oblation to water".

Yasna seventy-seventy-two are again a set of invocations to the divinities.

The Visperad

The Visperad (prayer to all patrons) is a assemblingcompilation of supplements to the Yasna. The Visparad is divided into twenty-three or twenty-four kardo (sections) that are interleaved into the Yasna during a Visperad service (which is an extended Yasna service).

The Visperad compilation has no integrity of its own, and is never recited individually from the Yasna. Visperad or Visprad is either a special Zoroastrian religious ritual, or the name given to a passage compilation within the greater Avesta compendium of texts.

The Visperad ceremony "consists of the rites of the Yasna, virtually unchanged, but with a liturgy extended by twenty-three subsidiary sections." These subsidiary sections (kardag) are then – from a philological perspective – the passages that make up the Visperad compilation. The standard abbreviation for Visperad section-verse pointers is Vr., though Vsp. may also appear in older sources.

The name Visperad is a short form of Avestan vispe ratavo, with an equivocal meaning. Subject to how ratu is translated, vispe ratavo may be understood as "(prayer to) all patrons" or "all masters" or the older and today less common "all chiefs." or "all lords."

The Visperad ceremony – in medieval Zoroastrian texts pertained to as the Jesht-i Visperad, that is, "Worship through praise (Yasht) of all the patrons," grew as an "extended service" for observing the gahambars, the high Zoroastrian festivals that observe six seasonal events. As seasonal ("year cycle") festivals, the gahambars are devoted to the Amesha Spentas, the divinites that are in custom identified with specific aspects of creation, and through whom Ahura Mazda realized ("with his thought") creation. These "bounteous immortals" (amesha spentas) are the "all patrons" – the vispe ratavo – who allocate the bounty of creation. However, the Visperad ceremony itself is devoted to Ahura Mazda, the ratûm berezem "high Master."

The Visperad compilationcompilation has no unity of its own, and is never recited individually from the Yasna. During a recital of the Visperad ceremony, the Visperad parts is not recited en masse but are instead interleaved into the Yasna recital. The Visperad itself exalts several texts of the Yasna compilation, including the Ahuna Vairya and the Airyaman ishya, the Gathas, and the Yasna Haptanghaiti (Visperad 13-16, 18-21, 23-24) Unlike in a regular Yasna recital, the Yasna Haptanghaiti is recited a second time between the 4th and 5th Gatha (the first time between the 1st and second as in a standard Yasna). This second recitation is executed by the assistant priest (the raspi), and is often slower and more melodious. In contrast to barsom bundle of a regular Yasna, which has twenty-one rods (tae), the one used in a Visperad service has thirty-five rods.

The Visperad is only performed in the Havan Gah – between dawn and midday – on the six gahambar days. Amongst Iranian Zoroastrians, for whom the seasonal festivals have a greater significance than for their Indian co-religionists, the Visperad ceremony has undergone substantial modifications in the twentieth century. The rite – which is technically an "inner" one demanding rite purity – is instead celebrated as an "outer" rite where rite purity is not a requirement. Often there is only one priest instead of the two that are actually needed, and the priests sit at a table with only a lamp or candle representing the fire, so avoiding accusations of "fire worship."

The Vendidad

The Vendidad (or Videvdat, a corruption of Avestan Vi-Daevo-Data, "Given Against the Demons") is an counting of various manifestations of evils, and ways to confound them. The Vendidad includes all of the 19th nask, which is the only nask that has survived in its entirety. The text consists of twenty-two Fargards, fragments arranged as discussions between Ahura Mazda and Zoroaster. The first fargard is a dualistic conception myth, followed by the account of a devastating winter on the lines of the downpour of mythology. The second fargard recounts the legend of Yima. The remaining fargards deal primarily with hygiene (care of the dead in particular as well as disease and spells to fight it. Fargards four and fifteen discuss the dignity of wealth and charity, of marriage and of corporeal effort, and the insult of unaccepted social behaviour such as assault and breach of contract, and specify the penances required to repent for violations thereof. The Vendidad is an ecclesiastical code, not a religious manual, and there is a degree of moral relativism apparent in the codes of conduct. The Vendidad's different parts vary widely in character and in age. Some parts may be comparatively recent in origin although the greater part is very old.

The Vendidad, unlike the Yasna and the Visparad, is a text of laws rather than the record of a religious ceremony. However, there is a ceremony called the Vendidad, in which the Yasna is recited with all the sections of both the Visparad and the Vendidad inserted at appropriate points. This ceremony is only performed at night. The Vendidad or Videvdat is a compilation of texts within the greater compendium of the Avesta. However, unlike the other texts of the Avesta, the Vendidad is an ecclesiastical code, not a religious manual.

The name of the texts is a contraction of the Avestan language Vi-Daevo-Data, "Given Against the Demons", and as the name suggests, the Vendidad is an enumeration of various manifestations of evils, and ways to confound them. As per the divisions of the Avesta as described in the Denkard, a 9th century text, the Vendidad includes all of the 19th nask, which is then the only nask that has survived in its entirety.

The Vendidad's different parts vary widely in quality and in age. Although some components are comparatively recent in origin, the subject matter of the greater part is very old. In 1877, Karl Friedrich Geldner identified the texts as being linguistically distinct from both the Old Avestan language texts and well as from the Yashts of the younger Avesta. Today, the Vendidad is separated as an "artificial" Younger Avestan text, that is, its language attempts to mime Old Avestan. In its extant form, the Vendidad is regarded to be a Magi (or Magi-influenced) composition. It has also been proposed that the Vendidad belongs to a particular religious school, but "no linguistic or textual argument allows us to attain any degree of certainty in these matters."

The Vendidad consists of twenty-two fargards or sections containing fragments arranged as discourses between Ahura Mazda and Zoroaster. In the past, among Zoroastrians themselves, this literary technique caused the Vendidad to be mistaken for a composition by one of the prophet's contemporaries.

The first section is a dualistic creation myth, followed by the description of a destructive winter comparable with the great floods of various other mythologies. The second section recounts the legend of Yima (Jamshid). Section 19 relates the temptation of Zoroaster, who, when urged by Angra Mainyu to turn from the good religion, turns instead towards Ahura Mazda. The remaining sections cover diverse reigns and regulations, through the adherence of which evils may be confounded. Broken down by subject, these fargards deal with the following topics (sections where a topic covered is in brackets):

Hygiene (in particular care of the dead) (3,5,6,7,8,16,17,19) and cleaning (9,10);

Disease, its origin, and spells against it (7,10,11,13,20,21,22);

Mourning for the dead (12), the Towers of Silence (6), and the remuneration of deeds after demise (19);

The sanctity of, and invocations to, Atar (fire) (8), Zam (earth) (3,6), Apas (water) (6,8,21) and the light of the stars (21);

The dignity of wealth and charity (4), of marriage (4,15) and of corporeal effort (4]

Statutes on unacceptable social behaviour (15) such as breach of contract (4) and assault (4);

On the worthiness of priests (18);

Praise and care of the bull (21), the dog (13,15), the otter (14), the Sraosha bird (18), and the Haoma tree (6.

There is a degree of moral relativism evident in the Vendidad, and the diverse reigns and regulations are not always conveyed as being absolute, universal and mandatory. In some examples, the description of prescribed behaviour is accompanied by a description of the penances that have to be made to repent for violations thereof. Such penances include:

Payment in cash or kind to the aggrieved; corporal punishment such as whipping; repeated recitations of certain parts of the liturgy such as the Ahuna Vairya invocation.

Althouth the Vendidad is not a religious manual, a section of it may be recited as part of a greater Yasna service. Although such extended Yasnas appears to have been frequently performed in the mid-1700s, it is very rarely performed at the present-day. In such an extended service, Visparad twelve and Vendidad one-four are inserted between Yasna twenty-seven and twenty-eight. The Vendidad ceremony is always performed between nightfall and dawn, though a normal Yasna is performed between dawn and noon.

The Vendidad might also be recited on its own, not accompanied by any rite activity: this ceremony is known as the Vendidad Sade.

Because of its length and complexness, the Vendidad is read, rather than recalled from memory as is otherwise requisite for the Yasna texts.

The recitation of the Vendidad calls for a priest of higher rank (one with a moti khub) than is normally essential for the recitation of the Yasna.

The Yashts

The Yashts (Yasts) are a compilation of twenty-one hymns in Younger Avestan. Each of these hymns invokes a specific Zoroastrian divinity or notion. Yasht section and verse pointers are traditionally abbreviated as Yt.

The word yasht is derived from Avestan yesti, "worship by praise," and several hymns of the Yasna liturgy that "worship by praise" are - in custom - also nominally called yashts. These "hidden" Yashts are: the Barsom Yasht (Yasna two), another Hom Yasht in Yasna nine-eleven, the Bhagan Yasht of Yasna nineteen-twenty-one, a hymn to Ashi in Yasna fifty-two, another Sarosh Yasht in Yasna fifty-seven, the praise of the (hypostasis of) "prayer" in Yasna fifty-eight, and a hymn to the Ahurani in Yasna 68. Since these are a part of the main litury, they do not count among the twenty-one hymns of the Yasht compilation.

All the hymns of the Yasht compilation "are written in what appears to be prose, but which, for a large part, may originally have been a (fundamentalally) eight-syllable verse, oscillating between four and thirteen syllables, and most often between seven and nine."

Most of the yazatas that the person Yashts are in praise of also have a dedication in the Zoroastrian calendar. The exceptions are Drvaspa and Vanant.

The twenty-one yashts of the compilation are:

	Yasht title	in praise of	extent
1.	Ohrmazd Yasht	Ahura Mazda	thirty-three verses
2.	Haft Amahraspand Yasht	the seven Amesha Spentas	fifteen verses
3.	Ardawahisht Yasht	Asha Vahishta of "Best Truth"	nineteen verses
4.	Hordad Yasht	Haurvatat of "Wholeness" and "Flawlessness"	eleven verses
5.	Aban Yasht	Aredvi Sura Anahita of the waters	132 verses
6.	Kwarshed Yasht	Hvare-khshaeta of the "Radiant Sun"	seven verses

7.	Mah Yasht	Maonghah of the "Moon"	seven verses
8.	Tishtar Yasht	Tishtrya, the star Sirius	sixty-two verses
9.	Drvasp Yasht	Drvaspa, guardian of horses	thirty-three verses
10.	Mihr Yasht	Mithra of "Covenant"	145 verses
11.	Srosh Yasht	Sraosha of "Obedience"	twenty-three verses
12.	Rashn Yasht	Rashnu of "Justice"	forty-seven verses
13.	Fravardin Yasht	the Fravashis	158 verses
14.	Warharan Yasht	Verethragna, "Smiter of resistance"	sixty-four verses
15.	Ram Yasht	the "good" Vayu	fifty-eight verses
16.	Den Yasht	Chista, "Knowledge"	twenty verses
17.	Ard Yasht	Ashi of "Recompense"	sixty-two verses
18.	Ashtad Yasht	khvarenah, the "(heavenly) glory"	nine verses
19.	Zam Yasht	Knowledge	ninety-seven verses
20.	Hom Yasht	Haoma	three verses
21.	Vanant Yasht	Vanant, the star Vega	two verses

The Siroza

The Siroza ("thirty days") is a numeration and supplication of the thirty divinities presiding over the days of the month. (Zoroastrian calendar). The Siroza exists in two shapes, the shorter (little Siroza) is a brief numeration of the divinities with their names in the genitive. The longer ("great Siroza") has complete sentences and sections, with the yazatas being addressed in the accusative.

The Siroza is by no means recited as a whole, but is a source for individual sentences committed to particular divinities, to be inserted at appropriate points in the liturgy depending on the day and the month.

The Khordeh Avesta

The Khordeh Avesta ("little Avesta") is both a selection of verses from the other compilations, as well as three sub-compilations that do not appear elsewhere. Taken together, the Khordeh Avesta is regarded the prayer text for general lay use. In a broader sense, the term Khordeh Avesta includes all material other than the Yasna, the Visparad and the Vendidad, as it is only the ceremonies contained in these three texts that are reserved for the priests.

The Khordeh Avesta is divided into four sections:

Five introductory sections, accompanied by excerpts from different parts of the Yasna.

Five Niyayishns "praises," addressed to the sun, Mithra, the moon, the waters, and the fire. In the main, the material overlaps with that of the Yashts. The Niyayishn to fire derives from Yasna sixty-two.

Five Gahs "moments of the day," addressed to the five divisions of the day.

Four Afrinagans "benedictions," each recited on a particular occasion: the first in honour of the dead, the second on the five epagomenal days that end the year, the third is recited at the six seasonal fetes, and the fourth at the origin and finish of summer.

Fragments

All matter in the Avesta that is not already present in one of the other categories falls into a "fragments" category, which - as the name suggests - includes incomplete texts. There are altogether more than twenty fragment compilations, many of which have no name (and are then named after their owner/collator) or only a Middle Persian name. The more important of the fragment compilations are the Nirangistan fragments (eighteen of which constitute the Ehrbadistan); the Pursishniha "questions," also known as "Fragments Tahmuras"; the Aogemadaeca "we accept," a treatise on demise; and the Hadokht Nask "volume of the holy scriptures" with two fragments of eschatological significance.

NON-RELIGIOUS SCRIPTURES

Only texts saved in the Avestan language count as holy scripture and are part of the Avesta. Several other secondary works are nevertheless important to Zoroastrian theology and scholarship.

The most noted among the Middle Persian texts are the Denkard ("Acts of Religion"), dating from the ninth century; the Bundahishn ("Primordial Creation"), finished in the eleventh or twelfth century, but containing older material; the Mainog-i-Khirad ("Spirit of Knowledge"), a religious conference on questions of faith; and the Arda Viraf Namak ("Text of Arda Viraf"), which is particularly important for its views on demise, salvation and life in the hereafter. Of the post-14th century works (all in New Persian), only the Sad-dar ("Hundred Doors, or Sections"), and Rivayats (traditional treatises) are of doctrinal significance. Other texts such as Zartushtnamah ("Text of Zoroaster") are only notable for their preservation of legend and folklore.

Arda Viraf

The Text of Arda Viraf is a Zoroastrian sacred text that describes the dream-journey of a adherent Zoroastrian through the next world. Due to the ambiguity inherent to Pahlavi script, Arda Viraf, the name of the supporter of the story may also be transliterated as Arda Wiraf, Arda Wiraz or Arda Viraz. The Arda of the name is an name of Viraf and is more or less translateable as "truthful" or "virtuous."

The date of the text is not known, but is generally assumed to be fairly late in the ancient history of the faith, probably from the period of the Sassanian kingdom, when Zoroastrianism experienced a state-sponsored revival. The fact that the "evil" Alexander of Macedon is referred to as a Roman suggests this period, in which the rivalry between the two kingdoms was intense. The text is frequently compared to Dante's Heavenly Comedy.

In the narration Arda Viraf is chosen for his piousness to undertake a journey to the next world in order to prove the accuracy of Zoroastrian notions, after an era when the land of Iran had been disturbed by the presence of confused and alien religions (probably a reference to Hellenising policies of the Seleucid dynasty). He drinks wine and a hallucinogen, after which his spirit travels to the next world where it is greeted by a good-looking woman named Den who symbolizes his faith and virtue. Crossing the Chinvat bridge, he is then conducted by "Srosh, the devout and Adar, the angel" through the "star track", "moon track" and "sun track" – places outside of heaven reserved for the virtuous who have nevertheless failed to conform to Zoroastrian reigns. In heaven itself he meets Ahura Mazda who shows him the spirits of the blessed (ahlav). Each person is described living an idealised version of the life he or she lived on earth, as a warrior, agriculturalist, shepherd or other profession.

With his guides he then goes down into hell to be shown the agonies of the evil, which are described in graphic detail. As in Dante, each evil person is allotted a form of suffering appropriate to their transgressions. For example, a woman who failed to feed her children decently is forced to consume her own flesh. Stress is placed on respect (Srosh), social authority, and order (Ard).

Having finished his visionary travel Viraf is told by Ahura Mazda that the Zoroastrian faith is the only proper and true way of life and that it should be preserved in both sucess and adversity.

Bundahishn

The Bundahishn, signifying "Primal Creation", is an account of Zoroastrian cosmogeny and cosmology, and reflects ancient Zoroastrian and even pre-Zoroastrian notions. Although the Bundahishn draws on the Avesta and develops ideas alluded to in those texts, it is not itself holy scripture. Unlike the texts of the Avesta, the Bundahishn is in the Middle Persian language.

Most of the sections of the compendium date to the eighth and ninth centuries. These portions of the compilation are roughly contemporary with texts of the Denkard, another substantial text of the Zoroastrian-Pahlavi canon. A final editing was not completed until the twelfth century.

The Bundahishn is the brief view of the world, and the battle of the powers of Ahura Mazda and Angra Mainyu for the control of the world. As per Bundahishn the first 3,000 years of the celestial year, Ahura Mazda produced the Fravashis and conceived the idea of his would-be creation. He used the insensible and motionless Void as a weapon against Angra Mainyu, and at the end of that period, Angra Mainyu was forced to submission and fell into a stupor for the next 3,000 years. Taking advantage of Angra Mainyu's nonappearance, Ahura Mazda produced the Amesha Spentas (Holy Immortals), along with the corporeal world, consisting of the sky, waters, earth, plants, the sacred white bull called Parvin, and Kayomars, the celestial man. What's more, he penetrated his kingdom with truth in order to prevent Angra Mainyu from achieving and ruining it.

Chidag Andarz i Poryotkeshan

The Chidag Andarz i Poryotkeshan, a Zoroastrian Pahlavi text, comprising the select advises of ancient sages, sums up the whole of Zoroastrian philosophy, what the followers should believe, practice and follow without doubt in order to benefit from the good that arises out of it. The holy scripture is also known as The Text of Counsel of Zartosht. The text in its totality is reproduced below.

1. Now it is faith that explores out causes, tangible and as they are, and then, acting as intermediary by means of reason (passes them on). So this must one know without venturing to doubt: "I have come from the unseen world, nor was I (always) of this world. I was produced and have not (always) been. I belong to Ohrmazd, not to Ahriman. I belong to the Gods, not to the demons, to the good, not to the evil.
2. I am a man, not a devil, a creature of Ohrmazd, not of Ahriman. My stock and lineage is from Gayomard. My mother is Spandarmad, (the Earth), and my father is Ohrmazd. My humanity is from Mashye and Mashyane who were the first seed and offspring of Gayomard.
3. To perform my function and to do my obligation means that I should believe that Ohrmazd is, was, and evermore shall be, that his Kingdom is undying, and that he is infinite and pure; and that Ahriman is not, and is destructible; that I myself belong to Ohrmazd and his Bounteous Immortals, and that I have no connection with Ahriman, the demons, and their associates.
4. My first (obligation) on earth is to confess the Religion, to practice it, and to take part in its worship and to be steadfast in it, to keep the Faith in the Good Religion of the worshippers of Ohrmazd ever in my mind, and to distinguish profit from loss, sin from good works, goodness from evil, light from darkness, and the worship of Ohrmazd from the worship of the demons.
5. My second (obligation) is to take a wife and to procreate earthly offspring, and to be strenuous and steadfast in this.
6. My third (obligation) is to cultivate and till the soil;
7. My fourth to treat all livestock justly;
8. My fifth to spend a third of my days and nights in attending the seminary and consulting the knowledge of holy men, to spend a third of my days and nights in tilling the soil and in making it fruitful, and to spend (the remaining) third of my days and nights in eating, rest, and enjoyment.
9. I must have no doubt but that profit arises from good works, and loss from sin, that my friend is Ohrmazd and my enemy Ahriman, and that there is only one religious way.

10. (This) one way (is that) of good thoughts, good words, and good deeds, (the way of) Heaven, of light and of purity, of the Infinite Creator, Ohrmazd, who was always and will ever be.
11. (There is also) the other way of evil thoughts, evil words, and evil deeds, (the way of) darkness, and of the finiteness, utter misery, demise, and evil which belong to the accursed Destructive Spirit (Ahriman) who once was not in this creation, and again will not be in the creation of Ohrmazd, and who in the end will be destroyed.
12. I must have no doubt but that there are two first principles, one the Creator and the other the Destroyer.
13. The Creator is Ohrmazd who is all goodness and all light:
14. And the Destroyer is the accursed Destructive Spirit who is all evil and full of demise, a liar and a deceiver.
15. Equally I must have no doubt that all men are mortal except only Soshyans and the seven kings (who help him).
16. I must have no doubt but that the spirit (jan) will be severed (from the body) and that the body (itself) will be dissolved. (Nor may I doubt) the three nights judgment (of the spirit at demise), [the raising of the dead and the Final Body] the crossing of the Bridge of the Requiter, the coming of the Soshyans, the raising of the dead and the Final Body.
17. I must (further) observe the law of chivalry (erih) and the Religion of the Ancients, and (I must) preserve my thoughts in morality, my tongue in truth, and my hands in doing what is good.
18. With all good men I must observe the law of chivalry,
19. Peace and concord in all good deeds I do.
20. In my dealing with the good (I must) always behave as per justice and the dictates of the Good Religion.
21. With whomsoever it may be, in past, present. and future time, I must act in a common virtue and in a common morality (ham-datastan).
22. Good deeds performed for the sake of the Law are of a higher value than those performed for one's own sake, and by them is salvation most assured.
23. I declare that I have received the Good Religion of the worshippers of Ohrmazd and have no doubts concerning it

not for any bodily or spritual comfort (that it may bring), not for a pleasant life or for a long life, nor yet because (I know that) my consciousness must needs part company with my body. I shall never apostatize from the Good Religion of the worshippers of Ohrmazd, and I have no doubts concerning it. I neither approve of nor respect other religions, nor do I lend them credence.

24. For it is plain that of thoughts, words, and deeds it is deeds (only) that are the criterion:

25. For the will is unstable, thought is impalpable, but deeds are palpable indeed,

26. And by the deeds that men do.

    In Man's body three roads have been laid out.

27. On these three roads three Gods (menok) have their dwelling, and three demons (Druj) seek to waylay. In thought Vohuman, (the Good Mind), has his dwelling, and Wrath seeks to waylay; in words Knowledge has its dwelling, and Heresy (varan) seeks to waylay; but in deeds the Bounteous Spirit (Ohrmazd) has his dwelling, and the Destructive Spirit (Ahriman) seeks to waylay.

28. On these three roads Man must stand firm, nor may he give up his heavenly (menok) prize for the sake of worldly goods, wealth, or earthly desire.

29. For the man who does not guard these three bastions within his body which I have mentioned, — his thoughts proceed from evil thought his words from evil speech, and his deeds from evil deeds.

30. Next must I be thankful; and by thankfulness (I mean gratitude) for that it is within my power that my spirit (ruvan) may not go to Hell.

31. For when a man passes from the loins of his father into the womb of his mother, then does Astwihad, ('the Dissolver of Bones' and demon of demise), secretly (menokiha) cast a halter round his neck which for his whole life's span cannot be shaken off, not through the power of a good spirit and not through the power of an evil;

32. But after he has passed away, that halter falls from off the neck of the man who is saved through the good deeds that he

has done, but the man who is damned is dragged to Hell by that very halter."

33. Whosoever is in the world must perform the office a certain number of times and must know what sins (he is liable to commit) with hand or foot, — unless he be deaf or dumb: in that case he cannot be accounted guilty. Should (a deaf or dumb man) perform (a religious office), then it should be the erpatastan, and he should know the commentary on it.

34. Fathers and mothers must teach their children this much concerning good works before they reach their fifteenth year. If they have taught them this much concerning good works, the parents may claim credit (?) for any good deed the child does; but if the child has not been (properly) instructed, then the parents are accountable for any sin it may commit on attaining majority.

35. Be agreeable to good works and do not have any part in sin. Be grateful for good things, contented in adversity, long-suffering in affliction (astanak), zealous in the performance of your obligation.

36. Repent of all your sins, and do not allow any sin that brings punishment with it to remain (unconfessed) for even a moment.

37. Overcome doubts (varan) and unvirtuous desires with reason (khrat).

38. Overcome concupiscence (Az) with contentment, anger with serenity (Srosh), envy with benevolence (huchashmih), want with vigilance, strife (anashtih) with peace, falsehood with truth.

39. Know that Heaven is the best place, that the kingdom of the spirit (menok) is the most pleasurable, that the mansions (deh) of the sky are the most luminous, that Heaven (Garothman) is a shining house, and the doing of good works brings great hope of the Final Body which passes not away.

40. So far as lies within your power, do not pay respect to evil men, for by commending what is wrong evil enters into your body and good is driven out.

41. Be diligent in the acquisition of learning (frahang), for learning is the seed of knowledge, and its fruit is knowledge, and knowledge reigns both worlds.

42. Concerning this it has been said that learning is an adornment in sucess, a safety in hard times, a ready helper in affliction (astanak), a guide in distress.

43. Do not make mock of anyone at all; for the man who mocks will himself be mocked, will lose his dignity (khwarrah) and be execrated; and rarely indeed will he have a decent or warlike son.

44. Seek every day the company of good men to ask their advice, for he who makes a habit of seeking the company of good men, will be blessed with a greater share of virtue and holiness.

45. Go three times a day to the Fire Temple and do homage to the Fire; for he who makes a habit of going to the Fire Temple and of doing homage to the Fire, will be blessed with a greater share of both worldly wealth and of holiness.

46. Take great care never to vex your father and mother or your superior lest your body become ill-famed (thereby) and your spirit see damnation.

47. Know that of all the countless adversities that the accursed Destructive Spirit devised these three are the most grievous, — the obstruction of the sight of the eye, deafness of the ear, and thirdly the Lie of discord (anashtih).

48. For it is revealed that for this reason does the Sun issue his command to men on earth three times a day.

49. At dawn he says, "Ohrmazd ever bids you who are men to be diligent in the doing of good works so that I may bestow earthly life upon you." (so) At midday he says, "Be diligent in seeking out a wife, in the procreation of children, and in your other duties, for until the Final Body (comes to pass) the Destructive Spirit and his abortions will not be separated from this world."

51. At eventide he says, "Repent of the sins you have committed that I may have compassion on you." For it is revealed that just as the light of the Sun comes down to earth, so do his words come to earth.

52. In this material world do not think, say, or do what is wrong (false) in thought, word, or deed.

53. Through the power of the Gods, and by way of knowledge and by consultation with the Religion be vigilant and zealous

(for good works), and consider that since the value of good works is so great and limitless, the Destructive Spirit strives his utmost to conceal (this truth) and to cause you misery, and Ohrmazd strives his utmost to reveal (the truth). Whosoever has knowledge of the Religion, let him be diligent in the doing of good works and be forever steadfast therein.

54. At the end of this millennium when the evil of the demons knows no limit and the Religion of Ohrmazd is much reduced and that of the unvirtuous is predominant, when discussions concerning the Law and Religion between good and virtuous men who know their obligation have ceased, when the deeds of Ahriman and the demons are done openly, — and the sign of this will be that there will be a (general) retrogression when creatures will be destroyed, those who break contracts and who have taken the part of the demons and opposed the religion will go free, and when throughout the length and breadth of the lands which acknowledge the Law of Ohrmazd (all) good creatures will despair on account of evil tyrants (azhidahakan), — then every man must add to his (inner) peace through (the power of) Vohuman, (the Good Mind), consult with Knowledge through the Religion, search out the way of holiness by knowledge, rejoice his spirit by means of generosity, show honour to rank by benevolence, seek a good name by manliness, collect friends by humility, make hope acceptable by long-suffering, store up (for himself) goodness by temperance (khem), and prepare the way to bright heaven by morality; for there shall he enjoy the fruits of his good works.

55. The body is mortal but the spirit is immortal. Do good works, for the spirit is (real), not the body, the next world is (real), not this world.

56. Do not abandon the care of the spirit and forget it for the body's sake.

57. Out of respect for persons (and out of forgetfulness) that all the goods of this world must perish, do not lust after anything that will bring punishment on your body and retribution on your spirit. Desire rather those things whose fruit is an everlasting joy.

58. Doing good is born of zeal, zeal of prayer, prayer of desire, desire of intellect, intellect of knowledge of the other world;

and knowledge (of the other world) is a weapon that was and is and (evermore) shall be. By it He is known Who creates all things anew, Who teaches (all) things, Who ordains all that should be done Who wills the good (sut) of all in this world and the next.'

REFERENCES

Avesta: Pahlavi, and Ancient Persian Studies in Honour of the late Shams-ul Ulama Dastur Peshotanji Behramji Sanjana. Strassburg, 1904.

Buch, M. A.: Zoroastrian Ethics. Baroda, 1919.

Chatterjee, J. M.: the Ethical Conceptions of the Gatha. Navsari, 1932.

Fluegel, M: The Zend-Avesta and Eastern Religions. Baltimore, 1898.

Madan, D. M.: Discourses on Iranian Literature. Bombay. 1909.

McNeile, H.: The Avesta and the Bible. Bombay, 1905. Moulton, James H.: The Treasure of the Magi. Oxford, 1917.

Namakiha-i Manushchihar: The Epistles of Manushchihar. Edited by B. N. Dhabhar. Bombay, 1912.Rawlinson, George: The Seventh Great Oriental Monarchy. London, 1816.

Rivayat, Pahlavi, accompanying the Dadistan-i Dinik: Edited by B. N; Dhabhar. Bombay, 1913.

Rivayat, Persian of Darab Hormazyar: Edited by M. R. Unvala with an Introduction by J. J. Modi. 2 vols. Bombay, 1922.

Shikand Gumanik Vijar: Translated from the Pahlavi-Pazand text by E. W. West. In *Sacred Books of the East*, vol. 24.

Vendidad: Pahlavi Text. Edited by Hoshang Jamasp. Bombay, 1907.

7

Teachings

Zoroastrianism is one of the most ancient religions of the world. It is almost an extinct religion, with a total number of followers hardly exceeding a few hundred thousand in the world. But the religion lives through other major religions of the world today such as Hinduism, Buddhism, Judaism, Christianity and Islam in such concepts as sacrificial rituals, conflict between good and evil, creator God, judgment day, resurrection of the dead, arch angels, heaven and hell, five daily prayers etc. In many ways Zoroastrianism is a bridge between the religions of the east and of the west.

Just as the Jews place their hope in Messiah, the Hindus on the coming Kalki Avatara, so also the Parsis have been looking forward to the birth of Saoshyant who will establish on earth righteousness and happiness.

There is no Tapas or austerity in Zoroastrianism in order that the body may not be weakened and rendered unfit for work. Rebirth is not found in the scriptures as accepted by orthodox Parsis, but it is taught in the fragments preserved by the Greeks and in the Desatir. Parsis perform prayers for the dead at stated fixed periods. They perform ancestor-worship and do anniversaries for the dead in an elaborate manner.

SPIRITUAL TEACHINGS

Zoroastrianism teaches that Ahura Mazda created man and gave him his body and mind. Ahura Mazda is the protector and nourisher of all. Man is responsible for his thoughts, speeches, and actions. Individual will and individual intellect are connected with the cosmic will and cosmic-intellect.

Ahura Mazda created this world in six periods. Mashya and Mashyana are the first man and woman created by God. During the deluge an underground palace 'Vara of Yima' was built for the protection of all creatures.

Zoroastrianism is a religion of absolute faith and unswerving devotion to Ahura Mazda. A devotee bows, prays, and sacrifices. He makes offerings unto the Lord. He prays and Ahura Mazda grants all his wishes. He prays to remove his sins by repentance.

Zoroastrianism teaches that the goal of life is to attain perfect eternal happiness through companionship with Ahura Mazda. The means for attaining the everlasting bliss is Asha or holiness. Holiness or purity is the soul of Zoroastrianism.

Pure thoughts, pure words, pure deeds—this is the famous axiom of Zoroastrian religion. This is the constantly reiterated rule of the Zoroastrian life. Pure thoughts, pure words, pure actions can be practised only through faith in the Ahura Mazda, the Lord of righteousness. The word Asha includes all the principles of morality. The word Asha comes in almost every chapter of the Zend Avesta. Zoroastrianism teaches that holiness is happiness, and that is the most precious gift of Ahura Mazda and that is the best offering to be presented to the Lord by the virtuous.

A Zoroastrian must act in harmony with the will of God. He should study the scriptures and perform his duty to God and his fellowmen. He should strictly observe the divine laws. Then only he will attain holiness and happiness.

REDEMPTION

The work of regenerating the world, which was commenced by Gayomard, the first man, and was looked forward to from the time of the Gathas, will be brought to completion and perfection by Soshyos, the last saviour. With Gayomard the curtain rose on the human drama. It will fall with the advent of Soshyos. Gayomard, Jamshid, Zaratusht, and all pious men who have worked for the betterment of the universe are among those that help in bringing about the final renovation. The great work proceeds with greater or lesser success according as mankind are stronger or weaker in the practice of righteousness at various periods. In two of his visions the prophet sees a tree with four and seven branches respectively. The branches are made of different metals and represent the various periods of the religious history of Zoroastrianism. The first and the golden branch represents the golden age of the faith under King Gushtasp, the silver and steel boughs symbolize a decadence, while the last, depicted by the iron branch, or age of the great catastrophe, is the period of the final overthrow of the kingdom, the overwhelming cataclysm that threatened to submerge the world except for the triumph of virtue and right. When the mighty work of reclaiming mankind from evil is accomplished, there will follow the Renovation of the universe. Those who work to bring this period nearer are said to be holding communion with Ohrmazd.

Ohrmazd sends his special messengers at various periods of chaos and confusion to save humanity from the clutches of Ahriman. This is clear in the Gathas as in the Younger Avesta. These Messianic heralds of the real truth to be embodied in the final Soshyos exemplify righteousness complete and translate the abstract teachings of religion into concrete actions that thus make the seemingly incomprehensible intelligible and tangible to the masses. The most prominent among these leaders in the last three millenniums, as noted before, are the three sons that are to be born miraculously to Zaratusht, from his seed through a supernatural conception by a maid, bathing in the waters of Lake Kans (an idea as old as Yt. 19), and the names of these three ideal promoters of mankind, as perpetuated in the forms current during the Pahlavi period, are Hoshedar, Hoshedar-mah, and Soshyos, who will appear at an interval of a millennium each. It is said that Zaratusht went three times near unto his wife Hvov, and that each time the seed went to the ground. On each of these three occasions, important for mankind, the spiritual seeds were caught up by the angel Neryosangh and intrusted to the keeping of Ardvisur, the divinity of waters, and from these sanctified waters they will be born in time to come, as miraculously conceived at different periods by three virgins. The advent of the all-beneficent renovators of the faith for the regeneration of the world will, be attended with portents and miraculous signs.

The Millennium of Hoshedar

A child is born to a virgin named Shemik-abu of the age of fifteen, who miraculously conceives Zaratusht's seed when she drinks the waters from a pool. The seed was emitted during the lifetime of Zaratusht and lay concealed in the waters until the maiden kindled the germs and became pregnant. The child thus immaculately born in the first of the three final millenniums of the world is named Hoshedar, a later modified corrupt transcript of the Avestan Ukhshyat-ereta. In the first of the last three thousand years of the world, before the final renovation and the resurrection, he holds, at the age of thirty, a conference with Ohrmazd and receives a revelation. When he returns from this divine conference, Hoshedar makes the sun stand still for ten days and nights to convince the people, of the world about the authenticity of his mission. During his millennium, righteousness, liberality, and all the virtues supreme will be practised by mankind more and more as the world slowly moves towards perfection during this aeon. Two-thirds of the people of Iran, according to the Pahlavi texts, will turn out righteous. The wisdom of the religion will constantly increase, the poverty of the people and the slaughter of cattle will decrease, as he is the benefactor that will help to remove the wickedness of the wolfish nature in mankind.

The Millennium of Soshyos

The world, according to the Pahlavi texts, which carry onward the ideal teachings of Zaratusht in the Gathas as developed further in the Younger Avesta, is ever striving and tending toward final betterment, and will reach perfection in the millennium of Soshyos. It needs only the final touch of this greatest of the renovators to bring about this result for the eternal welfare of the universe. Men by this time, when these millennial conditions have been reached, have ceased eating meat, and subsist on milk and vegetables. Even milk, according to the Pahlavi works, is gradually given up, and water and vegetables form the only food of mankind. The Bundahishn, moreover, adds that, before the Resurrection and the Renovation of the universe occur, men will give up milk, vegetables, and even water, and they will ultimately subsist without food of any kind, and yet not die. Still another Pahlavi text states that during the period of the fifty-seven years of the activity of this last apostle mankind will be able to subsist for seventeen years simply on vegetables, then thirty on water alone, and for the last ten years on spiritual food.

At this time, according to the texts, when the world is ripe to welcome the last of the prophets, a virgin named Gobak-abu conceives immaculately the third seed of Zaratusht in the same manner as her two forerunners had done. At the age of fifteen she becomes pregnant and gives birth to the most illustrious Soshyos in the realm of Khvaniras. When the final saviour is thirty years of age, the sun stands still in the zenith of the sky for thirty days and nights; through his supernal power the demoniac nature among men will be broken. He will then cause the Resurrection and the future existence. His body, which is as radiant as the sun, partakes only of spiritual food and he is clad with Kingly glory. Around him he looks with the power of six eyes and he it is that foresees the end of the Evil Spirit. He is the greatest renovator of the world. He comes to restore the dead to life, and to bring final perfection to the world.

Any kind of wickedness that may still be lingering, in spite of his supreme beneficence, will perish through his presence. The angels will enable mankind to co-operate with the great apostle Soshyos to rout Druj. In advance of his divine mission to the world he has met Ohrmazd in conference and has received the supreme sanction for his task. During the fifty-seven years of his work, he will drive out the drujes from the world, and will make the world eternally happy.

The Collaborators of Soshyos

Ohrmazd has ordained that Soshyos will be helped by certain great persons who have departed from the world, but who remain immortal and are still living in the body, and are yet to exert sway. The chief among these personages, potent for the eternal welfare of mankind, are, Peshyotan, Aghrerat, Parsadga, Urvatadnar, Narsih, Tus, Giv, Ibairaz, Ashavazd, with a thousand others. Kaikhusru will arise to help Soshyos in the raising of the dead; Peshyotan, or Chitra-mahan, will lend help with his hundred and fifty disciples. Still another Pahlavi passage speaks of fifteen men and fifteen women among the living that are to come to the help of Soshyos. They will all leaven the rest of mankind. Zohak, who is put in chains on Mount Demavand, shall even at the last, break loose from the bonds in which he has been confined, and as a monster-man will return to the world and disturb the righteous creation. At the command of Ohrmazd, his ministers Srosh and Neryosangh approach the body of Kersasp and raise it from the dead. The hero then rises up and slays Zohak. Soshyos and six of his companions, Roshn-chashm, Khur-chashm, Fradat-gadman, Varedat-gadman, Kamak-Vakhshishn, and Kamak-sud, all of which names have a spiritual significance, will divide the work between them, and each of them will act in one of the seven zones. Every one will miraculously communicate with the other of his six colleagues in the other zones. They will read each other's thoughts from a distance and will thus converse just as two men sitting close together would do. The work of the renovation of the world will last for fifty-seven years, the number already referred to. Full fifty years of this beneficent activity will be devoted to the seventh zone Khvaniras, where Zaratusht himself was the spiritual chief, and where Soshyos himself is working. All evil will perish during these fifty-seven years, and goodness prevail among mankind, and men will embrace righteousness and zealously practise religion before the final raising of the dead. Disease and demise, apostasy and vice, depravity and every fiendish influence, will perish during this period. The world will be restored to its primal state.

Resurrection of the Dead

The preliminary work of the renovators is to raise again to life all those who have died from the time of Gayomard, the primeval man, down to the last man Soshyos, and then give them their respective bodies. It is natural that the world could not at this period be quite empty of men. Those who happen to be living at the time when the period of renovation approaches near shall abstain from eating, live without food, and live so virtuously that even the offspring that are born unto them at this period will be of spiritual nature. All these, therefore, will be ready to enter the ranks of the dead who will now receive new bodies.

The dead will be made to rise from the place where they had yielded up their lives in the world. Zaratusht questions Ohrmazd in this connection, according to the Pahlavi texts, regarding the questions of forming again the bodies of the dead, inasmuch as the material frames of the dead have perished and been reduced to dust. Ohrmazd, thereupon, tells the prophet that even as it was possible for him to have created something from nothing, when nothing at all existed, and as he was able to create the sky and the earth, the sun and the moon, and the stars, fire and water, clouds and wind, grain and mankind, in fact everything that formerly had no existence, it would not be difficult for him at the Resurrection to form anew something that had already existed. Mohammed likewise tells those that doubt, that if God could create them out of nothing, it was certainly possible for him to bring them back to life after demise.

The spirit of the earth, the water, the plants, and the fire will at that time restore the bones, blood, hair, life, and other materials which had been committed to them by God in the beginning, and in this manner the bodies will be formed anew. And in another Pahlavi work it is said that just as it is easier to teach what once was learnt but was forgotten than it is to teach that which had never been learnt, and as it is easier to repair a house than to build a new one, even so is it easier to bring to pass the restoration of the creation than in the beginning the original creation out of nothing.

All those resurrected will be furnished with their bodily frames by the command of Ohrmazd. The first body thus raised up will be that of Gayomard, the father of mankind. Then will follow the first couple, Mashya and Mashyoi, and then the rest of mankind, whether righteous or wicked. Exceptions to this general statement are found in other Pahlavi texts, but the tone is in general the same. Men of demoniac nature, sodomites, apostates, and the hateful Afrasiab will not be given their bodies, for these arch-enemies of religion are no longer men, but have converted themselves into fiends and must consequently share the fate of their class.

Universal Judgment

A further arraignment at the judgment seat now takes place. The righteous and the wicked souls are now gathered together in one place and are subjected to the collective, or universal judgment. Every soul at this judicial session sees its good and its evil deeds, and the wicked man becomes as conspicuous as a white sheep among the black. Ohrmazd himself takes a final and decisive account of the souls, and pronounces definitely upon them, for he remembers in each detail the several individual judgments passed in connection with every one of the myriads of the wicked souls after their demise, as well as the just. From his judgment there is no appeal. The souls called together in this great and last judicial assembly recognize each other after the long separation. The father sees his son, and the brother meets his sister, the husband greets his wife, the relative welcomes his kinsman, and the friend inquires after the experience of his friend. Everyone eagerly narrates his or her account of the joys or sorrows during the long period of separation from their comrades of the material world. The wicked ones taunt their righteous friends or relatives with the bitter reproach that it had not been good on their part to have practised righteousness themselves, and yet to have left them unwarned in the indulgence of vice. The righteous weep for the wicked, and the wicked weep for themselves in the midst of this universal mourning while the righteous are being separated from the wicked and sent back to heaven. So far they had enjoyed bliss and felicity in their spiritual condition, they now enter heaven in body, and have the satisfaction of seeing even the bodily grievances of their earthly life adjusted.

Bodily Punishment

The wicked are now cast back to hell, where they suffer bodily punishment for three days. Hitherto their life in hell was torment of the spirit, now in the very body that on earth was instrumental in bringing the spiritual fall of the soul suffers materially. It is said that the wicked soul suffers three kinds of punishment at three different periods. Firstly, in this world during the earthly life; secondly, in hell from the night after the individual's demise up to the period of the Renovation in spiritual form; and thirdly, now for three days in hell in the bodily form.

Ordeal of Molten Metal

The final punishment of being tortured in hell and burnt in a river of molten metal for three nights, after Ohrmazd's judgment is given, is in store for the wicked souls. A comet, named Gochihar will fall from heaven and melt all metals and minerals in the earth, and will burn up the world in a general conflagration. A boiling flood of the metals of Shatravar will then flow over the earth, and the righteous as well as the wicked souls will be made to pass into it. In this glowing flood the wicked souls will be purged of their sins, so that they become wholly purified, while the righteous will feel as if they were walking in warm milk. The torture of the worst' sinners, such as Zohak, Afrasiab, and the rest, during these three nights is more intense than that of all others. This final conflagration brings freedom of the sinners from the prison of hell.

The righteous and the wicked shall no longer remain as divided, but unite into one. Then, following the great conflagration, there will be the final renovation of the world. The sinners who have been thus purified and purged of their sins by the fiery metal become worthy of eternal bliss; and that final punishment will absolve them of their sins. The entire creation of Ohrmazd now becomes virtuous. The wicked no longer remain wicked, but become righteous. The angels under whose influence they had done good deeds in the world approach them and give joy to them in the proportion of these good deeds. The happiness of the souls that were already righteous is far greater than that of the wicked who had been cleansed through torture and punishment. The erring children are now restored to the bosom of the Heavenly Father, and Ohrmazd now takes back the entire creation to himself.

Removing Imperfection from Material Bodies

The completion of heavenly bliss requires that it be everlasting. The human soul is immortal, but the body is not so. Therefore Soshyos and his companions prepare through an Izishna ceremony a nectar from the fat of the ox Hadhayosh and the white Hom juice, through a draught of which all beings become immortal forever and everlasting. Every one is given an immortal body and becomes as innocent in nature as cattle. The entire good creation is henceforth immortal. Any one who was a full grown man when he had died is given the appearance of a man of forty years of age; and those who died at an early age are given the stature of a youth of fifteen years. Husbands and wives united with their children live together, even as they lived and acted in this world, but there is no begetting of children. Their existence in paradise is accompanied by the full enjoyment of their reward for ever and ever. Those that had not given clothes as a righteous gift in the world and were now consequently without clothes themselves are provided with garments by the angels. They are hungerless and thirstless, undecaying and undying, undistressed and ever-beneficial. Neither a blow, nor a knife, nor a sword, nor a club, nor a stone, nor an arrow hurts the body, for it is now perfected and is immune from pain of any sort. Bodily ailments have vanished. The portals of eternal bliss are now flung open to the whole humanity.

Decisive Battle between the Good and Evil

Then will follow the last and decisive battle of the eternal war between the rival armies of Ohrmazd and Ahriman. Every one of the good spirits will combat with his adversary, and in every case the success will be on the side of the good. Ohrmazd assails Ahriman, Vohuman seizes on Akoman, Artavahisht on Indar, Shatravar on Sovar, Spandarmad on Taromat or Naonghas. Khurdad and Amardad on Tairev and Zairich, Truth on Falsehood and Srosh on Eshm. Druj will perish. Hell itself is burnt out. Ohrmazd comes down to the world and acts as the Zota, sacrificial priest, together with Srosh as his Raspi, and holds the sacred thread-girdle in his hands. The holy formulas confound the Evil Spirit, who, now impotent, rushes back to darkness by the same passage through which he had come out at the beginning of creation.

Demon and fiend, deceit and falsehood, strife and anger, hatred and ill-temper, pain and disease, want and greediness, shame and fear, all perish.- Evil of every kind disappears, and good of every kind is perfected. Ohrmazd at last becomes completely predominant, and his Kingdom of Righteousness is built upon the earth.

Humanity attunes its will to the will of Ohrmazd. All men now become of one will and remain of one accord in the faith of Ohrmazd, giving voice in song to the Glory of their Lord. On no account will their will be in conflict with the divine will, but will ever coincide with it. They now live in the blessed company of Ohrmazd, and work to exalt his glory.

DEVOTION TO GOD

Religion has formed a deeply integral part of mankind at all times. We glean from the records of early peoples the earliest gropings of the human mind in its endeavour to understand and interpret natural phenomena. At various stages of its evolution, religion rises from animism to a belief in cosmic and abstract gods. Each tribe had its local god or gods who gained or lost in power as the seats of their location rose or fell in political power. The fate of the gods fluctuated with the vicissitudes of their followers. The god who rose to power either absorbed other gods in his person or subordinated them as lesser gods or ministering angels in his own service. Some of these gods were embraced in the family of the great god as his son or consort, in case of a goddess, and formed a divine triad of father, mother, and son. When religious ideas approached abstract thinking, they were represented as the manifestations of the newly enthroned god or they were reduced to abstractions as the great god's attributes. When Babylon rose to power, its god Marduk absorbed all other gods, both of the north and the south, even his father Ea, and became the chief god of the whole of Babylonia. The legends of the earlier gods clung to his name and hymns formerly composed in their honour were now dedicated to him. Ashur, the local god of Assyria, eclipsed gods of other localities and rose to preeminence as his native city came to parmnount power. When Shamash outshone his many confederate solar gods, he became the supreme god, and the other gods who were formerly on a footing of equality with him were accommodated as his satellites. Sometimes when the fighting tribes were united by peace the rival gods of each tribe formed their divine union. For example, the sun god Ra who came to Egypt from Asia formed an alliance with the popular god Amen and the dual divinities, thereafter, came to be known as Amen Ra.

Ahura, Mazda, and Ahura Mazda

The name of God still retains its two elements separate. These have not yet coalesced into one word. In the metrical sections of the Younger Avesta the two elements are sometimes used apart from each other, or either one of the terms may be used to designate the Supreme Being, but in the prose compositions the collocation Ahura Mazda generally occurs as a compound phrase. In the formation of compounds, however, either Ahura or Mazda alone is used for the sake of convenience. The Ahura compounds such as Ahura-dhâta, 'created by Ahura,' Ahura-tkaesha, 'of the faith of Ahura,' or the adjectival form âhuiri, 'of Ahura,' invariably represent the divine lord Ahura Mazda. Similarly, the Mazda element in the compounds Mazda-dhâta, 'created by Mazda,' Mazda-yasna, 'worshipper of Mazda,' Mazdo-frasasta, 'taught by Mazda,' Mazdo-fraokhta, or Mazdaokhta, 'spoken by Mazda,' invariably stands for Ahura Mazda himself.

Ahura Mazda still holds sovereignty sway over both the worlds; his authority in the world of righteousness is undisputed, and his imperial right is unchallenged. He is the greatest and the very best of the angels. The Old Persian Inscriptions speak of him as the greatest of the divinities. The archangels and angels dutifully carry out Mazda's orders. Reverence for him has never abated, and adoration of him does not languish with the advent again of the old Indo-Iranian divinities. Like the dual divinities

Varuna-Mitra who received joint invocation during the Indo-Iranian period, Ahura-Mithra or Mithra-Ahura are invoked together. Ahura generally takes precedence and Mithra stands second in the compound, but in the Nyaishes composed in honour of Hvare Khshaeta or the sun and Mithra, as also in the Yasht dedicated to Mithra, the order is reversed and we have then Mithra-Ahura. He is yet the sublimest goal of human aspiration. The best of all sacrifices and invocations are those of Mazda.

The faithful acknowledge their indebtedness to Ahura Mazda and devoutly offer to him their homage and sacrifice. They worship him with the very life of the body, and they long to reach him through the medium of fire, through the Good Mind, through Righteousness, and through the deeds and words of wisdom, as well as through good thoughts, good words, and good deeds. Ahura Mazda, in fact, is implored to be their very life and limb in both the worlds. It is through the Best Righteousness that the true in heart aspire to behold the Lord to approach him, and to associate with him, The attainment of the companionship and the Kingdom of Ahura Mazda is the pious wish of the supplicant.

ETHICAL ACTIONS

Zoroastrian have a strong tradition of ethical action. Ethical action refers to initiatives that express our commitment to working for a better world for ourselves and our children and proclaim our belief in the worth and potential of all human beings. There are so many human needs and problems which call for a hands-on response. We're also aware of the importance of modeling an ethical approach to life, and we know that nothing contributes more to our own development as ethical human beings and to the vitality of our fellowship than an active involvement in confronting the ethical and social challenges that surround us.

Ethical action has two basic dimensions: community service and social issues advocacy. Community service is directed at helping organizations and individuals in the community. Every morally good action we do advances God's work on earth and brings us closer to the Wise Lord, but every evil action we do, no matter how small, retards that work and distances us from God. This is a sober and even stark way: everything is up to us. We cannot blame our bad actions on an independent Devil who made us do it, or on the inscrutable plan of an incomprehensible God. If we do wrong, it is our fault alone, having given in to our own hostile mentality.

The following are the ethical teachings of Zoroaster: To do good actions; to be pure in thought, word, and deed; to have a clean heart; to wish others' good; to speak the truth; to do charity; to be kind; to be humble; to attain knowledge; to control anger; to be pious; to respect parents, the teachers, and the old and the young; to utter sweet and pleasant words; to be patient; to be friendly towards all; to be contented; to feel shame for doing forbidden actions.

MESSAGE OF HARMONY AND LOVE

3,738 years later the message is still relevant. Still vital to our success in this life. Still vital to our success in delivering the ultimate goal of Zoroastrianism, Freshokereti - the renewal of the Earth. It empowers those who choose to accept it and live by it. We are not victims of a wrathful illogical God; we are not sinners; we do not have to submit to a powerful God (and his supposed representatives on Earth) to be saved; and we don't have to take on faith irrational concepts and beliefs.

Rather Zarathushtra empowered humans, perhaps for the first time, to understand how the world could be and how to work to perfect it. Basically, we become co-creative with Ahura Mazda.

Zarathushtra was the first prophet and philosopher to proclaim that there is one wise creator; that the world evolves according to some basic laws of goodness; that humans have an element of godliness in them that gives them the power to think and choose righteousness or goodness in everything we do; and finally, that humans can and should co-create and perfect the world through their good choices.

The principles of Zoroastrianism are based on truth and justice, connected with wisdom and tied together with the concept of free choice. And when they ask what the purpose of our existence is here on earth? We have the answer; it is to renew the world, through righteousness!

What we care about as a community, the things we do for the world and for others, may be the best indication of who we are as a community of Zoroastrians. The goal of the religion is not the happiness of the individual but making others happy.

Zarathushtra's message shifts the focus from an individualistic highly personal way of thinking to a much broader, less self-absorbed way of thinking, acting, and living. That is, doing what is good or "best" in each situation is often different than doing what is advantageous or convenient to an individual. This has implications for how we live our lives, how we interact with others in person and in a societal setting, and how we choose leaders. I like to think of Zarathushtra's message as that of the image of a butterfly flapping its wings in one part of the world and setting into motion a series of events perhaps causing a hurricane in another part of the world. Zarathushtra's message can be the wing moving people's minds in a small way completely changing the kind of life they lead — away from living a life focused on what's best for one alone, and towards living a good life that improves the world for all people and beings in the world.

It means we have to work towards perfection in every aspect of our lives. Each individual has God's most important attribute within him or her; the attribute of the Good Mind. Each individual has full freedom to choose to think and speak and act in good and righteous ways (according to the law of Asha). Those who choose to follow their good mind and transform good thoughts into words and action everyday and in each and every choice -large and small - help move the world closer to completion and perfection. In this way each person has the potential and ability to be a co-leader with God in renewing and perfecting this world.

As individuals we must continually strengthen our Good Mind - that ability to know the right path or choice in a situation - and the capacity for loving others within ourselves. We have to strive to understand and choose the right and good path in every choice we make in our lives, not for any reward, but because it is the right thing to do. This process starts within ourselves; and as we individuals are transformed, it affects our families, then our neighbors, then our communities, then our countries, and ultimately the entire world.

According to Zoroastrian teachings, Angra Mainyu is the architect of evil, the anti God principle, who represents evil, untruth, arrogance and demise and subjects people to torment once they come under his influence. He is emotionally unstable, lazy, lacks confidence, cowardly and ignorant, but has a blind ambition to overpower God and infest His creation by whatever means that are available to him. He is assisted in his effort by a host of evil entities, the Daevas and the Druj whom he created. Jeh, the primeval woman is his partner, who instigates him and reminds him of his duties, whenever he is depressed or frightened by the memory of God, and goads him into action. Despite his weaknesses and evil intentions, he is somehow endowed with the power to create his own forces. Though God is omnipotent, Zoroastrian texts do not give the impression that he is created by God, because God being pure light and truthfulness, cannot create evil that is centered in darkness, falsehood and malice. God will only destroy him when the times comes. Till then Ahirman exists by himself, presenting a problem to the forces of light. They have to contend with him and do all they can to maintain the sanctity and order of the worlds so that he remains confined to his own domain till God destroys him in a manner already planned by Him.

Zoroastrian religion is based on the belief that the world is a battle ground between good and evil forces, with far reaching consequences to the humanity, depending upon which side they join. Zoroastrian texts vary in their interpretations of this epic battle. According to one version Ahura Mazda is constantly opposed by an evil being called Angra Mainyu. The battle between the two will continue till the end of creation when God will ultimately triumph and confine the evil to one particular region, the hell. According to another version, at the beginning of creation, Ahura Mazda created the twin spirits, the good Spenta Mainyu andl Angra Mainyu or Ahirman. He gave them the freedom to choose between life, light and good on one hand and demise, darkness and evil on the other. Spenta Mainyu chose life, truth, light, order and goodness, while Angra Mainyu chose demise, darkness, chaos and evil. Spenta Mainyu presides over the world of Truth and Justice while the latter over the kingdom of lies or falsehood (Druj). The material world in between is a playground in which the opposing forces meet and determine the fate of human beings. Angra Mainyu is presently trapped in metals and material things and will continue to trouble people till God brings him to justice on the Judgment Day. Some later day texts describe the opposing twins as children of Zurvan or Time.

Traditional accounts favour the first version according to which in the beginning there was only Infinite Time. In it God and Angra Mainyu were both infinite and finite. They were infinite on one side where there were no boundaries to their domains. On the other side, they were separated by a great Void. Because the void limited their domain on one side, they were also finite. God was not only the more powerful of the two, but also omniscient. with the knowledge of the past, present and future. Before He even met him, He was aware of Angra Mainyu, residing on the other side of the Void. He also knew about their impending battle. But Angra Mainyu was not omniscient. He was also not as brave and courageous as God. He was weak, timid, ignorant and lazy. Fear and malice were his weapons. In the Infinite Time, when there was perfect balance in the universe, Angra Mainyu crossed the Void and saw God for the first time. He made an attempt to attack Him. God made a covenant with him, knowing well that the time to contain the evil was yet to come.

According to the covenant, God offered a truce to Ahirman, that would last for 9000 years. According to the agreement, God's will alone would prevail in the first three thousand years. The will of both would prevail in the next three thousand years during which the material world and things would become susceptible to the forces of evil and suffer from instability, demise and decay. The next three thousand years would begin with the birth of Zoroaster, who would spread the teachings of God among humanity and make them aware of the conflict between the forces of good and evil and prepare them for the final confrontation, teaching them the right way to live and support the forces of good. Another prophet would be born a thousand years later to continue the teachings. Finally at the beginning of the third millennium, a future son of Zoroaster would manifest on earth. He would be called Saoshyant. He would herald the Final Judgment Day, distribute the drink of immortality among people and help God and his forces destroy the evil for ever.

As projected by God, Ahirman attacked the material world when he was instigated by his partner, Jeh. He burst through the sky. He invaded the earth. He attacked the primeval man, the primeval ox and all the elements, namely, fire, water, earth and air. He attacked the stars, the planets, the plants and the animals. According to Zoroastrian beliefds, the presence of evil in the material plane makes our world unstable and ever changing. Evil renders the things in our world susceptible to decay, demise and disintegration. Mountains were formed when the evil pierced through the otherwise plain earth and caused earthquakes deep inside. It is also responsible in our world for droughts, deserts and the stench that comes sometimes from the earth. Smoke and black soot is formed when evil overtakes the fire. It makes air noxious with stinking smells, water susceptible to pollution and impurities, plants, men and animals to fever and sickness and the sun and the moon to eclipses.

Human beings are also susceptible to the invasion of evil forces. Especially, their minds and bodies can succumb to the influence of evil. Their minds and bodies can fall prey to evil thoughts and evil temptations. They can intentionally or unintentionally come into contact with evil things such as dead or putrid matter or contaminated water, air or earth. The Zoroastrians scriptures therefore urge men to be very careful in their day to day lives. living very responsibly, religiously and ethically, remembering God all the time and practicing righteousness by observing the three commandments taught by Zoroaster, namely: good thoughts, good words and good deeds. They are advised to protect themselves by chanting the sacred mantras like Ashem Vohu and Ahunwar mantra and abide by the instructions given in the scriptures to keep their minds, bodies and environment as pure and clean as possible.

The concept of duality, or the battle between good and evil forces is found in all religions. Rejection of evil and adoration of the divine for one's own good is the common theme that runs through all religious scriptures. However Zoroastrianism presents its in a rather dramatic way, not as something that has been happening only in some higher worlds between beings of light and darkness, but as something that has been happening right here, right now, in oneself and in every aspect of the material creation, in everything that one can see, touch, smell and feel. It presents it as an inherent problem of our existence, from which escape is possible, by a conscious and ethical choice, by practicing righteousness and emulating all the qualities represented by God and His six Immortal Beings.

REFERENCES

Bradke, P. von: Dyaus, Asura, Ahura Mazda. Halle, 1885.

Dina i Mainu i Khrat: Edited by Darab P. Sanjana. Bombay, 1895.

Dinkard: Books 3-9. Edited and translated from the Pahlavi text by Peshutan and Darab Sanjana. Vols. 1-19. Bombay. 1874-1919.

Dinshaw, V.: The Date and Country of Zarathushtra. Hyderabad (Deccan), 1912.

Govindacharya, A.: Mazdaism in the Light of Vishnuism. Mysore, 1913.

Haug, Martin: Essays On the Sacred Language, Writings, and Religion of the Parsis. 3d ed. Edited and enlarged by E. W. West. London, 1884.

King, L. W., and Thompson, R. C.: The Sculptures and Inscriptions of Darius the Great on the Rock of Behistun in Persia: a new Collation of the Persian, Susian, and Babylonian Texts. London, 1907.

Kohut, Alexander: The Jewish Angelology and Demonology based upon Parsism. Translated from the German by K. R. Cama. Bombay, 1883.

Neriosengh's Sanskrit Ubersetzung des Yasna: von F. Spiegel. Leipzig, 1861.

Nirangastan: Translated from the Avesta-Pahlavi text by S. J. Bulsara. Bombay, 1915.

Oriental Studies in honour of Cursetji Erachji Pavri: London, 1933.

Sanjana, Rastamji E.: The Parsi Book of Books, the Zend-Avesta. Bombay, 1924.

Sanjana, Rastamji E.: Spiritualism through Zoroastrian Eyes. Bombay, 1929.

Shayast-ne-Shayast: Edited, transliterated, and translated by Jehangir C. Tavadia. Hamburg, 1930.

Wadia, Ardaser S.: The Message of Zoroaster. London, 1912.

8

Moral Value System

The Arab world is now eclipsed by one firm and fierce religion. But, during the families of such nobles as the Achaemenids, a truly imposing and proud faith appeared; Zoroastrianism. The word of this religion was brought to the cosmos by the Persian prophet Zoroaster. The origins of the faith and the notions of Zoroastrianism were and still are the foundation of the religion. During time, the religion depleted in size because of Mohammed, who introduced and brought the faith of Islam into the world. Also, Zoroastrianism played a major part in everyday life. Because of its beliefs, Zoroastrianism could once again arise as a prevailing religion. This is not just because of its beliefs, but also that its origins as a religion are firm and present in many families today.

The faith of Zoroastrianism is founded mainly on two aspects of life. The people who tell the truth are on the side of Asha, and are know as the people of morality.

The others, who are know as the individuals of the lie, or the Druj, followed the dark way of evil. Zoroastrianism is a polytheistic religion which shows people ways of life but lets the individual make a choice of truth or lie. But, it is also believed in Zoroastrianism that a judgment day will occur when good will overcome evil. In this great battle, Ahura Mazda, the Master knowledge would fight Angra Mainya, the Fiendish spirit for control over the world. During this war between good and evil, Ahura Mazda and his supporters would defeat the evil Angra Mainya. Furthermore, all evil would be annihilated on earth in a trial by ordeal in which fire and molten metal would burn away all evil and only leave behind good.

It is considered that Zoroastrianism first appeared as a religion during the sovereignty of Darius I in Persia. Zoroaster, as he was know by the Greeks, proposed this religion to Darius I and it was accepted. It was believed that Zoroaster had seen an invision from the Master Knowledge Ahura Mazda. Zoroastrianism continued to grow under Grecian rule with the likes of the Seleucids ruling Persia. Also, under the Parthian Arsacids, Zoroaster was a prevailing religion. From 226-641 AD, Persia was finally back under Persian reign with the Sassanids. During this time, Zoroastrianism grew quickly and was the most powerful religion in Persia. Eventually under the Sassanids, who were of Zoroastrian belief, made Zoroastrianism the official state religion. This meant that everyone was now of this belief since that a king ordered it. Overtime, Zoroastrianism soon decreased in size mainly because of the rise of another religion, Islam. During the seventh century, Persia was slowly converted to the faith of Islam by the Arabs. Because of this, people of this faith were not safe in a dominate Islam society and most were faced with another quandary, demise. The Islamic people converted the Zoroastrian people with force. However, Zoroastrian still lives on in eastern parts in India because the Islam crusaders never reached this far away place.

Despite the fact that not much is know how Zoroastrianism played a role in the family of Persians, it is know that it did help their lives. Zoroastrianism brought the people of Persia a religion which based on two ideologies, old and new. Zoroastrianism had brought along many views from the past which included the Magi. This tribe of people, which produced the prophet Zoroaster, was though to have had a pre-Zoroastrian faith. But, after the rise of this faithfaith, they headed Zoroastrianism as priests and pretty much ran the temples of Zoroastrianism. They were though to have power over demons and this gave rise to the word magic. The main new theory of Zoroastrianism was that of good suppressing evil. With this combination of old and new, a very well balanced, high moral faith was produced.

Zoroastrianism has played a major role in the way our world works today. For example, this faith shows the people of the world very strong and virtuous morals such as telling the the true and telling lies. It was believed by them that truth defeats lies, which today is still taught. It is also seen as the right thing to do. Nevertheless, this faith knew that this would not always be the case and showed us that everyone has the choice of truth or lie. No one is ever forced to lie, it is there choice. This is what was instructed many centuries ago and it can been still seen like this today. There is no reason why Zoroastrianism could not develop to be powerful again because the beliefs which were used so many years ago have not substantially passed off or changed and are still seen in the same way. This is why Zoroastrianism is such a marvellous faith which should not be over looked, but cherished.

MORAL VALUES

Moral values are things held to be correct or incorrect or suitable or unsuitable. While ethics is sometimes described as 'innate' in humans, the scientific view is that a capacity for morality is genetically decided in us but the set of moral values is gained, through example, teaching, and imprinting from parents and society. Different civilizations have very different moral value systems. Moral values, along with customs, laws, conduct patterns, and beliefs, are the defining features of a culture.

Moral values are enforced, for example, by parenting, peer counselling, conscience, disapproval, shunning, and only in some instances by law. They were effective in small communities before laws were formalized. They can also be sustained by the notion of 'status', a notion which has many different meanings in different societies. There is today important disagreement over what role status plays in present-day society and of what it actually consists.

MORALITY IN LIFE

Most faiths teach systems of morals in order to encourage compliance and cooperation and to discourage nonconformity and cheating. In some faiths, ethic of self-sacrifice has functioned to promote loyalty to a group, thereby tactically promoting human survival. All faiths teach virtues, such as love, self-control, compassion, nonviolence, and knowledge, but differences in belief systems can give varying significance to these virtues.

Zoroastrian faith can be termed as 'natural', which is the innate capacity of all humans to arrive at a belief in the subsistence of a supreme being. Zoroastrian faith is liberal, comforting, egalitarian and contemplative, and encourages reliance on personal responsibility. A Zoroastrian cannot achieve deliverance either through states of trance, dreams, visions and healings, or through special signs and miracles, mystical experiences, oblations and sacrifices, cleaning and penance. In some faiths, possession of the human body by a mystical entity is a common form of interchange with the spritual world. However, for every Zoroastrian, relationship with God can only be expressed in terms of moral behavior because each person has the capability to contribute and improve the quality of human life and thus renew this world.

More than 3000 years ago, Zarathushtra disclosed to humanity that there is only One God whom he referred to as Ahura Mazda, literally meaning, "A Being having Super-Knowledge". As per Zarathushtra, Ahura Mazda produced the world in space and time through his creative faculty Spenta Mainyu (Best Mentality). Ahura Mazda not only let the world evolve into inanimate objects such as the sun, moon, stars and planets but also into living species such as the plants, animals and humans. The corporeal laws, such as the principles of gravity and electromagnetism came into subsistence, and natural selection which can weed out potentially dangerous genetic mutations govern the evolution of the world to this day.

Zarathushtra brought in the unique idea that the aim for human life is to emulate the characteristics of Ahura Mazda and help move His creation towards perfection. Ahura Mazda is intelligent and full of knowledge and has vouchsafed every human with Vohu Manah, a good mind, so that we can think and discern what is good and bad, and rationally select our own way in life. The human mind is the best gift that has been conferred on us by Ahura Mazda and we are the only species in the animal Kingdom capable of evaluating rationally and separating good from evil. By employing our mind we can be creative, constructive and progressive or unimaginative, destructive and ignorant. The freedom to select between, good and evil is the underlying principle of Zarathushtra's faith.

We should make our options only after heeding and reflecting and not make conclusions based on popularity or because we are forced to do so.

The dualism reflected in the Gathas is not celestial but moral; for good and evil are limited to the human mind, and thoughts, when translated into words and actions can produce good or bad results. Zoroastrianism is an ethical faith and teaches that mortals can achieve spritual completeness by fighting evil with Humata, Hukhta and Havarashtra (good thoughts, good words and good deeds).

As per Zarathushtra the world is governed through Asha or Arta, the old Indo-Iranian law of "truth and precision". Ahura Mazda is in accord with Asha and he wants us to promote this way of morality, which stands for order, evolution and progress. As per this law good deeds produce good rewards and evil deeds have bad results. Zarathushtra emphasized respect for the elements of nature, such as, fire, sun, moon, earth, water, and the seasons. If we do not live in concord with nature it would guide to catastrophic consequences. By following the way of Asha we can make this world a better place, not only for this generation but also for the generations to come.

Zoroastrians do not believe that good things in life are detrimental to the spritual life or that we should derogate the material world. For a Zoroastrian life has to be lived to it's fullest by making the right choices in order to bring about Frashokeriti, the final renovation of the world. Zarathushtra did not encourage the ideas of repudiation, celibacy and withdrawal of any form, because life is a true celebration to be lived with sincerity in order to bring pleasure and fulfillment both within oneself and to others. Humans are ultimately accountable for their choices and reap the consequences of their actions. The law of consequences is fashioned and delivered with knowledge and benevolence, and is not intended to punish but to deliver nirvana and understanding for what is true and right. Evil can be eliminated by making the wrongful become virtuous, and by changing their minds through knowledge and reason.

Zarathustra described Ahura Mazda's characteristic, Khshatra Vairya, as the rule of goodness, the heavenly power that guides all creations towards Asha. People who are wise and sincere can establish an ideal state that promotes corporeal, material and spritual progress of humans and the world towards Frashokeriti. Each person can strive to bring serenity to this world to promote happiness. If we live our lives with goodness towards all creations, then it can also shape others to goodness, and this in turn would launch a cycle of good deeds that goes on forever. Haurvatât, perfection, and Ameretât, immortality, are the rewards of a virtuous life. Khshatra and Âramaiti can guide humans to live in eternal bliss, the ultimate aim of the Zoroastrian doctrine.

Zoroastrian faith is simple because it is positive and life affirming, and the Zoroastrian way of life can be guide by moral perception and decision. The faith does not demand blind belief but reason and action on the part of every person. It is not a normative ethic, based on respect and fear, but rather an ethic of personal responsibility. The Gathas provide guidance for humans to reflect upon and act using their own good mind and clear conscience. Each person has an inherent right as well as responsibility to select the way of Asha, for Zoroastrians do not believe in predestination that God has decreed everything that will happen. The freedom to act goes hand in hand with responsibility for the effects of such actions. The mind of humans can accept to follow Asha, and through good thoughts, good words and good deeds, produce bliss or deviate from it and produce havoc. Those who follow the way of Asha walk on the way of morality and goodness, out of which comes happiness.

Each and every one of us can stand evil, follow the way of morality and enlightenment and help to guide this world to Frashokereti. Zarathustra says in Yasna 30.9 of the Gathas: may we be like those who make this world advance.

MORAL VALUES FOR LEADER

The shaping of leaders is one of the most important dimensions in the organisational field, it gives the basis for improvement of the intellectual assets of the companies and its competitiveness. The leaders are the creators and sustainers of an organizational culture that should be pointed to Quality, Excellence and Social Justice, among other values. The leaders make the differences in the success of the organizations.

Ethical leaders must base their actions in a Good Mind. A Good Mind provides the terminus a quo to build and maintain a solid and stable ethical leadership. The Zoroastrian perspective considers that a Good Mind invokes the person principles of rightheousness, knowledge and serenity. The leader embarked on this approach realizes the Truth and drives them to a flourishing and productive situation.

Truth is a very important value taken into consideration by the Zoroastrian View. Truth plays a predominant role in the life of man. It is Truth which prospers the creatures and makes the plants and waters increase, It is through the quest for Truth that good understanding arises in the spirit of man, an understanding that teaches him to further the principles of God in good thoughts, in good words and in good actions. It is Truth which also teaches man to discern between what is right and wrong. It is man's bond to Truth that gives full meaning to the subsistence of God and grants strength and enduring life to him as well.

In Zoroastrianism the leaders or priests go by different names, depending on the tasks they execute. In ancient times there used be several types of priests, organized into a power structure, whose functions have been now either deemed unnecessary or combined into others.

To the highest class of priests belonged matharans, who like Zoroaster, were empowered with writeric ability and composed the verses of the sacred holy scriptures, linked

There were atharwans, who like the vedic atharvan priests, were associated with fire and haoma rites.

A zaotar, like the hotr of the vedic faith, was an functioning or presiding priest of Yasna, who poured libations into the sacred fire to the accompaniment of rite chants.

Magi or magu were an exceptional class of priests empowered with occult cognition, magical powers and power of divination. They also interpreted dreams and performed divinatory rites to portend future. They were confined mostly to the western parts of ancient Iran and served in the courts of kings. Some of them wielded enormous political power and often came into conflict with the sovereigns they served.

Other classes of priests mentioned in the Zoroasrian texts, but comparatively lesser known, were mowbeds, herbeds and kirdars who existed at various times in the long and chequered history of the faith. The priesthood, as in vedic faith, is hereditary.

In the heydays of Zoroastrianism, the priests had the power to declare punishments or expiate the certain sins through cleaning rites. the following verse from Denkdar declares the grandness of a priest in cultivating virtue.

"The holy priest is the man to explain what is virtue; and by this explanation every spirit has to guide a good life. Every man obtains from the Dastur the knowledge of what to do and what not to do. A man lives in the world without sin by not injuring virtuous men, and then the man obtains the love of God. All men not having the benefit of the Dastur's true knowledge about every thing, they do not possess the knowledge of God, faith and virtue. How can an ignorant man know of virtue without the aid of a religious teacher? Therefore every one amongst men has the need of a teacher of the salvation from sin and the acquisition of virtue."

MORAL VALUES IN SOCIETY

The Zoroastrian society is established on the teachings of Zoroaster as per which followers of the faith have to:

- Declare perfect allegiance and dedication to Ahuramazda,
- Decline evil totally,
- Comply with the great qualities of Amesha Spentas,
- Believe in the holiness and divinity of God's creation,
- Show unshrinking commitment to virtuous living, practicing good thoughts, good words and good words,
- Adhere to the instructions of Zoroaster and other wise men of the Mazdayasnian faith and
- Pledge themselves to the Mazdayasnian faith

These predominant ideals of Zoroastrian religious doctrine are mentioned in the Yasna twelve of the Avesta, which is procreated below

Allegiance and Devotion to God

I curse the Daevas. I declare myself a Mazda-worshipper, a helper of Zarathushtra, unfriendly to the Daevas, fond of Ahura's teaching, a praiser of the Amesha Spentas, a worshipper of the Amesha Spentas. I ascribe all good to Ahura Mazda, 'and all the best,' Asha-endowed, splendid, xwarena-endowed, whose is the cow, whose is Asha, whose is the light, 'may whose blissful areas be filled with light'.

I select the good Spenta Armaiti for myself; let her be mine. I resign the theft and robbery of the cow, and the damaging and plundering of the Mazdayasnian settlements.

I want freedom of movement and freedom of dwelling for those with homesteads, to those who dwell upon this earth with their cattle. With reverence for Asha, and (oblations) offered up, I vow this: I shall nevermore damage or plunder the Mazdayasnian settlements, even if I have to risk life and limb.

Rejection of Evil Accordingto the Teachings of Zoroaster

I reject the authority of the Daevas, the evil, no-good, lawless, evil-knowing, the most druj-like of beings, the foulest of beings, the most damaging of beings. I reject the Daevas and their comrades, I reject the demons (yatu) and their comrades; I reject any who harm beings. I reject them with my thoughts, words, and deeds. I reject them publicly. Even as I reject the head (authorities), so too do I reject the hostile followers of the druj.

As Ahura Mazda taught Zarathushtra at all discussions, at all meetings, at which Mazda and Zarathushtra conversed;

As Ahura Mazda taught Zarathushtra at all discussions, at all meetings, at which Mazda and Zarathushtra conversed — even as Zarathushtra rejected the authority of the Daevas, so I also reject, as Mazda-worshipper and supporter of Zarathushtra, the authority of the Daevas, even as he, the Asha-empowered Zarathushtra, h[illegible] rejected them.

Belief in the Sanctity and Divinity of the Wo[illegible]

As the belief of the waters, the belief of the plants, the belief of the well-made (Original) Cow; as the belief of Ahura Mazda who produced the cow and the Asha-empowered Man; as the belief of Zarathushtra, the belief of Kavi Vishtaspa, the belief of both Frashaostra and Jamaspa; as the belief of each of the Saoshyants (saviors) — fulfilling destiny and Asha-empowered —so I am a Mazda-worshipper of this belief and teaching.

Pledge to follow the Three Commandments

I profess myself a Mazda-worshipper, a Zoroastrian, having vowed it and professed it. I pledge myself to the well-thought thought, I pledge myself to the well-spoken word, I pledge myself to the well-done action.

Declaration of Faith

I pledge myself to the Mazdayasnian faith, which causes the attack to be put off and weapons put down; [which upholds khvaetvadatha], Asha-endowed; which of all faiths that live or shall be, is the greatest, the best, and the most beautiful: Ahuric, Zoroastrian. I ascribe all good to Ahura Mazda. This is the creed of the Mazdayasnian faith.

PRACTICAL ASPECTS

Traditional values refer to those notions, moral codes, and mores that are passed down from generation to generation within a civilization, subculture or society. In its own right "traditional values" simply means the values coming from custom rather than any specific philosopher, moralist, or writer. Hence the "traditional values" of non-Western societies may be wildly at variance from any Zoroastrianism notion of Family values. Societies based on traditional values often embrace animism and ancestor worship rather than any Ibrahimic faith.

In Zoroastrianism those who oppose transition as being against the religious custom generally deem themselves to be a force for "traditional values." Radical elements of Hindutva are also intent to keep any Christian or other religious values from getting into their society, although their more contemporary views on Hindu law power make their relation to traditional values more complex than this implies. There are also Hopi traditionalists who wish to keep Christianity and other faiths from gaining a foothold amongst their people and who prefer that Native American languages be used instead of English, Spanish, and so forth.

Attempts at producing a kind of universalized "traditional values" has proved generally hard or even impossible. It is generally fair to say that usually traditional values tend, by definition, toward conservatism and that they often, but not always, accept some form of patriarchy as normative.

REFERENCES

Epistles of Manushchihar: Translated from the Pahlavi text by E. W. West. In *Sacred Books of the East*, vol. 18.

Firdausi: Le Livre des Rois, traduit et commente par Jules Mohl. 7 vols. Paris 1876-1878.

Firdausi: Translated into English by A. G. Warner and E. Warner. vols. 1-9. London, 1905-1925.

Gottheil, R. J. H.: References to Zoroaster in Syriac and Arabic Literature. In *Classical Studies in Honour of Henry Drisler*. New York, 1894.

Hodivala, S. K.: Parsis of Ancient India. Bombay, 1920.

Hyde, Thomas: Historia Religionis veterum Persarum eorumque Magorum. Oxford, 1700.

Indo-Iranian Studies: Being Commemorative Papers contributed by European, American and Indian Scholars in honor of Dastur Darab P. Sanjana. London, 1925.

Jackson, A. V. Williams: Researches in Manichaeism. New York, 1932.

Jamaspi: Edited and translated from the Pahlavi-Pazand iexts by Jivanji Jamshedji Modi. Bombay, 1903.

Menant, J.: Zoroaster. Essai sur la Philosophte religieuse de la Perse. 2d ed. Paris, 1857.

Meyer. Edward: Geschichte des Alterthums. Stuttgart, 1884.

Mills, L. H.: Our Own Religion in Ancient Persia. 1913.

Minu-i Khrat: Translated from the Pahlavi text by E. W. West. In *Sacred Books of the East*, vol. 24.

Mistri, R. H.: Zoroaster and Zoroastrianism. Bombay, 1906.

Modi, Jivanji J.: The Religious System of the Parsees. Bombay, 1885.

Moulton, James H.: Early Religious Poetry of Persia. Cambridge, 1911.

Moulton, James H.: Early Zoroastrianism. London, 1913.

Moulton, James H.: The Teachings of Zarathushtra. Bombay, 1916.

9

Movements

RELIGIOUS MOVEMENTS

Manichaeism

Zoroastrianism looks back to the Iranian prophet Zarathushtra, who may have lived anywhere from 1500 to 500 BC. Central to its view is a cosmic struggle between good and evil in which humans are called to participate. Ahura Mazda (later Ormazd), the creator of the universe, chose the good, while the evil spirit, Angra Mainyu (later Ahriman) chose the evil. These two are both primordial, but Ormazd will defeat Ahriman at the end of time. Its highly developed conceptions of spiritual beings and its eschatology probably influenced Jewish thinking in the later centuries BC. It uses fire as its central symbol, so that the Muslims called the Zoroastrians "fire worshippers." In the third century AD. Zoroastrianism was reorganized as the state religion of the Sassanian dynasty. After the Muslim conquest, most Iranians became Muslims, but Zoroastrian activity remained vigorous for some time. A small Zoroastrian community continues to exist in Iran and a larger one in India (the Parsis).

The Manichaean movement was founded by Mani (216–277AD.) and has an extremely dualistic view in which the material world is the realm of evil and darkness. Particles from the world of light have been captured and imprisoned in matter, and knowledge (gnosis) and highly ascetic practices are designed to free them and return them to their heavenly home. The movement spread widely and was strong for some centuries, being the official religion of the Uighur state in central Asia from 763 to 840. It was severely persecuted by both Christians and Muslims and died out by about the twelfth century.

The Mandaeans, located mainly in southern Iraq, are an ancient Gnostic sect, claiming John the Baptist as their prophet at least since Islamic times. They practice frequent ritual immersions (baptism).

Anquetil du Perron's Pioneer Work

The inexor-able decree of Providence had ruled that a new light from the West should dispel the darkness that had surrounded the pages of the sacred scriptures for ages, and add to their better under-standing and elucidation. European travellers who had visited India and Persia during the sixteenth and seventeenth centuries acquainted the people of the West with the religious beliefs, man-ners, and customs of the followers of Zoroaster. Hyde's masterly work on Parsi religion, which drew its materials from the works of the classical authors and the Persian version of the Sad Dar as well as from kindred works, appeared in 1700. Some im-portant Iranian manuscripts had been carried from India to Eng-land, and were now shelved as curios in the Bodleian library at Oxford.

To the energetic Frenchman, Anquetil du Perron, is due the credit of making the first systematic attempt to study the Avestan texts and place their contents before the Western world. Having come across a fac-simile of four leaves of the Bodleian manuscript, his curiosity was aroused, and with characteristic zeal he enlisted as a soldier in 1754 on a ship bound for India with the aim of bringing back to the Western world a knowledge of the sacred scriptures of Zoroaster. Unbounded enthusiasm, combined with the vigour of youth, enabled Anquetil to overcome the almost insuperable dif-ficulties that stood in the way of his literary enterprise. Having acquired from Dastur Darab, the High Priest of the Parsis of Surat, what inadequate knowledge he could get in those days, he returned home after six years of strenuous work and published the result of his studies in three quarto volumes in 1771. This publication created a stir in literary circles, and gave rise to a heated controversy. One school of thought of eminent scholars in Europe declined to attach any weight to the Frenchman's work, and denied that the grotesque stuff that he had placed before the world could ever be the work of so great a thinker and sage as Zoroaster, stoutly maintaining that Anquetil's Avesta was either a forgery or that he had been duped by the Indian Parsi Mobads. The falseness of this view, however, was ultimately shown.

The dis-interested labours of various scholars during the subsequent years fully substantiated Anquetil's pioneer work; and when the closer affinity between the languages of the Avesta and Sanskrit be-came generally known, the sacred texts began to be studied in the light of comparative philology, and the authenticity of the Avesta was completely proved. The seeds sown by Anquetil have since blossomed into fruitful trees in the West, but some decades passed after the publication of his work before Western scholar-ship penetrated into India.

We have already seen that the handful of the Parsi fugitives who immigrated to India after the final overthrow of the Persian kingdom in the middle of the seventh century had to face enormous difficulties in the earlier centuries of their settlement in the new home. The precarious condition in which they lived for a con-siderable period made it impracticable for them to keep up their former proselytizing zeal. The instinctive fear of disintegration and absorption in the vast multitudes among whom they lived created in them a spirit of exclusiveness and a strong feeling for the preservation of the racial characteristics and distinctive fea-tures of their community. Living in an atmosphere surcharged with the Hindu caste system, they felt that their own safety lay in encircling their fold by rigid caste barriers.

The community was divided regarding the question of ad-mitting lower classes of aliens into its fold. Though the prac-tice of an active religious propaganda had thus fallen into desuetude, the question of conversion does not seem to have died out entirely, for we find recorded in the Rivayat literature that a heated polemic regarding the subject was carried on during the latter part of the eighteenth century. With the beginning of economic prosperity, the Indian Parsis, we learn, were in the habit of purchasing male and female slaves of low Hindu castes. These slaves, in many cases, were invested with sacred shirt and girdle and admitted into the Zoroastrian fold by the priests at the request of their masters. Those members of the community who were opposed to the mingling of their blood with that of such a low class of people denied to these converts the full privi-leges of a true believer. The contesting parties applied to their coreligionists in Persia for their advice and decision in the mat-ter. The point made by those who favoured the cause of the the converts was that the Parsis of India who owned slaves for their work not only often had them admitted to the Mazdayasnian faith in accordance with the tenets of the religion, but also, without and religious scruples, partook of food prepared by them, and even permitted them, at the season festival to prepare the sacred cakes used for consecration and sacrificial purposes. It was urged that having allowed the converted slaves all such rights of a true Zoroastrian in their lifetime, certain priests as well as laymen objected to the corpses of these slaves being deposited in the Tower of Silence when they died. The Iranian high priests, in replying to their inquiring brothers in India advised them in the beginning to take precautionary measures in all such conver-sions that no harm should thereby be done to the religion and to the community. It was certainly an act of great merit, they pro-ceeded, to purchase alien children and bring them up as Zoroastrians. It was unfair and highly objectionable, they added, nay it was an inexpiable sin, to refuse these unfortunate people all the privileges of a believer after once admitting them into the Zoroas-trian religious fold. It is taught by the scriptures, they argued, that all mankind will be brought over to the religion of Mazda in the time of the future saviour prophets. It was, therefore, the pious duty of every true Zoroastrian to help this great cause by leading all to the path of righteousness. In the face of such commands, they concluded, those who denied to the proselytes the full rights of a faithful believer did not deserve to be called Zoroastrians.

On another occasion in reply to a question about the conver-sion of such low-class people, the Iranian informant wrote that even a man who dug graves or followed the profession of burning the dead (two inexpiable sins according to Zoroastrianism), should be admitted into the Zoroastrian fold, provided his admit-tance would not be harmful to the faith.

The fear that the community might be swamped by the un-desirable alien element was a reason why proselytizing fell into disfavour. We notice in that discussion that the different sections of the community were divided more on the social side of the question of proselytizing than on its religious side. The protest was chiefly based against the admixture of racial blood that the low class of the aliens introduced into the community. The Zoroastrians of Persia, who were trampled under the iron foot of their Moslem conquerors and had lived in servile state, saw no objection whatsoever in receiving converts even from the lowest strata of the non-Zoroastrian peoples. But the case was different with the Indian Parsis, among whom the improved social and economic conditions had aroused a keen sense of racial pride and consciousness of their past greatness. A very consider-able portion of the community, it seems, looked with disapproval upon the introduction of the undesirable element of alien races into their small numbers. This strong feeling was aggravated the more through the fact that such converts who sought admis-sion came always from the lowest classes. Members of the upper classes of the non-Zoroastrian communities were not heard knocking at the door of the Mazdayasnian fire-temples seeking admission. The community was not disposed to any kind of active religious propaganda. The cases of conversion were con-sequently confined either to the slaves brought up in Parsi fam-ilies or to the children born to Parsi fathers of their non-Zoroas-trian mistresses. Proselytizing came to be associated with the low type of fosovereignty element, and fell into disrepute.

A beginning of opposition to the idea of religious propaganda was thus made when the entire question of proselytizing came to be looked upon by the community with disfavour. No serious at-tempt has since been made by the Parsis of India to organize a proselytizing movement with the sole object of propagating their faiths But the desire on the part of some Zoroastrians to include in the faith children born to them by illegitimate intercourse with non-Zoroastrian mistresses, or by others seeking a matrimonial alliance with alien women and investing the children born of such unions with the sacred shirt and girdle, has prompted them to open the question from time to time to the present day. So bitter have been the controversies thus arising that they have stopped just short of physical violence.

Modernism Versus Traditionalism

The modern world is divided between Modernism and Tra-ditionalism. Religions rest on divine revelation. This revealed knowledge is static. Secular knowledge progresses with time and, by continuous research and discovery in the realm of the physics of nature and the laws of life, creates new knowledge. It knows no end and is ever new. It adapts itself to the times and satisfies the cravings of the thinking minds. From the earli-est times, religion spoke with authority on matters relating to the spirit. But there were physical problems for which the inquisi-tive mind always demanded solution. Science claimed to make new discoveries in the realm of physical researches. Religion adopted science as its handmaid and incorporated the discoveries of the scientists and the physicists and proclaimed them as the further divine revelation to mankind to explain physical ques-tions. The crude cosmologies and cosmogonies of the times when science was in its infancy were thus made integral parts of the religions of the world. The researches of modern science have rendered them untenable in the light of advanced knowledge. The doctrine of evolution has revolutionized man's outlook upon life throughout the world. Modern science has changed the atti-tude of the thinking people everywhere. The intellectual ferment and spiritual unrest have stirred the whole world. The enlight-ened youths are driven to disbelief. They are not happy in the state of disbelief. They are anxious to believe and secure peace of mind but they cannot honestly subscribe to the beliefs in which they are brought up. They are disbelievers despite themselves. This state of disbelief is produced by honest doubt.

Orthodoxy is obstinacy to forget anything old and learn anything new. Orthodoxy has always and everywhere professed that the doctrines, dogmas, rituals, and the established views of life that a people has inherited are fixed and right. All those that dissent from them are heterodox, other than right, not right, that is, wrong. Orthodoxy has always numbers on its side, for the average man is temperamentally timid and conservative and is unwilling to be disturbed in the thoughts and views he has in-herited with his birth. He seeks refuge in tradition and is con-tent to live secure in the dead past. All that is handed down from remote times and forms the tradition of the people is sacred. Orthodoxy is jealous of the views it holds and resents all opposition to them. It aims at making people religious in its own way. It moves about with prying eyes and spies on its neighbour's conscience and struggles to read his thoughts. When-ever it is powerful enough to inflict its will upon others, it clips the wing of thought, gags speech, and cripples action. The collective orthodox mind controls the thinking of the individual and drives the dissenters to secrete their thoughts in the lowest depths of their souls. Orthodoxy makes free thinking taboo and fails to see that high thinking is impossible without free think-ing. Orthodoxy is impervious to the influence of the times.

REFORM MOVEMENTS

Doctrinally, the Parsi reformists aim to synthesize Zoroastrian beliefs with the modern world. The existence of a divine being other than Ahura Mazda was denied and the Amesha Spentas were declared to be merely abstract nouns. Although the Pahlavi texts contradicted these theories, they were dismissed as a corruption of the original teaching of the prophet. The noted reformist Maneckji Dhalla summarised his own reformist position with five criticisms of Zoroastrian practice which all focused on 'excessive' ritual practices, such as the practice of ritual washing in cow's urine. In addition, Dhalla described demise in Christian terms as the freeing by God from the bondage of human life, an interpretation wholly at variance with orthodox Zoroastrian teaching on demise and belief in the essential goodness of life. For some reformists at the beginning of the 20th century, such as D.M. Madan, the Zoroastrian virtue of Wisdom became identified with western knowledge, in so doing, questioning the revelatory aspects of the faith. However, other reformists have not advocated such variant interpretations. For example, the contemporary reformer Khojestree Mistry reaffirms the orthodox doctrine of bodily resurrection in an attempt to re-interpret the religion of Zoroaster in its traditional form.

This school of thought known as the Parsi reform movement began in the late 19th century as a response to the impact of western culture.

The first translation of a Zoroastrian text was produced in the middle of the nineteenth century by Martin Haug who spent the 1860s in India, lecturing to the Parsis on his understanding of the prophet's teaching. His ideas were taken up by the reformists who used western philological methods to defend their sacred texts against Christian charges of polytheism and dualism. In particular, Parsi reformists such as Maneckji Dhalla (1875-1956) criticised various aspects of ritual practice, including the reciting of prayers by rote in Avestan, and denied 'irrational' elements of the religion.

The attempts by Dhalla and other Parsi reformists to present Zoroastrianism in western terms led to both a contradiction of traditional beliefs and an avoidance of doctrines which were unmistakeably Zoroastrian. Nevertherless, their presentation found widespread support and approval within the Parsi community and Dhalla's work has retained its influence amongst Parsis throughout this century. Contemporary Parsi reformists continue this process of reinterpretation. For example, the western-influenced scholar Khojestee Mistry believes he is reinterpreting the religion of Zoroaster in its traditional form; reaffirming orthodox doctrines such as bodily resurrection and the Pahlavi myth of the world renovation.

Crusade against the non-Zoroastrian practices engrafted upon Zoroastrianism. The compromises and concessions made on the part of the early Parsi settlers in India were needed to conciliate the prejudices of the Hindu rulers. The Parsis were a handful of people living in the midst of the teeming millions of India, and even the twelve centuries of their residence in this country have failed to merge them in the ocean of Indian human-ity. This fact is largely due to their intensely communal spirit, fostered by the dread of being assimilated into greater commun-ities, and of thus losing their individuality. But the average Parsi did not fail to borrow many superstitious customs and habits from the Hindus as well as from the Mohammedans dur-ing the later period. The Hindu augur and the Moslem diviner became important factors in the family life of the Parsis. These seers were called in to cast the horoscope of the new-born Zoroastrian child; they foretold the future, administered amulets to heal every sickness and disease in the family, prescribed charms to ward off the evil eye, exorcised demoniacal influences from persons possessed by the powers of darkness, and, in many ways, proved indispensable auxiliaries to a Parsi from birth to demise. The mediation of a Brahman or of a Mullah was often rated higher than that of a Mobad, and a Sanskrit mantra or an Arabic kalma was regarded more efficacious for the purchase of heavenly boons than an Avestan manthra. The Zoroastrian priest ruled in the fire-temple, but the non-Zoroastrian priest had a powerful sway over the hearts of the Parsi populace. With rich offerings did the faithful repair to the tombs of Moslem saints and to Hindu shrines. They laid their faith upon all altars and turned to strange gods in their extremities. The grandeur of the Mazdayasnian teachings had faded, and Zoroaster had partly ceased to be a living force in the spiritual life of the community.

Many alien customs had thus worked their way into Zoroastrianism. These were hard facts for the orthodox to admit but they were facts all the same. With the vigour of youth and with unquenchable zeal the reformers of that day undertook to liber-ate the community from the thraldom of superimposed non-Zoroastrian customs, and to wean it from superstitions.

The reformers protested against reciting their prayers par-rot-wise in an unintelligible language. The Avesta language had long since fallen into disuse. It was not a living language. Yet the belief in its being of celestial origin, the tongue in which Ohrmazd addressed his heavenly court, and even that in which Ahriman harangued his ribald crew, had preserved it as the only true vehicle for conveying prayers. The reformers now argued that it was meaningless to mumble an unintelligible gibberish which neither the priest himself nor the layman understood. Ejaculations and genuflexions were of no avail, when they re-cited their prayers in a dead language. No amount of such formulas would affect the character of the devotees and ennoble their thoughts. A prayer that had no subjective value was no prayer. It failed to awaken any ethical fervour, for a truly de-vout prayer should spur the spirit within to a higher life. This was not possible so long as the priest perfunctorily droned prayers, not a word of which was understood.

The orthodox vehemently retorted that the Avestan language was divine, and as such it possessed inherent magical efficacy. Miraculously composed as these Avestan prayers were, they had indescribable objective value; it was claimed, quite independent of the motive of one who recited them. The mere utterance of the sacred texts, without knowing in the least what they meant, would produce marvellous effect. The ultra-orthodox viewed the situation with pious dread and entertained serious apprehen-sion that, if once the community permitted the use of Gujarati or English compositions for daily prayers, nothing short of a revolutionary change would come, and with the lapse of time the Avestan texts would be supplanted by prayer-books composed in the modern vernaculars.

The reformers pointed out that there already exist some monajat prayers composed in Persian by some of the learned Dasturs even in their own lifetime, which the orthodox were using without any scruple at the end of their daily Avestan prayers.

A fierce controversy raged around this question, with the re-sult that the orthodox went on praying in their own way, and the reformers, neither having faith in the recital of their prayers in an unintelligible language nor having a proper substitute to sat-isfy their demand, went without prayers of any kind. And the situation remains, in large measure, unchanged up to this very day.

The Avesta text metamorphosed into an ungrammatical jargon. The reformers further said that the Avestan texts were recited with the most incorrect pronunciations. In vindication of their statement they quoted passages from the original texts and put by their side the corrupt formulas in vogue in the community. An example of this kind may not be out of place here, and we shall insert the text of Ahunavar, the most important Zoroastrian formula, first in its correct form and then in the corrupt form which obtains among a considerable portion of the community up to this hour.

This, however, did not trouble the orthodox, for they com-placently remarked that as long as they had implicit faith in what they recited, and recited it whole-heartedly, it mattered very little whether they used correct pronunciation or not. Ohrmazd looked to their hearts, and not to their sense of grammar and orthog-raphy. So long as their motives were good, their prayers were acceptable to the Heavenly Father.

The redeeming feature of this entire controversy has been a growing tendency in the community to avail itself of the help of the philologist, who has brought nearer home to them the correct and carefully edited version of their sacred scriptures, and they have consequently begun to recite their daily prayers from books that have based their texts on the standard and authorized ver-sion of the liturgy.

Too much ritualism, protested the reformer. The mechan-ical handling of the ritual, which was as much unintelligible in its real purport to the priest who performed it as it was to the lay-man who ordered it, failed to satisfy the new school. The ortho-dox maintained that although the priestly authorities themselves had lost the key of the mysteries of the ceremonies and were unable to understand their meaning, nevertheless untold good ac-crued to those who devoutly ordered such ceremonies for their own merit. They entertained a pious hope that the lost key would some day be recovered, and the hidden secrets brought to the light of the day.

The reformers urged that a vast structure of formalism and ritual had replaced the edifice of the simple faith, and religion had simply turned into ritualism. They dwelt especially on the subjective value of the ritual, and argued that however elaborate and expensive the ceremony might be, it was of no value if it failed to symbolize a moral idea for the faithful who ordered it. Ceremonial observances, they complained, were given greater im-portance than moral observance. Righteousness was identified with rituals. They were only a clothing of religion, but the ethi-cal substance of religion was of greater importance than the clothing itself. Religion, they urged, does not consist in laying up merit by ceremonials. The orthodox retorted that the ritual as such had an intrinsic value and inherent merit, and the more such rites were performed, the greater was the merit assured to the faithful. The new school said that these ceremonials may perhaps serve as a means of conveying ethical ideas to a back-ward people, but the Parsis were not a backward people. Hence they did not need them. Righteousness did not depend upon such ceremonial observances, but upon the purity of man's inner life. Besides, the ceremonials became an economic drain on the slender resources of the credulous poor, who incurred heavy debts for their performance, which was displeasing in the sight of Ohrmazd. The orthodox declared these statements an Ahrimanian onslaught upon the Mazdayasnian rites.

The progressives denounced the intercessory prayers for the dead. The philological researches had for the first time brought to the notice of the Parsis the fact of the sharp distinc-tion between man's soul and his Farohar. From what has been stated in the earlier pages, it can be clearly seen how this essential difference was lost sight of, as early as during the later Pahlavi period. The soul and the Farohar were taken to be one and the same by the Zoroastrians before the philologist pointed out the error. Priest and layman, the learned and the illiterate alike, believed implicitly that the souls of the dead profited by the ceremonials performed in their honour by their relatives in this world. The Avestan and Pahlavi passages, which speak of the coming of the Farohars to earth at the period of the Fravar-digan festival, seeking invocation and sacrifice, were understood by the entire Community as indubitably referring to the coming of the souls of the dead.

According to the general conviction, the supplications offered by the living procured either a remission of the sins committed by the deceased in this world, or else a specific merit for the good deeds he had done. It was this strong faith in the efficacy of the ceremonials to help the struggling soul in either making its way out of hell, or in ascending upwards through the graded heaven in the next world, that inspired the loving and dutiful survivors to order elaborate rituals for the spiritual welfare of the departed. Propitiatory offerings were made, and penitential prayers were recited to secure a better lot for the souls of the dead, and the performance of these periodical rites was most zealously observed. Rich viands were consecrated in the name of the deceased. Whatever kind of food or drink the departed ones had best liked in life were specially prepared. On the last day of the festival, moreover, when the souls were believed to leave this world and return to that beyond, food and drink were offered them to assuage the hunger and thirst on their return journey, while money in copper and silver was dedicated to them to meet their travelling expenses.

The recital of the Patit, or expiatory prayer, forms an im-portant part of the ceremonies performed in honour of the dead. The relatives and friends of the deceased still engage a priest to recite it, and do the same themselves for the expiation and wel-fare of the soul when it is embarking on its journey to the next world after demise. The devout generally keep up this observance daily for at least a month, or throughout the first year, or in many cases for a still longer period.

The reformers took up the question and said that Zoroastrian-ism enjoined that a man went to the abode of weal or woe ac-cording to his deserts, and that no amount of ceremonials per-formed by the living could either mitigate his sufferings or im-prove his condition in the spiritual world. His sins could not be atoned for by elaborate rituals performed in his name, nor would he be one whit the happier for them. It is true, they fur-ther said, that according to the scriptures, the benefit of the ceremonials performed for the dead accrues to the soul during the first three nights after demise, while it still hovers over the body, but from the period of the dawn of the fourth day, when justice is administered to the soul, and it is awarded its special place, the rituals do not affect its position. Any ceremonies per-formed after this day, that is, on the monthly and yearly anni-versaries or on any other occasions, are mainly for the Farohar of the dead man, and not for his soul. In fact, it was claimed, these rites are more for the interest of the living than for the imagined interest of the dead. Zoroastrianism, they said, never stood for any kind of vicarious salvation, for the question of salvation or damnation rested on the individual's own deeds. Neither would the expiatory prayers recited by the living wash out the sins of the dead, nor would the propitiatory sacrifices offered by them induce the heavenly judges to revoke their de-cision. As the man sows, so shall he reap, is the immortal truth taught by Zoroaster. Merit, they contended, cannot be purchased at a price, and sin cannot be expiated by proxy. It was destroy-ing the true spirit of the prophet's great religion to entertain such degrading ideas of vicarious expiation which had been fastened on Zoroastrianism.

These scathing criticisms seriously wounded the religious sus-ceptibilities of the orthodox, who became unsparing in the ve-hement denunciation of the reformers, charging them as reac-tionaries with carrying the religious barque to ruin. They branded the attempts of the reformers as blasphemous and as an irreverent prying into the divine work of Ohrmazd. Bitter words were exchanged between the rival parties, and abuses and invec-tives, ridicule and obloquy, became rampant over these and sev-eral other controversial questions.

The good sense of the disputants saved the community from being split into sects. The reformers were termed the Parsi Protestants and were charged with thinking in terms of Christianity. They were said to be fired by the sole ambitition of being original, and of setting at naught the achievements of their elders for the last three thousand years. The reformers replied that they were simply looking to antiquity for models for their conduct and were profiting solely by the vast experience of the past. But at the same time, they rejoined, the orthodox should remember that the ancients had tackled the religious and cere-monial questions that arose in their own days according to light that had prevailed in the past. Those of that day had not done the thinking for all times to come, with injunctions to the future generations to act in strict accordance with them. They alone had not the monopoly to think, and had not given the final man-date to acquiesce in all that they had believed. Besides, a return to the past could not being unalloyed happiness to the Parsis in the present times. The community, it was urged, cannot afford to transplant itself back to the age of the Vendidad. There was no use sticking to outworn forms and seeking to give them a new life. It was futile to attempt to support delusions, and the ortho-dox, they said, should not throw all possible shackles in the way of progress by hampering and paralyzing the well-meant efforts of the new school.

Such, in brief form, is the story of the opening of the conflict between conservative and free thought among the Parsis in In-dia, which rent the community into two sections. The rival parties, however, did not make any formal division between themselves. The reformers did not venture to contemplate so complete a break with the orthodox as would culminate in the establishment of a reformed Church. The orthodox could not excommunicate the reformers even if they would. The orthodox had to content themselves with condemning the reformers, and the reformers by satrizing the orthodox. Even to-day the main disputes over some of these vital problems remain much the same as they were nine decades ago, and the battle goes on, still to be won.

Parsi Theosophists

Inquiring minds seek a deeper meaning of life. At this period of transition, when the old practices seemed to have spent their force, and the younger generation was drifting towards in-difference in religious matters, there were other forces at work which heralded the rise of a new class of dissenters. Those of a prosaic and matter-of-fact turn of mind in the community had steadily doubted the statements that did not admit of a rational justification, and refused to believe in anything mysterious and mystical in religion. But human life cannot altogether be stripped of mystery. Rationalism is not the whole of human nature. Besides, the state of doubts and disbeliefs that prevailed in the community could not last long. Man is essentially a re-ligious being. He feels an inherent need in himself for some form of religious belief which would satisfy the yearnings of his spirit-that irrepressible heart-hunger of the human soul.

The Parsi priesthood, as custodians of the conscience of the community, zealously guarded and conserved the dogmatic teach-ings and traditions, but they were uuable to work for the adapta-tion of the traditional material to the contemporary situation. They were incapable, at the time, of helping the community in its religious crisis. Persons who thought that the rationalism of the new school ignored an essential part of human nature when it discarded the emotional side of man, to which man was indebted for some of his noblest virtues, yearned for new light. If that light did not come from within, they would welcome it from without. At this juncture the Theosophical Society opened its propaganda in India, and a number of Parsis eagerly em-braced the movement.

In the early eighties of the last century the Parsi members of the Theosophical Society entered the arena of religious controversy and gave new zest to it. They became a potent factor in shaping the religious beliefs of a section of the community through their active propaganda. Hitherto ritual ob-servances, theological dogmas, and ecclesiastical usages had oc-cupied a most conspicuous place in the religious controversies. The Parsi theosophists introduced metaphysical themes such as the nature of Being, a personal or an impersonal God, creation or emanation, rebirth, and such like for discussion. This is significant as an indication of a higher phase in religious polemics. They showed a strong tendency towards mysticism in religion. They did not flee from the sight and sound of man and withdrew themselves to the fastness of the jungle, nor did they mortify their flesh, but their code of ethics comprised the ascetic virtues, tempered by the spirit of the age.

Zoroaster and his disciples, the theosophical interpreters said, wrote in a mystic language which conveyed a double meaning. The exoteric, or surface meaning, was intended for the vulgar, and the esoteric, or inner meaning, was designed only for the initiates. The adepts of various periods were the ones who possessed the mysterious key to the chamber of hidden truths. The last of such Parsi adept was Azar Kaivan, who died at Patna in 1614. With his demise this key was lost. Occult science alone, it was asserted, could explain and vindicate the allegorical teachings of Zoroaster. Providence had blessed the founders of the Theosophical Society with the possession of a master-key that opened the secret cham-bers of the hidden knowledge of all religions. The Zoroastrian theosophists applied this key to Zoroastrianism to unravel the mysteries of its exoteric teachings. They aimed at an adjust-ment of the fundamental Zoroastrian concept according to the standard philosophy of their society, which was an eclectic sys-tem drawing its materials mostly from Hinduism and Buddhism.

The theosophists summarily rejected the method of the philologist adopted in interpreting the sacred texts. In their zeal for discovering great truths buried under the seemingly simple texts, but alleged to be pregnant with deep meaning, these esoterics often invested legends and myths with a symbolic sig-nificance, and included much in the sphere of serious literature that could be relegated to the realm of poetry. They alleged that the philologists, being bound by the fetters of literalism in the interpretation of the sacred texts, generally took a statement at its face value and adhered to the surface meaning. The theosophists chose to lean upon the miraculous and mysterious, rather than to follow the recognized canons of the method of reasoning. Consequently, the sense of proportion, critical acumen, the his-torical sense, accurate thinking, and such preliminary requisites of modern scholarship became conspicuous by. their absence in most of their interpretations. Flashes of vague thought came to be regarded as inspiration, and visions as verities.

Passage after passage in the Zoroastrian scriptures was ex-plained to signify what it did not mean in the original. The fol-lowing may be adduced as a specimen: The pastoral people in Ancient Iran had found a faithful sentinel in the dog, and that animal, as shown by the Avesta, occupied an exalted place among the Iranians from the earliest ages; three chapters of the Vendidad in fact were devoted to this indispensable companion of the household, All scholars in accord with the traditional inter-pretation have naturally taken these passages as the fragments of an old Iranian canine literature. But the theosophists branded this explanation as absurd, and discerned in the chapters an alle-gorical description of conscience and its workings. Space here precludes the citation of other examples of this kind.

When the linguists challenged such interpretation of the an-cient texts, they were informed that their inability to reconcile themselves to the new esoteric explanations was due to the fact of not having yet sufficiently developed their spiritual faculties. They were dubbed 'mere philologists,' 'dry-as-dust' grammarians. Highly pungent bitterness was marked in the controversy carried on between the two parties. The theosophists in this controversy denounced the philologists, and the philologists denounced the theosophists.

The advocacy on the part of the theosophists of the revival of the past, and their seeing in such a revival the sole panacea of communal ills, whether real or imaginary, their readiness to al-lege religious sanction for the time-hallowed customs, matched with their zeal for ritual, and their eagerness to vindicate the sacred ceremonies by giving strained allegorical interpretations to explain them, won for them the applause of the orthodox party, who cast in their lot with them. Inasmuch as the Parsi, theosophists declared that they were working to bring out the youth of the community from the, trough of materialism, and endeavoring to defend Zoroastrianism against innovations of the reformers, they were regarded as the pillars of faith and the guardians of the edifice of ceremonialism.

Avestan prayers, however unintelligible, were declared the most efficacious owing to their occult significance. We have already seen the arguments advanced by the reformers against addressing to God prayers in a language unintelligible to the sup-pliant, and we have noted the discussion that followed. We now need only notice the part that the theosophists took in the con-troversy. The syllables composed in the Avestan texts, they averred, were so mysteriously adjusted to each other in the prayers, that they produced vibrations on the ethereal plane, when pronounced. The potency of such rhythmical sound was so great that, like every good thought that flashed out with strong occult force and sent forth a good "elemental," it created forms in the ethereal world, attracted good "elementals," and repelled evil ones. Every single sentence conveyed an occult meaning, and the prayers composed in the celestial tongue of the prophet and other seers had an unspeakable efficacy conducing to the welfare of the individual concerned, but their renderings into any modern vernacular would make them totally ineffectual as prayers.

Zoroastrianism in the light of theosophy. These followers of an eclectic philosophy, and interpreters of the divine scriptures through a claimed knowledge of occult and hidden meanings, ap-plied the theosophic principles of explanation to the teachings of Zoroaster, and adapted them to the Zoroastrian theology. Such an interpretation, however, led them to credit the religion of Zoroaster with ideas that in no period of its religious history were ever included in its sphere.

When these theosophic interpreters of Zoroastrianism were reminded that the thoughts they claimed to read in the canonical Zoroastrian works were not there, they argued with a doubtful historical perspective that if they did not meet them in the plain words, in the authentic texts, it was because the twenty-one Nasks of the prophet had not been preserved. If the bulk of the Zoroastrian canon had not been irrevocably lost, they should un-doubtedly have found such doctrines to be indissolubly associated with the cardinal texts of the Zoroastrian faith. Every Iranian student knows that the historical sources and records of the teachings of the prophet that were in vogue at any particular period of Zoroastrian history have not perished altogether Some-thing of every period, whether the Gathic, Avestan, Pahlavi, or the later periods, has fortunately survived the vandalism of the conquering hordes and the ravages of time, and consequently has come down to the present day. For example, in the controversy regarding the rebirth theory, to which we shall advert below, the theosophic interpreters, having recourse to similar arguments, stated that we should have found the theory of transmigration of souls taught in the Zoroastrian works, if these had reached us intact. It might be pointed out, however, that the fragmentary works of all periods of Zoroastrian history have come down to us; they contain the authentic teachings on the life after demise, but they all persistently and systematically speak of only one bodily life on the earth, and never once suggest the theory of rebirth.

Zrvan Akarana as an impersonal God in the theosophic light. The theosophists attempted a readjustment of the Zoro-astrian doctrine of a personal God, or rather in accordance with their theory of an impersonal God. Personality, they alleged im-plied limitation and was a characteristic of the finite. A personal God meant that the godhead was a limited God, and therefore an incomplete God. In Zrvan Akarana, or Boundless Time, the Parsi theosophists saw this impersonal neuter being of whom nothing could be predicated. This supposititious being was the rootless root from which issued Ohrmazd. Ahriman was but Ohrmazd's manifested shadow. Zrvan Akarana, the primeval im-personal principle, according to their interpretation, was like a central fire from which all creation had emanated. The indi-vidual was only a vital spark, and his final resting-place was in it. Passionately loving the light, the moth finally immolated it-self in the flame; in like manner the individual had to throw off the illusory shackles of personality and be merged in the Universal, the One. This doctrine is certainly not Zoroastrian, be-cause through the whole history of the religion individuality is not an illusion. It is ever a stern fact. Personality is not an im-perfection, but it is the highest expression of life, that ultimately strives for the divine. Not the losing of individuality and the loss of the personal self, and not the weakening of personality, but the gaining and strengthening of it, is the Zoroastrian ideal. This has been the truth taught by Zoroastrianism in the striving for the highest aims comprehensible to mankind from the remot-est antiquity.

Zrvan was extolled above Ohrmazd, who was ranked by them as a mere manifestation of Time. The one was elevated by de-basing the other. The personal God who could be loved and feared, who responded to the gentle aspirations of the human heart, was dethroned to make room for a monistic principle that might answer the stern canons of cold intellectualism, but which evaporated into an unthinkable abstraction and mercilessly left its hapless votaries without a word of solace or hope. Affection, love and devotion, however, can centre about some personality only. We find in the authoritative teachings of the Zoroastrian Church that Ohrmazd knows no peer, and he always sits supreme at the head of the divine hierarchy.

These modern votaries of Zrvan were, however, not to be confounded with the Zarvanite sect of old, which looked to Zrvan Akarana as a personality as much defined as Ohrmazd. We have already seen that, in postulating impersonated Time as the orig-inator of Ohrmazd and Ahriman, the sect aimed at supplanting Zoroastrian dualism by monotheism, in order to save their re-ligion from the so-called stigma of dualism. Not so the theoso-phists, who grafted this new feature on the pure teachings of Zoroaster. They did not personify Time, but reckoned this ab-stract principle of Time as higher than Ohrmazd himself, because, in common with all mystic schools, they held the idea of an im-personal God as the highest category of philosophical thought.

Zoroastrianism declared by the thesophic claim to be in-complete without the doctrine of transmigration of souls. From first to last Zoroastrianism, like Judaism, Christianity, and Mohammedanism, shows no sign of this theory of rebirth. But this dogma occupied a pre-eminent place among the theosophists, being, in fact, one of the most conspicuous characteristics of their doctrines. To teach man to attain liberation from the bondage of rebirth was the ultimate aim of their ethics. It was not re-garded by the theosophists as one of the many solutions put for-ward by the human mind to solve the mysteries of the life after demise, but as the only rational explanation that satisfied human instinct of justice, and the only solution of the anomalies in this world. They persuaded themselves that the theory was fast becoming a recognized truth in the West, and that, at no distant date, it would be hailed as an inexorable law of nature proved with scientific certitude.

With a view to investing their state-ments with scriptural authority they tore one or two passages from their context, and basing their arguments on these, they declared that they had unearthed the theory from the labyrinth of Zoroastrianism. When the Dasturs and other Parsi scholars asserted, in accord with all Iranian scholars of the West, that in no period of the religious history of Iran was metempsychosis ever hinted at in the remotest form, and that the passages re-ferred to had no bearing upon the question, they retorted that the scholarship of the scholars must be at fault, for so great a master as Zoroaster simply could not fail to have taught this fundamental truth.

But this was not all. Enthused by a zeal for the theory, they went a step further and alleged that Zoroaster himself was an Amshaspand incarnate. This is contrary to the spirit of Zoroastrianism. The sacred books speak of the prophet as the greatest of the mortals, the most brilliant among men; even as the star Tishtar is among the infinite stars, 1 and as the noblest soul whose ideal is a leaven of righteousness to humanity. He is the highest and the greatest ideal of human perfection, the very embodiment of piety. The Gathas give a distinctly visualized image of the personality of Zoroaster. His life is surrounded by a nimbus of miracles in the later period, and most extravagant legends are woven about his personality, but after all that the human language can sing in his praise, he is simply a man, and not an arch- angel incarnate. So was he during life, and so he is after demise.

These modern successors of the Parsi Yogists of the seven-teenth century have caused several members of the community to drift towards a growing fondness for occult mystery. Many men and women, with or without higher education, are seen to-day running after any form of occultism that they come across. These continue to interpret and explain the sacred texts on the allegorical basis, with overweening presumption, common to the occultists of all ages and places, they claim to be the only cor-rect interpreters of Zoroastrianism and are busy producing a novel type of Zoroastrian ideological literature.

REVIVALIST MOVEMENTS

Awakening of the Communal Conscience

The advent of the British in India, and an era of peace, justice, and security of life and property, ushered in by them, opened a new page in the history of the Parsis. Having a ready scope, the means of adaptation, and also elasticity in their religion, they now began to assert their latent capacity, and soon emerged from the obscurity in which they had lived, to become henceforth the foremost people in India in matters educational, industrial, and social. They came in the vanguard of progress, amassed vast fortunes, and munificently gave away large sums in charity. This un-precedented economic prosperity helped the revival of learning among the Zoroastrians. The new epoch of the revival of learn-ing gave new hopes for a period of formation and life. Various educational institution had been founded, and the Parsis faced the problem of the responsibility of universal franchise in the world of letters. The average Parsi child of both the sexes en-tered the schools founded on European lines by the community during the first half of the last century, in various centres of Parsi population, and education on Western standards spread with accelerated rapidity.

The new knowledge profoundly modified the religious con-ceptions of the young. The inroads of Western ideas and culture undermined the old ideals, and modified many of the beliefs sanctified by ages. It was the opening of a new age for the Parsis, in which they witnessed the waning of the power of au-thority and the waxing of the demand for the verification of religious truths. The transition from the old to the new was bound to be disruptive. The new spirit that had taken hold of the community stirred it to its lowest depth. It threatened the community with an intellectual revolt from the new school. The reaction was bound to come, and come it did. It was violent as all reaction is apt to be, and it ended in indifferentism. The popular creed as propounded by the traditionalist exponents and orthodox formalists failed to carry conviction to their intellect. They wanted to verify their doubts and refused to believe that which, as they said, was not in accord with reason. The glowing accounts of the reward and retribution of the materialized heaven and hell ceased to act upon the imagination of the educated classes. The imaginings of Viraf failed to exert any restraining influence over the tendency to sin. The inspired visions of this seer, about the scenes of the hereafter, depicting the pleasures of the souls of the blessed in paradise and the agonies of the wicked in hell, which satisfied the spiritual cravings of their elders for ages, failed longer so to do in the case of the new generation. The waters of Ardvisur had inundated the regions of hell and quenched the blazing fire, the horrors of hell had vanished into thin air, and the apocalyptic account of Viraf no longer presented to the minds of the enlightened youth what they had to the strictly orthodox. A treatment of the unfortunate souls, such as was portrayed traditionally, seemed to them monstrous, and subverting man's idea of the goodness of Ohrmazd. They thought them to be crude and archaic. The germs of new thought were sprouting among the young, and they viewed these theological problems with a changed attitude. They gradually became estranged from all beliefs that had been instilled into them from childhood. They aimed at reconciling religion and contemporary knowledge, and bringing religious beliefs and practices into closer relation with the intellectual ways and thought. Parsi orthodoxy resented it.

An illiterate priesthood failed to satisfy the intellectual wants of the enlightened youth. The Parsi priesthood had long before degenerated into ignorance. The situation was not keenly felt so long as the laity was equally illiterate. But now when the latter sought enlightenment, the clergy had kept less and less abreast of the times. During the long period of twelve centuries, very few priests rose above mediocrity. The priest hitherto had acted as an intercessor between the layman and Ohrmazd, and through elaborate ritual had undertaken to gain for him divine help, being duly paid to recite penitential prayers for the expia-tion of the sins of the living, and to sacrifice for the purchase of paradise for the dead. The youth of the new school argued that there was no more need of the Mobad's mediation between him and his Heavenly Father. He demanded that the priest should act as a moral preceptor, a spiritual ministrant to his soul. This, in those times, the priest could not do. He could not widen his religious outlook and adapt himself to the demand of the younger generation.

The youth now grew up without religious instruction and gradually gravitated towards indifferentism. The apathy, cal-lousness, and disregard towards religion on the part of the edu-cated youth waxed stronger day by day, and culminated in an atmosphere of agnosticism that withered the beliefs in which they were brought up. Agnosticism became the threatening evil of the day.

Western Method of Scholarship in India

Up to that time the Avestan texts had been almost wholly interpreted by the Zoroastrian authorities through the help of their Pahlavi translations. The original Avestan texts had remained largely unintelligible with-out the Pahlavi version. It was not then known that the Gathas were composed in metre, much less the fact that some other minor texts were also metrical. The rudiments of Avestan gram-mar that various inflections modified the meaning of a word had been a long forgotten fact. This was due to the circumstance that, owing to the inflectional poverty of the Pahlavi language, the translators had resorted to the use of particles and very often had even dropped this only means of indicating the syntactical relation of words in a sentence, and had contented themselves with rendering an inflected Avestan word by its uninflected crude Pahlavi equivalent. Firdausi and other Moslem writers were the sole informants of the Parsi scholars regarding the ancient and legendary history of Iran. As these did not record the do-ings of the Achaemenian Kings, the Parsi community remained without any inkling of the greatness and glory of the illustrious Parsi Kings of the great Persian kingdom. European history had now for the first time startled the English-educated Parsi youth with the information that there once flourished a mighty dynasty of rulers whom the modern Parsi can claim as his kith and kin. The truth had been denied for centuries to their legitimate descen-dants in India and Persia that a Cyrus or a Darius, a Xerxes or an Artaxerxes, who had carried the Persian banner in war to the farthest ends of the world, were historically their own core-ligionists.

In vain did the august Farohar of Darius hover round the rock of Behistan for over two thousand years in pious expecta-tion of some Parsi traveller who would one day trace his steps to this hallowed place, climb the rock to read the great King's record, make it known to the world, and thus earn the royal mon-arch's blessings whispered in the solemn silence by as many tongues as there were wedges and angles in the letters of the carved inscriptions.

Such, in short, was the deplorable state of Parsi scholarship when comparative philology came to its aid from the West and opened a new era of critical study in the field of Iranian re-searches.

Introduction of the science of comparative philology among the Parsis. Since the year 1771, when that worthy pioneer of romantic renown in Iranian studies, Anquetil du Perron, pub-lished his volumes containing the first European translation of the Avesta, or Sacred Book of Zoroaster, great strides forward have been made in Europe and America in the realm of Iranian research. The field is now replete with the lasting monuments of Western scholarship whether in the department of standard editions of the sacred texts or the compilation of grammars and dictionaries or again in the preparation of scientific translations as well as in making exegetical, philological and archeological re-searches. The service that these scholars have rendered to the Parsis is greater than can ever be expressed.

To K. R. Kama, Parsi pioneer of the Iranian studies on West-ern lines in India, who had studied the Avestan texts in Europe under the German savant Spiegel, is due the credit of introducing among Parsi scholars the science of comparative philology and the scientific method of interpreting their sacred books. The inauguration of this new era belongs to the early part of the sec-ond half of the last century.

Textual criticism brings startling revelation for the Parsis. The first outcome of the critical study of the Avestan literature, as may be judged from intimations given above, was the discov-ery made by the Western scholars that the grammar, style, and internal evidence of the extant Avestan texts show that they were not composed at a single period and by one person, but that they were the products of many persons who worked at various times. Scholars such as these undertook to determine the approximate dates of the component parts of the Avesta. The Gathas were shown to be the oldest in time of composition and the authorship of a considerable portion, if not all, of these hymns was ascribed to Zoroaster himself. The prophet's work, it was said, was continued by his immediate disciples, and must have extended over a very long period after him, even though the immediate impression made by Zoroaster himself may be ac-knowledged to have become fainter in succeeding generations. The religion of the Younger Avesta had departed in certain re-spects from the religion of the Gathas, and the subsequent com-positions showed signs of degeneration both in substance and style. The simple and abstract spirit of the Gathas was blurred if not lost, and the development of the later texts tended to be-come more complex and concrete. We breathe a different atmos-phere, they declared, when we pass from the Gathic to the Later Avestan field. Nature-worship, which Zoroaster strove to sup-plant by a higher type of ethical religion, was shown to have been reinstated in these later texts. The masses could not be weaned from the beliefs that loomed large in their eyes, and thus, the scholars maintained, many practices abolished by Zoroaster were later resuscitated by the clergy.

Startling indeed were these new ideas that philological re- searches brought to the Parsis, who had been accustomed to at- tribute indiscriminately all Avestan compositions to Zoroaster himself and who never approached their own sacred books with a historical perspective.

Back to the Gathas was the war-cry of the new school. This critical estimate of their scripture by the Iranian scholars of the West greatly influenced the young Parsi scholars in India. They now hailed the Gathas as providing a self-sufficient religious system in themselves. They claimed to have discovered the only true mirror in which the genuine teachings of Zoroaster were, re-flected. The Later Avestan texts were declared to render nuga-tory the pristine purity. An exuberant outgrowth of dogmatic theology and ceremonial observances, they asserted, had sup-planted the buoyant simplicity of the Gathic teachings, and simply' represented a decline from the pure teachings of Zoroaster. The names of the Amshaspands in the Gathas were considered to be merely descriptive of the attributes of Ohrmazd. These attributes, they insisted, had crystallized into concrete beings, thus convert-ing the monotheistic religion of Zoroaster into a veritable system of polytheism. Tradition, they argued, attributed to Zoroaster doctrines that he never preached. They advocated a return to the original purity of the faith by stripping off the accretions that had gathered round the pure canon of the prophet, thus removing the haze of ignorance and bigotry that had overclouded the light of their excellent religion.

All this was highly sacrilegious to orthodox ears. Such state-ments roused the strong resentment of the community and elicited vehement protests from priests and laymen alike. The new school was assailed on all sides. More sober opinion intervened to modify the sweeping assertions, and declared that while the Gathas, of course, should be taken as the norm, there should also be admitted into the Zoroastrian canon such parts of the later scriptures as were in accord with the Gathic spirit; but whatever could not be traced to the Gathas was adventitious, and therefore not deserving of acceptance. The problem at once arose as to who was going to distinguish the authoritative from the un-authoritative and a new controversy opened amid still more bit-ter feelings.

Gathas

The salient feature of dualism in the Iranian faith has ever been the chief point assailed by the non-Zoroastrians, both in ancient and modern times, whenever they have entered into re-ligious disputations with the followers of the prophet. They have laid the doctrine of two gods to the charge of Zoroastrianism. The accidentals of the controversy have varied materially in their character at different periods, but the main point of contention has ever remained the same. We have already seen how ve-hemently the learned prelates of the Pahlavi period strove to vin-dicate this characteristic feature of the Zoroastrian teachings. Far from considering it a weak point, they hailed it the only possible solution of the problem of evil. Not so their modern descendants. The repeated attack of the Christian missionaries, and the strong influence of the Western literature, which hailed monotheism as the highest category of theology, brought about an unprecedented change in this belief; and so powerful has this influence been, that we hardly ever find even at this day any learned Parsi priest or layman marshalling arguments in vindi-cation of the doctrine. Attempts are now generally made either to explain it away by ingenious arguments or to speak of it apologetically.

Haug was the first to bring it to the notice of the Parsis that the leading idea of the Gathas was monotheism. Ahura Mazda, he declared, is the supreme godhead, who has produced the two rival principles Spenta Mainyu and Angra Mainyu as his twin spirits. Separated as they seem, they are united in action. They are indispensable to each other in the formation and conduct of the universe. They are the creative and the destroying, construc-tive and destructive powers of God, and are as inseparable from each other as day and night. The opposition rests with the two rival spirits, and nowhere in the Gathas does Angra Mainyu, the Evil Spirit, stand in direct opposition to Ahura Mazda. This fundamental distinction, he said, is lost sight of in the late period, and we find in the Vendidad that the Good Spirit Spenta Mainyu is identified with Ahura Mazda himself, and the Evil Spirit Angra Mainyu stands in direct antagonism to God. The Parsi scholars who were ever in search for some new arguments to remove the so-called weak point of their faith eagerly embraced this new explanation, which, they thought, saved the Gathas at least from the stain of dualism. If the Vendidad and other later works introduced it in the Zoroastrian theology, it was a decided fall, they claimed, from the original pure monotheism. The prophet himself never taught dualism, they argued, and it is unfair to ascribe that doctrine to him, for which the enlightened youth had to blush before modern criticism!

REFERENCES

Aogemadaecha: The Pazand and Sanskrit texts, edited and translated into German by Wilhelm Geiger. Erlangen, 1878.

Aogemadaecha: Translated into English by James Darmesteter. In Sacred Books of the East, Vol. 4, second edition.

Chatterjee, J. M.: the Ethical Conceptions of the Gatha. Navsari, 1932.

Cheyne, T. K.: Book of Psalms, its origin, and its relation to Zoroastrianism. In Semitic Studies in Memory of Rev. Dr. A. Kohut. Berlin, 1897.

Collected Sanskrit Writings of the Parsis: Part 1. Khorda-Avesta. Part 2. Ijisni. Part 3. Mainyoi Khard. Part 4. Skanda Gumani Gujara. Edited by Sheriarji D. Bharucha. Bombay, 1906-1913.

Cumont, Franz: Texts et monuments relatifs au culte de Mithra. 2 vols. Paris, 1893.

Pahlavi Zend-i Vohuman Yasht: Edited by Kaikobad A. Nosherwan. Poona, 1899.

Pavri, Jal C.: The Zoroastrian Doctrine of a Future Life. New York, 1926.

Rawlinson, George: The Five Great Monarchies of the Ancient Eastern World, Chaldea, Assyria, Babylon, Media, and Persia. 4 vols. London, 1862-1867.

Rawlinson, George: The Sixth Great Oriental Monarchy. London, 1813.

Rivayat, Persian of Hormazyar Framarz and others: Their Version with Introduction and Notes by B. N. Dhabhar. Bombay, 1932.

Rosenberg, F.: Le Livre de Zoroastre (Zaratusht-Nama) de Zartusht-i Bahram Pajdu. St. Petersburg, 1904.

Sad Dar: Translated from the Pahlavi-Pazand text by E. W. West. In *Sacred Books of the East*, vol. 24.

Sad Dar: Edited by B. N. Dhabhar. Bombay, 1909.

Sanjana, Darab P: Zarathushtra in the Gathas and the Greek and Roman Classics. Translated from the German of Geiger and Windischmann. Leipzig, 1897.

Sanjana, Rastamji E.: Zarathushtra and Zarathushtrianism in the Avesta. Leipzig, 1906.

Shatroiha-i Airan: Translated from the Pahlavi text by Jivanji Jamshedji Modi. Bombay, 1899.

Zand-i Khurtak Avistak: Pahlavi Text. Edited by B. N. Dhabhar. Bombay, 1927.

Zatsparam: Translated from the Pahlavi text by E. W. West. In *Sacred Books of the East*, vol. 5.

10

Reformers

In Zoroastrianism, whenever religion was perceived to be in danger of getting misrepresented at the hands of a few ignorant souls, reformers came out to channelize the faith away from deformations. They were concerned with the protection of the essence of religion, which is devotion to God; they did their best to rid religion of unwanted elements who tampered with its true nature and practice. The first thing the reformers did was to use the native language of the people to teach the truths of religion. These reformers also decried ostentation and hypocrisy.

REFORMERS IN EARLY PERIOD

Tiridates I of Armenia

Tiridates I was King of Armenia beginning in AD 53 and the founder of the Arshakuni Dynasty, the Armenian line of the Arsacid Dynasty. The dates of his birth and demise are unknown. His early sovereignty was marked by a brief interruption towards the end of the year 54 and a much longer one from 58 to 63. In an agreement to resolve the Roman-Parthian conflict in and over Armenia, Tiridates (who was the brother of Vologases I of Parthia) was crowned king of Armenia by the Roman king Nero in AD 66; in the future, the king of Armenia was to be a Parthian prince, but his appointment required approval from the Romans. Even though this made Armenia a client kingdom, various contemporary Roman sources thought that Nero had de facto ceded Armenia to Parthia.

In addition to being a king, Tiridates was also a Zoroastrian priest and was accompanied by other magi on his journey to Rome in AD 66. In the early 20th century, Franz Cumont speculated that Tiridates was instrumental in the development of Mithraism, which—in Cumont's view—was simply Romanized Zoroastrianism. This "continuity" theory has since been collectively refuted. Tiridates is one of the principal characters in George Frideric Handel's Radamisto and Reinhard Keiser's Octavia operas.

Darius the Great

Enthroned in Peresepolis, the magnificent city that he built, Darius I firmly grasps the royal scepter in his right hand. In the left, he is holding a lotus blossom with two buds, the symbol of royalty.

Darius, a member of the Achemenides family, rose to the throne of the Kingdom of Persia by taking part, in 522, in a plot to assassinate Smerdis, who had assumed the Kingship that same year at the demise of his brother Cambyses on his way back from Egypt. Both Cambyses and Smerdis were sons of Cyrus the Great, the founder of the Persian Kingdom. Darius, on the other hand, was a remote cousin of them. The story of the plot of Darius and six other high-ranking Persians to assassinate Smerdis, who, they pretended, was not the son of Cyrus by that name, but an impostor, a Medean magus posing for Cyrus' son, who, by their account, had been murdered earlier at the request of his own brother Cambyses, is told by Herodotus in his Histories. It offers him an opportunity to put in the mouth of three of the conspirators, when time comes to decide how tu rule the kingdom, three speeches, one in favour of democracy, one in favour of aristocratic oligarchy, the rule by a small group of persons chosen among the best citizens, and the last one, by Darius himself, who eventually prevails, in favour of monarchy, supposed to be the very best of all three regimes, each taken at its best.

If Cyrus and Cambyses built the Persian kingdom by conquering a terrritory spanning from the Ionian coast west to India east, and from Scythia, Caucasus and the southern shores of the Black and Caspian Seas north to Lybia, Egypt and the shores of the Persian Gulf south, it is Darius who organized its administration. He moved his residence to the Elamite city of Susa, which became the administrative capital of his kingdom and where he had a gigantic palace built for himself. He divided his vast kingdom into satrapies headed by Satraps and submitted to an annual tribute, and built roads across the kingdom to ease the communications required to administer such a huge territory (Herodotus in his Histories gives a description of the road leading from Sardis, the capital of Lydia, along the Ionian coast, which had become the siege of a satrapy, to Susa). He also directed the building, in his native country of Persia, of another palace at Persepolis.

But Darius was not merely an administrator and, after curbing several rebellions in various parts of the kingdom during his first year in power, he also continued the politic of expansion of his ancestors, toward the east in India, as well as toward the west and Europe, starting with Thracia. In 499, some Ionian Greek cities of the satrapy of Lydia, under the leadership of Aristagoras of Miletus, rebelled against the Persians and set fire to Sardis. It was not until 494, with the naval victory of the Persian fleet at Lade, off the shores of Miletus, and the recapture of Miletus, that the rebellion was completely curbed. Having thus subdued the Ionian Greeks, Darius set out to conquer the rest of Greece, which led to the first Persian War. But his troops were stopped by the Athenians at the battle of Marathon in 490. It was left to his son Xerxes to lead a second attempt in 480, with no more success.

Darius' sovereignty marks the apogee of the Persian Kingdom, which started to crumble by the mere fact of its size after his demise, until it was conquered by Alexander the Great.

The sovereignty of Darius spans most of the period covered by Herodotus' Histories, a part going from the middle of book III to the beginning of book VII. In the Phædrus, Plato cites Darius at the side of Solon and Lycurgus, the half legendary lawgiver of Sparta, as examples of successfull lawmakers. And in the Laws, the Athenian stranger praises Darius for the way he ruled his country, but reproaches him not to have learned from Cyrus' mistakes in raising his children, and to have done the same mistakes with his son Xerxes, that is, to let him have a pampered childhood he himself didn't have, not being the son of a King. In the Menexenus, faithful to the rules of the funeral oration he is caricaturing, he exalts the power of Darius only to give more lusters to the Athenian victory at Marathon.

REFORMERS IN MEDIEVAL PERIOD

Xerxes

Xerxes became King of Persia at the demise of his father Darius the Great in 485, at a time when his father was preparing a new expedition against Greece and had to face an uprising in Egypt. According to Herodotus, the transition was peaceful this time. Because he was about to leave for Egypt, Darius, following the law of his country had been requested to name his successor and to choose between the elder of his sons, born from a first wife before he was in power, and the first of his sons born after he became King, from a second wife, Atossa, Cyrus' daughter, who had earlier been successively wed to her brothers Cambyses and Smerdis, and which he had married soon after reaching power in order to confirm his legitimacy. Atossa was said to have much power on Darius and he chosed her son Xerxes for successor.

After quelling the revolt of Egypt, Xerxes finally decided to pursue the project of his father to subdue Greece, but made lengthy preparations for that. Among other things, remembering what had happened to Mardonius' expedition a few years earlier (his fleet had been destroyed by a tempest in 492 while trying to round Mount Athos), he ordered a channel to be opened for his fleet north of Mount Athos in Chalcidice. He also had two boat bridges built over the Hellespont near Abydus for his troop to cross the straits.

The expedition was ready to move in the spring of 480 and Xerxes himself took the lead. Herodotus gives us a colorful description of the Persian army that he evaluates at close to two million men and about twelve hundred ships. Modern historians find these figures irrealistic, if only for logistical reasons, and suppose the army was at most two hundred thousand men and the fleet no more than a thousand ships, but this still makes an impressive body for the time.

Xerxes' expedition moved by land and sea through Thracia, the fleet following the army along the coast. It didn't meet resistance until it reached Thessalia, where the Persian army defeated the Spartans and their allies at the pass of Thermopylæ while, on sea, neither the Persian nor the Athenian fleet could win the decision in the battle that took place near Cape Artemisium, along the northern coast of the island of Euboea. Because of Themistocles' decision to evacuate Athens, Xerxes managed to take the city and set fire to the temples of the Acropolis, but his fleet was soon after destroyed by the Athenian fleet of Themistocles at the battle of Salamis.

After this defeat, Xerxes returned to Asia via the Hellespont, leaving part of his army in Greece under the command of Mardonius. But the following year, after having taken Athens a second time, the Persian army was defeated, in September of 479, at Platæa, near Thebes in Boeotia, in a battle that lasted 13 days, in which Mardonius was killed while, at about the same time, what remained of the Persian fleet was destroyed by a Greek fleet under the command of the Spartan general Leutychides off Cape Mycale, a promontory of the Ionian coast, north of Miletus, facing the island of Samos. This was not the end of the war between Persia and Greece, but it was the end of the incursions of the Persian army on mainland Greece. And without a fleet, Persia had to abandon control of the sea to Athens. Xerxes died in 465, assassinated probably upon order by one of his sons, Artaxerxes, who succeeded him.

In the Laws, Plato compares Xerxes to Cambyses in that, as him, he was victim of his education at the court, unlike his father Darius, who was not a son of King. And he goes on to say that it is almost impossible for someone raised in an extremely rich family to become virtuous, and to explain thus why there was no other great King of Persia after Darius. But it is Xerxes who serves as an example to Callicles in the Gorgias to show that the stronger should have a greater share.

Kartir

Kartir Hangirpe was a highly influential Zoroastrian high-priest of the late 3rd century AD. and served as advisor to at least three Sassanid kings. Kartir was probably instrumental in promoting the cause of Mazdaism (as opposed to Zurvanism, the other - now extinct - branch of Zoroastrianism), for in his inscription at Naqsh-e Rajab, Kartir makes plain that he has decided that there is a heaven and there is a hell, thus putting himself at odds with the principles of (fatalistic) Zurvanism. Nonetheless, it was during the sovereignty of Shapur I to whom Kartir was first appointed advisor - that Zurvanism appears to have developed as a cult, and this contradiction remains an issue of scholastic dispute.

Simultaneously, Kartir is also considered to have been a significant force in an iconoclastic movement that would result in the loss of favour of the shrine cults, an alien (to Indo-Iranian religious tradition) form of worship inherited from the Babylonians and instituted six centuries earlier by Artaxerxes II as an instrument for tax collection. It was during Kartir's time as high-priest that the shrines were - by law - stripped of their statues, and then either abandoned or converted into fire temples.

According to his own inscriptions, Kartir rose to power during the sovereignty of Shapur I, to whom he served as advisor and accompanied on travels. Shapur's son Hormizd I appointed Kartir Moabadan-Moabad, 'priest of priests', a position Kartir ruthlessly used to promote his own position and to punish lower-ranking priests whose opinions he considered contrary to his own. Under subsequent kings, Kartir called for the persecution of adherents of other religions, in particular Manichaeans, whose prophet Mani was sentenced to demise by Bahram I, very likely on the instigation of Kartir and even though Shapur I had previously been a patron of the prophet. The persecution ceased during the sovereignty of Narseh, probably after the demise of the high-priest. Kartir is not well attested in sources other than his own inscriptions on the Ka'ba-i Zartosht (at Naqsh-e Rustam) and at Naqsh-e Rajab.

Azar Kayvan

Azar Kayvan was a Zoroastrian high priest of Istakhr and native of Fars who emigrated to the Gujarat in Mughal India during the sovereignty of the King Akbar and became the founder of a Zoroastrian school of ishraqiyyun or Illuminationists. Exhibiting features of a Zoroastrianized Sufi order, this school became known as the Sepassian.

Details regarding Azar Kayvan's life are scanty and are mainly culled from the hagiographical literature of the school. This hagiography places Azar Kayvan, son of Azar Gashasb, and his ancestry back to Sasan the Fifth then through Sasan the First to the Kayanids, Gayomart, and finally to Mahabad, the figure who appeared at the very beginning of the great cycle of prophecy, according to the "Bible of the Prophets of Ancient Iran," and who seems to be none other than the primordial Adam. His mother was named Shirin; her ancestry goes back to Khosrow I Anushiravan. According to the Dabestan-i-Mazahib, as a young boy Azar Kayvan showed signs of his calling to the contemplative life.

Through dreams and visions he received the teaching of the ancient sages of Iran, which allowed him to give extraordinary replies to questions which were asked of him at the madrasa where he was a student, and which won him the nickname Zu'l-'Olum (master of the sciences). Internal references in the biography by his devotees allow us to determine that his residence was at Estakhr (about a hundred kilometers north of Shiraz), where he spent the first thirty or forty years of his life in contemplation and where he assembled his first assembly of disciples.

Around 1570, drawn by the religious revival which was taking place in India around the King Akbar, he left with them to settle down in the town of Patna in the Gujarat, where he lived until he died at around eighty-five years of age. Amongst his students, certain of these hagiographical sources place key Shi'ite Muslim theosophical figures of the Safavid philosophical revival at Isfahan within his circle.

Notably among these figures was Shaykh Baha' al-Din Amili and Mir Findiriski, on whose behest the latter seems to have translated a major Tantric yogic text from Sanskrit into Persian. According to some scholars, Dastur Meherji Rana, who had influenced Akbar and founded the famous lineage of Parsi high priests at Navsari, was a disciple of Azar Kayvan.

REFORMERS IN MODERN PERIOD

Maneckji Nusserwanji Dhalla

Maneckji Nusserwanji Dhalla also abbreviated M. N. Dhalla, was a Zoroastrian priest and religious scholar.Dhalla is best known for his criticism of the orthodox factions within the Parsi community. In particular, he was stringently opposed to the excessive ritualization of religious practice, including that of the use of the Towers of Silence. In his autobiography, he was also critical of the orthodox refusal to accept converts, noting that "the permanent blockade to an influx from outside, the abandoning of the fold by an increasing number of both men and women, and the ever-falling birth-rate of the community.

Maneckji Dhalla was born on September 22, 1875 in Surat, India into a family of Godavara priests. At age 3, he was sent with his father Nusserwanji Dhalla to Karachi (then a city in the Sindh province of British India, and today lies in Pakistan), where his father had subsequently employed.

In 1890, at the age of 15, Dhalla began his training for the priesthood. Shortly thereafter he interrupted his studies in order to work and so augment the family's meagre income. In 1894, Dhalla became editor of a monthly magazine Goolshan-e-Danesh. Two years later, Dhalla acquired ownership of the magazine but was forced to shut it down when funds ran out a few months later. The debt incurred would remain with him for many years.

Dhalla completed his clerical training on March 21, 1895 at the age of 20 and his first lecture as a full-fledged priest was on atash, fire. In the next three years, he published six booklets (in the Gujarati language) on various aspects of the Zoroastrian religion. On September 21, 1900, just shy of his 25th birthday, Dhalla delivered his first public lecture in Bombay (present day Mumbai), the first of what would become a lecture tour of the Indian subcontinent.

The lecture series made him famous among the Parsi community, and in August 1901 Dhalla was accepted at the postgraduate degree program in Avestan and Pahlavi studies at the Sir Jamsetjee Jejeebhoy Madressa in Bombay. He graduated in 1904, having completed the five-year course in just over three.

In May 1905 and with the financial support of Parsi, Dhalla continued his studies at Columbia University in New York City, where he studied under the personal tutelage of A. V. Williams Jackson, an authority on the Avestan language. Even with the preparatory assistance of Shapurji Saklatvala and Jivanji Jamshedji Modi, New York was initially quite a culture shock for Dhalla, who until his arrival in the United States had never even worn fosovereignty attire.

Nonetheless, and with great pecuniary discipline, for the next three years Dhalla studied Iranian languages and Sanskrit as majors with minors in philology and philosophy. He received a Master's degree in 1906. Following the publication of his thesis on The Nyaishes or Zoroastrian Litanies, Dhalla was awarded a Ph.D. in May 1908.

The experience at Columbia University gave Dhalla a new outlook on life and he began observing religious literature from a new angle. He renounced conventional religion and his fascination for ritualistic religion faded. He now considered ethics as the highest form of religion and embraced the path of devotion. His antagonism for western culture turned to amity. Although it would be later said that his time at Columbia had made him felt attracted to mysticism, Dhalla unambiguously says the opposite in his own autobiography.

On April 22, 1914 Dhalla and his wife again sailed again for the United States, where Dhalla was to have his book Zoroastrian Theology published. While there, Dhalla delivered a series of lectures on 'The Culture of the East' under the chairmanship of Williams Jackson.

In September 1921 Dhalla, accompanied by his wife and son (Nariman, who would eventually also study at Columbia), again proceeded to New York, this time to have his book Zoroastrian Civilization published. On the way, the family also spent four months in Iran and Iraq, where Dhalla again gave a series of lectures. Although Dhalla was appalled at the living conditions (not just of Zoroastrians), he found that the still-medieval infrastructure afforded him with opportunities for closer contacts with the people that he would have had with more modern forms of transportation. In New York, Dhalla delivered lectures whenever the opportunity arose. Following the publication of his book, Dhalla and family returned to Karachi via London, Paris, Berlin, Vienna, Milan, Rome, and Naples, and felt the effects of the war that had ended only three years previously. Following a five-week layover in Bombay, they returned to Karachi in July 1922.

In 1929, Dhalla journeyed again to New York to attend Columbia University's 175th anniversary celebrations, and at which he received an honorary Doctor of Letters (Litt.D.). His book Our Perfecting World: Zarathushtra's Way of Life was subsequently published there and he again delivered lectures. On his return journey – this time eastwards – he was surprised to discover that he was known in Japan. It turned out that a newspaper article on him had recently been published. Dhalla was upgraded to a first class cabin for the onward journey to Karachi.

In June 1935, Dhalla was awarded the title of Shams-ul Ulema by the British colonial government. In January 1938, Dhalla again travelled to New York, where his magnum opus The History of Zoroastrianism was then published.

On June 24, 1942 his wife Cooverbai died of a stomach affliction. She was 65. Dhalla continued to write and give lectures until 1954. He died in 1956, aged 79. He was succeeded as High Priest of Karachi by Godrej Sidhwa.

Godrej Sidhwa

Ervad Godrej Sidhwa was born in Karachi, Pakistan, in 1925, and studied Avesta, Pahalvi, Persian & Pazend languages, plus Ancient Iranian literature at M.F. Cama Athornan Institute, Andheri, Mumbai, for 6 years. He got initiated into the Zoroastrian priesthood by going through the Navar and Maratab initiation ceremony from Iranshah Atash Behram, Udvada, India. His initiation as a priest accounts for the "Ervad" ('Reverend') title.

Godrej has been the instructor of Zoroastrianism and Ancient Iranian History at the B.V.S. Parsi High School and Mama Parsi Secondary School, Karachi, for the last 45 years. He was appointed as the Honorary Lecturer in Zoroastrian Theology at colleges in Karachi for the Zoroastrian students. He was also appointed as Examiner in Zoroastrian Theology by the University of Karachi, Pakistan, for the Bachelor's degree program. After the demise of Dasturji Dr. M. N. Dhalla he took up all the duties of the late Dasturji, in the religious as well as the social areas.

Ervad Sidhwa has lectured on Zoroastrian Theology in India, Pakistan, Iran, Canada, UK, USA and UAE. He has also lectured on Zoroastrianism at University of California, Berkeley. On several occasions he has been invited by the Government of Pakistan to discuss the Human Rights and problems faced by religious minorities in Pakistan.

He is the Honorary Secretary of The Karachi Parsi Anjuman Trust Fund, Karachi Athornan Mandal, and Joint Honorary Secretary of Dr. Dhalla Memorial Institute since its inception in 1965. He is also a jury delegate of Karachi Parsi Matrimonial Court, Government of Sindh, Pakistan, since 1960.

Meher Baba

Meher Baba was an Indian mystic and spiritual master who publicly declared in 1954 that he was the Avatar of the age. He led a normal childhood, showing no particular inclination toward spiritual matters, until age of 19, when a short contact with the Muslim holy woman Hazrat Babajan triggered a seven-year process of spiritual transformation. He contacted other spiritual figures he called "the five perfect masters," and settled in Sakori with Upasni Maharaj before beginning his public work. The name Meher Baba, meaning "Compassionate Father," was given to him by his first followers.

From 1925 to the end of his life, Meher Baba maintained silence, and communicated by means of an alphabet board or by unique hand gestures. He spent long periods in seclusion, often fasting, but would intersperse these periods with wide-ranging travels, public gatherings, and works of charity, including working with lepers, the poor, and the insane. He gathered numerous Western followers during several world tours, which he continued despite serious car accidents in the US and India. He wrote books on metaphysics (God Speaks) and on the life of the spirit (Discourses). For several years beginning in 1949, he traveled incognito about India in what he called "The New Life." On February 10, 1954, Meher Baba declared that he was the Avatar (an incarnation of God).

Concerned by an increasing use of LSD and other psychedelic drugs, in 1966 Meher Baba addressed their use and discredited any alleged spiritual benefits. Despite deteriorating health, he continued his "universal work," which included fasting, seclusion, and meditation, until he died on January 31, 1969. His samadhi (tomb-shrine) in Meherabad, India has become a place of international pilgrimage.

Meher Baba's metaphysical views are most notably described in his books Discourses and God Speaks. His cosmology incorporates concepts and terms from Vedanta, Sufism, and Christianity. Meher Baba upheld the concept of nonduality, the view that diverse creation, or duality, is an illusion and that the goal of life is conscious realization of the absolute Oneness of God inherent in all animate and inanimate beings and things. Meher Baba compares God's original state to an infinite, shoreless ocean which has only unconscious divinity — unaware of itself because there is nothing but itself. From this state, God had the "whim" to know Himself, and asked "Who am I?" In response to this question, creation came into existence. In this analogy, what was previously a still, shoreless Ocean now stirred, forming innumerable "drops" of itself or souls.

According to Baba, each soul pursues conscious divinity by evolving: that is, experiencing form in seven "kingdoms" — stone/metal, vegetable, worm, fish, bird, animal, and human. The soul gathers sanskaras (impressions) in each form; these impressions lead to further evolution expressed by taking new, more complex forms. With each new form, increasing consciousness is gained, until the soul experiences and discards forms from all the evolutionary kingdoms. The final form of the soul's evolution is the human form. Only in the human form can the soul experience its own divinity, by entering into involution, through which it gradually eliminates all impressions which cause the appearance of separateness from God.

Baba asserts that in the human form, the soul becomes subject to rebirths, the "involuntary process of assocation and disassociation of consciousness". The purpose of rebirth is to provide the opportunity for liberation from illusion. The soul reincarnates innumerable times in all conditions of life encompassing the whole range of human experience (e.g. man/woman, rich/poor, powerful/weak, etc.).

Eruch Jessawala

Eruch Byramshaw Jessawala born in Bombay, India, was a close disciple of the silent Indian master Meher Baba, and one of his mandali (close disciples). Eruch was also the primary interpreter of Meher Baba's alphabet board, and later his unique sign language.

Eruch was born in Bombay to Zoroastrian parents, Beheram and Gaimai Jessawala. His father Beheram was an engineer with a high post in the Indian government in Nagpur, the capital of central provinces at that time. Due to constant relocations of his father, Eruch was placed in an orthodox Zoroastrian boarding school in Nashik, India at the age of 6. When his father eventually bought an estate, Eruch was transferred to a Catholic school at the age of 8 where he excelled as a student, eventually planning to study engineering like his father.

According to Eruch the first time he remembered meeting Meher Baba was in 1925 at the age of nine on a trip with his family to Ahmednagar. Twelve years later, while Eruch was preparing to study engineering, Meher Baba called him to Panchgani and asked him, "Will you leave everything and come to be with me?" To this Eruch answered, "By your grace anything is possible." Thus Eruch Jessawala joined Meher Baba as his disciple in 1938 at the age of 21.

Meher Baba was silent for 44 years, from 1925 until his passing in 1969. Eruch Jessawala was Meher Baba's main interpreter, interpreting both his English language alphabet board and later his sign language. Eruch Jessawala also dictated from the alphabet board Meher Baba's major book God Speaks, wrote the ninth chapter of that book working from a chart by Meher Baba under Baba's direct supervision, and wrote the book's conclusion. Eruch's stories of his life with Meher Baba were also published during his lifetime.

Eruch survived Meher Baba's demise by 32 years, continuing to live at Meherazad and working for the Avatar Meher Baba Perpetual Public Charitable Trust in the trust office in Ahmednagar until his own demise in 2001. He continued to be an inspiration for followers and disciples of Meher Baba from the east and west until the end. Eruch was well known for his acute talent for telling stories of Meher Baba's life, and his books are taken from those accounts.

REFERENCES

Arda Viraf: The Pahlavi text, edited and translated by Hoshangji Jamaspji Asa, Martin Hang, and E. W. West. Bombay, 1872.

Arda Viraf Nameh: The Original Pahlavi Text with Persian version of Zartosht Behrain in verse, edited by Kaikhusru J. Jamasp Asa. Bombay, 1902.

Avesta: The Sacred Books of the Parsis. Edited by Karl F. Geldner. Stuttgart, 1885-1896. (For Yt. 22-24 and the Avestan Fragments see N. L. Westergaard's Zendavesta, Copenhagen, 1852-1854.).

Avesta: Translated into French by C, de Harlez. Livre Sacré du Zoroastrisme. 2 éd. Paris, 1881.

Bradke, P. von: Dyaus, Asura, Ahura Mazda. Halle, 1885.

Brodbeck, A.: Zoroaster. Leipzig, 1893.

Buch, M. A.: Zoroastrian Ethics. Baroda, 1919.

Bundahishn: Translated from the Pahlavi text by E. W. West. In *Sacred Books of the East*, vol. 5.

Bundahishn: An Untranslated Chapter of the Bundehesh. Edited and translated by Jivanji Jamshedji Modi, in Journal of the Bombay Branch of the Royal Asiatic Society. Bombay, 1902.

Ganj-i Shayigan: The Pahlavi text, edited and translated by Peshutan Dastur Behramji Sanjana, Bombay, 1885.

Gatha: Translated into English by J. M. Chatterjee. Navsari, 1933.

Gathas: Translated into English by K. E. Punegar. In *the Journal of the K. R. Cama Oriental Institute*, No. 12. Bombay, 1928.

Geiger, Wilhelm: Civilization of the Eastern Iranians in Ancient Times. Translated from the German by Darab Dastur Peshutan Sanjana. 2 vols. London, 1885, 1886.

Geiger, W., and Windischmann, Fr.: Zarathushtra in the Gathas and in the Greek and Roman Classics. Translated by Darab P. Sanjana. Leipzig, 1897.

Moulton, James H.: The Treasure of the Magi. Oxford, 1917.

Namakiha-i Manushchihar: The Epistles of Manushchihar. Edited by B. N. Dhabhar. Bombay, 1912.

Neriosengh's Sanskrit Ubersetzung des Yasna: von F. Spiegel. Leipzig, 1861.

Nirangastan: Translated from the Avesta-Pahlavi text by S. J. Bulsara. Bombay, 1915.

Oriental Studies in honour of Cursetji Erachji Pavri: London, 1933.

Pahlavi Zend-i Vohuman Yasht: Edited by Kaikobad A. Nosherwan. Poona, 1899.

Pavri, Jal C.: The Zoroastrian Doctrine of a Future Life. New York, 1926.

11

Major Sects

Zoroastrianism had its factions, sects and different schools of thought, particularly during the tolerant periods of the Median, Achaemenian and Parthian kingdoms (708 BC. to 224 AD.) but they endured a setback during the secular rule of the Sassanians (224-652 AD.). The ruling school prevailed. It is this school that has survived with its beliefs, customs and customs after the downfall of the Sassanian Kingdom to this day. There are three major sects, the Shahenshahis of India known as Parsis, the Qadimis of Iran, and the Faslis. The main difference is the calendar issue. The Shahenshahis and the Qadimis use a "non-intercalating" calendar of 360 days. However, their New Years are one full month of 30 days apart. The Faslis have a complete calendar of 365 days, 5 hours, 48 minutes and 45.5 seconds. The year begins on the first day of spring, on about 21 March. The Parsis have three sub-divisions of "Traditionalists." They are the common disciple, the Ilm-e Khshnumists, and the Pandole Group. The last two are occult schools. The Iranian Zoroastrians, all following the Fasli calendar, have no sub-divisions.

The reform movement begun in the nineteenth century by Parsi scholars has led Zoroastrians to turn to the fundamental teachings of Zarathushtra as given in the Gathas. Iranian Zoroastrians have almost all become reformers. The reform movement among Parsis, although begun by them, has been sluggish. Zoroastrian settlers in Western countries are turning more and more to reformation.

The three sects in Zoroastrianism are Restorationists, Progressives and Isolationist, or Closed Faith. In general, of all three groups, the breakdown as to the Avesta is as follows:

Most Progressives accept some of the Yashts, the Vispered and the Haptanghaiti as obligatary. Some do not. No liberal believer accepts the Vendidad, nor the Pahiavi writings as binding.

The Isolationists are almost solely Parsis and called themselves Traditional Mazdayasnies. They claim to believe in all the so called twenty-one Nasks of the Sassanian, recompiled Avesta, most of which are not existing. (the Sassanian recompiled the Avesta and by their own admissions, elected themselves the arbitrators of what to include and what not to include in it). In practice they do not keep most of the regulations of the Vendidad. Their main interest is to avoid conversions, so that their caste is not polluted by the inferior raavans of Non-Zarathushtis (Raavan is the Parsi perversion of the Old Avestan Urvan, which means self, or spirit).

The Restorationists simply have retorted to the only compositions of Zarathushtra. In doing so they have detected many things. Main among them is that the New Avesta directly contravenes the teachings of Zarathushtra in many instances and violates the spirit in which they were given. They also fail to find no elaborate rites in the Gathas. So the Restorationists make Zarathushtra's Gathas, the sole rule and authority for faith and practice. The Haptanghaiti and other sherds in Old Avestan have value only as far as they elaborate on some Gathic point and not directly oppose a Gathic teaching. The Visperad is seen as a description of the Festivals and exercises of some early Zarathushtis, but not in anyway definitive. The Yashts and Nyashes are seen as largely unaccepted, as are the Vendidad and the Pahlavi writings.

Reformation is spreading among Western Zoroastrians, but North America has groups of both Parsis and Iranians. Some, such as the the Zarathushtrian Assembly, are avowedly reformist, and some are avowedly traditionalist (such as the Traditional Mazdayasni Zoroastrian Anjuman).

SHAHENSHAHIS

A Shahenshahis is a fellow member of a Zoroastrian society based primarily in the Indian subcontinent. All Shahenshahis outside of India name either India or Pakistan as their home country or country of hereditary origin. Shahenshahis are came from Persian Zoroastrians who migrated to the Indian subcontinent over 1,000 years ago. More recent Zoroastrian immigrants are known as Iranis.

The term ' Shahenshahis ' is not evidenced in Indian Zoroastrian texts until the seventeenth century. Until that time, such texts consistently use either Zarthoshti, Zoroastrian or Behdin. The twelfth century Sixteen Shlokas, a Sanskrit text in praise of the Parsis and apparently written by a Hindu is the earliest documented use of the term as a symbol for the Indian Zoroastrians.

The term 'Parsi' was used by the Indians to denote anyone from Greater Iran, regardless of whether they were actually ethnical Persians or not. In any case, the term 'Parsi' is itself "not necessarily an indication of their Iranian or 'Persián' origin, but rather as indicator - apparent as several properties - of ethnic identity". Moreover, (if heredity were the only factor in a determination of ethnicity) the Parsis - per Qissa - would count as Parthians. The term Parsiism (or Parsiism) is characteristicd to Anquetil-Duperron, who in the 1750s - when the word Zoroastrianism had yet to be coined - made the first elaborate report of the Parsis and of Zoroastrianism, therein mistakenly presuming that the Parsis were the only remaining followers of the faith.

Although the Parsis in the first place migrated from Persia, most Indian Parsis have lost social or familial ties to Persians. Many do not share language or recent history with them. Over the centuries since the first Zoroastrians arrived in India, the Parsis have incorporated themselves into Indian society while simultaneously maintaining their own distinct customs and customs (and thus ethnic identity). This in turn has given the Parsi society a rather peculiar standing - they are Indians in terms of national affiliation, language and history, but not typically Indian (constituting only 0.006% of the total population) in terms of consanguinity or cultural, behavioural and religious practices.

The definition of who is (and who is not) a Parsi is a matter of great argument within the Zoroastrian society in India. Generally accepted to be a Parsi is a person who is a) directly descended from the original Persian refugees; and b) has been formally admitted into the Zoroastrian faith. In this sense, Parsi is an ethno-religious designator.

Some members of the society additionally contend that a child must have a Parsi father to be eligible for initiation into the faith, but this assertion is regarded by most to be a infringement of the Zoroastrian principles of gender equality, and may be a remnant of an old legal definition of Parsi.

An often quoted legal definition of Parsi is based on a 1909 ruling (since invalidated) that not only specified that a person could not become a Parsi by converting to the Zoroastrian faith (which was the case in question), but also noted that "the Parsi society consists of:

- Parsis who are came from the original Persian emigrees and who are born of both Zoroastrian parents and who profess the Zoroastrian faith.
- Iranis from Persia confessing to the Zoroastrian faith.

The offsprings of Parsi fathers by alien mothers who have been duly and properly accepted into the faith.

This definition has since been overruled several times. The equivalence principles of the Indian Constitution invalidate the patrilineal restrictions expressed in the third clause. The second clause was contested and overturned in 1948. On appeal in 1950, the 1948 ruling was continued and the entire 1909 definition was deemed an dictum, that is, a collateral opinion and not legally binding (re-affirmed in 1966).

Nevertheless, the opinion that the 1909 ruling is legally holding continues to persist, even among the better-read and moderationist Parsis. In the February twenty-one, 2006 editorial of the Parsiana, the fortnightly of the Parsi Zoroastrian society, the editor noted that several adult children born of a Parsi mother and non-Parsi father had been inducted into the faith and that their choice "to embrace their mother's faith speaks volumes for their commitment to the faith." In recalling the ruling, the editor noted that although "they are legally and religiously full-fledged Zoroastrians, they are not regarded Parsi Zoroastrians in the eyes of the law" and hence "legally they may not avail of [fire temples] specified for Parsi Zoroastrians" (Parsiana 2006).

The Ilm-e-Kshnoom

The Ilm-e-Kshnoom (science of ecstasy) is a school of Parsi-Zoroastrian doctrine established on a mystical and occult, rather than literal, rendition of religious texts. As per the disciples of the sect, they are followers of the Zoroastrian faith as preserved by a clan of 2000 persons called the Saheb-e-Dilan ('Masters of the Heart') who are said to live in complete isolation in the hilly recesses of the Caucasus (alternatively, in the Alborz range, around Mount Damavand).

There are few apparent indications that a Parsi power be a follower of the Kshnoom. Although their Kusti prayers are very similar to those used by the Fassalis, like the rest of the Parsi society, the followers of Kshnoom are divided with respect to which calendar they maintain. There are also other small differences in their recitation of the liturgy, such as repeating of some sections of the longer prayers. Nevertheless, the Kshnoom are extremely conservative in their ideology, and prefer isolation even with respect to other Parsis.

The biggest society of followers of the Kshnoom lives in Jogeshwari, a suburb of Bombay, where they have their own Fire temple (Behramshah Nowroji Shroff Daremeher), their own housing settlement (Behram Baug) and their own newspaper (Parsi Pukar). There is a smaller density of disciples in Surat, where the sect was founded in the last decades of the 19th century.

At its core, the struggle is a manifestation of centuries-old anxieties and fears of assimilation and the loss of identity. However, in questions of practice, the conflict is (almost) pedantic. In cities with larger Parsi communities, there is almost certainly at least one fire temple run by priests that are not exclusionist. In any event, the Zoroastrian religion does not dictate worship in a fire temple, so in theory, a Zoroastrian who has been banned from entry to a particular temple could worship from his/her own home.

It has been traditional, in Mumbai and Karachi at least, for dead Parsis to be taken to the Towers of Silence where the corpses would quickly be eaten by the city's vultures. The reason given for this exercise is that earth, fire and water are all regarded as sacred elements, which should not be defiled by the dead. Therefore, burial and cremation have always been forbidden in Parsi culture. The problem today though is that in Mumbai and Karachi the population of vultures has been drastically reduced, due to broad urbanisation, as well as due to poisoning by the anti-inflammatory drug diclofenac which is often given to humans and cattle. As a result without vultures the bodies of the departed are taking too long to decompose and this has upset certain sectors of the society. Solar panels have been installed in the Towers of Silence to speed up the decomposition process but this has only been partially successful. There is a debate raging among the society as to whether the prohibition on buryings and incinerations should not be lifted. A committee comprising both liberal and conservative Parsis was set up to try and find an answer to the problem.The tower of silence in Mumbai is located at Malabar Hill. It has been said that residents of Malabar Hill and surrounding areas have also complained against this practice. Parsis are now given an option of burying versus the tower of silence demise rite.

QADIMIS OF IRAN

Qadimis in Iran have had a long history, being the oldest religious society of that nation to last to the present-day. Prior to the Muslim Arab invasion of Persia (Iran), Zoroastrianism had been the main faith of the Persian people.

Since the decline of the Sassanid Zoroastrian kingdom by the Arab subjugation of Persia, Qadimis in Iran have faced much religious favouritism including forced conversions, torments, as well as being identified as najis and impure to Muslims, making them unfit to live alongside Muslims therefore driving them to evacuate from cities and face major sanctions in all senses.

Although the ancestries of Qadimis are ill-defined, it was during the Sassanid period that it gained far-flung acceptance, and many of the Sassanid kings were at least to some extent Qadimis. Qadimis enjoyed royal sanction during the Sassanid era but no traces of it remain beyond the tenth century.

Qadimis regarded Ahura Mazda not the transcendental Creator, but one of two equal-but-opposite deities under the domination of Zurvan. The fundamental Qadimis belief made Ahura Mazda (Middle Persian: Ohrmuzd) and Angra Mainyu (Ahriman) twin brothers that had co-existed for all time.

Commencing from the early twentieth century, Tehran, the nation's capital, experienced rapid movements from all Iranian minorities. The Qadimis population increased from about fifty merchants in 1881 to 500 by 1912.

During the sovereignty of the Pahlavi dynasty, Qadimis changed from being one of the most oppressed minorities in Iran to a symbol of Iranian patriotism. This belief carried on all the way through the 1979 Islamic revolution of Iran when Ayatollah Sadughi in defence of Qadimis declared that "We Muslims are like the branches of a tree, if our roots are cut off, we shall shrivel up and die", also the last prime minister before the revolution Shapour Bakhtiar held an anti-Khomeini meeting in Los Angeles on the day of the Qadimis Mehregan festival (1980), in tribute to true nationalism.

The Iranian revolution of 1979 and the ultimate establishment of the new theocratic Islamic Republic posed many initial setbacks for religious minorities. Today, the Qadimis society in Iran is estimated by some to number some 22,000 - half the size of that in subsistence before the 1979 Islamic revolution.

Like the Armenian, Assyrian and Persian Jewish communities, Qadimis are formally accepted and on the grounds of the 1906 Constitution allocated one seat in the Iranian Parliament, currently held by Esfandiar Ekhtiari Kassnavieh.

Zurvanism

Zurvanism is a now-finished branch of Zoroastrianism that had the deity Zurvan as its First Principle (primordial creator deity). Zurvanism is also known as Zurvanite Zoroastrianism. In Zurvanism, Zurvan is the hypostasis of Time (and Space). The name, as it appears in Middle Persian, comes from Avestan zruvan-, 'time', with the same range of significance as in the English language. The name "Zurvan", like 'time', also appears in other belief systems, but in those faiths are only nominally related to the Zurvan of Zurvanism.

Unlike Mazdean Zoroastrianism, Zurvanism regarded Ahura Mazda not the otherworldly Creator, but one of two equal-but-opposite divinities under the domination of Zurvan. The fundamental Zurvanite belief made Ahura Mazda (Middle Persian: Ohrmuzd) and Angra Mainyu (Ahriman) twin brothers that had co-existed for all time.

Though the particulars of the origin and growth of Zurvanism remain cloudy, it is generally accepted that Zurvanism was a branch of greater Zoroastrianism; that the philosophy of Zurvan was a sacerdotal response to resolve a perceived inconsistency in the religious texts and that this philosophy was probably brought in during the second half of the Achaemenid era.

Zurvanism revelled in royal authorization during the Sassanid era (226-651 AD.) but no traces of it remain beyond the tenth century. Although Sassanid era Zurvanism was surely influenced by Hellenic doctrine, whether Zoroastrian Zurvan was an adaption of an antecedent or foreign divinity of Time has not been once and for all established.

Non-Zoroastrian histories of typically Zurvanite notions were the first traces of Zoroastrianism to reach the west, which misguided European scholars to reason out that Zoroastrianism was a monist faith.

The earliest evidence of the cult of Zurvan is discovered in the History of Theology, attributed to Eudemus of Rhodes. As quoted in Damascius's Difficulties and Solutions of First Principles (sixth AD.), Eudemus reports a faction of the Persians that regarded Space/Time to be the primaeval "father" of the rivals Oromasdes of Light and Arimanius of Darkness.

Most of what is known of Zurvanism throughout the Sassanid period is from contemporary Christian Armenian and Syriac references. The Kartir inscription at Ka'ba-i Zartosht and the edict of Mihr-Narse are the only contemporary native sources that reveal anything about Zurvanism, the latter being the only native evidence from that period that is honestly

Zurvanite. The few other Persian language commentaries on the faith of the Sassanid period were all compiled after the fall of the kingdom.

Although the Armenian and Syriac sources describe the faith of the Sassanids as having been clearly Zurvanite, the later aboriginal commentaries are mainly Mazdean and with only one exclusion do not mention Zurvan at all. Of the remaining so-called Pahlavi texts only two, the Menog-i Khrad and the Selections of Zatspram reveal a Zurvanite propensity. The latter is regarded to be the latest Zoroastrian text that provides any evidence of the cult of Zurvan. The foreign accounts of the Zurvanite father-of-twins doctrine is supported by only a single Persian language source, the Ulema-i Islam, that, nevertheless the title, is evidently by a Zoroastrian.

There is no clue of any worship of Zurvan in any of the textbooks of the Avesta, even though the texts (as they live today) are the result of a Sassanid era editing. Zaehner proposes that this is because the person Sassanid sovereigns were not always Zurvanite and that Mazdean Zoroastrianism just happened to have the whip hand during the important period that the canon was finally written down. In the texts compiled prior to the Sassanid period, Zurvan appears twice, as both an abstract notion and as a minor divinity, but there is no evidence of a cult. In Yasna 72.10 Zurvan is invoked in the company of Space and Air (Vata-Vayu) and in Yasht 13.56, the plants grow in the manner Time has ordained as per the will of Ahura Mazda and the Amesha Spentas. Two other points of reference to Zurvan are also present in the Vendidad, but though these are late additions to the canon, they again do not demonstrate any proof of a cult. Zurvan does not appear in any listing of the Yazatas.

The beginnings of the religious cult of Zurvan remain debated. One view believes Zurvanism to have formulated out of Zoroastrianism as a reaction to the liberalisation of the late Achaemenid era form of the faith. Another belief proposes that Zurvan existed as a pre-Zoroastrian divinity that was incorporated into Zoroastrianism. The third opinion is that Zurvanism is the product of the contact between Zoroastrianism and Babylonian/Byzantine faiths.

Surity nevertheless is that by the Sassanid era (226–651 AD.), the divinity "Infinite Time" was well founded and enjoyed royal backing. It was during the sovereignty of Sassanid King Shapur I (241-272) that Zurvanism appears to have developed as a cult and it was presumably in this period that Greek and Indic notions were introduced to Zurvanite Zoroastrianism.

It is nonetheless not known whether Sassanid era Zurvanism and Mazdaism were separate factions, each with their own establishment and priesthood, or simply two dispositions within the same body. That Mazdaism and Zurvanism contended for attention can been guessed from the works of Christian and Manichean polemicists, but the doctrinal incompatibilities were not so utmost "that they could not be settled under the broad aegis of an imperial church."

Following the decline of the Sassanid Kingdom in the seventh century, Zoroastrianism was step by step replaced by Islam. The former continued to live but in an increasingly decimated state and the remaining Zoroastrians appear to have bit by bit returned to the Mazdean philosophy prescribed by Zoroaster in the Gathas. By the 10th century, Zurvanism had ceased to exist, leaving Mazdaism the sole left over form of Zoroastrianism.

Why the cult of Zurvan disappeared (while Mazdaism did not) remains again an issue of scholarly argument. Arthur Christensen, one of the first exponents of the theory that Zurvanism was the state faith of the Sassanids, suggested that the rejection of Zurvanism in the post-conquest era was a response and reaction to the new agency of Islamic monotheism that brought about a measured reform of Zoroastrianism that aimed to establish a stronger orthodoxy. Zaehner is of the notion that the Zurvanite priesthood had a "strict orientation which few could endure. Moreover, they interpreted the Prophet's message so dualistically that their God was made to appear very much less than all-powerful and all-wise. Reasonable as so absolute a dualism power appear from a purely rational point of view, it had neither the appeal of a real monotheism nor had it any mysterious element with which to nourish its inner life."

Another possible account advocated by Boyce (1957:308-309) is that Mazdaism and Zurvanism were separated regionally, that is, with Mazdaism being the predominant tendency in the regions to the north and east (Bactria, Margiana, and other satrapies closest to Zoroaster's homeland), while Zurvanism was outstanding in areas to the south and west (closer to Babylonian and Greek influence). This is backed by Manichean evidence that indicates that third century Mazdean Zoroastrianism had its stronghold in Parthia, to the northeast. Following the fall of the Persian Kingdom, the south and west were relatively quickly assimilated under the banner of Islam, while the north and east remained autonomous for some time before these areas too were absorbed. This could also explain why Armenian/Syriac watchings reveal a distinctly Zurvanite Zoroastrianism, and inversely, could explicate the strong Greek and Babylonian influence on Zurvanism.

REFERENCES

Aerpatastan: Translated from the Avesta-Pahlavi texts by S.J. Bulsara. Bombay, 1915.

Andarz-i Atarpat-i Maraspand: The Pahlavi text, edited and translated by Peshutan Dastur Behramji Sanjana. Bombay, 1885.

Balsara, P. P.: Ancient Iran. Its contribution to Human progress. Bombay, 1936.

Bartholomae, Christian: Altiranisches Wörterbuch. Strassburg, 1904.

Benveniste, Emile: the Persian Religion according to the chief Greek Texts. Paris, 1929.

Bharucha, Sheriarji D: A Brief Sketch of the Zoroastrian Religion and Customs. Bombay, 1893.

Dinkard: Books 3-9. Edited and translated from the Pahlavi text by Peshutan and Darab Sanjana. Vols. 1-19. Bombay. 1874-1919.

Dinkard: Books 7-9. Translated from the Pahlavi text by E. W. West. In *Sacred Books of the East*, vols. 37, 47.

Jackson, A. V. Williams: Zoroastrian Studies. New York, 1928.

Jackson, A. V. Williams: Researches in Manichaeism. New York, 1932.

Shatroiha-i Airan: Translated from the Pahlavi text by Jivanji Jamshedji Modi. Bombay, 1899.

Shayast la-Shayast: Translated from the Pahlavi text by E. W. West. In *Sacred Books of the East*, vol. 5.

Shayast-ne-Shayast: Edited, transliterated, and translated by Jehangir C. Tavadia. Hamburg, 1930.

Zand-i Khurtak Avistak: Pahlavi Text. Edited by B. N. Dhabhar. Bombay, 1927.

Zatsparam: Translated from the Pahlavi text by E. W. West. In *Sacred Books of the East*, vol. 5.

12

Demographic Propagation

Zoroastrianism is an umbrella term to depict the overall notions and practices of Parsis, Qadimis of Iran and the Faslis. Nowadays there are around 200,000 Zoroastrians in the world. Zoroastrianism proceeded to change, develop and mutate with shifting social circumstances and new migrations though none challenged it as much as the religion of Islam.

The overspread of Zoroastrianism thoughts elsewhere has been significant throughout Europe and North America as well as Asia and Australia. Zoroastrianism priests have journeyed west, and Westerners have been deeply affected. Zoroastrianism belief, imagery and doctrine offer a very different form of spiritual understanding from that practiced in the West. It has produced waves of groups inspired by Zoroastrianism.

Zoroastrianism derives its names from its founding father Zarathushtra, the Persian prophet, whom the Greeks denoted as Zoroaster. Zoroastrianism also goes by the epithet Parsiism, a name derived after Parsis, a group of ancient Iranians or Persians, who transmigrated to India in the seventh century AD after the decline of Sassanid dynasty to escape ill-treatment in the hands of Islamic encroachers who occupied the country and used several means to convert the crushed to the new faith. A small but vibrant society of Parsis continue to practice this ancient faith in India and lend richly to its ethnical, religious and cultural diversity.

ORIGIN

Not very much is known about the personal history of Zoroaster. There is no agreement among historians as to the times in which he survived. As per the most faithfull followers of the faith he lived some time around 6000 BC. However founded on the linguistic and other proof historians tend to place him between twelfth and sixth century BC.

Zarathushtra likely lived long before the Buddha and Mahavira. Therefore it would be more acceptable to place him nearer twelfth century BC rather than sixth, the period during which the Vedic people were making themselves as a religious society in the Indian subcontinent. There is also a contention about the place of his origin. As per one popular hypothesis, he came from a family of noble men who lived at Rhages or Ragha, discovered to be Ravy, a suburb in Tehran. Others think that he was probably born outside Iran in some part of Central Asia.

To them Zarathustra introduced the notion of one supreme God above all, following a series of insightful spritual experiences he underwent, in which Ahura Mazda, the most eminent God of Zoroaster faith, appeared to him personally and conveyed to him the highest cognition. It is said that when he was about thirty, as he was drawing water from a well, a gleaming angel named Vohu Manah, appeared to him in a vision and led him into the front of Ahura Mazda. Ahura Mazda declared himself to Zarathustra as the most eminent, everlasting and ethical God and through a series of visions conveyed to him the knowledge of Zoroaster faith and its many secrets with a command to spread them among his people. The teachings of Zoroaster are now preserved in the seventeen hymns known as the Gathas in the Yasna part of the Zend Avesta, the Zoroastrian's scripture. Zoroaster lived among people who believed in the plurality of spirits and deities whom they worshipped.

They also divided up the Gods into three classes, representing with the social order which they followed. Of them they regarded Varuna and Mitra as the highest and most ranking lords (asuras). Zoroaster did not entirely reject the prevailing notions about divinities, but introduced the practice of monotheism, announcing Ahuramazda as the highest and virtuous creator God and dispenser of justice, aided by six or seven other divinities known as Amesha Spentas each personifying certain qualities which humans should aim for for and train in order to receive the prize of heavenly life when they leave this world. He also did not entirely get rid of the reigning rites and animal sacrifices, but only those that involved some decadent practices. He also kept back the fire cult and haoma sacrifice.

After obtaining enlightenment, Zarathushtra changed some close members of his family to his commandment. But largely he was not successful in convincing people to the new religion. However after several years, he was able to convert king Vishtaspa and many of his ministers and court functionaries. He remained in his court for some time. As per a legend he got his daughter married to Jamasp, a minister in Vishtaspa's court. We do not know distinctly how his life ended.

The commandments of Zoroaster began to disperse among the people of Persia and bordering states mainly through nomadic tribes. When Cyrus became the king of the vast Persian kingdom, he made Zoroastrianism accepted throughout Egypt, Greece, Persia and parts of India, mainly with the help of Magi, a priestly society that came originally from Medes. In all probability the three Magi who visited Jesus at the time of his birth in Bethlehem, belonged to the same priestly society. Zoroastrianism suffered a temporary fall in Persia when Alexander captured Persia in 331 BC.

However it was resurrected again in third century AD, when the Sassanians brought down the Parthenians and established their dynasty. The Sassanians made Zoroastrianism as their state faith. They recognized the spiritual authority of the priests as an authoritative part of their political power and gave them special prerogatives to propagate the faith among the people. The state and the faith therefore became inseparable during their time, a notion that was similar in many regards to the one followed by the Romans when they accepted Christianity as the state faith. During this period the Magi made an inflexible rendition of the teachings of Zoroaster and announced any resistance to it as heresy and high treason.

Zoroastrianism suffered a serious blow in Persia when the Sassanid dynasty came to an end in seventh century AD, with the Muslim conquest. The encroachers submitted the followers of the old faith to ill-treatment and discrimination. As a result of their actions the faith vanished from the country, first in the cities and then in the rural areas, leaving a few adherents most. Some took flight and went to India where they settled first in Gujarat and then in other parts of the country, especially Mumbai. They continue to live today in India as Parsis, a vibrant society who played a significant role in the economical improvement of India. They comprise the single largest Zoroastrian society in the world.

Those who remained behind, endured ill-treatment in the hands of Muslim sovereigns for several centuries. They got a relief when Reza Sha Pahlavi overthrew the rule of the Qajar dynasty in 1925 and established his rule. There are still a handful of Zoroastrians in Iran, guessed to be about 30000, who practice the ancient faith, especially in the provinces of Yazd, Kerman, Fars, Tehran, Khuzestan and Kohgilouyeh and Boyerahmad. The Iranian state laws acknowledge Zoroastrians as a religious minority, along with Christians and Jews. It is however appropriate to say that it is in India that Zoroastrianism found its safe harbour, where its followers still practice the ancient faith without the fear of abuse or prejudice

EARLY RISE

It is the oldest revealed faith known to us. As such, it is closely related to most other world faiths; its philosophy lies at the very base of civilized society. It was about 3,800 years ago when something else surprising happened among the people. In the East, in the land of Bactria, appears Zarathushtra, a descendent of those survivors of the ice age, and it was clearly in Zarathushtra's revealings that the answer came.

Given that reason practiced well in a society leads to knowledge, it is not surprising that Zarathushtra elevated Ahura Mazda, meaning the "Wise Lord," truly the "Master of Knowledge" itself, to the highest level among the pantheon of early Iranian Gods. Although it is the earliest monotheistic view known to us, a view that likely had a profound impact on later faiths, Zarathushtra and his supporters were hardly concerned with complex theologies during his time. They had other problems to deal with, as already mentioned, so what was to become the Zarathushtrian faith was largely pragmatic in its outlook.

They were survivors of the ice age, and fire had played a significant role in their culture for generations. With Zarathushtra, fire would now take on a mysterious symbolical meaning. Fire would represent enlightenment, the illuminated mind. To this day, every time we see a candle burning in a church, synagogue, mosque, or temple, its flame means much the same thing. But for most of us, we have forgotten that it was once, literally during the ice age, the difference between life and demise.

Now, with Zarathushtra's divine revelation that we have free will to select between what is better for us and what is not, maybe for the first time, we see a link now with another of the world's faiths. Judaism, in the second section of Genesis, deals with the same subject. The adaptation in Genesis is an archetypical story for teaching. Good and evil are no longer seen as a great encounter of celestial forces. Instead, they are seen as delicate influences in our day-to-day decisions. Now, underlying the principle of free will to choose, as conveyed by Zarathushtra, are some very significant notions that apply as much today and in the future as they did back then. The ûrst of these recognizes how we think. One of our fundamental thought processes, and the one that can cause us the most trouble, is polarized thinking. That is, thinking in terms of good or evil, the truth or the lie, light or dark, hot or cold, positive or negative, rich or poor, and so on. Zarathushtra's divine revelation assumes that we often think this way, and this has backlashes in later philosophical growth.

The second notion recognizes how we learn. We learn by making selections and, given our all-too-human helplessness, every choice may not always be the best one. Zarathushtra's revelation thus expects a some degree of failure, it forecasts forgiveness among people, it favours guiding by example rather than by vengeance, and thus arrives early at the golden rule found later on in Leviticus, the Gospel, the Hadith, and other holy scriptures.

The third notion recognizes how we act together. To select, each man and woman for his or her self, implies freedom as a complete reality in society. This was perhaps the most radical notion to be derived from Zarathushtra's revelation of free will. Given that some 3,800 years has passed since the time of Zarathushtra, it remains to this day the least formulated notion, the hardest to put into practice.

Thus, Zarathushtra's revealing of free will thus tells us much about how we imagine, how we learn, and how we interact wih each other. It is not an inactive statement, but an active process. As such, the notion of free will also has many significances in Zoroastrian thought.

One significance is aim. In Zoroastrianism, each and every person has an aim, and that aim is to help make this a better world, and that is best done by making good choices.

Nowadays, those who profess the Zoroastrian faith number only a few hundred thousand out of six billion people. But the inheritance of Zarathushtra's revealing has touched every corner of the world, and likewise, Zoroastrianism has also been influenced by other faiths. Indeed, today it is quite a challenge to study Zoroastrianism outside of the circumstance of our contemporary views on faith. We have discussed a little about its relation with Judaism, because the Tanakh shares many remarkably similar, if not exactly the same, revealings, and the history of the Jewish people was closely interwoven with the Zoroastrian in early times. Zoroastrianism is also intimately related to Hinduism, with whom its holy scriptures share a closely associated language, and many traditions, names, and the like are related. Because of is great history, it can be reasoned that Zoroastrianism laid the basis for the great family of monotheistic faiths, including Judaism, Christianity, Islam, along with most of Hinduism, and others that share a monotheistic view.

With a little awareness about Zoroastrianism, it is not too hard to see that the author of the Gospel of Matthew tries to sway not only Jews that Jesus of Nazareth is the Messiah foretold by the Hebrew prophets, but also the deliverer promised by Zoroastrianism. Hence, in Christianity, we ûnd not only the magi (Zoroastrian priests) accrediting the birth of Jesus, but there is also the deduction declared by the Apostle's Creed: that "Jesus died, and was buried; he descended into hell; the third day he rose again from the dead." It happens to be a succession that is virtually alike an ancient Zoroastrian metaphor. Today, Christianity's deep sense of love ûnds a welcome home in Zoroastrian thought.

Zoroastrianism today is a energetic, living faith, its philosophies live on in other faiths world-wide, and are at the base of civilized societies everywhere. The world today faces grievous challenges posed by immense increases in population, great economical disproportion and social deficiency, and serious environmental damage. Yet the Zoroastrian view is an ever-optimistic one. It reminds us that we already have the great gift needed to solve our problems today and in the future. We have the power to reason. If we select to do so, we can think good thoughts, speak good words, do good deeds. We can surely change the world in which we live. Hope is with us always, until the end of time.

FACTORS RESPONSIBLE FOR RISE

Today only about 125,000 individuals still follow the religion first propagated by the prophet Zarathustra in Central Asia some time between 1500 and 600 BC., and the biggest density is in Bombay. They are known as the Parsis-the people from Pars, or ancient Persia-the land they fled during the Middle Ages to continue their faith amid the spread of Islam.

The astounding rise of the Parsis from peaceful agriculturists and craftsmen to key builders of contemporary India helps support the belief within the society that they are a chosen people. After the exodus from Persia (now Iran), the fortunes of the society changed a second time with the rise of British power on the subcontinent. The Parsis, less suspecting and hostile toward the new comers from the West, became arbitrators and agents for the colonizers. They embraced contemporary education and collected fortunes in commerce and industry. They went on to make contributions in an assortment of fields, from politics, law and nuclear physics to cinema and sport, while their charity helped build Bombay. Today, India's biggest industrial kingdom, the Tata group, is headed by a Parsi, as is Godrej, the country's largest privately owned conglomerate. The late Prime Minister Rajiv Gandhi's father also came from the society. The ardour with which the Parsis still pursue certain trades is best illustrated by their unique surnames.

Unlike other invaders who came to India to loot, plunder and dominate, the Parsis imbibed with a quiet self-respect into India's history and added their extraordinary genius in every walk of life. As intelligent expats, while guarding their own ethnic, cultural and religious individuality with ferocious pride, they were always aware of their status and made friends wherever they went. As an ethnic group, Parsis have excelled in a way no other society has and it would seem that their breeding and strong religious belief may be the cause for this. There is, in the Zoroastrian religious doctrine, a simplicity that defies challenge. Be good, do good, think good and fight evil. Be accountable for yourself and don't blame others. Listen to your scruples but laugh and enjoy life. Look after your own people, and so on. From the time a child is able to understand social kinetics, right and wrong are clearly outlined and the child is made accountable for his/her thoughts, words and deeds. No wonder that when a Parsi child goes wrong, the whole society hangs its head in sorrow and disgrace.

Starting with commerce and industry, through law and literature, including the armed forces, and traversing the arts, music and nuclear science, Parsis always gave more than they took from their assumed land. A large number of Parsis settled in Bombay when famine affected Gujarat in 1790. The city's universal outlook and its dynamic vitality brought out the Parsi's natural gusto for life. And it became a springboard for some of the most gifted men and women from that society to take flight in their varied fields of expertness.

The names of renowned Parsis roll off like a absolute who's who of famous Indians: Dadabhoy Naoroji, Fali Nariman, Homi Bhabha, JRD Tata, Madam Bhikaji Cama, Ratan Tata, Sam Maneckshaw, Sir Jamshedji Tata, Soli Sorabji, the Godrej clan, the Wadias, Zubin Mehta, and others too numerous to list.

The outstanding success of the small but limited society, however, has carried the seeds of its own end. The most Westernized of all of India's ethnic groups, the Parsis tend to be well-educated and middle-class. They in general prefer to marry late and, like contemporary couples everywhere, typically have just one or two children, or none at all. The ban against religious conversion obliges most Parsis to select partners from within the group, and generations of in-breeding have added to genetic-related disorders. Religious custom also blocks Parsi parents from adopting non-Zoroastrian children. The result is a increasingly aging and reducing population. The Bombay journal Parsiana keeps track of births and demises among the Parsis. Last year it recorded around 1,000 demises in Bombay, and only about five hundred births among the city's Parsi population of roughly 55,000.

In spite of such forecasts, the Magi hold tight their beliefs. "It's a kind of collective death wish-the decisions of the conventional leadership go against the long-term endurance of the Parsis," tells Ava Khullar, who has published extensively on the demographic death trap. Indeed, many individuals feel the Magi's rigid interpretings are not in keeping with the principles of the faith. But many Parsis in India view the society as if it's yet another exclusive class to which you can belong only by merit of your birth. Religious conversions now are being done only in North America, mostly on the proposal of migrants from Iran's small, lasting Zoroastrian society. In India, the high priests-following a practice more distinctive of the Hindu upper castes-do not permit non-Zoroastrians to enter their fire-temples, or even the stone towers where the Parsi dead are still consumed, as in ancient times, by vultures.

To help save the Parsis, a secular council of society leaders in Bombay, the Parsi Punchayat, produced a new scheme that subsidizes Parsi parents who want to give birth to a third child. Forty Punchayat-sponsored babies have been born in the last five years, counting a set of triplets. But the plan isn't likely to stop the slide. Once members of a mature society choose for late marriages and fewer children.

ZOROASTRIANISM IN OTHER PARTS OF WORLD

In Iran

In 1990 there were roughly 33,000 Zoroastrians in Iran. They speak Farsi and are based in Tehran, Kerman, and Yazd. Zoroastrianism initially grew in Iran during the seventh century BC. Later, it became the official faith of the Sassanid Kingdom, which ruled over Iran for approximately four centuries before being demolished by the Arabs in the seventh century AD. After Iran's incorporation into the Islamic kingdom, the bulk of its population was slowly converted from Zoroastrianism to Islam, a process that was likely completed by the tenth century.

Throughout the Qajar era there was significant prejudice against Zoroastrians. In the mid-nineteenth century, several thousand Zoroastrians migrated from Iran to British-ruled India to recover their economical and social status. Many finally acquired wealth in India and later on expended part of their fortunes on advancing conditions in the Zoroastrian communities of Iran.

The stress placed on Iran's pre- Islamic inheritance by the Pahlavis also helped Zoroastrians to accomplish a more respected place in society. Many of them migrated from Kerman and Yazd to Tehran, where they amassed substantial wealth as merchants and in real estate. By the 1970s, younger Zoroastrians were entering the different professions.

Like the Christians and Jews, the Zoroastrians are accepted as an official religious minority under the Constitution of 1979. They are allowed to elect one spokesperson to the Majlis and, like the other lawfully accepted minorities, may seek work in the government. They in general enjoy the same civil liberties as Muslims. Although Zoroastrians probably have encountered individual examples of prejudice, they have not been oppressed because of their religion.

Causes of the Fall of Zoroastrian Iran

The Byzantine King, Heraclius gave the first blow to undermine the Zoroastrian Sasanian Iran. He overcame the Persians in 622 AD. and in 627 AD. he invaded Atropatene (Azerbaijan) and demolished the Great Fire Temple and entered the Tigris states. Chosroes Abarvez or Parviz 'the victorious' sought to resist him but before he could do so he was traitorously murdered by his son Shiroe who assumed the name of Kavadh and ascended the throne as Kavadh II in 628 AD. Shiroe was born out of Chosroes' marriage to a Christian Princess, Shirin. This execution was the beginning of the end of Zoroastrian Iran. It is interesting to note that Chosroes Parviz had succeeded in extending the frontiers of the Sasanian Kingdom almost to the limits of the Achaemenid Kingdom, but at the vital junction he was denounced by his son.

It is an irony of fate that Kavadah II who murdered his father to grab the throne died inside a year in an outbreak and succeeded by his infant son Ardashir III who was killed by Shahrbaraz, a General of the Persian Army who captured the throne, in turn being murdered during his sovereignty of two months. Lawlessness set in and ensued in the succession of short-time sovereigns, Yazdegerd, the son of Shahriyar, and grand-son of Chosroe was found in Istaker fire-temple and he came to the throne in 633 AD. He became the last Sasanian King. A perfect setting was in order for the tribal brutality of united Arab Bedouins to cast the final blow.

The lengthy exhausting aggressions reduced the power and power of both Iran and Byzantium, opening the door for a newly issuing force from the Arabian desert to confront both the states and faiths. After several face-offs, the fate of the Sasanian Kingdom was sealed in the battle of al-Qaadisiyah on the Euphrates canal, near al-Hirah where to make matters worse, Rustam, the Sasanian Supreme Commander-in-Chief was killed. Ctesiphon, the Sasanian capital with all its vast wealth was now at the mercy of the triumphant Arabs. Yezdegerd fled to Media and with the help of his Generals formed new opposition and the last battle was fought at Nehavand, south of Hamadan which finally put an end to all hopes of recovering the Kingdom. This was the offset of the blackest age of Zoroastrianism. Yezdegerd sought asylum in one state after another until at last in 651 AD., he was killed near Merve by a miller for his jewels clad sword. With the fall of the Kingdom, the fate of its faith was also sealed.

It is essential to comprehend the backdrop of the emerging force of the Arabs to realize what made them achieve triumphs over one of the mightiest Kingdoms in history. The prophet Muhammad had made Medina, his adopted city and Mecca, his birth place, centers of an Arabian movement that Muslim Arabs grew into a world wide movement by the subjugation of Iran. Arab tribalism beyond urban fringes was less easily broken than idols. It was implanted in the desert sparsity that led to war and careful counting of a tribes' male offspring. After Mecca and Medina became Muslim, it was necessary to secure loyalty of all the other desert Arab tribal people. In the process of doing this, wars over water holes, bare pasturages, men-at-arms and camels were expanded into international campaigns of expansion.

The weakness of Sasanid Zoroastrian Iran helped the expansionism process. As noted when Yazdegerd III, the last Zoroastrian Sasanian sovereign came to the throne in 632 AD, the year of Muhammad's demise, he inherited an kingdom weakened by Byzantine wars and internal discord. After the sad end of the Sasanids, century after century Zoroastrian faith was oppressed in Iran and little by little it disappeared, except for a few living adherents who remain to the present day in Yazd and a few other places. Other Zoroastrians migrated to western India where they are now concentrated in Bombay (Mumbai). These Parsis have preserved their sacred writings by carefully producing hand written manuscripts and faithfully following their religious teachings so also those who stayed behind in Iran, maintained their ancient faith till the present times.

Currently some Parsis and Iranian Zoroastrians (after the fall of the Shah) have migrated to Western countries to better their aspects. They both are facing courageously new social and family values and their children may be at great danger of being imbibed ethically and culturally into the major faiths of the West. But they do not have to fear for the worst, as the present course towards better realizing of their faith together with inherited strength of Zoroastrianism will give them no cause of concern in keeping their faith intact.

In Pakistan

Before independency of Pakistan in 1947, main urban centres in what is now Pakistan were home to a flourishing Parsi business society. Karachi had the most outstanding population of Parsis in Pakistan and were mostly Gujarati-speaking. After independence, absolute majority of Pakistan's Parsi population migrated to India, notably Bombay, however a number of Parsis still remain in Pakistan and have enrolled Pakistani public life as welfare workers, business folk, and diplomats. The most outstanding Parsis of Pakistan today include Ardeshir Cowasjee, Byram Dinshawji Avari, Jamsheed Marker, as well as Minocher Bhandara.

DEMOGRAPHICS

In 1996 the number of Zoroastrians in universe was guessed to be "at most 200,000" India's 2001 Census found 69,601 Parsi Zoroastrians. In Pakistan they number 5,000, mostly living in Karachi. Anglo America is home to 18,000–25,000 Zoroastrians of both South Asian and Iranian background. Iran's figures of Zoroastrians have ranged widely; the last census (1974) before the revolution of 1979 revealed 21,400 Zoroastrians.

Few, if any, disciples remain in the Central Asian regions that were once regarded the traditional stronghold of Zoroastrianism, i.e. Bactria which is in Northern Afghanistan, Sogdiana, Margiana and other areas close to Zoroaster's homeland.

In the Indian census of 2001 the Parsis numbered 69,601, representing about 0.006% of the total population of India, with a concentration in and around the city of Mumbai. Due to a lowly birth rate and high rate of expatriation, demographic trends project that by 2020 the Parsis will number only about 23,000 or 0.002% of the total population of India. The Parsis would then cease to be called a society and will be labelled a "tribe". By 2008, the birth-to-demise ratio was 1:5 - 200 births per year to 1,000 demises. However, As per some other sources, "The World

Almanac And Text Of facts" distributed by St Martin's Press, printed in the U.S.A. the current population world wide is 2,728,000.

There are very few Zoroastrians left in the world. They mainly live in India and Iran. There are only about 200,000 Zoroastrians left and their population keeps on declining steadily. It is often found in the Zoroastrian society that they tend to marry late and often do not produce children. These are one of the primary reasons why their population is diminishing. Moreover, since Zoroastrianism does not accept children of mixed marriage and inter-religious marriages, they lose several new inclusions into their faith.

Zoroastrianism has prospered in the modern age. They were quick to admit the new changes. Parsis are the founders of many fields in India. Some prestigious and famous Parsis are J.R.D Tata, a business magnate and a noteworthy philanthropist, Pherozshah Mehta and Dadabhai Naoroji, two very authoritative early freedom fighters in India against the imperialistic powers, the director of the Philharmonic Orchestra, Zubin Mehta, Freddie Mercury of the rock band 'Queen' and the popular and critically applauded writer, Rohinton Mistry.

REFERENCES

Andarz-i-Khusro-i-Kavatan: The Pahlavi text, edited and translated by Peshutan Dastur Behramji Sanjana; Bombay, 1885.

Bahman Yasht: Translated from the Pahlavi text by E. W. West. In *Sacred Books of the East*, vol. 5.

Carter, G. W.: Zoroastrianism and Judaism. Boston, 1918.

Casartelli, L. C.: The Philosophy of the Mazdayasnian Religion under the Sassanids. Translated from the French by Firoz Jamaspji Jamasp Asa. Bombay, 1889.

Cumont, Franz: The Mysteries of Mithra. Translated from the French by T. J. McCormack. Chicago, 1903.

Dhalla, M. N.: Zoroastrian Theology. New York, 1914.

Dina i Mainu i Khrat: Edited by Darab P. Sanjana. Bombay, 1895.

Hodivala, S. K.: Zarathushtra and His Contemporaries in the Rig Veda. Bombay, 1913.

Hodivala, S. K.: Parsis of Ancient India. Bombay, 1920.

Hodivala, S. K.: Indo-Iranian Religion with parallelisms in the Hindu and Zoroastrian Scriptures. Bombay, 1925.

Hoshang Memorial Volume: Bombay, 1918.

Mills, L. H.: Zarathushtra, Philo, the Achaemenids and Israel. Leipzip, 1905, 1906.

Mills, L. H.: Avesta Eschatology compared with the Books of Daniel and Revelations. Chicago, 1908.

Mills, L. H.: Our Own Religion in Ancient Persia. 1913.

Shikand Gumanik Vijar: Translated from the Pahlavi-Pazand text by E. W. West. In *Sacred Books of the East*, vol. 24.

Taraporewala, Irach, J. S: Some Aspects of the History of Zoroastrianism. Bombay, 1928.

Wadia, Ardaser S.: The Message of Zoroaster. London, 1912.

Wilson, John: The Parsi Religion. Bombay, 1843.

13

Socio-Political Influence

SOCIO-POLITICAL IDENTITY

The ancient Indians and ancient Iranians had many in things in common. They revered many identical Gods, spoke languages of common ancestry, performed rites that had many things in common both in the method and mode in which they were executed and the intention for which they were executed. Their religious beliefs and practices drew motivation from similar sources. The ancient Iranians spoke Avestan which was a sister language of Sanskrit, spoken by the Vedic Indians. Both groups worshipped several Gods and performed elaborate sacrificial rites (yagnas or yasnas) at the end of which they feasted and drank an heady drink called Soma in India or Haoma in Iran.

The Iranians recited verses to appeal toancient Gods just as the Indians performed rites to appeal to the gods of the celestial region. Some of the gods they worshipped had similar names, such as Airyaman, apam Napat, Atharvan/Atar/Agni, Sraosa/Brihapsati, Mitra/Mithra, Vauy/Wayu, Tvastar/Thworeshter, Datar/dadar, Indra/Werethragna, Varuna/Rashnu. Usha/Usa, Yama/Yima, Vayu/Vay, and so on. Both groups believed in the existence of a three level universe consisting of an upper heavenly region, a middle atmospheric region and the earth. Some of the language they used in the practice of rites was also similar such as zaotar and hotar, athaurwan and atharvan, manthra and mantra, asha and arta and so on.

By the way, at some stage in their maturation, both groups parted their ways and acquired differences. Some of the differences may be due to the geography and some to the new political and social growths that took place in the relevant parts. They also came into contact with new faiths and new religious ideas of other customs that came from across the borders through conquests or through traders, merchants and migrants or grew indigenously. While the vedic Indians interacted with the pre-vedic customs of India, dating back to the Indus period and even earlier, the ancient Iranian faith which was rooted in the vedic beliefs, faced opposition from Zoroastrianism, which was steadily emerging in the region as the most structured and appealing faith of ancient Iran, backed by the support of some sovereigns and the teachings of Zoroaster who clamed he had a direct communication with God and obtained the seal of support to spread the new ideas.

Zoroaster advanced Ahura Mazda as the most eminent God and brought in the element of monotheism in an otherwise polytheistic faith of ancient Iran. He brought in the practice of revering one God, (Madayasna), in contrast to the Vedic practice of worshipping multiple divinities (devayagna). He laid more stress on ethical living rather than on rite purity and sacrificial ceremonies as the predominant idea of religious practice. There was no place in his teachings for the old practice of sacrificial rites involving animal and human sacrifices, which were deemed harrowing and brutal and antithetical to the revealings received by him. He brought into focus a dynamic universal God as a protector of the virtuous and opposed to evil, in place of an enigmatical and passive God who remained in the background while the gods battled with various dark forces and claimed heavenly authority to themselves. However he did not cast aside old faith altogether.

He continued with those ideas, deities, practices and philosophies that fitted well in his new commandments and declared the rest to be antithetical to the new tenet. As a result most of the former devas, who were found to be in direct opposition to the precepts represented by God were categorized as diabolical spirits and unworthy of honour and worship. Zoroaster added into focus the ethical dualism comprehended in the entire creation as an ongoing battle between the armies of good and evil, a fight that was already perceived in the ancient faith but interpreted rather anecdotally. He shifted the focus of the faith from rite purity to ethical purity and from person divinities to a central God, who combined within Himself all the qualities represented by them as their lord, creator and sustainer.

His instructions portrayed the battle between good and evil beyon[d] the known religious speculation, as an honourable battle of universa[l] proportions between the originative forces of good led by God and th[e] negative forces of evil led by an anti-God principle. This ethical view o[f] faith as the means to maintain the spritual purity of not just men but th[e] entire creation, resulted in the polarization of the classic deities into two groups, the followers of Truth (ashawan) and the followers of falsehood, the former portrayed as benignant and good, representing the ideals to be cultivated by men; and the latter as vicious, damaging and destructive forces, constituting the dangers to which humanity power yield if they were careless. What the ancient Iranians practiced was a custom that was grounded in the history of their ancestors and their beliefs, without being unfriendly to new ideas. What the new prophet taught was an inflexible new tenet that had elements of intolerance and rigidity, which was so feature of the new faiths that descended upon earth a few centuries later in the Mediterranean and engulfed nation after nation blotting out all traces of ancient faiths.

In the process of this social and religious turbulent in the ancient Iran, some well known popular divinities of the ancient world, like Indra, Natasya (Naonhaitya) and Rudra (Saurva) lost their status as recipients of rite honours. The reasons are not difficult to find. All the Gods, who lost their status as divinities in the new faith, possessed qualities and indulged in actions that could not be categorized strictly as pure and virtuous as per Zoroastrian values. From a purely honourable point of view, they had characters with shades of gray, suggestive of pollution, which would disqualify them, in the new faith, as beings of pure light or forces of a just and virtuous God. In a faith that rested on the base of inflexible purity and an unequivocal approach towards good and evil, it was not possible to continue their worship and still convince the new converts about the importance of purity and morality.

So all the accepted gods of the old custom that seemingly possessed questionable qualities were pushed into the dark side and disqualified from receiving sacrificial oblations. Those who fitted into the new collection with their emblematic virtues, such as Mithra and Yama (Yima), continued to obtain the honours as forces of light. In a move that smacked of religious intolerance, but for reasons understandable from a Zoroastrian viewpoint, Zoroaster declared that impure Gods should not be worshipped and no sacrifices should be offered to them. He introduced new reigns for the sacrificial rites, forbidding certain old methods and practices which were used to appeal to them, such as the haoma rites involving heady drinks, which were pleasing to the daevas.

Vedic and the Zarathushtrian faiths were much less different than was generally supposed and that the three way partition of devas, asuras and daevas was not an entirely strange classification to the Indian custom as it was familiar to the habitants of Kashmir who had contacts with both. Indian authors brought into focus the same dichotomy between the heavenly and evil forces in the Puranas, with Vishnu or Shiva as a Supreme Being, acting as an adjudicator between the two, in a language that was recognizable to the Indians.

The list of familiar divinities and notions will make it clear that the Zoroastrian faith is essentially the same as the Vedic one. The presence of Indra in the list of the daevas seems to mirror the deputation of Indra that started in the Puranic times where instead of connecting to Svar through the intermediate region of which Indra is lord, a direct worship of the Great Master was stressed. This innovation is not counter to the Vedic system since the triple division is a recursive order. The devas are a part of the good forces in the Zoroastrian system under the label of yazata.

The Zoroasatrian mythos remembers the Vedic sages and heroes such as Kavi Susravah (Kay Khosrau), Kavi Usanas (Kay Us). The names Ksatra Virya (Shahriyar) and Suvarn ah (Khwarrah, Farrah) helped the logic of late Persian names. The daeva in contemporary Persian are known as deev.

The commonness of the fire rite is well known. Less known is the rite of the nine-nights (barashnom i noshab) which is like the Indian rite of the same name (navaratri). The No Roz occurs on the day of the spring equinox just as the festival of Indra.

Due to the geographic closeness, there was a regular swap of ideas and practices between India and Iran from the early Vedic period till the Mughal period. As early as 1400 BC, the Hittites and the Mittanis were common with the Sanskrit names of many Indian Gods. Their kings bore Sanskrit names. Like the ancient Iranians, they probably followed a faith that bore many likenesses with the Vedic faith of ancient Indians. Afghanisthan and Baluchistan acted as the linking link between the two regions. India was known to the Persians, in the Avestan, as Hapta Hindu (Sapta Sindhu), a land that existed beyond Kubha (Kabul), Kurmu (Kurrum) and Gomti (Gomal.

King Darius ruled a kingdom which included parts of India. He used an Indian army that was well fitted and fit to fight, with infantry, archers, cavalry and chariots. The Persians continued to hold on parts of India till Darius III (300 BC). The intrusion of Alexander added further to the cultural exchanges. The continued bearing of Persians on the Indian soil led to the intermingling of ideas and practices. Indian goods were admired in Persia. So was the knowledge of metallurgy and other sciences, while components of Persian architecture found their way into many monuments built curing the Mauryan rule.

The Mauryan king Chandragupta hired women bodyguards of likely Persian origin and adapted the hair washing ceremony of the Persian kings. In the religious field a number of new developments took place in the Indian subcontinent. The Vedic faith transformed itself into a complex faith incorporating the best of all the persisting ideas of the time, challenged by Buddhism and Jainism and other rival customs. In Persia the opposite happened. Zoroastrianism developed into an organized faith. Its strict adherence to the teachings of Zoroaster, intolerance of other faiths and puritanical approach to religious practice, made any changes in its fundamental fabric impossible, till it met its own match in Islam several centuries later and was altogether wiped out from Iran.

ZOROASTRIANISM AND POLITICS

Zoroastrianism is always rejuvenated, its substance spread across, its revitalization, its reverberating call heard by all even if it is given some limited freedom. Therefore the first battle is to obtain freedom to deliver the message, extend consciousness and enabling the subsistence of Zoroastrianism.

Democracy is the simplest and right way to accomplish the aims of a noble life, to be able to invite all to Zoroastrianism, to be able to call others to Zoroastrianism. It is the space for a free and honourable nation to have the right to choose, evaluate the sovereign, change governments without takeovers and without bloodshed.

The gist of democracy is that the public, the people can select the sovereigns who are going to manage them; the people having the right to choose, criticize and terminate; and the people are not pushed to accept systems, trends, and policies which they do not agree to and they are not ill-treated. They are free to hold elections, referendums, assuring majority rights, defending minority rights, having opposition, have multi parties, have press freedom and protecting the independence of the judiciary.

Zoroastrianism has laid down universal basic rights for humanity which are to be observed and honoured in all circumstances. For example, human blood is sacred and may not be spilled without solid justification; it is not allowed to oppress women, children, old people, the sick or the wounded; women's honour and virtue must be respected; the hungry must be fed, the naked clothed and the injured or diseased treated medically irrespective of whether they belong to the Zoroastrianism society or are from other communities. These, and other provisions have been laid down by Zoroastrianism as basic rights for every man by virtue of his status as a human.

FUNDAMENTALISM

By way of introduction it may be expressed that in Zoroaster's religious teachings the warring realms of good and evil, light and darkness, right and wrong, embodied respectively as Ormazd and Ahriman, or the ancient Persian God and Devil, are represented as in eternal conflict. Yet, while these two opposed principles, which struggle for the mastery of the spirit of man, are primeval and coeval in the world, they are not coeternal, because Ormazd will triumph in the end and Ahriman will be eradicated forever. Man will help in bringing about this triumph.

Man is Ormazd's own tool and belongs by birthright to the kingdom of good. But God has produced him as a free agent, empowered with the power to choose, of his own volition, between that which is correct and that which is wrong. Upon his choice, however, his own redemption and his share in the final victory of good will depend. Every good deed that man does increases the power of good; every evil he commits increases the kingdom of evil. His weight thrown in either scale turns the balance in that direction. Hence man ought to select the good and support the hosts of heaven in the struggle to conquer the legions of hell, thus bringing about the era, at which time the Saoshyant, or Savior, will emerge, the resurgence of the dead and the final judgment will take place, 'the good kingdom, the wished-for kingdom' will be founded, and the world will be revived and made perfect as per will.

Obligation consequently rests upon man, and, because of his free will of choice, he will be held to strict answerability hereafter; it was, furthermore, for the particular purpose of guiding humanity toward the general choice of right that Zoroaster conceived himself to be sent by Ormazd on his assignment as prophet.

Thus while Zoroaster's religious doctrine, as presented in the sacred text of the Avesta, centuries before Christ, and further grew in the patristical Pahlavi literature of Sasanian times and later, is dualistic in its doctrine, it has powerfully monotheistic tendencies in that it postulates, with affirmative hope, the ultimate victory of Ormazd; and it is quintessentially ethical since it gives to the philosophy of dualism a moral value by placing obligation upon man as a free agent . After this universal presentation by way of preface, we may take up and discuss in turn the

Avestan and Pahlavi texts that touch upon the liberty of the will, supplementing these from later sources.

As for the Avesta, the 'Holy Gathas,' or 'Psalms of Zoroaster,' are the oldest and most hallowed part of the sacred texts. In certain stanzas of these, for example Yasna 45. 2; 30. 3-5, the underlying opposition and all imbuing fight between the two Primordial Spirits is clearly brought out; and it is plainly stated, in Yasna 30.5, that from the beginning 'the Evil (Ahriman) chose (varata) to do the worst things; the Holiest.Spirit (Ormazd), who wears the firmest heavens as a robe, chose Morality, and (so do those) who gladly will gratify Ahura Mazdah (Ormazd) by right acts.' The original choice made by the Primal Spirits thus forms the prototype and serves for an example to guide man in making his own choice.

This idea is more clearly conveyed in the next Gatha (Ys.31.2), in which Zoroaster presents himself as the guide and master because, owing to the teachings of the evil, 'the better way to select is not clear in view. He therefore exhorts his hearers to live 'as per Morality,' so as to win the prize of the Kingdom of Mazdah (stanza 6), whom he glorifies (7-8), and then turns to the special subject of volition and choice. This, as we understand the next two stanzas (9-10), is presented first as a allegory or parable, under the guise of which the cow (an animal sacred in Zoroastrianism) is given the option to select between the thrifty husbandman, who cares for the cattle, and the non-husbandman. The cow (unlike 'Buridan's ass' between the two bundles of hay, as familiar in the scholastic doctrine) makes the right choice at once without wavering; and then in the next two stanzas (11-12) man's freedom to determine and practise his own belief by word and deed, and thus decide his fate, is brought out.

The Pahlavi, or Middle Persian, writings belongs to the period of the Sasanian Kingdom and the centuries directly after the Muhammadan conquest of Persia, thus dating roughly from the third to the tenth century AD. This Zoroastrian patristical literature, as it may be called, consists largely of translations of Avestan texts and of writings on general religious subjects rather than on philosophical topics. For that reason there are fewer allusions to metaphysical questions than we power otherwise expect; but the policy of the freedom of the will is implied throughout in the ethical writings of the followers of Zoroaster after the Arab conquest, and we know that this tenet was explicitly branded as 'Magian' by their defeatist conquerors, thus showing that it continued to prevail. In the

Pahlavi texts themselves, moreover, there are various direct as well as indirect references to the principle.

In the first place, in the Bundahishn, which is an old Pahlavi work based on the Damdat Nask, one of the lost texts of the original Avesta, there is directly indicated a choice made by the Fravashis-those pre-existent spritual counterparts, or guardian aces, who were the heavenly prototypes of material creations afterward produced to leave for a time their heavenly state and assume a bodily subsistence on earth, in order to overcome finally the opposition of Ahriman and become 'perfect and immortal in the future subsistence, for ever and everlasting.'

The fact that orthodox Mohammedans looked suspiciously at the Magians, or Zoroastrians, and especially the priesthood, as being proponents of the philosophy of free will can readily be shown, and it has a special bearing on the subject. In fact, within Islam itself, owing partially to Neo-Platonic and other influences, the free-will principle gave rise to internal dissident sects. Thus in the religious and philosophical developments during the golden age of Islam in the earlier Abbasic period we have the Muslim schismatical factions of the Kadarites, or Partisans of Free Will, and their branch the Mutazilites, Separatists, or Seceders, both of which were fully impregnated with the doctrine of free decision as opposed to the fatalistic predetermination of the Quran.

The philosophy of free will is a principle still acknowledged by the Zoroastrians today, as certain of the writings of their priests and temporalty well show. It may justly be added, moreover, that although, owing to several changes and variations, there remain in the world only a small number of followers of the ancient creed of Zoroaster-about eleven thousand in Persia and something over a hundred thousand in India-these two disciple communities of Parsis and 'Gabars' prove, by their high honourable standards and their practice in life, how unwaveringly they have maintained the historic doctrine of their faith, which teaches man's free choice between right and wrong and which lays upon him the obligation of accounting for that choice in the afterlife.

CONTEMPORARY POLITICS

After Zarathushtra died and many centuries later, new texts were written, not by Zarathusthra, but by clerics in this new era where there was Judaism, Christianity, and Islam. These texts were written, the text called "Vendidad," which is very dissimilar from what Zarathushtra had to say and are not his direct words.

In the Vendidad, there are other sorts of limitations. Zoroastrians don't have a Holy Father or a figurehead or someone who makes all the decisions: Zoroastrianism is all about the person and about using your mind and making the right choices.

A lot of new Zoroastrians are marrying Hindus and Christians; whoever they fall in love with now. So, also, in India, the argument is becoming more exciting because the younger generation is calling into question what their, parents and grandparents instilled and forced them to believe.

While some of the Parsi involvement with the British as well as in the Indian Freedom Movement has been authenticated, the role of Parsis in government and in serving the Nation historically goes back much further. There were Parsi attendants at the Mughal Court who obtained favours for deeds and actions performed. At many local courts, such as Jamnagar and Baroda, Paris were nominated as both Diwans and Treasurers and were valued for their sincerity and uprightness. They were also trusted Hakims or Doctors to several Kings. Historically, the upswing and their enrolling into public service in large numbers came with the European arrival in India.

The Parsis worked as mediators or agents because they could interrelate with both Indians and Europeans and had no caste barriers to prevent social dealings. Thus, their service in both British and pre-British days and after Independence needs to be studied and documented. Research into the Parsi bearing at the Mughal Court is starting to yield worthful information. Their service as watch fixers, and their rewards by the Kings need documentation. King Akbar's interaction with the Vada Dastur Meherjirana in the conceptualization of his Din-e-Ilahi faith and his interest in the Zoroastrian faith needs further study, perhaps, through Mughal Court records.

Besides being Diwans of Jamnagar, Baroda and parts of Gujarat, Parsi attendants and consultants functioned in the States of the Deccan as well as at the Nizam's royal court at Hyderabad. Many plans which amended the lives of the people and the economic system of the states were planned by them e.g. the transporting of Deccan cotton to cloth mills at Mumbai.The Peshtanshahi Sikka of Hyderabad is the only Indian coin to be named after a Parsi as an honour for the services he rendered the Nizam and Hyderabad State. In the fields of educational activity, social service, reforms, helping plague victims, the uplift of women, the labour movement, the Indian Factory Act and other politically linked reforms, Parsis played a guiding role e.g. Bengalee, Malabari.

Dadabhai Naoroji, Sir Pherozeshah Mehta and others were moderationist leaders in the struggle for Indian Freedom. A revolutionary leader who spent much of her life in exile was Madame Cama who designed and raised the Indian flag for the first time.

The historical origins of Parsis in business life came through their role as translators and professional mediators between the Dutch and the Indians. They were weavers who introduced Chinese silk and fabric weaving into India. As chiefs and carpenters in the building of ships and dockyards, Parsis were innovators. The Wadias were ship builders, some even skilled engineers although today they are acknowledged for their input to commerce and industry. At another level, Parsis were known as skilful Hakims and Vaids, some following the Unani system and other herbal cures as well as the profession of bone setting still preserved by the Madhivala family and others practicing in Gujarat. Because of their professional links, the Parsis became westernized very rapidly and shifted to the urban centres of Surat and Mumbai. They laid great emphasis on education and the British finding them valuable for their designs took great pains to breeding their ambitions.

REFERENCES

Aogemadaecha: The Pahlavi Texts of, Edited by B. N. Dhabhar in *Indo-Iranian Studies in honour of Dastur D. P. Sanjana*, p.117-130. London, 1925.

Avesta: Translated into English by James Darmesteter and L. H. Mills. In *Sacred Books of the East*, vols, 4, 23, 31.

Bundahishn: Edited by T. D. and B. T. Anklesaria. Bombay, 1908.

Cama Memorial Volume: Edited by J. J. Modi. Bombay, 1900.

Dabistan: Translated from the original Persian by Shea and Troyer. 3 vols. Paris, 1843.

Dinshaw, V.: The Date and Country of Zarathushtra. Hyderabad (Deccan), 1912.

Encyclopaedia of Religion and Ethics: Edited by James Hastings. 12 vols. Edinburgh, 1908-1921.

Epistles of Manushchihar: Translated from the Pahlavi text by E. W. West. In *Sacred Books of the East*, vol. 18.

Haug, Martin: Essays On the Sacred Language, Writings, and Religion of the Parsis. 3d ed. Edited and enlarged by E. W. West. London, 1884.

Henry, Victor: Le Parsisme. Paris, 1905.

Kohut, Alexander: The Jewish Angelology and Demonology based upon Parsism. Translated from the German by K. R. Cama. Bombay, 1883.

Lazarus, M. E.: The Zend-Avesta and Solar Religions. New York, 1852.

Lehmann, Edvard: Zarathushtra. Kobenhavn, 1899.

Modi Memorial Volume: Bombay, 1930.

Moffatt, J.: Zoroastrianism and Primitive Christianity. In *Hibbert Journal*, 1903, p. 763-780; *ibid*, 1904, p. 347-359.

Moulton, James H.: Early Religious Poetry of Persia. Cambridge, 1911.

Moulton, James H.: Early Zoroastrianism. London, 1913.

14

Religious Rituals and Traditions

Zoroastrian doctrines and rites should be studied within the historical context. The elabouration and propagation of rite practices over time must be elucidated in order to comprehend fully the values attached to beliefs and practices, as Zoroastrians and their culture cannot be separated from their heritage. It would be foolish to set aside the zoroastrian rites and deny the importance of past experience, both person and communal, on perception and faith.

In Zoroastrian rites a symbolic relationship is established among the actions, words, objects and substances used in the rites and the religious world itself. This relationship transmits the beliefs that underlie rite practices to the Zoroastrian participants in terms of the basic principles of zoroastrianism. The revelatory encounter with symbols, although present in everyday life, occurs most forcefully within the religious and social parameters of rite practices.

As per Zoroastrian doctrine, every religious rite serves more than a limted corporeal function; it aids in the final renovation of the entire world. The Pahlavi commentary to the Videvdat (Vendidad) emphasizes: "Purity of man [and] purity of the spirit is best from birth (5:21)" thus the Zoroastrian cleaning rites not only cleanse the corporeal body but also purify the spirit through prayers uttered during such rites.

The theological linking of the spirite and material aspects of the world in the Gathas froms the basis of every action. All thoughts, words and deeds can serve to further the triumph of Ahura Mazda over evil, Anghra Mainyu. Truth over deceit/lie. It is firmly believed that only by adhering to the creed of "good thoughts, good words and good deeds" (Av. Humata, Huxta, Hvarshta; phl. Humat, Huxt, Huwarsht) can a Zoroastrian act in accordance with the will of Ahura Mazda and the laws of his religion. Also the celestial and ethical dualism present in the

Zoroastrian faith provides the basis for all the rites in both doctrine and practice.

The purity of the spirit and body is being embodied by the religion itself such as one finds in the cleaning rites of Padyab, Barashnum, Nahn and other minor rites. The other major rites like performing Yasna ceremony and even outer rites first require the Zoroastrian priests to undergo such cleaning rites before performing any major or minor rites.

The Zoroastrian beliefs and rite practices are integrated into the religion over 3500 years and are doing well. Zoroastrianism without its intricate religious rites will not survive. Both beliefs and rite practices are integrated into the religion and presented as a unified part of the planned and purposeful work of Ahura Mazda and they connect the material and spirite worlds thus making the entire world a holy singularity whose purity must be maintained at all times and all His seven creations must remain in the untainted state (in perfect ecological balance) to further His plan of renovation by making the subsistence brilliant and ushering the triumph of truth over lie and deceit.

RELIGIOUS RITUALS

Prayer is the heavenward soaring of the spirit on wordy wings. Man has always prayed. Primitive man who did not understand natural phenomena worshipped power in the invisible beings whom he feared. He humbled and humiliated himself before them, and strove to placate and mollify them. His more enlightened descendants began worshipping goodness or knowledge or morality in gods. Prayer in its origin is instinctive and it gradually grows rational and moral. Man has always wearied God with his extravagant demands. He has prayed that fortune may drop from the skies. He has fancied gods would do miracles for him. And he has always expected that gods should answer all his prayers. His mental and moral progress has purified prayer. Naturally, he prays for his health and vigour of body, for food and riches, for offspring and long life. In his nobler mood, he prays for purity of mind and heart. He prays that God may strengthen him to fight temptation, vice, and sin. When he falters and falls, he feels contrition for his misdeeds, strips his heart bare before God and implores him to wipe out his transgressions.

When his troubles are sleeping and the world smiles upon him, man sometimes forgets that he owes the happy turn in his life to God and prays not, or, if he prays he prays with his lips what he disowns with his heart. Some sorrow, some disaster throws him again on his knees. When darkness and gloom hang heavily upon him, when he is plunged into deep dejection, when he is cast down by the sense of his utter helplessness, when he thinks the world is giving way beneath his feet then to God he turns for succour. With uplifted hands and on bended knees, he unburdens himself of his afflictions, seeks strength in prayer and prays with his heart on his tongue. In his infinite mercy, God beckons him near, softens his bitterness, chases away his anxiety, strengthens him to triumph over his hardships, and fortifies him against the assaults of vice and sin. The soothing gleam of joy dawns on his sorrowful life and, with God as his rock, he finds himself on safe soil.

Homage, invocation, sacrifice, and the outpouring of prayer are the various expressions of the inward longings of man to commune with the heavenly, to enter into mutual intercourse with him. Those are outlets through which man pours forth his heart to the fountain of all bounty. The person who surrenders himself to unseen powers, who kneels down in humility at the altar, who with uplifted hands pays homage to the hidden forces behind the rising sun or the waxing moon or the roaring ocean, and who carries an oblation to the fire or a libation to the waters is psychologically greatly affected. Such attitudes of spirit have great subjective value, for they deeply influence man's character. Prayer is the highest type of expression through which man conveys to his Heavenly Father his feelings of joy and sorrow, gratitude and love, hope and fear, or in his hunger and thirst for the heavenly grace lays down his grievances before him, confesses his guilt, craves for help, seeks mercy. Dedication is the first requisite. Mere mutterings of a few formulas with the lips, while the heart does not pulsate with dedicational fervour, are no prayer. Where there is no such prayer, there is no dedication; and where there is no dedication, there is no religion.

A host of gods claimed man's homage. Gods were bountiful and benevolent. Men prayed to them. Prayers were mostly petitions for gifts of health, long life, offspring, cattle, chariots, riches, and victory over enemies. In Egypt prayers were offered to Amen and Amen-Ra at Thebes, Re-Horus at Heliopolis, Ptah at Memphis, who rose to great eminence and drew a large concourse of worshippers to their shrines. In Babylonia and Assyria hymns were composed in honour of Marduk and Ashur, Shamash and Anu, Nergal and Ninib, and other gods and goddesses like Ishtar. Men and women humiliated themselves, exalted the divinities, addressed them with honourific names as wise, creators, powerful and merciful, sang paeans to them and prayed to them. Gods were bountiful and men prayed to them for long life, numerous offspring, and wealth.

The Vedic Aryans invoked gods for specific gifts which were in their power to bestow. Agni and Prajapati were asked to grant them fulfilment of their desires and to shower wealth upon them. Agni and the Maruts were asked to give heroic offspring and sucess. Men besought Agni to be near them for their welfare and to be of easy access as a father is to his son. The Adityas were invoked to guide them to the way of pleasantness. Ushas was implored to give them good luck and glory and riches. Indra was besought to render them help in their conflict with the black-skinned Dasyus and to enable them to ward off their enemies. Indra and Varuna were asked to confer upon them pleasure and objects of their desires. Yama was invoked to grant them long life upon earth and happy life in the company of gods in heaven. Men dreaded Rudra's wrath and prayed humbly to avert his ill-will. Men prayed to gods and sought safety against hostile demons who worked for harm.

Power of Prayer

Ahura Mazda hears prayers even in thought. Virtuous thinking is prayer. Such prayer lifts man to Ahura Mazda. Potent is the power of prayer unto Ahura Mazda, says Zarathushtra. Like unto Ahura Mazda, Zarathushtra addresses his prayers to Vohu Manah, Asha, Khshathra, and Armaiti, either as Ahura Mazda's characteristics or as the eternal beings representing holy virtues. He pours out his spirit in passionate supplication to Ahura Mazda and longs to win his love. With hands lifted in fervent homage and with dedicational hymns, he yearns to come to Ahura Mazda. He praises and beseeches Ahura Mazda to be his own. Steeped in dedication, he comes to him with worship and praise. He seeks to approach Mazda with songs of praise and invocation. Through morality of Asha and good deeds of Vohu Manah, he says, he will come to Ahura Mazda worshipping with words of praise. He is anxious to behold his maker and to hold converse with him. He implores Ahura Mazda to come to him through Vohu Manah. In another place he beseeches Ahura Mazda to come in his person through Asha and Vohu Marrah. He is eager to win Ahura Mazda, Vohu Manah and Asha for himself. He desires to know when being enlightened he will See Ahura Mazda, Asha, Vohu Manah, Sraosha, and the throne of Ahura Mazda. He appeals to Ahura Mazda, Asha, Khshathra, and Armaiti to come to him; to hearken unto him and have mercy upon him. The disciple long to dedicate their songs of praise to Mazda, Asha, and Vahishta Manah and say that they will never incur their provocation. The songs of praise and homage, the prayers and good deeds of the virtuous are stored in Garo Demana [Garothman], the Dwelling of Song.

Bountiful Ahura Mazda is munificent in showering his gifts upon humanity and he knows what is best to give. Zarathushtra implores him to give what pleases him. He prays for long life; that he may be enabled to perform the good deeds of the Holy Spirit through morality. He asks him to apportion all good things of life and further the life of the body through Vohu Manah and Khshathra as per his will Vigour and endurance are the essential qualities that enable man to fight evil and cling to morality and Zarathushtra prays for them.

These benedictions are the earthly counterparts of weal and immortality, the heavenly boons represented by Haurvatat and Ameretat, and Zarathushtra asks Ahura Mazda to bestow them upon him through Vohu Manah as per his commandments. He prays for the possession of spirite riches of Ahura Mazda, the riches that form part of the life of Vohu Manah. He beseeches Ahura Mazda to come unto him for help in his need with Vohu Manah, Asha, Khshathra, and Armaiti. He asks Ahura Mazda to shower his benedictions upon the man who approaches him with invocation. He prays for that heavenly benediction, the power of Ahura Mazda which he gives through Vohu Manah unto the holy man who furthers morality through words and deeds tinged with religious knowledge. He invokes upon all the benedictions of Ahura Mazda, Vohu Manah, Asha, and Armaiti, who are all of one will. His best prayer is heard and his ardent wish is fulfilled that those who once opposed his teachings have now come over to the faith to embrace the words and deeds of his religion and Ahura Mazda has extended to him the life of felicity now and for ever.

Zarathushtra faces bitter opposition from those who have played upon the credulity of the ignorant and the superstitious and have prospered thereby. He invokes Ahura Mazda for the frustration of their mischievous machinations. Even prophets are moved with indignation and virtuous wrath against evil-minded persons who guide humanity to destruction. Jesus, the incarnation of gentleness, denounces the Scribes and Pharisees with prophetic rage as fools and hypocrites, serpents and vipers; he overthrows the tables of money-changers, and casts them out of the temple with a whip of small cords. Zarathushtra exhorts those who seek Vohu Manah's benedictions to put down violence and cruelty. He implores Armaiti not to let evil sovereigns govern the land, Bendva is the powerful foe who thwarts Zarathushtra's work of winning over men and women to morality, and he prays unto Ahura Mazda for his downfall. He calls such persons liars, deceivers, and evil.

The Manthras

The prophetic word of great moral significance is called Manthra, corresponding to the Vedic Mantra. Both in Iran and India they turn into spells of magical charms. Ahura Mazda has, in one will with Asha, made them. Zarathushtra prays that he and Vishtaspa may successfully declare them. Whoso explains these sacred formulas unto the wise reaps joy. Zarathushtra is the friend of one who chants them with homage; and invokes Ahura Mazda to help him through Asha. He rouses all those that recite them to religious life. He gains the best prize who declares the true words of morality, weal, and immortality. He who follows morality under the inspiration of the Manthras gains weal and immortality. Those who do not base their conduct upon these salutary words as the prophet himself thinks and does, will be in the woe in the end. Grehma the opponent of the faith and his evil followers who harass the messenger of Ahura Mazda's holy words will go to the dwelling of the Worst Thought. Zarathushtra seeks to know how will he rout evil by the holy words of Mazda's ordinance. With these sacred formulas on their tongues, he says, he and his disciples will convert the evil to their Lord. The words of the evil are also called Manthras, and the prophet exhorts his hearers not to listen to them, because they bring destruction and demise to the settlements of the disciple.

Rites and Sacrifices

Gods required to be propitiated that they power extend their favour to men. When men began to guide settled agricultural life, they began to offer the first fruits of the harvest and produce of the cattle as thanksgiving oblations to them. With growing sucess they prepared rich repasts of sumptuous food and wine and invoked them to alight on the hpermitted place where ceremonial rites were performed, or kindled fire to despatch the sacrifices to heaven on its flaming tongues. Thus were the gods as well as the ancestral dead treated at sacrificial repasts everywhere. The Indo-Iranians were not behind other peoples and their sacrificial oblations consisted of milk and melted butter, grain and vegetables, flesh of goats and sheep, bulls and horses, and the exhilarating Soma-Haoma beverage. Elaborate rites and sacrifices offered to obtain coveted boons, to gain the remission of sins, and to stave off the terrors of hell. The consecrated food was partaken of by the sacrificers to reap the merit. The altars were reeking with the blood of animals that were sacrificed to innumerable gods. Zarathushtra does away with such sacrifices and purifies rites.

Rite is not religion; but it is a powerful aid to religious life. It feeds the emotional nature of man which plays the most outstanding part in religious life. It inspires dedicational fervour and purity of thoughts. Zarathushtra presumably utilized this formal side of religion to stimulate religious emotion and inspire virtuous conduct. Custom ascribes the division of society into priests, warriors, husbandmen, and artisans to the initiative of King Yima of the Golden Age of Iran. Zarathushtra does not recognize this fourfold professional order of society in the Gathas. He does not mention âthravan, 'the protector of fire' or priest. The Later Avesta speaks of the sacerdotal class by the title of âthravan. The Pahlavi texts continue to employ this priestly designation, and in addition speak of it as magopat, or magpat, corresponding to the Greek form Magi or Magus. Zarathushtra uses the forms derived from maga, 'great,' but it cannot be said that he uses them in reference to the priestly class. A threefold division of society appears in the Gathas, and Zarathushtra gives each one altogether different names. They are called xvaetu, airyaman, and verezena, probably indicating his immediate disciples, the nobility, and the functioning classes respectively.

The Later Avestan texts speak of distinct functionaries who officiated at the sacrificial ceremonies. The head of this group is zaotar, corresponding to Skt. hotar, 'the sacrificer.' Zarathushtra speaks of himself as a zaotar in one passage though with an ethical implication only. As a zaotar, he seeks the vision of Ahura Mazda and longs to hold communion with him. The food offered as a ceremonial oblation is known in the Avestan texts as myazda, and Zarathushtra says that the disciple will offer myazda with homage unto Ahura Mazda and Asha. He alludes once to draonah, 'thc sacred cake,' which forms an indispensable article of oblation in the later period. He speaks of it probably in the sense of the ambrosia and asks Haurvatat and Ameretat to confer it upon him for ever.

SOCIAL RITUALS

Temperance

In Zoroastrianism there is a great deal of emphasis on leading a balanced life. The body is susceptible to evil where as the spirit is immune from it. But both are deemed important for practicing morality and doing what is desirable for the creator. While living upon earth one should aim to "seek the maintenance and sucess of the body without injury to spirit and preservation of the spirit without injury to the body," One should avoid excesses of all kinds, such as covetousness, lustfulness and unseasonable chatter. The body and spirit should be well maintained by practicing the three commandments preached by Zoroaster: good thoughts, good words and good actions. Actions should be guided by the principle of moderation for the greater good of oneself and others. The body should not be subjected to extreme harshness but kept strong so that it would be immune to the the evil forces. Whether it is drinking wine or eating food, the guiding principle is whether such acts are impairing one's ability to think good thoughts, speak good words and do good actions.

Performance of sacrificial rites, paying visits to the fire temple, oblation prayers, following the teachings of Zoroaster and reciting the sacred verses are the recommended methods to live virtuously in this world. Fasting is not a recommended religious practice. Zoroastrianism does not find any virtue in renouncing the world or becoming a monk. There is no place for asceticism or renunciation either. It does not entertain the notion of spirite liberation. The spirits are already liberated. They are in the material world, for a specific purpose, as per God's decree, who commanded them to be upon earth and wait for end of the world. Man's obligation is to fulfil that purpose, not escape from it. Monkhood and monastic orders are therefore not recognized institutions in Zoroastrianism. Followers are advised to guide normal and healthy lives safeguarding themselves against the dangers posed evil forces. They should live virtuously, doing their part, get married and beget children, cultivate the good qualities represented by the six Amesha Spentas and keep the good in them alive and active.

Sudre

Zoroastrian wear, Sudre, a white upper garment, as a symbol of purity, and kusti, a sacred thread, around their waists. They are worn for safety. It is believed that those who do not wear these are mysteriously harmed by the evil forces. They are also used to profess one's faith in the religion. As per Denkard, those who do not wear kusti or Sudre are "equal to men of alien religion and not considered to belong to the true faith." In Zoroastrianism it is "a sinful act to keep the body unclothed with the Sudre and to wear Sudre without the girdle of the kusti." The kusti is made of 72 strands of lamb's wool. Each strand symbolizes a chapter in the Yasna. It is wound three times around the waist, signifying the three great commandments, namely, humata (good thoughts), hukta (good words) and harshvata (good deeds). A sacred mantra is chanted while tying or untying the kusti. Custom demands that the kusti is worn in the middle of the body to signify the importance of balance and moderation in human life.

Naujote

In Zoroastrianism, young boys and girls are admitted into the society through an initiation ceremony called Naujote. It is usually performed when a child is of seven or nine years age. In exceptional cases the maximum prescribed age is 15. Age is important because a child is initiated into the religions only when he has enough awareness and maturity to make an intelligent decision to become a follower of God and live a life of morality. Unlike in Vedic religion, in Zoroastrianism the initiation ceremony is performed for both boys and girls without any discrimination. During the ceremony, the initiate is given a sacred bath and made to wear Sudre (white garment) and kusti (sacred thread) to signify the beginning of their lives on the spirite path.

Yasna

Like the yajna of the Vedic people, yasna is a sacrificial rite, performed daily in the morning hours by two qualified Zoroastrian priests at a designated sacred place in a fire temple. In Zoroastrianism rites are an important aspect of religious practice. Apart from the material gains that may accrue, they are performed to enhance and invigorate the purity and morality of the world in general and people in particular, so that they remain immune to the forces of evil. In a yasna, the priests usually chant the sacred manthras and make sacrificial oblations symbolically to the sacred fire, which is a symbol of god and seek His benedictions. The Yasna is therefore is a tool of morality, the practice of which is equal to the practice of the three commandments of God, namely to practice as well as live in the company of good thoughts, good words and good actions.

Apart from its ethical implications, the yasna has a symbolic significance. The various sacrificial items used in the yasna symbolically represent some aspects of God's invisible creation. The fire used in the sacrifice represents God Himself as a symbol of light and recipient of the oblations, and also Asha Vahishta or the spirit of Purity and Morality. The barsom, the twigs or the metal wire, used in the sacrifice, represents the connecting link between the visible and the invisible aspects of creation. The metal implements used in the rite such as the cups, saucers and the stands represent the sky and Kshatra Virya, the creative power of God. The earth and the stones used in the construction of the rite place represent the earth and Aramaiti, the spirit of dedication. Milk, butter and the hair from a white bull represent the animal kingdom and spirit of Good Mind. The fruit, haoma (wine or a sacred drink) and pomegranate twigs represent plant kingdom and the spirit of Ameretat or Immortality. Consecrated water represent the waters of the world and Haurvatat or the spirit of Purity and Wholeness. The priests themselves through their virtuous conduct represent humans as a part of the heavenly force.

Ahuna Vairya

Just as the Hindus chant Gayatri mantra and consider it as very sacred, the Parsis chant Ahuna Vairya Mantra which is considered to be very sacred by them. as per the holy scriptures of Zorastrianism, Ahura Mazda uttered this manthra at the time creation and apparented the whole creation. He also used it to drive away Angra Mainyu when he tried to invade the kingdom of God. As per the Zoroastrian texts, Angra Mainyu was so terried upon hearing the manthra that he fell back into the abyss and remained their stupefied for 3000 years. The significance of this mantra is such that chanting of it is considered to be equivalent to chanting of all the sacred texts. By chanting it continuously, the Parsis believe that one can drive away forces of darkness both within and without.

The first line of the verse says that just as a ahu (king) is powerful on earth, a ratu (a seer or a great spirit) is powerful everywhere because of his Asha. The second line of the verse says that the gifts of Vahumano are for those who work for the Master of life. It means that Vahumano bestows his boons (love and purity of thought) upon those who indulge in good thoughts and good actions as per the heavenly will of God. The third line of the verse says that the Supreme power of God is bestowed upon him who considers himself as the helper of the meek and the lowly. The third line thus lays special emphasis on the notion of Sraosha or service.

Three Commandments

As per Zoroastrian principles men of faith should live upon earth doing what is desirable for the Creator. Through knowledge they should come to know what God wants and do it for His sake. The best way to achieve it is by practicing morality through the three commandments given to them through Zoroaster. The three commandments are humata (good thought), hukhta (good word), and havarshta (good deeds). As per Zoroastrian beliefs, good thoughts keep the mind free from impurities. Holy thoughts are the source of good words and good deeds. Through good thoughts, good works and good deeds one can communicate with

Vohu Mano and other heavenly entities. They enhance the power of the good forces in the world and increase their numbers. They also weaken and slow down the influx of evil forces. Men should be aware of how evil works in the world, how they make the thoughts, words and deeds of men contaminated with destructive vices. When men think evil thoughts, they attract evil into themselves. When Ahirman enters a person, Vohuman departs from there, leaving him entirely to the evil. What awaits such a fallen and contaminated person is agonizing suffering in the hell.

Social Divisions

Ancient Zoroastrian society was organized more or less like the Vedic society into four classes consisting of priests, warriors, husbandmen and artisans. The obligation of the priestly class was to maintain the religious purity by performing the religious rites and invocations as per established procedures and preserving their purity and sanctity, practicing morality and keeping themselves free from heresy, greed, trafficking, attention to trifles and non-belief. The obligation of the warriors was to defeat the enemy and keep their country well protected. safeguarding themselves against violence, dissincerity, cruelty, ostentation, pride and arrogance. The obligation of the husbandmen was to cultivate the lands and keep the world invigorated and populous, staying away from ignorance, envy, ill-will and maliciousness. The obligation of the artisan class was to do labour using their skills and charge fair wages for the work rendered and protecting themselves from vices such as unbelief, ingratitude, improper recitation of prayers, laziness and abusiveness.

Vices

The following vices of the four classes are listed in the Menog-i Khrad:

- The vices of priests are heresy, covetousness, negligence, trafficking (sudakih), attention to trifles, and unbelief in the religion.
- The vices of warriors are oppression, violence, promise-breaking, unmercifulness (an-avokhshaga-vandih), ostentation (dakhshih), haughtiness, and arrogance.
- The vices of husbandmen are ignorance, enviousness, ill-will, and maliciousness.
- And the vices of artisans are unbelief, want of thanksgiving, improper muttering of prayers, moroseness, and abusiveness.'

CEREMONIAL RITUALS

Birth Ceremonies

The birth of a child is a very auspicious event in a Parsi house. It was so also in ancient Persia. As per the Vendidad, Ahura Mazda says:- "I prefer a person with children (puthrânê) to one without children (aputhrâi)." Even the very ground, where lives a man with his children, is described as feeling happy. Cultivation and a good supply of food to people are recommended, because they make humanity healthy and able to produce a healthy progeny. To be the father of good children was a benediction from the Yazatas, like Tishtrya, Mithra, Haoma, and Atar, and from the Fravashis. To be childless, was a curse from the Yazatas. Domestic animals, when ill-fed and ill-treated, cursed their masters, that they may be childless. Childlessness was something like a punishment from heaven. Kingly splendour (khwarrah) was associated with those who were blessed with children. As per the Shayest Na-Shayest, one of the advantages of having children was "that the obligation and good works which a son performs are as much the father's as though they had been done by his own hand."

A Zoroastrian woman often prayed for a good, healthy child. A Zoroastrian man and woman prayed before their sacred fire for a good, virtuous child. A woman without a child felt as sorry as a fertile piece of land that ia not cultivated. She prayed for a husband who could make her a mother of children.

Among the Achaemenians, a wife who gave birth to many children was a favourite with her husband, who did not like to displease her in any way. Children being the choicest gift of God, their lives were, as it were, pledged by parents for the solemn performance of an act. We read in Herodotus: "Next to prowess in arms, it is regarded as the greatest proof of manly excellence to be the father of many sons. Every year, the King sends rich gifts to the man, who can show the largest number: for they hold that number is strength." Strabo also says a similar thing. We learn from the writings of the Christian Martyrs of Persia, that the ancient Persians, did not, for the above reasons, like the prohibition against marriage among the Christians in the case of holy young Christian girls.

In the Avesta itself, we find no references to any ceremony or rite during the state of pregnancy. The only allusion we find is this:- Women on finding themselves enceinte prayed before Ardwisura for an easy delivery, and then for a codevout supply of milk at their breast for their children. The allusion to these prayers suggests, that there may be some formal ceremonies accompanying those prayers, but we do not know what they were.

Shayaaast ne-Shayest directs, that, when it is known that a lady of the family has become pregnant, a fire may be maintained most carefully in the house. The Saddar also gives this direction. We have the remnant of this injunction in the present custom of some of the modern Parsis, who on the occasion of the completion of the fifth and seventh months of pregnancy, light a lamp of clarified butter in their houses. The reason, assigned for this in the Pahlavi and Persian books, is that the fire, so kindled in the house, keeps out daevas, i.e., evil influences from the house. Again, a fire or a lamp is even now taken to be symbolical of the continuation of a line of offspring. For example, it is not rare to hear, even now, words like these "Tamâro cherâg roshan rahê" i.e., "May your lamp be always burning." This benediction is meant to say: "May your son live long, and may your line of descent continue." The ancient Iranians believed that there were many chances of the children to be born being males, if the males were stronger than the females at the time of notion.

As per the Avesta, in the state of pregnancy, a woman is to be looked after very carefully. It is wrong for the husband to have sexual intercourse with her in her advanced state of pregnancy, which, as per the Rivayats, commences with the fifth month. She is to abstain from coming into contact with any dead or decomposing matter, even with a thing like one's tooth-pick which may contain germs of one's disease.

During pregnancy, the modern Parsis have no religious ceremonies or rites. On the completion of the fifth month of pregnancy one day is celebrated and known as "Panch mâsiûn," i.e., the day of the fifth month. Similarly, a day is observed on the completion of the seventh month, and is known as Agharni. These days are observed as auspicious days of rejoicing only in the case of the first pregnancy. They are observed not in accordance with any religious injunction or with religious ceremonies or rites. The expectancy of a child being a joyful event as said above, these days — especially some day after the completion of the seventh month — are observed as joyous occasions, when the lady who is enceinte is presented with suits of clothes by her parents, relatives, and friends and especially by the family of her husband. The husband, is in turn, presented with a suit of clothes by the wife's family. Sweets are sent out as presents by the husband's family to the bride's house and to near relations and friends. In these sweets, one prepared in the form of a coconut has a outstanding place. A cocoanut typifies a man's head and so it is a symbol of fecundity. Some of the customs observed on these occasions are more Indian in their origin and signification than originally Persian or Zoroastrian.

In the case of the first delivery, it generally takes place in the house of the wife's parents. A room or a part of a room, generally on the down-floor, is prepare an set apart for the purpose. As the Vendidad says, the place for delivery must be very clean, dry and least-frequented by others. It appears, that in former times, such places were specially provided in Parsi houses on the down-floors. Parsi houses in those times had generally spacious down-floors that were used for all purposes. The upper floors were low, and were rather like lofts. So, the down-floors provided proper places for delivery, as enjoined in the Vendidad. But, as, with changed circumstances, Parsi houses of today are not what they were before, and as, at present, in storied houses in big towns, the down-floors are generally the worst part of the houses, places of delivery at the down-floor are now-a-days properly condemned as unhealthy. In the case of a house or a place where no delivery has taken place before, religious-minded persons generally take care that a religious ceremony may be performed there before the delivery. In other words, they get the place consecrated. A priest or two say and perform the Afringan prayer and ceremony over the place. At times, even the Baj prayer is recited. It seems that one of the lost nasks (books), the Husparam, had special chapters on the subject of parturition.

On the birth of a child, a lamp is lighted and kept burning, for at least three days, in the room where the lady is confined. The Saddar says: "When the child becomes separate from the mother it is necessary to burn a lamp for three nights and days — if they burn a fire it would be better — so that the demons and fiends may not be able to do any damage and harm; because when a child is born, it is exceedingly delicate for those three days." Some people keep the lamp burning for ten days and some for forty days, the latter number being generally observed as the period of confinement.

On delivery, the mother is enjoined to remain apart from others. She is not to come into contact with fire, water, and other furniture of the house. In the case of those that give birth to still-born children, it is enjoined in the Vendidad, that they must thus remain apart for 12 days. This period has been latterly extended, as described m the later Pahlavi and Persian books, to forty days in all cases of delivery. Now-a-days, a Parsi lady has generally forty days of confinement after delivery. The Saddar says: "During forty days it is not proper that they should leave the child alone; and it is also not proper that the mother of the infant should put her foot over a threshold in the dwelling (i.e., leave the house) or cast her eyes upon a hill, or it is bad for her menstruation."

Some families, following the Hindu custom, observe the fifth day after birth, known as pachory (i.e., the fifth day), and the tenth day, known as dasori (i.e., the tenth day), as gala days, but these days have no religious signification.

During the above forty days, the lady is in a state of isolation. She is not to come into contact with anybody and with any part of the ordinary furniture of the house, especially wooden furniture and linen articles. Her food is to be served to her on her plate by others. Those who have to come into contact with her have to bathe before they mix with others. Even the medical attendants had to do so, but, now-a-days, this sanitary rule is more honoured in the breach than in its observance. The original injunction may, among some other reasons, have been intended to observe "purity" in order to prevent the spread of the diseases to which women in this state are subject.

At the end of forty days, which is the period of confinement, the lady has to purify herself by a bath before ordinarily mixing with others. At first she takes an ordinary bath and then goes through what is called 'nân,' a contraction of the Sanskrit word "snaan " which is a sacred bath. A priest, generally the family priest, administers that bath with consecrated water.

All the bedding and clothes of the woman, used during the forty days of her confinement after delivery, are rejected from ordinary use. They are enjoined to be destroyed, lest they carry germs of disease among others. But, now-a-days, that injunction is not strictly followed. They are given away to sweepers.

Formerly, a mother in child-birth first drank a few drops of the sacred Haoma-juice, which was squeezed and consecrated in a fire-temple. The Persian Farziât-nameh of Dastur Darab Pâhlan says, that a new-born child should be made to drink a few drops of this juice. If the consecrated Haoma-juice may not be had, one may pound at home a few Haoma twigs and a few leaves of the pomegranate tree in water with the recital of an Ahunwar and give the juice for the first drink. In the Hom Yasht, Haoma is said to give fine healthy children to women. Haoma was symbolatical of immortality. Anquetil Du Perron42 refers to this religious custom as prevalent in his time. But now-a-days this custom is rarely observed, and in place of the Haoma-juice, a sweet drink made of molasses or sugar is given to the child as a first auspicious drink.

Herodotus refers to the custom of naming the child among the ancient Persians. We infer from what he says, that the parents waited for some time after birth, and then, watching the corporeal and mental characteristics of the child, gave them such names as indicated their characteristics. In the case of modern Parsis, many name the child after an immediate deceased ancestor. A Parsi name is made up of three names. The first is his own personal name. The second is his father's name and the third is his surname or family name. Now, it is the first of these three, that is the proper name of the child; and in the case of that name, many prefer to call a child by an immediate ancestor's name.

This process of naming the child has one particular religious significance, and it is this: In all religious ceremonies, during life or after demise, a person's name is recited as he or she is named at the time of his or her birth: This name is called Janam-nâm or birth-name. In his or her Naojote, i.e., sacred shirt and thread ceremony, marriage ceremony, or any other ceremony enjoined by him or her during lifetime, the birth-name is recited together with the father's name. In all the ceremonies after demise, the name is similarly recited. In the case of a female, her personal name is recited together with that of her father as long as she is not betrothed. But after betrothal, her name is recited together with that of her husband. As a lady's name is recited with her huband's in all ceremonies after betrothal, the ceremony of betrothal is known as "Nâmzad shudan" in Persian, meaning "to be named," or nâm pâdvun in Gujarati meaning "to give a name."

Herodotus says of the old Achremenian times, that "their names, which are expressive of some bodily or mental excellence, all end with the same letter." Looking to the names as given in the Avesta, we find that they mostly end in 'a'. The same or similar names when given by Greek writers end in 's'. This can be easily seen from a list of Iranian names given by Rawlinson with their corresponding forms in Greek writings.

We find from stray allusions here and there in the Pahlavi and Persian writings, that, at times, children were named after, or in memory of, some particular events at the time of their birth. For example, names like Rustam and Kobâd are associated with some particular events at the time of their birth. Herodotus47 speaks of Persian names as expressive of their corporeal form. Thus we read in the Khushro Shirin of Nizami that the father of Khusro Parviz named the child Khusru, because he saw him 'kinglike' (Khusravi) in appearance.

As for the names derived from the Zoroastrian Yazatas or angels, children are at times named after some particular Yazatas, if they are born on the days of the month bearing the name of those Yazatas. For example, a male or female child born on the day Mihr, the 16th day of a Parsi month, may be named Meherji or Meherbai respectively.

The birthday of a Parsi child and especially the first birthday, is an important day. No religious rites are enjoined as necessary. But the parents generally like to celebrate the day in what one may call, a religious way. After a bath and a new suit of clothes, the child is generally sent with some sandalwood to an adjoining Fire-temple. There, the ash of the sacred fire is attached to its forehead. Some of those, who can afford, get a religious ceremony, known as Fareshta performed. That is generally done on the first birthday. This ceremony consists of the recital of prayers in honour of the 33 different Yazatas or angels, and indicates, that God's benedictions are invoked upon the child, and that it is wished that it may be blessed with all the corporeal characteristics and mental virtues over which God has directed these Yazatas to preside.

From a strictly religious point of view, there is nothing special to be remarked in the case of the childhood of a Parsi child. It is held to be innocent and not liable or subject to the performance of any religious duties or rites. If God forbid, the child dies before the Naojote [navjote] or the investiture of the sacred shirt and thread, its funeral ceremonies are on a lower scale. In the recital of the funeral prayers, the child is spoken of as 'Khûrd,' i.e., small or young. This appellation signifies that the deceased person was too young and that it had no responsibility for duties or rites as a Zoroastrian.

Marriage Ceremonies

As per the Parsi books, marriage is an institution that is favoured by the Almighty God. As per the Vendidad, Ahura Mazda says: "O Spitama Zarathushtra! Indeed, I thus recommend hereunto thee, a man with a wife above a Magava (i.e., an unmarried man) who grows up (unmarried), a man with a family above one without any family, a man with children above one who is without children." The very ground where a married man lives is represented as feeling happy. Zarathushtra asks: "O Creator of the corporeal world! Which is the second place on the earth that feels happy?" Ahura Mazda replies: "That (place is happy), over which a holy man builds a house with fire, cattle, wife, children, and good followers."

The reason why marriage is recommended in Parsi books is that there is a greater likelihood for a married person than for an unmarried one to be able to withstand corporeal and mental afflictions and to guide a religious and virtuous life.

Marriage being thus considered a good institution and well-nigh a religious obligation, recommended by religious scriptures, a Parsi considers it a meritorious act to help his co-religionist to marry. The Vendidad says: "If a co-religionist — be he brother or friend — comes to thee with a desire for a wife, get him married to a wife." To bring about the marriage of a maiden, who has reached her puberty, with a good righteoun man, is considered to be very meritorious and an act of atonement for a sin.

We learn also from Herodotus, that in ancient Persia, the State encouraged married life. He says: "Next to prowess in arms, it is regarded as the greatest proof of manly excellence to be the father of many sons. Every year the King sends such gifts to the man who can show the largest number, for they hold that number is strength."3 Thus, from very ancient times, marriage is considered among the Parsis to be a most important event in one's life.

After the several vicissitudes of fortune that the society has passed through, it is difficult to determine how many and which of the present several marriage customs of the Parsis are originally Zoroastrian or Persian. But this much can be said with well-nigh a certainty, that the strictly solemn or the religious part of the ceremony, wherein the priests take part, is more or less originally Persian.

The nuptial ceremonies of the marriage-day are preceded by several other ceremonies. When the match is arranged, an auspicious day is fixed for the betrothal. The new moon day, or the first day (Hormazd) of the Parsi month, or the twentieth day, over which Behram [Warharan], the angel of Victory, is believed to preside, are generally considered to be auspicious days. Now-a-days, the parties generally fix such auspicious days or the days most convenient to them. But still it is not rare, especially in the Mofussil towns, for the parties to resort to Hindu astrologers to name one or more auspicious days for the betrothal or marriage or such other auspicious events.

Matches are generally arranged by the parents with the consent of the children, though, now-a-days, there are many cases of marriages where marrying parties make their own choice. In the latter case, they generally consult the parents. Mutual friends of the two families generally carry messages and bring about the arrangement. The Pahlavi Pand-nâmeh of Aderbad Marespand recommends this process. The marriages of the three sons of Faridoon and the marriages of Rustam with Tehemina and of Kaus with Soudabeh were, as we learn from Ferdowsi, thus arranged. Upto late, and even now to a certain extent, professional match-makers were not unknown.

On the betrothal day, at first, the ladies of the bridegroom's family go to the house of the bride and make her money present in silver coins. Then the ladies of the bride's family go to the house of the bridegroom and make him a similar present. These reciprocal presents of silver coins form the only important part of the ceremony.

The ladies return to their houses, after a little refreshment, mostly consisting of fish, sweets, curd, plantains and sugar. The modern Parsi term for this ceremony is Adrâvvûn, but the older term is Nâm pâdvûn, which is derived from the Persian term 'Nâmzad kardan,' i.e., to name. It is so called from the fact that after the betrothal, the brides took the names of the bridegrooms.6 As per the Parsi custom, a girl's name is always connected with her husband's in religious ceremonies after the betrothal, even if, by some chance or accident, marriage does not take place. This shows that betrotha was considered to be a solemn ceremony for a marriage contract. Nuptial songs are generally sung on this occasion.

The next ceremonial occasion is that of Divo, i.e., a light. It is so called because early in the morning of a day fixed for the occasion, an oil lamp is lit in the house of each party. The ladies of each of the two families go in turn to the house of the other, and place a silver coin in the lamp there. This occasion is considered more important than that of the betrothal, because, on it, formal presents of clothes and rings are made. When the matches are arranged, the betrothal is hastily determined upon, to give a formal stamp, as it were, to the arrangement, The parties then have no time to prepare mutual presents and gifts; so, this second occasion, the day for which is fixed leisurely, is more important than the betrothal, for the formal presents of gifts, The first wedding rings are generally presented by both the parties on that day.

The next important occasion is that of Adarni, It is the occasion, on which, the dowry given by the bride's father, is presented to the bride-groom's family. On several other occasions of holidays between the betrothal day and the marriage day, several presents are sent to each other's family, mostly from the family of the bride to that of the bridegroom. The marriage occasion is one, when the mothers of the bride and the bridegroom, expect presents of clothes from their own parents. If the parents are dead, it is considered to be the obligation of the brother or brothers to present a suit or suits of clothes to the sister. A nuptial song is generally sung on such an occasion.

An auspicious day is fixed for the marriage. In some families, even now, it is the astrologer who determines which day is auspicious for the marriage. The new moon day and the full moon day are auspicious. Tuesdays are inauspicious.The marriage festivities generally last for four days. The first of these is called mândav-saro, when a twig of a tree, generally a mango-tree, is planted near the door, symbolic of a wish for fertility. The second and the third days are known as Varadh-patra days when religious ceremonies in honour of the dead are performed.

Coming to the ceremonies of the day of marriage itself, the bride and the bridegroom take in the morning or in the afternoon, a sacred bath with consecrated water. This sacred bath is known as nân. The Parsi marriages are generally performed in the evening, just a little after sunset. The bridegroom generally sits in the compound of the house or bungalow in a promiscuous place in the midst of a company of several male friends and relations. The bride and the lady guests are accommodated with seats within the building.

Marriage is considered to be an event which must be celebrated, not quietly, but with some eclat. It must be celebrated in the presence of an assembly (anjoman) who can bear witness to the event.

Marriages were performed in ancient Iran, with pomp. It says that the drums and fifes which played at marriage gatherings announced the marriage to the people of the town or village. The assembly of males that gathers on marriage occasions is called Shahjan, (i.e., the assembly for the royal bride).

The bridegroom puts on the usual ceremonial dress of the Parsis, which is a loose flowing dress, full of folds and curls. This flowing dress is always white in colour. The bridegroom holds a shawl in his hand, a shawl being considered in India a symbol of respect and greatness. He has the mark of a Kunkun (red pigment) on his forehead.

The red pigment mark on the forehead of a bride is always round and that on the forehead of a bridegroom always long and vertical. The reason is this: the long vertical mark of the male symbolizes a ray of the sun, and the round mark of the female symbolizes the moon. A handsome man is compared by Oriental writers with the sun, but the beauty of a woman is always compared with that of the moon. The sun is always represented in ancient pictures, as a round disc with shooting rays. Again, the sun, through his rays, is a fructifying agent, but the moon is represented as a conceiving agent. She absorbs the rays of the sun. Just as the sun is a fructifying agent, and the moon a conceiving agent, so is man in his relation to woman. Hence it is that the mark on a man's forehead is long and vertical like the rays of the sun, and that on a woman's forehead round like the moon.

The bridegroom has a garland of flowers round his neck as a symbol of sweetness and geniality. The bridegroom is called var-râjâ, i.e., husband-king. For this particular occasion of marriage his position is taken to be elevated.

Some of the assembled friends and relations then make their presents to the bridegroom and his father. The presents mostly consist of shawls or rings or money in cash. The bride and her parents receive similar presents from their friends. Up to a few years ago, these presents, especially those in cash, were very common. Small presents of cash up to Rs. 5 were not necessarily paid into the hands of the parties, but were given into the hands of a friend or relation, who acted as a receiver or collector for the occasion. He put down in a book the names of the donors and the amount of their money-gifts. Such money-presents used to payoff a part of the marriage expenses. The memo kept by the receiver proved to be of use to the parties when, on similar occasions of marriages in the family of their friends, they had to make similar presents in return.

It appears from the Avesta, that in old Iran, it was more customary for the bridegroom to give marriage gifts to the bride than for him to take from her. The obligation of the father of the bride, and in his absence or demise that of the brother was confined to that of presenting an ear-ring (gaoshâvarê) to the bride. The sum of 2,000 silver dinars and two gold dirhems, referred to in the Pahlavi Paêwand-nâmeh, recited at the marriage, seems to be the average standard which an ordinary bridegroom of moderate means was expected to provide for his bride.

An hour or two before the celebration of the marriage, the ladies of the bride's family and the bride's friends, form themselves in a procession, and carry for the bridegroom, to his place, presents of clothes and some other valuables. The houses of the bridegroom and the bride have a kind of wedding powder called chauk spread over their thresholds on such merry occasions. A nuptial song is again sung on such an occasion. They return to their place after this presentation. The assembly, then, forms itself into a procession, headed by the officiating priests and the bridegroom and followed by the ladies who carry with them what is called varni, i.e., a present from the var, (i.e., the bridegroom) to the bride. The procession is sometimes preceded by a band of music. As per the Pahlavi Denkard, one of the objects of playing music on the occasion of a marriage is to inform the whole town, especially the neighbourhood, that a marriage has been celebrated. The procession26 goes to the house of the bride, where the marriage generally takes place. A nuptial song is generally sung on this occasion.

The procession goes to the place of the bride, and its members are accommodated with seats, the males in the compound and the females within the house. The door of the house of the bride is decorated with a hanging string of flowers, called toran (i.e., arch) and the sideposts which support the doors are marked with Haradh (turmeric) mixture. This kind of decoration is observed on the door of the bridegroom's house also. A nuptial song is sung on this occasion.

After the assembly is seated, the bridegroom enters the bride's house. He is welcomed at the door by the mother of the bride. He is made to stand at the threshold where several ceremonies are performed to welcome him and to wish him good luck. A fresh Kunkun mark is made upon his forehead, and a little rice is stuck upon the moist Kunkun mark and thrown over his head. Rice is considered to be the symbol of plenty and sucess. Hence the sprinkling of rice plays a outstanding part on many occasions of joy for wishing good luck. The officiating priests also, in performing the religious ceremony, and in invoking the benedictions of God upon the couple, sprinkle rice over them. Before the recital of the marriage benedictions, the bride and the bridegroom also throw upon one another a handful of rice. Some fond mothers make the bride and the bridegroom eat a few grains of rice thus besprinkled over them in the marriage ceremony.

An egg is then passed round his head three times, and then thrown upon the ground and broken. This seems to be the remnant of the old custom of animal sacrifice. It signifies that if there be any evil destined for the person it may pass off to the egg and be destroyed with it.

A coconut is then similarly passed round the head three times and then broken. A little water is then poured in a tray, which is passed round the head three times, and then the water is thrown at the feet of the bridegroom. Once in the evening, the ladies of the bride's family present before the bridegroom a water-pot (called var-behendoo, i.e., a pot presented to the husband, (var), as a part of the dowry), and make him dip his hand in it. While doing so, he drops a silver coin into it as a return gift, and as a mark of his appreciation of their gift. At one time it was customary that the feet of the couple were washed with water just after the performance of the marriage ceremony. When Parsis began to put on English-fashioned boots, it being a little troublesome to remove the boots, the custom was to wash the tip of the boots with a little water.

After the welcoming ceremonies on the threshold, the bridegroom is made to cross the threshold without placing his foot upon it. The bride also, when she goes to her husband's, is made to cross the threshold. The threshold is crossed with the right foot, which is always considered auspicious.

When the bridegroom enters the house to be married he is further welcomed with a song. Having entered the house, the bridegroom takes his seat first, and waits for the bride, who comes in after a short time, to take her seat. The bridegroom sits on the right hand of the bride. The right hand side is a place of honour, and so it is occupied by the husband who is considered to be the leader of the bride.

The bridegroom and the bride take their seats facing the East. There are two stools on one side of each of the chairs. On these are placed two metallic trays full of rice, which is to be thrown by the officiating priests over the couple while reciting their marriage benedictions. On the stool by the side of the chair on which the bride is to take her seat, stands a small metallic pot containing ghee (clarified butter) and molasses.

A servant stands there holding a censer with burning fire in one hand, and a little frankincense in the other. On the two stands there are two burning candles, one, by the side of the bridegroom, and the other, by the side of the bride.

Then two persons are made to stand before them, one by the side of the bridegroom and the other by that of the bride. These are the marriage witnesses. The nearest relations generally stand as witnesses. It is usually married persons, not bachelors, who stand as marriage witnesses.

Before being seated by each other's side, the bride and the bridegroom are first seated opposite each other, separated by a piece of cloth held between them as a curtain. Now begins what we may call the religious ceremonies. Two priests present themselves for the performance of these ceremonies. The senior officiating priest gives the right hand of one into the right hand of the other. Then a piece of cloth is passed round the chairs of both so as to enclose them in a circle. The ends of the cloth are tied together. This is, as it were, strictly speaking the tying of the marriage-knot. This is done with the recital of the sacred formula of "Yatha Ahu Vairyo."

After tying the knot of the ends of the cloth, which, as it were, encloses them into a circle of unity, the priest fastens with raw twist their right hands which are grasped by each other. This rite is called Hathêvârô, i.e., hand-fastening. The above sacred formula is recited during this rite also. It is the family priests who are entitled to the fee of hand-fastening, even if the ceremony is performed by other priests.

In the ceremony of hand-fastening, the raw twist is put round the hands seven times. After fastening the hands, the raw twist is passed round the pair seven times, and then, finally, it is passed seven times round the knot of the cloth which passes round their chairs. During all this process, the sacred prayer of Yatha Ahu Vairyo is recited.

At the end of this ceremony, at a signal given by the senior priest, the servant who holds the fire-vase places frankincense on the fire. At this signal, the curtain of cloth, which is held between the couple, is dropped, and the couple throw on each other a few grains of rice which they hold in their left hands. This throwing of rice is accompanied by a clapping of hands by the friends and relations who have assembled there.

The above ceremony of holding the cloth-curtain between the bride and the bridegroom, and then dropping it after the fastening of the hands, signifies that the separation that hitherto existed between them no longer exists now, and that they are now united into the bond of matrimony. As long as the curtain was held, they sat opposite each other, but on its removal, they are made to sit side by side. This also signifies that they, who were up to now separate, are now united together.

The putting on of raw twist round the couple seven times also indicates union. The raw twist itself can be easily broken, but when several threads are twined into one, they cannot easily be broken. So it signifies that the tie of union into which the couple is now bound may not easily be broken.

The throwing of the rice by the marrying couple upon each other is watched with great interest by their friends, especially by the ladies, who urge their respective friends, the bridegroom or the bride, to look sharp and throw the rice first when the signal is given. The one that throws rice first over the other is said to win. This is, as it were, a race of love. "Who won, the bridegroom or the bride!"

This is to signify that one who throws rice first, thereby indicates that he or she will be the foremost in loving and respecting the other. The clapping of hands expresses the approval and good-will of the assembly for the union. The priests also, during the recital of the benedictions, throw rice over the marrying couple. To throw rice or some such other thing over the marrying couple as a symbol ot good luck and sucess seems to be an old custom. Ferdowsi refers to it in the case of Zal's marriage (akik va zabarjad bar afshândand).

The marriage rite is repeated at midnight. Anquetil du Perron says that it is a remnant of the old custom of Persia where, in the town of Kerman, the marriage ceremony was performed at midnight. In many families, the practice of repeating the ceremony at midnight and of the address in Sanskrit is not resorted to now. The performance of the above ceremonies and the recital of the address, complete, what we should call, the solemn part of the celebration of marriage. But there are certain other customs and observances, which, though very rare in Bombay, are observed to a certain extent in the Mofussil towns. It is the ladies who observe them. Moreover, they are now rather looked on more with an idea of merriment than with that of any solemnity.

The first observance of that kind is that of uniting Chheda cheddi, of fastening the skirt of the garments of the couple. The nearest friend or relation of the couple ties the skirts of the jâmâ (the flowing dress) of the bridegroom with that of the sâree of the bride. Thus united, the bride goes to the house of the bridegroom. The process of fastening the skirts is accompanied by a song. This custom also signifies the act of uniting the two into the bond of marriage.

The next rite is that of "washing the feet" of the couple with water. That was more practicable about forty years ago, when almost all Parsis put on native shoes without stockings. But now, owing to the inconvenience of taking off English shoes and stockings, only the front tip of the shoes is washed with a little water. The signification of the custom may be that of washing away all past mistakes and driving away all evils and misfortunes. More probably, it signifies a kind of welcome. In India, visitors who come from some distance, are first given some water to wash their feet soiled by a long walk. At times, a lady hid the shoe thus removed and did not return it unless paid a rupee.

The next rite was that of making the couple partake of food from the same dish. In doing so, each gives to the other, morsels of food of which dahi or curd form a part. This rite signifies that now, being united in the bond of marriage, they have to board together and to share each other's pleasure and grief. This repast is known as "Dahi-Koomro" from the fact that dahi (curd), which is considered an auspicious substance of food on gay occasions, formed the essential part of the dish.

Another peculiar custom now almost obsolete is that of making the couple plays Eki Beki which is a form of play. Both have several rupees in their hands. One, without letting the other know, takes a certain number in the right hand, and asks the other whether the number is eki (odds} or beki (even). If the other guesses the number right, he or she is said to win. Perhaps the signification is the same as that in the rite of throwing the rice referred to above, wherein the one who won, guaranteed, as it were, his or her desire to love the other more ardently than she or he would do.

A nuptial song is sung at the close of the wedding ceremony. After the celebration of the marriage, the bride accompanies the husband to his house. A nuptial song is sung by the ladies, when the bride is taken to her husband's house, and another is sung when the bride enters the house of her husband.

After the celebration of the solemn part of the marriage ceremony, most of the guests were entertained at a marriage feast. All, or some of these, except the fifth, are proposed as per the directions of the host, and some one among the guests proposes that of the host. At some marriage feasts, a piously inclined host adds to the above list that of the dear departed ones as "Asho Farohar ni yâd," i.e., "the remembrance of the devout departed ones." In other communal feasts, while proposing this toast, and the first on the list, viz., that in remembrance of the sacred name of God, fragrant frankincense is ordered to be placed on the family hearth. No speeches are made while proposing them. At large gatherings, there are professional health-proposers. Loud and clear voice is their only qualification for the work. They simply give out the toast with a loud voice, and at times, when the dining parties are very large, they go round the tables, repeating the words for giving the toasts several times, so that all may hear. These toasts are drunk generally while dining, not at the end of the dinner.

As to the menu, fish, which is considered a symbol of good omen and luck, is essential. No marriage feast can be complete without it.

Again, a course of some kind of sweets is essential. Meat is not generally eaten in marriage feasts. It appears from Anquetil that the reason why meat was prohibited in India, was, that formerly, at Surat, which was at first the head-quarters of the Parsis, a large number of Hindoo guests was invited. As Hindoos consider it irreligious to slaughter animals for food, to spare their feelings, meat was prohibited. But, from an account of the proceedings of a meeting of the society, held in Bombay on the 18th of October 1823, and convened to consider some steps to regulate funeral and marriage expenses, it appears that meat was prohibited on marriage occasions from the point of view of economy.66 Meat courses were thought to be expensive.

Funeral Rites

The main principle, at the bottom of the Parsi custom of disposing of the dead and at the bottom of all the strictly religious ceremonies enjoined therewith, is this that the body, when the immortal spirit has left it, should, preserving all possible respect for the dead, be disposed of in a way the least harmful and the least injurious to the living. For properly understanding the Parsi ceremonies that relate to the disposal of the body, one must look to the ancient Zoroastrian ideas of sanitation, segregation, cleaning, and cleanliness as expressed in the Vendidad, one of their Avesta Scriptures.

When a person dies, the relations begin to make preparations for the disposal of the body. At first, a part of the house on the down-floor, where the body is to be placed before its removal to the Towers, is washed clean with water. The shroud or the dress with which the body is to be covered is also washed beforehand in the house. The shroud or the dress with which the body is covered is white and made of cotton. It need not be new. Old clothes may be used for the purpose after being washed. Unnecessary wastage of clothes over the dead bodies is forbidden.

When a case is given up as hopeless, the relations send for two or more priests, who assemble round the sick bed of the dying person and say, for his benefit, the Patet, which is a prayer for the repentance of one's sins. The priests are paid in money and corn for their services. This is called the Akhiânah1 ceremony because during this ceremony, priests are presented with grain.

This part of the funeral ceremonies is not generally performed. The origin of this custom seems to lie in the fact that a person must always say his repentance prayer [patet], and repent of his sins. If he is conscious and able, he must do so at the approaching moment of demise. His near relations and friends may join in the last prayers. If the recital of the whole patet is not possible, the recital a short time before demise, of the Ashem-Vohu formula by the dying person himself, if he is able, or by some relation, if he is unable, is considered meritorious. The Hadokht Nask says that the recital of the Ashem-Vohu formula2 at the very end of life, praising good thoughts, good words, and good actions, and condemning evil thoughts, evil words, and evil actions is, in point of greatness, goodness and excellence equal in value to the whole or the region of Khwaniras with its cattle and leading men. The purport of all this is to say that if a man at his dying moment could honestly say that he led a devout life and repented of all his sins, that life is worth more than the country of Khwaniras with all its riches.

In the Vendidad, a shorter period or mourning is enjoined to the surviving relations of a virtuous person (Dahma) than to those of a sinful person (Tanu-peretha). As per custom, the Dahma or the virtuous in this case is one who has said his repentance prayer or recited the Ashem Vohu; and the Tanu-peretha or the sinful is one who has not said that prayer or recited that formula. A longer period of mourning is enjoined for the sinful, because, in his case, the surviving dear ones have not only to mourn his loss, but have to mourn for the fact that he has not led a good life, and as such has to meet with punishment.

Upto a few years ago, a short time before demise, a few drops of the consecrated haoma juice were poured into the mouth of the dying person. The haoma4 plant being an symbol of immortality, its juice is poured to impress an idea that, after all, the spirit of a man is immortal. As the Tree of Life is guarded by the Cherubim and the Sidra by 70,000 angels, so the haoma-i saphid, or the White Haoma, is guarded by 99,999 Fravashis or the guardian spirits. Sometimes, instead of the juice of the haoma plant, if it was not available at hand, the juice of a few grains of pomegranate, the leaves of which are considered essential in some of the Parsi ceremonies, is dropped into the mouth of the dying person.

A short time after demise, the corpse is washed throughout, first with a little application of gaomez and then with water, generally with well-water. A clean suit of clothes, washed at home, is then put over the body. It is afterwards destroyed and never used for any other purpose. The kusti or the sacred thread is then put round the body by some near or dear one, with the recital of the Nirang-i-kusti, or the Ahura Mazda Khudae prayer. The corpse is then placed on a cot. Then two persons keeping themselves in touch with the body sit close by, and somebody recites the

Ashem Vohu prayer very close to the ear of the deceased. The relations then meet or embrace the deceased for the last time. In Persia, the person washing the corpse puts on woolen gloves.

After this time, the dead body is supposed to fall under the influence of Druj-i-Nasush, i.e., the evil influence of Decomposition or Destruction. It is considered that to touch the body then is dangerous for the living, lest they should catch contagion and spread disease. Only the corpse-bearers are permitted to come into contact with the body. If somebody else touches the body, he has to go through a process of cleaning or a sacred bath taken under the directions of a priest.

The body is now given in charge of two persons who are generally trained to their work. They are first required to take a bath and put on a clean suit of clothes. They perform the Kusti, i.e., ungird the sacred thread and put it on again with a prayer, and then recite a part of the Srosh-baj prayer. Then holding a paywand between them they enter the room where the corpse is placed.

The Paywand: To hold a paywand means to be in close contact or touch with each other. This is done when two persons hold a piece of cloth or cotton tape between them. This is intended to show that they are associated or united in doing a thing and are ready to co-operate and sympathise with each other. When these two persons enter into the room, holding the 'paywand' between them, the two relations who are sitting by the side of the deceased leave their places and entrust the body to them. They place the body on the ground on a clean white sheet of cloth and put on the shroud over it. The whole of the body except the face is covered with cloth. In some parts of Gujarat even the face is covered with a padan.

The corpse is then lifted from its place by the above-mentioned two persons and put on slabs of stones in a corner of the front room. The hands are arranged upon the chest crosswise. In some of the towns of Gujarat, the old Avestic method of placing the dead body on a plot of ground previously dug in the house, instead of on slabs of stone is still in practice. The ground is dug out a few inches deep and a layer of sand is spread over it. The corpse is placed on the ground thus prepared. The body is placed on the ground or on the slabs in a position which would avoid the head pointing towards the North.

In all the ceremonies of the Parsis, the north side is as a rule generally avoided. The children while going through the naojote [navjote] ceremony for the purpose of putting on the sacred shirt [sudre] and thread [kusti], the marrying couple going through the Ashirvad or marriage ceremony, and the priests in all their religious rites and ceremonies never face the North. This is due to the fact that the ancient Iranians, the ancestors of the Parsis, had a natural hatred for the North, from which side proceeded all kinds of dangers and evils whether climatic, corporeal or mental. The Vendidad says that the Druj-i-Nasush, i.e., spirit of Destruction runs from the northern direction in the form of a fly. Even the wind from the northern direction was believed to be stinking.

The winds from the northern cold regions brought sickness and demise in Persia. Again, the marauduers from Mazenderan, Gilan, and other adjoining regions in the North brought destruction and demise in many Iranian families. These people of the North were depraved and wanting in many moral qualities. On the other hand, the South was considered a very auspicious side. The winds from the South were healthy and invigorating. Coming from the South, they brought rain and plenty. The wind blowing from the south purified the atmosphere all round. Thc wind blowing towards the spirit of a virtuous man, when it (the spirit) passes on to Heaven on the dawn of the third night after demise, was said to be sweet-scented and fragrant and to have come from the south. Owing to the belief based on these facts and considerations, the North was always avoided.

After placing the corpse on slabs of stones, one of the two persons, draws round the body three Kashas or circles with a metallic bar or a nail. This is intended to show that the ground within the circle is temporarily set apart for the corpse, and that nobody is to go to that part of the ground lest he should catch infection.

In ancient Persia, almost all houses were provided with separate apartments for placing the corpse before its removal to the Towers of Silence. In the case of the poor who could not afford to have such separate apartments there was a separate house for the purpose in every street. The poor carried their dead to such houses before removing them to the Towers. "Ahura Mazda said: 'In every house, in every street, they should make three katas (separate parts of ground) for the dead' ".

It is said that even now, such separate houses are provided in the Parsi streets in Persia where the parties take their dead and perform the funeral ceremonies before removing them to the Towers of Silence. Such houses are known as "margzâd". Up to late, some of the mofussil towns of Gujarat had such separate houses for the dead in Parsi streets. They were known as Nasâkhânâs, i.e., the houses for the dead bodies. Every

Parsi town has a Nassâ-Khânâ, but now it is generally used as a depot for the biers, the slabs of stones above referred to, the shrouds and such other requisites for the removal of the dead. The Bahman Yasht speaks of it as Nasâi-kata (corpse-chamber).

It is enjoined that the place to be chosen for such apartments or houses for the dead should be free from dampness, should be the least frequented by men and animals, and should be far away from the place where religious ceremonies are performed. The Vendidad says: "Ahura Mazda said that (they must choose) in the house of a Mazdayasnian the cleanest and the driest place which is the least frequented by cattle and beasts of burden, by the fire of Ahura Mazda, by the barsom spread through piety and by the holy man". After having placed the body on one side of the ante-room, either on slabs or on a part of the ground dug and specially prepared, the two persons, who were up to now arranging all these things, now leave the house, still holding the paywand between them. They then finish the Srosh Baj prayer, a part of which they had recited before commencing their work.

The Sagdid: One of the ceremonies is that of the Sagdid. The word 'Sagdid' is made up of sag, a dog, and did, sight, and means "the sight of a dog." A dog, usually a four-eyed (Chathru-chashma) dog, i.e., a dog with two eye-like spots just above the eyes, is made to see the corpse.

As regards the purpose why the sagdid is performed, various reasons are assigned: Some say that the particular class of the spotted (chathru-chashma, or the four-eyed) dog had the characteristic of detecting whether life in the body of a man was extinct or not. It stared steadily at the body if life was extinct, and did not look at it at all if life was not altogether extinct. Thus the purpose for the sagdid among the ancient Iranians was to ascertain, before the disposal of the body, whether life was really extinct. Others characteristicd the sagdid to some supposed magnetic influence in the eyes of the dog. There were others who connected the sagdid of the dog, which of all animals is the most disciple to his master, with the idea of loyalty and gratitude that must live between the living and the dear departed ones. M. Abel Hovelacque thinks that the respect which the Mazdayasnians professed for the dog may be due either to a recollection of ancient belief of which the correct meaning may have been

lost or to a special motive. That motive may be the expression of the recognition of the dog's valuable services in a society where the country life, agriculture, and the breeding of the cattle played a role of great importance. Again, others considered the dog to be symbolical of the destruction of immoral passions.

The Sagdid is performed twice during the process of putting on the shroud and is repeated in every Gah15, as long as the corpse is in the house. It is repeated just when the new Gah begins. It is enjoined that in case a dog is not procurable, the Sagdid of flesh-devouring birds like the crows and vultures may be permitted; that is to say, it will do, if a flesh-eating bird happens to pass and see the corpse from above.

After the first sagdid, fire is brought into the room in a vase and is kept burning with fragrant sandalwood and frankincense. This is done with a view to destroy the invisible germs of disease that may be floating in the air in the room where the corpse is placed before its removal to the Tower of Silence.

Then a priest sits before the fire and recites the Zend-Avesta till the time of the removal of the corpse to the Tower [dakhma], and keeps the fire burning. It is not absolutely necessary that a priest should recite prayers at this time. Any person in the house can recite prayers and keep the fire burning. The priest and all other persons are enjoined to sit at a distance of at least three paces from the corpse, so that in case the deceased died of an infectious disease, there may be no danger or risk to the health and life of the living.

The corpse may be removed to the Tower [dakhma] at any time during the day. As it is enjoined that "the Mazdayasnians should expose the body to the Sun," (Vend. V, 13), the removal of the body at night is strictly forbidden. If demise takes place early at night, the body is removed the next morning; but, if it takes place late at night or early in the morning, it is removed in the afternoon. In the case of an accidental demise, a long interval is generally permitted. The Vendidad says, that in a such a case, the decomposition does not commence as early as in the case of a body that was suffering from illness, but commences after one Gah, or one period of the day; and so, it is not detrimental to the health of the living to keep the body some time longer.

The corpse-bearers must be at least two, even if the deceased were a mere infant that could be carried by a single person. "Nobody should carry the dead alone". If the body is heavy, it must be carried by four, six, eight, ten, or any such even number. A pair, or the number two, plays a outstanding part in all the ceremonies for the disposal of the dead body and that pair always holds a paywand between them. After demise, the body must never be left alone or in the company of only one person.

After washing it, there must be always two persons sitting by its side. Again the persons, who put on the shroud and place it on slabs of stone in a corner of the house before its removal to the Tower, must be two. The priests who say the last funeral prayers at the house are also two. The persons who attend the funeral procession to the Tower also go in pairs of two and two, holding a paywand in the form of a handkerchief between them. A single person should never attend the funeral. The injunction of having pairs in all these funeral ceremonies is intended to produce a view of sympathy and mutual help.

The Recital of the Baj: The corpse-bearers, on entering the house, place the bier by The recital of the the side of the corpse and then "take the Baj." They then recite a formula in a suppressed tone which says:

We do this as per the dictates of Ahura Mazda, as per the dictates of the Amesha Spentas, as per the dictates of the holy Sraosha, as per the dictates of Adarbad Marespand [Mahraspandan], and as per the dictates of the Dastur of the age.

By the recital of this formula, known as the Dasturi formula, they declare that they undertake to perform all the ceremonies for the disposal of the dead as enjoined in the religious books and as directed by the Head-priest of the time. Then they sit silent by the side of the corpse. If they have at an any occasion to speak, they speak with a kind of suppressed tone, without opening the lips, which is said to be speaking in baj.

The Geh-Sarna Prayer: Then follows the "Geh-Sarna" ceremony, i.e., the recital of the Gatha. Its recital was intended as a sermon and exhortation to give moral courage to the survivors to bear up with fortitude the loss of the deceased and as a safety against the spread of disease.

In this Geh-Sarna ceremony, two priests perform the Padyab-Kusti, and, after reciting the prayers for the particular Gah, go to the chamber where the dead body is placed, and standing at the door or inside the door at some distance from the body, and holding a paywand between them, put on the padan over their face, take the baj and recite the Ahunavaiti Gatha which treats of Ahura Mazda, his Amesha Spentas or immortal archangels, the future life, resurrection, and such other subjects. After reciting nearly half of the Ahunavaiti Gatha, they stop for about a minute. The corpse-bearers now lift the corpse from the slabs of stone on which it is lying and place it over the iron bier. The two priests now turn towards the bier and recite the remaining half of the Ahunavaiti Gatha.

If the deceased person is a pregnant woman in the fifth month of her pregnancy when the child is supposed to have some life, the geh-sarna ceremony is enjoined to be performed by two pairs of priests.

When the recital of the Gatha is finished, the final Sagdid is performed, and then the relations and friends of the deceased who have by this time assembled at the house, have a last look of the deceased. In such an assembly, the females assemble in the house, and the males outside the house or in the street. The males, one by one, pass before the corpse, have a last look, and out of respect make a bow, which process is called sijda.

Immediately after the removal of the body from the house, Gomez, i.e., the urine of the cow, is be-sprinkled over the slabs of stone on which the body was placed and over the way by which the corpse-bearers carried the body out of the house. The slabs of stone are now generally removed from the house immediately after the removal of the body.

The Gomez or cow's urine is spoken of as Nirang, because its application or use is generaily accompanied by the recital of a nirang, i.e., a prayer formula. Cow's urine was believed by the ancient Zoroastrians to possess disinfecting properties. So, in order to destroy the germs of impurity and disease, if any, it was besprinkled on the place where the dead body was placed. For the same reason, cow's urine played a outstanding part in cleaning impurities attached to things that came into contact with the decomposing matters of men and animals. Such things are first asked to be purified or washed with cow's urine and then with water. Utensils or articles of furniture made of wood, clay, or porcelain that come into contact with a decomposing body are condemned altogether. Being porous, they are held to have possibly caught the germs of disease from the dead body and are therefore considered to be unsafe for further domestic purpose.

The Funeral Procession: When the bier leaves the house, out of respect for the deceased, all the male relations and friends of thc family that have assembled at the house of the deceased, or at times only the elders, follow the bier for some distance from the house or upto the end of the street. There, they make a last bow to the deceased and stand aside, giving way to those relations and friends who wish to accompany the funeral procession to the Tower of Silence [dakhma]. These follow the bier at a distance of, at least, thirty paces. The rest of the assembly now disperse. Before entering into their houses or places of business, they wash their face and other exposed parts of their body and perform the kusti. All those who go with the funeral procession to the Tower are clothed in full white dress. They arrange themselves in pairs of two, hold a paywand between them, take the baj and silently march to the Tower. The procession is headed by two priests.

The Disposal in the Tower: When the bier reaches the Tower, at first it is put on the ground outside and the Nassasalars uncover the face of the body. Those who have accompanied the funeral procession pay their respects and have a last look from a distance of at least three paces. Then sagdid is once more performed and that for the last time. In the meantime, the gate of the Tower which is kept locked with a metallic lock is opened. The Nassasalars who had fetched the corpse out of the house and entrusted it to the carriers and who have accompanied the corpse, now resume charge of the body. They lift up the bier and carry it into the Tower. They remove the body from the bier and place it on one of the 'pâvis'.36 They then tear off the clothes from the body of the diseased and leave it (the body) on the floor of the Tower.

On the Nassasalars completing their work in the Tower and on their locking the Tower, notice is given, by a clapping of hands by a servant, to all those who have accompanied the funeral procession and who have by this time taken their seats at some distance from the Tower, to say that the body is placed in the Tower. They all get up from their seats and finish the baj, i.e., recite the rest of the Srosh-baj, of which, before joining the procession, they had recited only a part. They now leave off the paywand and recite a short prayer which says: "We repent of all our sins. Our respects to you (the spirits of the departed). We remember here the spirits of the dead who have the spirits of the holy." They then apply cows's urine [gomez] to the exposed portions of their body and then wash them with water.

The Tower: The Tower of Silence wherein the dead bodies are exposed to the sun and to the flesh-eating birds, is generally built on the top of a hill or on an elevated ground. On such an elevated place, an isolated spot, away from human dwellings, is chosen for the Tower. Its construction all along is just in accord with the view held in the performance of the ceremonies for the disposal of the dead, viz., the sanitary view, which enjoins that, while disposing of the dead body with all respect due to the deceased, no injury or harm should be done to the living. The Tower is a round massive structure built throughout of solid stone. A few steps from the ground guide to an iron gate which opens on a circular platform of solid stone with a circular well in the centre.

Segregation: Not only should a man not come into contact with the dead body, but even utensils and other articles of furniture should be kept away from the corpse. If wearing clothes have been defiled by the sweat, vomit, etc., of the dead, they should be altogether rejected and destroyed. If not defiled, they may be purified by the "Gomez" and water. If the clothes are made of leather they must be washed thrice with "Gomez," rubbed with dry earth thrice, washed with water thrice, and exposed for three months in the air before being used again. If they are made of woven cloth, which is more porous than leather and therefore likely to carry more germs of disease and infection, the above process of cleaning and washing must be repeated six times, and they must be exposed to the air for an era of six months. Even the clothes thus purified cannot be used again for religious purposes or for ordinary domestic purposes, but they can be used for other petty purposes.

Utensils for domestic purposes, if they have come into contact with a dead body, require to be washed several times as per the specific gravity of the metal of which they are made. If the utensil is made of gold, it requires one washing with "Gomez" and water and a rubbing with dry earth. An utensil of silver, which is more porous than gold and therefore likely to carry more contagion, requires two similar cleanings and washings. An iron one requires three, a zinc one four, and a stone one six washings. An utensil of porcelain, wood or clay is to be condemned altogether. In the same way, if accidentally a dead body happens to come into contact with stores of grain or of drinking water it is enjoined to reject and condemn a certain quantity in the near vicinity of the body.

Thus, at the bottom of all religious injunctions and restrictions in connection with the funeral ceremonies and the disposal of the dead body, lies the sanitary principle of segregation, prevention of contamination and infecticn, and the idea of observing simplicity and equality.

The Uthamnu Ceremony: In the Uzerin Gah of the third day, a ceremony is performed which is called the "Oothamnâ" [Uthamnu] The friends and relatives of the deceased and a few priests meet together in an assembly. The particular prayers of the Gah, the Srosh Hadokht (Yasht XI.) and the Patet are recited. A Pazand prayer with the Khshnuman of Sraosha is recited, wherein the name of the deceased is announced and the safety of Sraosha is implored for him. This is an occasion for the announcement of charities. This ceremony and this assembly are very important, because, at the end of the ceremony, the relations and friends of the deceased generally announce donations to charity funds in the naiyat or memory of the deceased and to commemorate his name. The Parsi society of India has given many lacs of rupees in public charity. Of this sum, a large part was announced at these funeral gatherings of the third day after demise.

The Parsis have another custom of commemorating the name of a deceased person if he be a great public benefactor. At the conclusion of the above "Oothamna" ceremony on the third day, the head priest generally, or in his absence an "akâbar," i.e., a leader of the society, proposes before the assembled Anjoman, i.e., the public assembly, that the name of the deceased public benefactor, whose benefaction or good deeds he enumerates, be commemorated by the society consenting to remember the name of the deceased in all the public religious ceremonies in the Dhup-nirang recital. This proposal is sometimes seconded by somebody, or very often it is just placed before the assembly without any formal seconding. When nobody opposes that proposal, silence is taken as consent, and thenceforth the name of the deceased is recited and his spirit is remembered in all public religious ceremonies. If the deceased public benefactor has done benevolent acts for the good of the whole Parsi society, in whatever part of the world they be, his name is recited and remembered by the whole society. If the deceased has done good and benevolent acts for the good of the society of his own particular town or district, the Anjoman of that town or district alone begins to appeal tohis name in the religious ceremonies. For example, the name of Sir Jamsedjee Jejeebhoy, the first Parsi Baronet, who rose from very poor circumstances to be a merchant prince of India, and who gave large sums of money in charity, not only for his own co-religionists but for all sections of the mixed society of India, is remembered in the religious ceremonies by the whole Parsi society of India.

OHER RITUALS

The Kushti is the sacred cord that a Zoroastrian child is empowered with on the day of his or her Navjote ceremony. Along with the sudreh, or sacred shirt, the kushti is a weapon that a Zoroastrian uses to fight against the evil forces around and within. Although most Zoroastrians make a reasonable effort to wear the sudreh and kushti as much as possible, very few know how to correctly tie the kushti around the waist. If this article can teach just one person how to tie the kushti correctly, it will be time well spent. The kushti ceremony requires three prayers to be recited. First comes the Kem-na-Mazda, which is preceeded by "kshnothra ahurae mazdao" and one Ashem Vohu. While reciting the Kem-na- Mazda, many Zoroastrians hold the front of their kushti with both hands, while others don't. This just seems to be a difference in custom. After the Kem-na-Mazda, the kushti is untied - first the back knots and then the front. Initially, it is held folded in half, with the left thumb in the center and the right thumb and forefinger grasping both threads of it about 20 inches (50 cm) away. It should be held at chest level directly in front, and the arms should not be extended.The kushti is retied while reciting the Hormazd Khodae prayer.

While reciting certain words, certain actions should be performed: Hormazd Khodae (3 times): bow down and touch forehead to kushti Dushmata, Duzukhta, Duzvarashta: gently whip the right side of the kushti three times, once on each word Manashni, Gavashni, Kunashni: starting at the center, make three loops on the kushti (right, left, right in that order) You should be holding the kushti with three loops on it with your hands together Haithya varstam: release the loops and put the kushti on your waist. Wrap the kushti around you once, with the left side going over the right at the back. Then, at the front, tie two knots while reciting the two Yatha Ahu variyo prayers. For the first knot, you should start by placing the right side over the left, vice versa for the second. The thread should be dropped into the hole to produce the knot on the word "shaothannanam" The two back knots are tied during the final Ashem Vohu. For the first knot, start by placing the left side over the right, vice versa for the second. The thread for the first knot should be placed in the hole at the first word "ushta" (fifth word in Ashem Vohu) The second knot must be completed before the Ashem Vohu is completed. After the kushti is tied, hold the front with both hands and recite the Jasa me Avanghe Mazda prayer.

Many people only perform the kushti prayers once or twice a day, and some don't perform it at all. Ideally, it should be performed when waking up, before going to bed, and after showering or using the restroom. However, for those who have not been brought up with the habit of performing it on a regular basis, it is best to perform it once or twice a day until one is comfortable with the procedure. The sudreh and kushti are special weapons that are empowered upon a Zarathushti child at the Navjote ceremony in order to fight against evil. Evil is prevalent and unavoidable in our world, but luckily Ahura Mazda has given us the tools we need to overcome it. The sudreh and kushti, when properly worn, are extremely powerful tools. Wearing them, and performing the kushti prayers with faith and dedication, will enable all Zoroastrians to fight against evil and elevate their spirite spirit to a higher level. Prayer is food for the spirit.

REFERENCES

Avesta: Pahlavi, and Ancient Persian Studies in Honour of the late Shams-ul Ulama Dastur Peshotanji Behramji Sanjana. Strassburg, 1904.

Bilimoria, N. F.: Zoroastrianism in the Light of Theosophy. Bombay, 1896.

Dadachanji, F. K.: Light of the Avesta and the Gathas. Bombay, 1913.

Dadistan-i Dinik: Translated from the Pahlavi text by E. W. West. In Sacred Books of the East, vol. 18.

Darmesteter, James: Haurvatat et Arneretat. In Bibliothèque de l'Ecole des Hautes Etudes, vol. 23. Paris, 1875.

Darmesteter, James: Ormazd et Ahriman. Paris, 1877.

Dastur, M. N.: The Moral and Ethical Teachings of Zarathushtra. Bombay, 1928.

Dinkard: The Complete Text. Edited by D. M. Madan. 2 vols. Bombay, 1911.

Firdausi: Translated into English by A. G. Warner and E. Warner. vols. 1-9. London, 1905-1925.

Fluegel, M: The Zend-Avesta and Eastern Religions. Baltimore, 1898.

Fox, W. S., and Pemberton, R. E. K.: Passages in Greek and Latin Literature relating to Zoroaster and Zoroastrianism translated into English in *the Journal of the K. R. Cama Oriental lnstitute*, No.14. Bombay, 1929.

Mills, L. H.: Zarathushtra and the Greeks. Leipzig. 1903. 1904.

Minu-i Khrat: Translated from the Pahlavi text by E. W. West. In *Sacred Books of the East*, vol. 24.

Mistri, R. H.: Zoroaster and Zoroastrianism. Bombay, 1906.

Modi, Jivanji J.: The Religious System of the Parsees. Bombay, 1885.

Modi, Jivanji J.: The Parsis at the court of Akbat and Dastur Meherjee Rana. Bombay, 1903.

Vendidad, Vispered, Yasna, Pahlavi Texts: Edited by F. Spiegel in Avesta Die Heiligen Schriften der Parsen. Wien, t853.

15

Society

SOCIAL ORDER

The question of whether or not change is acceptable in religion is a question that will never, never go away. Change can be either for the better or for the worse. Zoroastrians follow a set of rules, beliefs, and values which have been followed by their ancestors for generations, and many think that these things shouldn't be experimented with or changed.

On the other hand, some people believe that it is okay to change the religion if desired. Desire to change religion is all around us. Some people do not wear sudreh-kusti, people want to pray in English, and some want to marry non-Zoroastrians. Others denounce these things, on the grounds that they are un-Zoroastrian. To make the entire picture clear we will present the reasons for and against religious change in chart form.

Religious doctrine has been transmitted orally for generations. This may have resulted in flaws and mistakes over time. We should do our best to correct the mistakes.

Our religion must suit our lifestyle and our home. We now live in different countries than in the past and we must make accommodations in our doctrine so that our lives are simpler.

Man has the power to think and reason, and if in his judgement religion must be changed, then obviously it can be.

Religion is man's connection with God. Therefore we must follow it as God wants us to follow it, not as we want to follow it. God told us how to follow our religion (through prophet Zarathushtra and other messengers), so we must follow it as he told us.

Prophet Zarathushtra and other saints who revealed the Zoroastrian religion to us were spiritually enlightened messengers from God Himself. We humans cannot challenge what the prophets taught us.

Attempting to change your religion is like telling God that you know better than Him what is right and what is wrong. Can we question God?

SOCIAL CONDUCT

Ethics is the discipline dealing with what is good and bad and with moral duty and obligation. Ethics has been called the science of the ideal of human character. A deeper study takes us to the gigantic tree of philosophy and there we see it as a branch of normative science as distinguished from the formal sciences. History of thought in the so-called Western civilization begins with Greece. So the earliest signs of Ethics begin in the 5th century BC. Since then, we have the Greek schools of Ethics, early Christian Ethics, Ethics after the Reformation, Ethics since Darwinism, and the recent trend, since Bertrand Russell, is that Ethics should mean complete participation in the life of society with the freedom to express one's nature.

Zoroaster lived 3770 years ago. He lived his life in eastern Iran. Zoroaster, like his contemporary Rig Vedic rishis, composed his songs that have survived in his very words to this day. The same holds true about volumes and volumes of Indo-Iranian poetic literature. They are the proof of the capacity of human memory. We had a Professor of Persian Literature in the Tehran University who had over 70,000 couplets in his memory. One thousand to 20,000 couplets are a common thing in the memories of literature teachers in the Indo-Iranian countries.

How many couplets did Zarathushtra compose to preserve his Doctrine? Only 241 stanzas that make 17 songs! They are Gâthâ, meaning "Sublime Songs." Here is the booklet of some 40 pages. Too small to hold a Doctrine! Let us see if our remark is true.

A quick glance shows that it has 93 answering questions, a masterpiece of poetry that makes the questions provide their own answers and more over, provoke thoughts. The songs define what is good and what is bad, and at the same time speak of the full freedom of will to make the choice. Learning wisdom helps to make the right choice. Ignorance keeps one in dark. Good brings better returns and bad results in bad consequences. Experience makes one grow wiser, a process that helps every individual to ultimately make the right choice. The good choice leads to perfection and perfection knows no defect, decay or demise. It means eternity. They explain the establishment of a free democratic way of life by the wise people for the wise people. And the songs guide one to study his/herself, the society, the environment, and the universe to realize, through his/her good mind, the wisdom that creates, regulates, maintains and promotes the Cosmos. That wisdom, a reality, an essence, is the Creator, Maintainer, and Promoter of the Universe. Zarathushtra coins a name for IT. Mazdâ, which means Super-wisdom and since it is a reality, it is also Ahura, the Essence, the Being. He has two words to describe what we say 'God': Mazdâ Ahura or Ahura Mazdâ - The Super-wisdom Essence.

With Mazda Ahura in mind, the songs become simultaneously loving Prayers to God and kindly Guidance to Mankind. Naturally they have no myth, no magic, no miracle, no legend, and no story to tell. Just a prayerful guidance.

Zarathushtra uses some twenty abstract terms to prescribe the way of promoting mental and physical faculties of soul to achieve perfection and immortality. He calls them "the Primal Principles of life." They are the universal principles of existence, the natural way of living. They, at the same time, make the faculties that have been endowed to mankind.

Of these asha, precision, has been mentioned more than 150 times and merezhdika, compassion, only once. We shall only briefly define those mentioned most in the Gathas:

Spenta Mainyu, the progressive mentality stands for the creative faculty of God. It creates, sustains, and promotes the creation. It leads to perfection and immortality. It makes mankind to be creative, maintainer and promoter of society and the environment.

Vohu manah, the good mind is the source of all that is good and wise. It was through his own good mind that Zarathushtra discovered, understood, and reached God. Good mind leads to refined speech, which, in turn, turns into noble actions. Zarathushtra's doctrine rests on three pillars—Humata, Hûkhta, Hvarshta—Good thoughts, Good Words, and Good Deeds. Good mind helps one to discriminate between good and bad. It defines the sources of happiness and sorrow. In fact, it is the bliss some call "heaven." Two other cognate abstracts are khratu, intellect, and chisti, comprehension, which enhance one's knowledge for better work.

Asha or arta is the old Indo-Iranian law of "truth, precision, righteousness" that governs the universe-the stars, sun, moon, earth, seasons and all. It is precision and order in the universe that points to the Creator, Maintainer, and Promoter. It has been enacted to maintain the creation. It is the road to perfection. In human society, asha is the right thing, done at the right time and right place, and with the right means to obtain the right result. This promotes a society to perfection. It ensures justice for all. It safeguards the rights of every member of society. It provides every individual with what he or she has contributed to society. Asha in a society sees that neither the society nor any individual exploits any person. And, above all, asha gives freedom of thought, word and deed to every member.

Seraosha is the divine voice one gets in tune with after one is fully conversant with good mind and righteousness. It is the guiding inner self of a person. It is divine inspiration.

Âthra, fire in the Gathas is mental light, warmth, and energy, three qualities that help one become as creative as one can. The physical fire, used as the best of altàrs, represents the mental âthra, a sublime object to observe and mentally to see the light, feel the warmth and enjoy the energy to translate Good Thoughts into Good Words and Good Deeds.

Ushtâ is enlightenment that comes through meditation, concentration of mental faculties. It is the true happiness that radiates happiness to others without any discrimination, social or otherwise.

Daênâ is clear conception. It is "conscience" in an individual and "religion" for a fellowship of individuals who actively join to promote the living world in accordance with the Primal Principles of Existence.

Good mind, precision and other principles create perfect order. Zarathushtra calls it khshathra. It means settlement, dwelling, domain, dominion, and sovereigntyty. It is the "desired," the "good," and the "chosen" government of the righteous, yet it belongs to God. It is the "ideal" order on the earth established by human beings who are wise, enlightened, experienced, sincere, and above all devoted to the promotion of the living world. It is mental and material, spiritual and physical democracy.

Fresho-kereti, continuous refreshing, renewing and modernizing keeps the good order up-to-date, in fact up-to-minute. Progress, progress, progress! A Zoroastrians pledges to modernize the world in his/her daily prayers.

Âramaiti, serenity and tranquility, thrives under a good progressive order. A tranquil order promotes health and happiness. Mind and body grow together to evolve into:

Haurvatât, entirety, perfection. Evolution to entirety means continuity, and continuity stands for immortality—ameretât. Entirety and immortality make human beings godlike and make them live in eternal bliss, the ultimate goal of the Zarathushtrian doctrine.

Zarathushtra uses more principles among abstract qualities that could help mankind to make the world an ideal place to live in peace and harmony with every living being, and to achieve the divine eternity ordained by God.

It is these Primal Principles that make his Ethics. They make a guiding map for the wise to reach the destination. And a map need not run into hundreds of pages of prescriptions and proscription. Forty pocketbook pages of Seventeen Songs suffice to make a good traveler to undertake the journey and reach the destination safe and sound.

The Seventeen Songs are a map that guides the traveler to reflect. The Zoroastrian Doctrine of Ethics is reflective and not prescriptive. Its seventeen songs provoke one's thinking faculty to think, to ponder, to consider and to decide on the basis of time, place and means. Yes, reflective, renovative and inventive. That makes it ever fresh, ever modern. Prescriptions and proscriptions fall behind and get outdated.

Good and Evil

Because of the sufferings in what appears to be a hostile world of natural disasters and human cruelties, the existence of "evil" has all along posed a perplexed problem. Intellectuals of all ages and lands have tried to solve it. Most of them have acknowledged it as a stubborn fact of life.

People's attitude towards evil range from optimism, pessimism, cynicism to skepticism. There are those who do not believe in evil and state that it does not exist; those who argue that just as darkness is nothing but the absence of light, evil darkens where good does not shine; those who say that one cannot fight evil and therefore should submit to it; those who want to escape evil and retire from the world by leaving behind all human wishes and desires; and those who acknowledge shortcomings and want to overcome them by facing them. People necessarily do not belong strictly to one of these broad classifications. Many share a little of each theory and have mixed philosophies, or express different ideas at different times.

People are divided again on the source of evil. Those who believe in a strict patriarchal/matriarchal divinity/divinities and see the sufferings as punishments for wrong deeds. Those who think that just as there are good and bad chiefs and kings, there are good and evil entities, which bring happiness or misery. Those who believe that the gods have created human beings as their toys and enjoy playing around with them. Those who believe in a rebel divinity who is causing all the trouble. Those who are dualists and maintain that both good and evil are primal and co-existing. Those who see the two as positive and negative poles that meet to create energy and existence. Those who see the world as imperfect or in its infancy, and that its sufferings are the experiences toward perfection. All have their logic, philosophy, stories, legends, or myths to elaborate. Many believe that evil exists in the universe and many confine it, some in vague terms, to the human world.

Zarathushtra observes the universe as a good creation of God and sees no evil in it. It is a cosmos — an orderly harmonious system. However, there are indications that he sees the universe in its infancy, complete in every form but growing to perfection and immortality.

As regards good and evil, he confines both to human mind, not outside, not in the cosmos. Man thinks and thinks constantly. His thoughts are good or bad, beneficial or harmful. When translated in speech or action, they yield the result — good or bad.

The two represent the duality only and only in the human mind and within the human society. The dualism in the Gathas is pure ethical in nature.

The criterion for "better" or "more progressive" thought, word, and deed is the beneficial effect on the human society in particular and the world in general. If not, it is "bad" or "retarding."

TRADITIONAL VALUES IN SOCIETY

The Gathic dualism lies only in "asha," "right, precision, righteousness" and "druj," "harmful, wrong". The human world is divided into two camps: the righteous, truthful and progressive, and the wrongful, retarding and destructive. The Gathas advocate a free, peaceful, prudent, and progressive society, both in spirit and matter. Spirituality makes people realize the divine in creation, and conceive the force and order — the wisdom — behind it. It makes them conceive God. It promotes them to commune with God, and be godlike. Materiality makes people understand their social environment and the living world. It teaches them the philosophy of living and letting others live, and of living in harmony with nature.

Only responsible men and women make the Gathic society. Carefree and parasitic people have no place in it. A person, be he or she wise, naive, strong, or weak, has his or her responsibilities in the society. Zarathushtra stands for freedom of thought, word and deed, and stands against suppression and exploitation. He condemns all "wrong done by evil power, deeds, words, conception, and mind." He repeatedly reminds people that good has a good reward, and bad has a bad consequence. And to be good is to be selflessly good.

In a true Zarathushtrian society, all are free to work for a better world without harming others. Every person receives in reward what one does in renovating human life. Every task is undertaken by fully qualified persons; the better the qualifications, the higher the position. Society is led by the very wise. Men and women are equal and their superiority lies in their wisdom and righteousness. Race, color, class, and nationalism have no place in it. The smallest unit in the society is the family, then the community, next the country, the fellowship, and last the world. The Zoroastrian society is global.

Zarathushtra speaks very little about a world from which no one has returned to tell us the tale. He never indulges in speculations. He does not thrive on speculations, but on conclusions from what one discovers and understands. He mentions certain terms, which give one an idea of a higher and sublimer spiritual life. They are the "House of Song," "House of Good Mind," and the "Eternal Best Existence of Good Mind." Only once, he uses the term "future existence." It is where one lives with God. The language is so that one understands that such a sublime state is both mental and physical in this world, but only mental when the soul attains its perfection and immortality.

But if a person lives a life of "harmful, wrong" in a human society, promotes an evil and deceitful government, sows seeds of discord among people, disregards social rules and regulations, and takes pleasure in harming the living world, he or she suffers the consequences of his or her actions and teachings, and remains in the "House of Wrong." He singles out bad rulers and evil priests as the foremost among such persons. Another term for this is the "House of the Worst Mind." The soul of a wrongful person returns from the "sorting bridge" back into the world of deceit. This bridge separates the righteous from the wrongful. The righteous progress but the wrongful remain in the world to perfect themselves. Does this mean rebirth or that the soul lingers on without a physical body until it is perfected? Perhaps, but only a thought provoking hint without any speculations.

This does not mean that there is no salvation for the wrongful. Their souls suffer the consequences of their words and deeds until they realize the divine truth and choose to turn righteous, and work for their own perfection and immortality. This life is but a refinery in which the souls are refined to perfection. To sum up, the pristine doctrine of Zarathushtra's "heaven and hell" is more of a mental bliss and torment than the two physical places reserved for ultimate sensual enjoyment or suffering.

The resurrection with all its details of how the dead would rise for the final judgment is again absent in the Gathas. The consequences of people's words and deeds in this world and the progress toward perfection and immortality are a continuous process. There are no pauses, no waiting. God's creation moves forward and we, souls and bodies, are a part of it.

Zarathushtra is the foremost in founding a universal religion. He taught to learn, consider and choose his Divine Doctrine first to practice and then teach and preach to others - all with a "sweet tongue" and with logic. He trained the first missionaries. Yet we have no reports at all of force, push, dictation, insistence, persuasion and temptation. The teaching was free and the listening free. "Hear the best with your ears, ponder over it with your bright mind and then, each of you, man and woman, decide for yourself to choose or not" was the watchword.

Through the history of one thousand years of Zoroastrian supremacy, we have not a single report of any religious war. No religious war with the Roman Kingdom and no religious war with the Christian Byzantine Kingdom. Religious wars between nations of different religions are only 1500 years old.

Culture

It is with these guiding ethics that the Zoroastrian Doctrine cultivated a culture, a culture that was based on knowledge, order, participation, cooperation, federation, alliance, and devotion. We see it in bloom when Cyrus the Great (550-529 BC.) united the ever-fighting nations of Afro-Eurasia into the first so-called kingdom. We see the comparatively peaceful occupation of lands with no enslavement and destruction followed. We see the captive nations freed and fully rehabilitated. We see freedom of worship, ownership, settlement, trade, travel, and above all, tolerance. We see transcontinental highways. We see what we know as pony postal service. And we see monetary coins and standard weights that facilitate commerce.

This brought unprecedented peace and prosperity over a vast area that had been wasted by wars. It brought the nations close to one another so much so that they began exchanging their knowledge and culture. From "a" Armenians to "t" Thracians, in all 26 nations pooled their skills to promote from "a" of architecture to "z" of zoology. And it was during these days, the Achaemenian era of 220 years during which we see knowledge advanced with rapid steps. Science boomed and bloomed forth. We have the Greek philosophers appear and almost disappear with the downfall of the kingdom at the hand of Alexander of Macedonia.

The Macedonian occupation did not crush or change the situation. It divided the federation into a number of camps. Yet the urge of unity put an end of the division within a century. But the Zoroastrian unity of globalization was not restored. The world split into the Roman Kingdom in the west and the Parthian in the east. Parthians as Zoroastrians showed tolerance towards all other nations and religions.

CASTE SYSTEM

The caste system, a complex network of interdependent yet separated, hereditary, endogamous, occupationally specialized, and hierarchically ordered social groups, the origins of which are definitely from the tribal, religious and cultural differences between various groups that can be seen anywhere in the entire world. However, the distinction between the tribalism in the rest of the world and the tribalism as a social institution in the Indian continent is its complexity and its persistence. Caste as an institution transcends religion. Brahmins, Muslims, Jains, Buddhists, Parsis, Sikhs, Vaishnavites, Shaivites, Veera Shaivites, Shaktites, Christians, Secular humanists, and others any where in the world and in India are all subject to the overarching dictates of the tribe. Attempts to break the caste system were made time and again from the days of Lord Buddha. Religions like Buddhism, Veera Shaivism, etc., succeeded momentarily, but the system always resurrected itself with vengeance. Even Islam failed to destroy this tribalism, e.g., Muslim Pashtoons of Afghanistan are different from other Muslims of Afghanistan, Muslim Kurds of Turkey are different from Turkish Muslims, Mohajirs of Pakistan are different from the rest, and so on.

Zoroastrian reform in the social terms seems to have been an accompaniment o the social changes that were happening as a result of the Aryan settlement in Iran and the pressure of their neighbours to the west, powerful civilisations of Mesopotamia. In face of scarce agricultural land, constant military threat, and the need to organise and form coherent political systems, another need for a uniting idea was evident. So,

Zoroastrianism, a belief system that is certainly uniting and also emphesises the duty of classes to obey their superiors, could be an indispensable tool in the hands of the new political rulers. The same process can be traced in India, where while not abandoning the polytheistic system, a caste system was formed that held each member of the society responsible for assigned duties.

In Iran, since the integration of local inhabitants to the Aryan society seems to have happened in a longer period of time, and since this social system was well formed prior to the Aryan contact with the locals, the formation of a caste system did not become an issue. Instead, the situation, especially the existence of laws in the civilised societies of the plateau and different climactic and land endowments, pressured the Iranians to form a new and coherent socio-political system that would enable them to become a political power and replace their predecessors. So, the foundations of the Median and Achaemenid power were laid in the pre-historical formation of Aryan, and indeed "Iranian" (i.e. Aryan and non Aryan), social system.

In modern Zoroasterian society there is no caste system.

STATUS OF WOMEN

Zoroastrian religion does not discriminate between men and women. Leaving aside the differences with regard to religious observances and role responsibilities, both the sexes are treated equally in the religious texts. Unlike in the Vedic religion there is no preferential treatment for male children. There is no such argument that male children are necessary for the deliverance of parents into the ancestral world. The initiation ceremony, Naujot is performed for both male and female children. Of the six Immortal Beings created by God, three are feminine and three are masculine. Both men and women have equal importance in protecting the sanctity and divinity of the world. Children are advised to honour both mother and father equally.

According to the Zoroastrian theories of creation, both men and women originated from the seed of Gayomard, the primeval man. When he was attacked by the evil forces, before passing away, he gave forth seed. The seed developed into Matro (Mashye) and Matroyao (Mashyane). They grew up from the earth like a plant united below the waist, whereby it was difficult to know who was male who was female. Ahura Mazda separated them from each other and changed them from plant into the shape of man. The Bundhahishn narrates the subsequent events in the following manner.

- Owing to the gracelessness which they practiced, the demons became more oppressive, and they themselves carried on unnatural malice between themselves; they advanced one against the other, and smote and tore their hair and cheeks.
- Then the demons shouted out of the darkness thus: 'You are man; worship the demon! so that your demon of malice may repose.'
- Mashye went forth and milked a cow's milk, and poured it out towards the northern quarter; through that the demons became more powerful, and owing to them they both became so dry-backed that in fifty winters they had no desire for intercourse, and though they had had intercourse they would have had no children.
- And on the completion of fifty years the source of desire arose, first in Mashye and then in Mashyane, for Mashye said to Mashyane thus: 'When I see thy shame my desires arise.' Then Mashyane spoke thus: 'Brother Mashye! when I see thy great desire I am also agitated.'
- Afterwards, it became their mutual wish that the satisfaction of their desires should be accomplished, as they reflected thus: 'Our duty even for those fifty years was this.'
- From them was born in nine months a pair, male and female; and owing to tenderness for offspring the mother devoured one, and the father one. 23. And, afterwards, Ohrmazd took tenderness for offspring away from them, so that one may nourish a child, and the child may remain.

Code of Behaviour for Women

Zoroastrian scriptures suggest that women are prone to the temptations of evil and therefore should be kept under regular watch. Women are expected to follow the example of Spenta Aramaiti and cultivate the qualities of love, devotion, sincerity and perfection. According to Arda Viraf, women who are desirous of going to heaven should honor water, fire, earth, trees, cattle and sheep and all the good creations of God. They should perform the religious ceremonies sincerely and offer prayers and service to God and the spiritual beings. They should show reverence and obedience to their husbands and lords and should practice the faith of Mazdayasnians without doubt. They should practice good thoughts, good words and good actions and abstain from sin. Adultery and unnatural intercourse are regarded as sins of heinous kind.

The Denkard classifies women on the basis of their conduct into four classes: "good as well as bad; not bad, and good; not good, and bad; and neither good nor bad. From among these any woman who is not bad and is good should be selected to manage household affairs and to give happiness and comfort to the master of the house. And to keep oneself free from unhappiness she who is good and bad ought not to be obtained; and (men) should positively keep aloof from choosing, from among the two descriptions of women mentioned above, her who is not good and is bad, over her who is neither good nor bad."

The Meno-i-Khard describes the best of women as "The woman who is young, who is properly disposed, who is faithful, who is respected, who is good-natured, who enlivens the house, whose modesty and awe are virtuous, a friend of her own father and elders, husband and guardian, handsome and replete with animation is chief over the women who are her own associates."

The wife of one's choice who is tied by a marriage ceremony should always be treated with affection and without niggardliness.

One should strive to increase progeny by going to her

She should be made a sharer in the good gained from righteous deeds.

A maiden wife should be given good dowry. And a wife who was previously widow should be given lesser dowry.

One should maintain physical intimacy and have sexual intercourse with her several times. No limit is prescribed, but thrice a month is considered reasonable.

As far as possible both men and women should avoid second spouse. Such an act is not considered meritorius.

Laws of Inheritance

The following laws of inheritance are mentioned in Dadestan-i Denig.

- As to the sixty-first question and reply, that which you ask is thus: How stand the shares in the inheritance (mirato) of property among those of the good religion, and how is it necessary for them to stand therein?
- The reply is this, that in the possession of wealth the wealth reaches higher or lower, just like water when it goes in a stream on a declivity, but when the passage shall be closed at

the bottom it goes back on the running water (puy-avo), and then it does not go to its after-course.

- When there is nothing otherwise in the will and private, property goes to a wife or daughter who is privileged; if one gives her anything by will then she does not obtain the share (dash) pertaining to her.
- Whenever a share for a son is not provided by it, every one has so much and the wife who may be a privileged one has twice as much; and the share of that one of the sons, or even the wife of a son, who is blind in both eyes, or crippled in both feet, or maimed in both his hands, is twice as much as that of one who is sound.
- And it is needful that he who was in the father's guardianship shall remain in guardianship, as when a father or mother is decrepit and causing awe (chagarin), or of a nurture different from that of the guardian — or a child of his brother or sister, or a father, or one without nurture apart from him, is without a guardian — the ready guardianship of a capable man, and the shelter and nourishment that have become inadequate are as indispensably forthcoming from the possessors of wealth, of those who have taken the property, as that taking was indispensable.
- If there be no son of that man, but there be a daughter or wife of his, and if some of the affairs of the man are such as render a woman not suitable for the guardianship, it is necessary to appoint a family guardian; if there be, moreover, no wife or daughter of his it is necessary to appoint an adopted son.

Marriage

Zoroastrian scriptures prohibit inter religious marriages. Followers are urged to marry within the religion to ensure the practice of righteousness without any complications. The texts suggest to select women who are wise and modest and firmly anchored in the religion. As for the son-in-laws they should be good natured, honest and experienced, even though they may be poor.

REFERENCES

Inostranzev, M.: Iranian Influence on Moslem Literature. Translated by G. K. Nariman with Supplementary Appendices from Arabic Sources. Bombay, 1918.

Jackson, A. V. Williams: Zoroaster, the Prophet of Ancient Iran. New York, 1899.

Meillet, A.: Trois Conferences sur les Gathas de l'Avesta. Paris, 1925.

Modi, Jivanji J.: A few events in the early history of the Parsis and their dates. Bombay, 1905.

Modi, J. J.: The Religious Ceremonies and Customs of the Parsees. Bombay, 1922.

Moulton, James H.: The Teachings of Zarathushtra. Bombay, 1916.

Pazend Texts: Collected and Collated by E. K. Antia. Bombay, 1909. Two Afrins, three Patits tr. into Eng. from Spiegel's German translation by A. H. Bleeck in *Khordah Avesta* Hertford, 1864. Seven Afrins, Sitayishes, and other Pazend prayers tr. into Gujarati by Phiroze E. Masani in *Pazend Prayers Series* Nos. 1, 2, 3. Bombay, 1916, 1920, 1931.

Ragozin, Z. A.: Media. New York, 1888.

Jamaspi: Edited and translated from the Pahlavi-Pazand iexts by Jivanji Jamshedji Modi. Bombay, 1903.

King, L. W., and Thompson, R. C.: The Sculptures and Inscriptions of Darius the Great on the Rock of Behistun in Persia: a new Collation of the Persian, Susian, and Babylonian Texts. London, 1907.

Lord, Henry: The Religion of the Parsees. London, 1630.

Madan, D. M.: Discourses on Iranian Literature. Bombay. 1909.

McNeile, H.: The Avesta and the Bible. Bombay, 1905.

16

Festivals

It is essential and necessary for every Zoroastrian(Zartoshti) to try to keep alive the religious traditions and customs, that have been passed from generation to generation to this day. The great history of our forefathers, that glowed with a special color in each period is a mirror of the culture and human characteristics of the period

The more we, Zoroastrians, think about and study our past history and customs, we realize the more about the greatness and broad-mindedness of our ancestors and good social consequences.

In Iran, the researchers of ancient Iran and Avesta language, think that Zartosht was born on Khordad Rooz in the month of Farvardin (March 26th) in the year 1768 BC. Some historians have said that Zartosht was born about 680 BC. While Plato, who praised Zartosht, gives Zartosht's birthdate around 6000 BC.

Zoroastrianism teaches hard work: every Zoroastrian has a duty to advance the cause of human progress, and work for the advancement of the civilization with his or her useful and constructive work. It teaches not to hinder the progress of humanity with idleness. Idleness, begging, withdrawing from life, are forbidden. Zartosht teaches free thinking and generosity to his followers. Zoroastrians should try to live in freedom and express their thoughts truthfully and freely. Zartosht does not force his religion on anyone, but asks everyone to listen to his teachings. Then every man and woman is to choose and decide for himself or herself.

In ancient Iran, people believed in working and feasting together. They believed that crying was a sin. They tried to have festivals throughout the year. Every month, when the name of the day and the name of the month was the same, that day would be celebrated at feast day. Hence twelve feast days for the twelve months. These were:

1. Farvardingan or Froodog: On the day of Farvardin in the month of Farvardin. This day is for remembrance of those who have passed away The words Farvardin and Fravahar are from the same root. It means a spirit which dwells in every man and animal for guidance and protection. People go to the cemetery on this day and remember the dead with a prayer. Iranian Zoroastians call this day Froodog. Hindus also have a ceremony like this called Pitara. The Catholics on the first day of November, which is called Toussaint (for the dead) go to the cemeteries and put flowers and plants on graves.
2. Jashn-e-Ardibeheshtgan: On the day of Ardibehesht in the month of Ardibehesht. Ardibehesht, (its Avesta word is Ashavahishta) represents cleanliness, purity and truth. It protects fire in all shapes everywhere.
3. Jashn-c-Khordadgan: On the day of Khordad in the month of Khordad. Its Avesta word is Orvatata, which means health and well-being. It protects water in any form in rivers, lakes seas and oceans.
4. Jashn-e-Tirgan: On the day of Tir in the month of Tir.

The day before Tirgan day, people cleaned their houses and on Tirgan day, people wore new clothes and a silken thread around their wrists. The feast lasted for ten days. Tir in Avesta is Teshtar, which is the name of a bright start. Avesta scholars have translated it to Sirius and is named as the Rain-Star.

There is a legend that during the war between Iranians and Touranians, in the Kingdom of Manuchehr, the Pishdadian King, Afrasiab was winning the war and had encircled Manuchehr with his forces. They agreed that someone would spring an arrow from the top of the Damavand Mountain. Wherever the arrow landed that would become the borderline between the two countries. Aarash who was great with the bow and arrow, went to the top of the Damavand and released an arrow. It is said that the arrow landed on a tree near Gaihoon River. This is were they selected to be the border line between the two countries.

GAHAMBAR

Gahambar means 'in time,' and refers to the six seasonal Zorastrian (Parsi) festivals. Gahambar can be translated to mean 'full time' or 'proper season'. King Jamshed was the first person to observe this festival.

Like Hindus, the Parsis observe six seasons. They are originally agricultural festivals. Each festival is five days in length and corresponds to one of the six days of creation in Zoroastrian cosmology. They days and their associations are: Maidhyozarem (heaven), Maidhyoshem (water), Paitishhayem (earth), Ayathrem (plants), Maidhyarem (animals), Hanaspathmaedem (man). During the rituals, tribute is paid to the phases or elements responsible for the creation of the world.

Four liturgical services are performed during the first four days, and the fifth day is reserved for communal interaction. Celebrations begin with a benediction ceremony called Afrin. It is a prayer of love and praise in remembrance of one's ancestors.

Every holy day is divided in 5 watches. Each watch is presided by an angel. The yaztas (angels) and the fravashis are honoured next in the Baj prayers. This is followed by the main Parsi rite, the Yasna. The last of the four customs for social service is the Pavi. It is a prayer for the particular Gahambar being celebrated. The priest and the faithful pray together during the Pavi.

On the fifth day of the Gahambar, there is a solemn feast. People can either donate or serve at the feast. Those who participate are expected to recall not only the blessings bestowed by the seasons, but also the seven main acts that a good Parsi must perform.

The Maidhyozarem Gahambar (heaven), is celebrated from the 41st day after Navroz. The second one, called Maidhyoshem (water), is observed 60 days later. Paitishhayem (earth) falls 75 days after that. Thirty days later, comes Ayathrem (flora and fauna), which celebrates creation and the prosperity that it brings. The fifth Gahambar, Maidhyarem, is celebrated 80 days after the fourth. The last of the six Gahambars, Hanaspathmaedaem, is observed 75 days after Maidhyarem.

As Zoroastrianism developed, Gahambars assumed religious significance. First gahambar is celebrated on the 11th day of the Parsi month Ardibenesth; second on 11th day of Tir; third on 26th day of Shehenever; fourth on the 26th of Meher; fifth on 6th of Dai; sixth on the 1st day of Gatha.

Gahamabar has become an important community feasts by all Parsis all over the world. Parsis hold public feasts in Bagh. Such feasts are not popular today. Gahambar is a community festival and pays tributes to God and Creation. It is also one that reinforces feelings of brotherhood. It is aimed at reminding Parsis of their roots and the good deeds that a true Parsi must do.

These deeds are radith (being charitable), rastih (being truthful), celebrating the Gahambars, observing the three-day ceremony after demise, worshipping god, building lodgings for the poor, and wishing everyone well.

Now-Rooze Festival: This festival has been one of the greatest festivals It has been continued since a very ancient time. All the writers attribute Now-Rooz to King Jamshid. Ferdousi said, "Now-Rooz starts on the first day of spring - Hormozd day - in the month of Farvardin." In ancient times, the festival would last for a month. Today in Iran this festival lasts for thirteen days.

Omar Khayyam in his book of Now-Rooz writes, "the sun completes its circle in 365 1/4 days and every four years a day is added. This extra day is called Avardad. King Jamshid learned about this and called it Now-Rooz, a new day and called for celebration. This occasion is celebrated every year on that day.

Five days before the new year, Panjeh or Muktad, Zoroastrians in Yazd, Kerman, and other cities and villages used to plant and grow Shesha. On the day of Now-Rooz all Zoroastrians prayed and gave thanks to Ahura Mazda. Afterwards, they would greet each other and wish each other a happy Now-Rooz and new year. They would use rose-water and sweets to greet each other.

If there had been a demise in a family, the family members would first go to visit that family and express their condolences. Thereafter, all would go to Atash-Bahram, or Aderian, or Dar-e-Mehr to pray and thank Ahura Mazda. Then they would wish each other a happy new year.

The Zoroastrian association in each locale would arange for the community to come together at a center on the second day, Bahman-Rooz, to celebrate the Now-Rooz, together.

Today in Iran there is a big festival during Now-Rooz and new year Family members and friends visit each other and send greeting cards to those who are away Khordad-Rooz in the month of Farvardin is the birthday of our prophet, Zartosht This day falls on the 26th of March. Zoroastrians celebrate this day.

KHORDAD SAL

The birth anniversary of Zoroaster or Prophet Spitaman Zarathushtra is celebrated as Khordad Sal in August-September. It falls sometime on the sixth day of the Parsi month of Farvardin. In some old Parsi texts, this day is also spoken of as the Navroz-I-Khas, which means 'special new year's day'. Even the real New Year's day is referred to as Navroz-I-Am, meaning 'common new year's day'.

The religious lore and texts of the Parsis mention the festival and its importance. In the olden days, the king and nobility, especially, observed Khordad Sal as Navroz-I-Khas. It is said to be the day on which many historic events of old Iran are said to have happened. Later, it came to be observed solely as Zarathushtra's birthday.

Zoroaster or zarathusthra was the founder of the religion. The exact year of Zarathushtra's birth is not known, but it is accepted that he was born in the beginning of the first millennium BC. Similarly, the day of his birth is also not known precisely.

On this day, Parsis wear new clothes; the house is cleaned and decorated with rangolis. Parsis arrange fragrant flowers prepare delicious meals. The ritual of Jashan, or thanksgiving prayers are offered at the temples. A grand feast is prepared to mark the occasion.

ZARTHOST NO DEESO

It is observed as the demise anniversary of Zoroaster. It is not a celebration but a mourning day for Parsis. It falls on June, on Khorshed roz, Dae mah (11th day, 10th month) of the Zoroastrian calendar.

It is believed that Zoroaster was killed in a temple while he was praying. It is marked as a sombre occasion. According to another belief, Zarathushtra in his 77th year was killed in a fire-temple by the Turanian army. It is also said that on this day, Zarathushtra ascended for the skies. Other sources believe that Zarathushtra died in his sleep or was killed by a murderer.

On this day, discourses on life and work of Zoroaster are held. Special prayers are recited and Zoroastrians go to the Fire Temple to pray. There aren't any elaborate celebrations. Zarthost No Deeso is observed in Mumbai and Gujarat particularly.

Fravahar

Fravahar which is called Fravashi in Avesta means progress and that man should aim high and try to lead a progressive life. Fravahar is like a luminous torch which shines and makes light all around it. In religious books, Fravahar is presented as an old man with a bright hallow who has two wings which are spread out and is going through a ring. The top as well as the bottom of the man is divided into three layers:

- The spread out wings are symbols of progress and advancing forward.
- The top three layers are symbols of good thoughts, good words, and good deeds
- The circle in the middle through which the old man is going symbolizes the world and man's desires for the earthly things, which one must face,
- The three layers at the bottom represent Dodgmat, Dodghookht, and Dodgvaresht, bad thoughts, bad words, and bad deed from which man has to stay away.

The symbols for a Zoroastrian are:

1. Good thought, good word, and good deed
2. Sedrah and Koshti, which are outward symbols.

Sedrah is a loose shirt with short sleeves and without collar made from a white cloth. In the front, there is a cut from the neck to near the chest at the end of which is a small pocket. This pocket is called Kissah-e-Kerfah.

In Avesta, sedrah is called Vohwnanu Vaslra, which means the clothes of good thought. In ancient times, sedrah was made of hide, wool, cotton and silk.

Koshti is made of seventy two strings of lamb wool. The seventy two strings represent the seventy two Yasnas. It is divided into six sections. Each of which has twelve strings, which represents the six Gahanbars and twelve months. Tying it around the waist three times, represents good thoughts, good words, and good deeds. With the first knot, Zoroastrians acknowledge that there is one God. The second knot represents that Zoroastrian religion was sent to us by God. The third knot represents Zartosht as our prophet The fourth knot is the symbol that we accept the principle of good thoughts, good words, and good deeds.

Sedrah and Koshti are said to have been before Zartosht and ascribed them to King Jamshid of Pishdadian. In ancient times, Zoroastrians used to make their children wear sedrah and koshti at the age of fifteen.

In Tiryasht, Kardeh six, paragraphs four and five, it is written, " Oh Zartosht Spintaman - Teshtar Rayoumand and Kharoumand wise appeared in the first ten nights in the shape of 15-year old youth. Bright with shinning eyes, tall and very strong. This is taken as the age for wearing sedrah and koshti. It is an age when a youth becomes mature and strong..."

On the day of ceremony, a large white cloth is spread in the middle of a room. A light or candle is placed on its four corners. An Afringan, with fire in it is placed in the middle of the cloth, along with a plate of sandal wood, etc. There is also a tray of dried fruits and nuts such as almonds and walnuts As well as coconuts and sweets which the Iranian Zoroastrians call Lork. There are also flowers, oregano (Abshen) rice, and sanjed.

The boy or girl, after a bath, wears sedrah and white clothes and enters the room and sits in such a way that he or she faces the sun. The mobed(s) sits facing the boy or girl The mobed(s) first recite Hormazd Yasht or Atash Nyaish. Then move to the side where the boy or girl is standing at this time and helps him or her to wear and tie the koshti with the Koshti Avesta.

After this, the mobed(s) recite Mazda Yasnu Ahmi and then Pyman-e-Din or Din-No-Kalmoh. The mobed(s) then finishes his prayer with Tandorosti prayer.

Dastoor Ardeshir Azargoshasb has said that it is good for our community to accept those who marry non-zoroastrians. His reason for this is that our numbers are small and we can't let them exit our community and religion. He also reasons that our religion is based on free thinking and freedom of choice. The meaning of Din-No-Kalmoh is as follows:

"O most truthful knowledge, concerning the noble religion of (the)Mazda-worshippers, given by Mazda (and) affecting 'Asha' the Divine Law of Righteousness. A religion (which is) noble (and) just, as well as complete and effectual, which God has made known for the people of this world; such it is which Zarathushtra has (himself) brought, a religion which is the religion of Zarathushtra (and) which is the religion of Ahura Mazda [and is] given unto Holy and Righteous Zarathushtra (for spreading it among mankind)."

NAVROZE

Navroze is the traditional Iranian new year holiday celebrated by Iranian, Turkic and many other peoples in West Asia, Central Asia, South Asia, Northwestern China, the Caucasus, the Crimea, and the Balkans.

Navroze marks the first day of spring and the beginning of the Iranian year. It is celebrated on the day of the astronomical vernal equinox (start of spring in northern hemisphere), which usually occurs on March 21 or the previous/following day depending on where it is observed. As well as being a Zoroastrian holiday, it is also a holy day for adherents of Sufism and the Bahá'í Faith. In Iran it is also referred to as an Eid festival, although it is not an Islamic feast. Alawites and Nizari Ismaili Muslims also celebrate Navroze.

The term Navroze first appeared in Persian records in the second century AD, but it was also an important day during the time of the Achaemenids (648-330 BC.), where kings from different nations under the Persian kingdom used to bring gifts to the king (Shahanshah) of Persia on Navroze.

The first day on the Iranian calendar falls on the spring equinox, the first day of spring. At the time of the equinox, the sun is observed to be directly over the equator, and the north and south poles of the Earth lie along the solar terminator; sunlight is evenly divided between the north and south hemispheres.

Due to its antiquity, there exists various foundation myths for Navroze in Iranian mythology. In the Zoroastrian tradition, the seven most important Zoroastrian festivals are the six Gahambars and Navroze which occurs at the spring equinox. According to the late Professor. Mary Boyce: It seems a reasonable surmise that Navroze, the holiest of them all, with deep doctrinal significance, was founded by Zoroaster himself. Between sunset of the day of the 6th Gahanbar and sunrise of Navroze was celebrated Hamaspathmaedaya (later known, in its extended form, as Frawardinegan). This and the Gahanbar are the only festivals named in the surviving text of the Avesta.

The Shahnameh, dates Navroze as far back to the of Jamshid, who in Zoroastrian texts saved mankind from a killer winter that was destined to kill every living creature[6]. The mythical Persian King Jamshid (Yima or Yama of the Indo-Iranian lore) perhaps symbolizes the transition of the Indo-Iranians from animal hunting to animal husbandry and a more settled life in human history. In the Shahnameh and Iranian mythology, he is credited with the foundation of Navroze. In the Shahnama, Jamshid constructed a throne studded with gems. He had demons raise him above the earth into the heavens; there he sat on his throne like the sun shining in the sky. The world's creatures gathered in wonder about him and scattered jewels aound him, and called this day the New Day or No/

Now-Ruz. This was the first day of the month of Farvardin (the first month of the Persian calendar). The association with Jamshid can be seen that in Persian, the festival is also called Navroze-i-Jamshidi.

he Iranian scholar Abu Rayhan Biruni of the 10th century AD., in his Persian work "Kitab al-Tafhim li Awa'il Sina'at al-Tanjim" provides a description of the calendar of various nations. Besides the Persian calendar, various festivals of Arabs, Jews, Sabians, Greeks and other nations are mentioned in this book. In the section on the Persian calendar, he mentions Navroze, Sadeh, Tiregan, Mehregan, the six Gahanbar, Parvardegaan, Bahmanja, Isfandarmazh and several other festivals. According to him: It is the belief of the Persians that Navroze marks the first day when the universe started its motion.

Today, the festival of Navroze is celebrated in many countries that were territories of, or influenced by, the Persian Kingdom: Iran, Iraq, Afghanistan, parts of the Middle East, as well as in the former Soviet republics of Tajikistan, Uzbekistan, Azerbaijan,Turkmenistan, Kazakhstan, and Kyrgyzstan. It is also celebrated by the Zoroastrian Parsis in India and Pakistan as well by certain Iranic inhabitants in Pakistan's Chitral region. It is also celebrated by the Iranian immigrants from Shiraz in Zanzibar. In Turkey, it is called Nevruz in Turkish, Sultan Nevruz in Albanian. In some remote communities located in parts of western Iran, the holiday is referred to as Nuroj, which literally means New Day in the Kurdish language.

Khane Tekani

Persians (Tajiks) and other groups (Kurds, Armenians, Aserbaidjanians, Balochs and various turkish nations) start preparing for the Navroze with a major spring-cleaning of their houses, the purchase of new clothes to wear for the new year and the purchase of flowers (in particular the hyacinth and the tulip are popular and conspicuous).

In association with the "rebirth of nature", extensive spring-cleaning is a national tradition observed by almost every household in Persia. This is also extended to personal attire, and it is customary to buy at least one set of new clothes. On the New Year's day, families dress in their new clothes and start the twelve-day celebrations by visiting the elders of their family, then the rest of their family and finally their friends. On the thirteenth day families leave their homes and picnic outdoors.

During the Navroze holidays people are expected to visit one another (mostly limited to families, friends and neighbours) in the form of short house visits, which are usually reciprocated. Typically, on the first day of Navroze, family members gather around the table, with the Haft Seen on the table or set next to it, and await the exact moment of the arrival of the spring. At that time gifts are exchanged. Later in the day, the first house visits are paid to the most senior family members. Typically, the youth will visit the elders first, and the elders return their visit later. The visits naturally have to be relatively short, otherwise one will not be able to visit everybody on their list. A typical visit is around 30 minutes, where you often run into other visiting relatives and friends who happen to be paying a visit to the same house at that time. Because of the house visits, you make sure you have a sufficient supply of pastry, cookies, fresh and dried fruits and special nuts on hand, as you typically serve your visitors with these items with tea or sherbet. Many Iranians will throw large Navroze parties in a central location as a way of dealing with the long distances between groups of friends and family.

Some Navroze celebrants believe that whatever a person does on Navroze will affect the rest of the year. So, if a person is warm and kind to their relatives, friends and neighbours on Navroze, then the new year will be a good one. On the other hand, if there are fights and disagreements, the year will be a bad one.

One tradition that may not be very widespread (that is, it may belong to only a few families) is to place something sweet, such as honey or candy, in a safe place outside overnight. On the first morning of the new year, the first person up brings the sweet stuff into the house as another means of attaining a good new year.

Haft Sin

Haft Sin or the seven 'S's is a major tradition of Navroze. The haft sin table includes seven specific items starting with the letter 'S' or Sin. The items symbolically correspond to seven creations and holy immortals protecting them. The Haft Sin has evolved over time, but has kept its symbolism. Traditionally, families attempt to set as beautiful a Haft Sin table as they can, as it is not only of traditional and spiritual value, but also noticed by visitors during Navrozei visitations and is a reflection of their good taste.

REFERENCES

Dawson, M. M.: The Ethical Religion of Zoroaster. New York, 1931

Desatir: Published by Mulla Firuz Bin Kaus. Persian and English. 2

vols. Bombay, 1818.

Gottheil, R. J. H.: References to Zoroaster in Syriac and Arabic Literature. In *Classical Studies in Honour of Henry Drisler*. New York, 1894.

Inostranzev, M.: Iranian Influence on Moslem Literature. Translated by G. K. Nariman with Supplementary Appendices from Arabic Sources. Bombay, 1918.

Jackson, A. V. Williams: Zoroaster, the Prophet of Ancient Iran. New York, 1899.

Meillet, A.: Trois Conferences sur les Gathas de l'Avesta. Paris, 1925.

Modi, Jivanji J.: A few events in the early history of the Parsis and their dates. Bombay, 1905.

Modi, J. J.: The Religious Ceremonies and Customs of the Parsees. Bombay, 1922.

Moulton, James H.: The Teachings of Zarathushtra. Bombay, 1916.

Pazend Texts: Collected and Collated by E. K. Antia. Bombay, 1909. Two Afrins, three Patits tr. into Eng. from Spiegel's German translation by A. H. Bleeck in *Khordah Avesta* Hertford, 1864. Seven Afrins, Sitayishes, and other Pazend prayers tr. into Gujarati by Phiroze E. Masani in *Pazend Prayers Series* Nos. 1, 2, 3. Bombay, 1916, 1920, 1931.

Ragozin, Z. A.: Media. New York, 1888.

Rapp, A.: The Religion and Customs of the Persians and other Iranians as described by the Grecian and Roman Authors. Translated from the German by K. R. Cama. Bombay, 1876-1879. Sanjana, Rastamji E.: Zarathushtra and Zarathushtrianism in the Avesta. Leipzig, 1906.

Sanjana, Rastamji E.: The Parsi Book of Books, the Zend-Avesta. Bombay, 1924.

17

Religious Places

RELIGIOUS PLACES IN INDIA

Sanjan Atash Behram

The Sanjan Atash Behram was the first sacred fire of the Parsis in India. Three hundred years after it was installed, Sanjan was invaded by Muslims, but the Sanjana priests managed to rescue the Atash Behram and carried it about 14 miles from Sanjan to a cave on an isolated hill named Bahrot,. Here, protected by jungle and sea, they guarded it for the next 12 years, and then when conditions were quieter, they took it to Bansda, a little town some 50 miles inland, where it remained for two years. During this time, the fire was kept in a metal vase so that it could be transported easily and the tradition of enthroning a sacred fire on a stone altar was broken. The Atash Behram was for some years without a fixed abode until Changa Asa, a layman from Navsari, came to Bansda to pay homage to the fire. On his return he proposed to the Bhagarias, a group of Parsis living in and around Navsari, that they should invite the Sanjana priests to bring the sacred fire to Navsari. The Bhagarias sent the invitation which the Sanjanas accepted and the fire was safely installed in Navsari. Ever since the establishment of the community's sacred fire in Navsari, the town became the center of Parsi religious life and the Bhagarias and Sanjanas lived together harmoniously. The Sanjana priests tended the fire and supported themselves from the offerings made to their fire, while the Bhagaria priests performed all other rituals and ceremonies for the Zoroastrian laity of Navsari. The first Dar-i-Mihr was founded in Navsari in the early 12th century.

In 1572 AD. King Akbar of the Mogul Dynasty of India took over Gujarat. He was a wise King who was interested in the various religions of his subjects and he held a religious discussion at his court. Meherji

Rana, a learned Bhagaria priest, was selected by the Zoroastrians to represent their community. He impressed the King so favourably, that Akbar ordered that the sacred fire be kept burning at his court day and night, according to the custom of the ancient Persian Kings. The Jizyad, a tax imposed on all non-muslims, was also abolished for the Parsis.

As Navsari prospered, the Parsi community grew and the Sanjanas began to encroach on the Bhagaria's rights to perform all ceremonies. Friction between the two groups increased and led to a law suit before a Hindu court which gave a decree that the Sanjanas must keep to their original agreement to serve the fire only. The Sanjanas decided that they would rather leave Navsari and in 1741 did so, taking the Atash Behram with them. A year later they installed it in a new temple at the village of Udwada, where it burns to this day.

The removal of the sacred fire distressed the Bhagarias and they resolved to consecrate an Atash Behram of their own in Navsari. With the help from the Parsi community and the priests of Surat, a new Atash Behram was enthroned in 1765. The Sanjanas were naturally a little jealous of this new Atash Behram, for it became a rival to their own 800 year old fire. They feared that fewer pilgrims would now come to remote Udwada, and so they evolved a legend to enhance its dignity. They created the new word "Iranshah" for it and humors were spread that the first Parsi settlers had brought it with them from Iran and it was somehow linked to the Xhavarenah of the ancient Kings of Persia. This legend is widely believed among the Parsis who continue loyally to make the pilgrimage to this day.

In the eighteenth century, Surat became an important port of trade and commerce and during the next century and a half it was the largest center of Zoroastrian population in the world. The earliest consecrated Adaran fire was founded in Siganpur, not far from Surat, by Lovji Wadia, (shipbuilder) in the later half of the eighteenth century and another one was founded in Surat proper in 1771 AD. An Atash Behram was installed in Surat in 1823 AD.

Meanwhile, Bombay became a British possession in 1661 and the East India Company set out to make it the most flourishing port of India. This brought in a steady flow of Parsi settlers and Dar-i-Mihrs were established in 1672 by Hirji Waccha and in 1709 by Banaji Limji and the second Adaran of India was founded in 1735 by Maneckji Seth.

Between the eighteenth and nineteenth centuries, more than 50 Adarans were established in India as far a Karachi (1848) and Calcutta (1839).

Today there are eight Atash Behrams in India:

- Udwada Anjuman(Shenshai) built in 11th century AD.
- Navsari Anjuman(Shenshai) built in 1765
- Surat Vakil (Kadmi) built in 1823
- Surat Mody (Shenshai) built in 1823
- Bombay Dady Seth (Kadmi) built in 1783
- Bombay Wadia (Shenshai) built in 1830
- Bombay Banaji (Kadmi) built in 1894
- Bombay Anjuman (Shenshai) built in 1898

The first two and the last Atash Behrams listed above are called Anjuman, meaning society, because they were built from donations made by various Zoroastrians. All others were entirely financed by private donations made by the respective families. Shenshai and Kadmi are the different calendars followed by the Zoroastrians.

Iranshah Atash Behram

According to Parsi (Indian Zoroastrian) legend, when (over a thousand years ago) one group of refugees from (greater) Khorasan landed in Western Gujarat, they had the ash of such a fire with them. This ash, it is said, served as the bed for the fire today at Udvada. (Boyce & Kotwal, 2006)

This fire temple was not always at Udvada. According to the Qissa-i Sanjan, 'Story of Sanjan', the only existing account of the early years of Zoroastrian refugees in India and composed at least six centuries after their arrival, the immigrants established a Atash-Warharan, 'victorious fire' at Sanjan. Under threat of war (probably in 1465), the fire was moved to the Bahrot caves 20 km south of Sanjan, where it stayed for 12 years. From there, it was moved to Bansdah, where it stayed for another 14 years before being moved yet again to Navsari, where it would remain until the 18th century. It was then moved to Udvada were it burns today.

Although there are numerous eternally burning Zoroastrian fires today, with the exception of the 'Fire of Warharan', none of them are more than 250 years old. The legend that the Indian Zoroastrians invented the afrinagan (the metal urn in which a sacred fire today resides) when the moved the fire from Sanjan to the Bahrot caves is unsustainable. Greek historians of the Parthian period reported the use of a metal vase-like urn to transport fire. Sassanid coins of the 3rd-4th century AD. likewise reveal a fire in a vase-like container identical in design to the present-day afrinagans. The Indian Zoroastrians do however export these and other utensils to their co-religionists the world over.

The Iranshah Atash Behram at Udvada near Surat has the distinction of having the oldest sacred fire of Parsis in India. Consecrated in 1742, this holy fire was brought by Iranian refugees to Udvada, shortly after their arrival at Sanjan in South Gujarat. This is the most important pilgrimage site for the Parsi sect of India. It also houses the Dasturji Koyaji Mirza Hall and the WZO Museum.

Udvada is a quaint coastal village 206 km north of Mumbai. It is situated between the Union Territory of Daman and the district town of Valsad. The nearest railhead Udvada is on the Virar-Surat section. The National Highway 8 from Mumbai to Vapi Juntion via Manor leads to Udvada.

RELIGIOUS PLACES OUTSIDE INDIA

The Special Fires

The desert province of Yezd, in Iran, is an ancient Zoroastrian stronghold. Even today a number of ancient spiritual fires are preserved in its sleepy little villages. The fire that burns in the village of Sharifabad is said to be more than 2,000 years old. Also, the only Atash Behram other than the eight that burn in India is in Yezd.

There are also the legendary "flying fires". This is not to say that one can see them fly. Not much can be written about these special fires except to say that one must experience the spirituality of these fires rather than just read or talk about them.

According to oral tradition, the Zoroastrians of Yezd believe that generations ago these special fires came flying into certain Zoroastrian villages like Cham and Zainabad. These special fires were typically found crackling and glowing on a cypress tree in the village. One could rationalize that lightening may have struck the tree or the intense desert heat may have triggered a spontaneous fire. But there is no denying the fact that these fires have a natural origin. Over the decades devout "Atashbands" (keepers of the Holy Fire) have preserved these Fires with great devotion and piety. Several miracles and legends are associated with these fires. As they say, 'the proof of the pudding is in the eating' and many (including this writer) have experienced a spiritual transformation after praying before these special fires.

The Holy Shrines

There are also a number of Holy Shrines, which the locals revere as "Pir" (ancient/holy). These mountain shrines consist essentially of sacred rocks in high and lonely places. According to folklore, after the defeat of Yazdagird III (the last Zoroastrian monarch of Sasanian Iran) at the hands of the Arab invaders, his family not only had to flee from the palace but were separated and had to roam about in the wilderness. The invaders were in hot pursuit of Yazdagird's wife and daughters. It is believed that when everything seemed lost, the princesses prayed to Dadaar Ahura Mazda for help, whereupon the mountains opened up and took them in.

For some, these stories may seem far-fetched and difficult to believe. But for Zoroastrians in Iran, the ' Pirs' and the stories wound around them are an article of faith. If you ask them if they really believe in these stories, they shoot back: "Do you believe in Ahura Mazda? Do you believe He is Good, All-knowing and Powerful? Do you believe that He created this entire universe, which also include these mountains? If you do, then what makes you think He cannot do something as simple as opening up a mountain to protect a sincere devotee and save her from the clutches of evil-doers?" This simple but logical argument often leaves the sceptic speechless.

The five sanctuaries and one other in the plain near the city of Yezd, were in communal trust. Each village looked after the shrines in its own fields and lanes, but all joined together to care for these six. To visit any of them on any occasion was an act of much merit, but the merit was greatest when one joined in the yearly pilgrimage at the time appointed. Each pilgrimage lasted officially for five days, like each of the major festivals."

Seti Pir

Seti Pir is situated east of Yezd and it is the shrine that marks the place where Yazdagird's queen (Shahbanoo Hastbadan), the mother of the princesses, Banu-Pars and Hayat-Banu, herself fleeing from the Arabs, jumped into a deep well, together with her two attendants, to save her honour. Seti Pir is, therefore, regarded as the mother of the other five great Pirs.

There is also a fascinating account of how the shrine came to be built. A Zoroastrian from Yezd was imprisoned and sentenced to demise for entering the holy city of Meshed. In those days, no non-Muslim could enter the city of Meshed, just as even today no non-Muslim can enter the holy city of Mecca. In prison, the Zoroastrian had a dream in which he was told the story of Seti Pir and asked to prepare himself to make the story known to others and build a shrine on the spot he would find himself the next morning. Indeed, the next morning, the Zoroastrian found himself not in his prison cell, but in Yezd. It appears, on verification, it was found that prison records in Meshed did indicate a Zoroastrian having "escaped" from prison.

Banu-Pars

According to legend, Yazdegird's daughter, Banu-Pars, fleeing from invading Arabs, came alone to the head of the Yezdi plain. Tired and thirsty, she requested a peasant for something to drink. He milked his cow for her but, just as the bowl was full, the animal kicked it from his hands. Since the Arabs were drawing close, she had to go on with a parched throat. Turning towards the mountains, she stumbled up a dry riverbed. She begged the "Stone of the Curse" to open and take her in, but it remained unmoved. She went on further into the mountain and cried out to Dadaar Ahura Mazda for help and He opened the rock before her and she hastened in, never to be seen again. However, a piece of her dress was caught, it is said, by the closing stone. Iranians claim that their grandparents had seen the fragment of cloth, pieces of which were cut and taken away by pilgrims over years, as a sacred relic. Today, there is no trace of the cloth in the natural cleft in the sacred rock. Childless women are known to have their wishes fulfilled after praying at this Pir.

Pir-e-Sabz

Situated on the northeastern side of the Yezdi plain one has to drive through miles of dry desert. And, then, suddenly, out of nowhere, a patch of green can be seen on the mountain – a mountain oasis, more popularly known as Chak-Chak or Pir-e-Sabz. Here, the sacred rock (where the princess 'Nek Banu' or 'Hayat Banu' is believed to have been taken in) is high up on the steep face of a great limestone mountain, besides a pool of water. This pool is fed by a spring that flows, seemingly miraculously, out of the bare cliff above. The course of the trickling water is green with maidenhair fern (believed to be the hair of the princess) and the huge old plain tree which shades the sacred rock is believed to have grown from a stick on which the princess leant and which she thrust into the ground before vanishing. This tree is said to catch fire and renew itself phoenix-like, every thousand years. By the pool, there is also a giant willow which age has bent right over so that the trunk and branches spread across the water and down to the rocks beyond.

From the foot of the mountain, one can see a honeycomb of terraces and little buildings clinging like a Tibetan monastery to the rock face. The climb all the way to the uppermost bungli is steep but not impossible to climb. The devote, though ailing from arthritis, rheumatism and heart disease have been known to climb all the way up to offer their respects at this Holiest of Holy shrine in Iran. What refreshes one and all immediately, is a drink of the water that trickles out of the mountain. The locals call it Aab-e-Hayat, or the Water of Life, and it is as sacred to them as the water of the river Ganga is to the Hindus or Zam-Zam to the Muslims. Local Iranians believe that the water stops trickling form the mountain if a woman in a state of menses approaches it. On the other hand, the flow increases if more pilgrims come to pay homage. Whether a dozen pilgrims come or five thousand, there is always sufficient water for everyone's need even in the summer, provided the laws of purity are observed.

The view from the uppermost terrace at Pir-e-Sabz is stupendous and if one is sensitive enough, one can visualize how the tired and thirsty princess must have come running to this mountain, how she must have prayed for protection and aid. Pir-e-Sabz is also symbolic of the victory of good over evil. No wonder when the Iranian Zoroastrians come back from their annual pilgrimage in the mountains, they come back stronger in their beliefs and conviction in their great religion.

Pir-e-Nauraki

Pir-e-Nauraki is situated at the foot of a mountain of the same name, in the valley of Gaigun. According to one source, the shrine is dedicated to an unnamed princess of Yazdagird. According to the other source, it is dedicated to "Naazbanu", the daughter of a Zoroastrian Governor.

The shrine is a mountain oasis in the middle of a vast and barren desert. The mountains (with patches of snow on the top, even in late spring) at some distance, provide a beautiful backdrop. The air is fragrant with the perfumes of the variety of flora and fauna that abound the shrine.

Pir-e-Hrist

The shrine rests on the crest of a ridge, which rises from the shingle of a plain, set in a ring of mountains. A maid by the name Morvarid serving the royal household, fleeing with a child of the royal family is believed to have been taken in by the mountain here.

Yezd

The province of Yezd is surrounded all over by mountain and desert. Kerman and Fars lie to the south, while Isfahan is to the west of Yezd.

The highest mountain in this province is Shirkuh (or Milky Mountain, so named due to the perpetual snow cover, even in summer) which is 4,055 m. high.

The city of Yezd is a typical desert city with extreme temperatures in summer and in winter. To beat the summer heat, the residents of Yezd have badgirs, or wind-towers, which is an ancient and natural method of air-conditioning. The construction of badgir and qanat (or underground water channels) is a skill known only to a few families of Yezd and is believed to be an ancient Zoroastrian innovation.

The architecture of the villages is fairly standard – mud houses appearing plain and simple from the outside, but generally well furnished from within. Each house generally has a courtyard – some even with fishponds and pomegranate trees. The rooms have natural cooling systems and openings in the roof for natural light to filter in.

The "Dokhma" (towers of silence) are a major tourist attraction in Yezd. Curious westerners, especially Germans, come in large groups to study and admire this ancient system for the disposal of the dead, which sadly has been abandoned in favour of burial for nearly a quarter of a century in Iran. With the hot desert sun and the 'dokhmas' situated on remote hilltops far from civilization, the system was working effectively. However, excessive westernization under the Pahlavi regime made certain Zoroastrians living in Tehran embarrassed of this 'archaic system'. Although the Zoroastrian villagers in Yezd were happy and comfortable with this natural and effective system, the 'urban intellectuals' spurred by the Late Mohammed Rezasha Pahlavi, brought sufficient pressure on the simple villagers to change the centuries old system of 'dohkmenashini'.

The Zoroastrian villagers are truly a simple, warm and friendly people. They love meeting fellow Zoroastrians who come as tourists or pilgrims and their hospitality and graciousness is legendary. Even the poorest Zoroastrian family would not allow a visitor to leave without a cup of tea, 'sherbet', sweets or fruits.

REFERENCES

Govindacharya, A.: Mazdaism in the Light of Vishnuism. Mysore, 1913.

Gray, L. H.: The Foundations of the Iranian Religions. Bombay, 1929.

Grundriss der Iranischen Philologie: Herausgegeben von W. Geiger und E. Kuhn. 2 vols. Strassburg, 1895-1904.

Hadokht Nask: The Pahlavi text, edited and translated by Hoshangji Jamaspji Asa, Martin Haug, and E. W. West. Bombay, 1872.

Indo-Iranian Studies: Being Commemorative Papers contributed by European, American and Indian Scholars in honor of Dastur Darab P. Sanjana. London, 1925.

Jamaspi: Edited and translated from the Pahlavi-Pazand iexts by Jivanji Jamshedji Modi. Bombay, 1903.

King, L. W., and Thompson, R. C.: The Sculptures and Inscriptions of Darius the Great on the Rock of Behistun in Persia: a new Collation of the Persian, Susian, and Babylonian Texts. London, 1907.

Lord, Henry: The Religion of the Parsees. London, 1630.

Madan, D. M.: Discourses on Iranian Literature. Bombay. 1909.

McNeile, H.: The Avesta and the Bible. Bombay, 1905.

Rawlinson, George: The Five Great Monarchies of the Ancient Eastern World, Chaldea, Assyria, Babylon, Media, and Persia. 4 vols. London, 1862-1867.

Rawlinson, George: The Sixth Great Oriental Monarchy. London, 1813.

Rezwi, T.: Parsis: A People of the Book. Calcutta, 1928.

Rivayat, Pahlavi, accompanying the Dadistan-i Dinik: Edited by B. N; Dhabhar. Bombay, 1913.

Rivayat, Persian of Darab Hormazyar: Edited by M. R. Unvala with an Introduction by J. J. Modi. 2 vols. Bombay, 1922.

Sad Dar: Edited by B. N. Dhabhar. Bombay, 1909.

Sanjana, Darab P: Zarathushtra in the Gathas and the Greek and Roman Classics. Translated from the German of Geiger and Windischmann. Leipzig, 1897.

Sanjana, Rastamji E.: Spiritualism through Zoroastrian Eyes. Bombay, 1929.

18

Art and Iconography

Zoroastrianism as a religious faith with its beginning in ancient Iran, which exist even in modern times is possibly the world's oldest continuing religion. The founding father of Zoroastrianism, Zarathustra, preached around 600 BC, a monotheistic religious message, much of which is found in the collection of sacred writing, Avesta. Inside the History of Religion the teachings of Zarathustra has been used in order to explain the development of the three major monotheistic religions, Judaism, Christianity, and Islam, but there has never been proven any clear examples of influence between the belief systems. Zoroastrianism is also called Zarathustrism, Mazdaism and Parsism. Parsism is the term used today among the believers in India, the largest Zoroastrian society of today. Modern Zoroastrianism counts about 150,000 believers in India, 60,000 in Iran, and perhaps 50,000 in the rest of the world.

HISTORY

Although, in the West, Iranian art and culture have traditionally been known as Persian, the inhabitants of the country have long called it Iran, rather than Persia, and themselves Iranians, rather than Persians. In accordance with popular usage, however, the term "Persian" will be used here to refer to the period before the advent of Islam in the seventh century AD; that is, the period of the ancient Persian empires; as well as the preceding prehistoric times. Large numbers of ceramic vessels and clay figurines survive from the prehistoric period. Architecture and sculpture predominated during the period of the first two Persian empires sixth century BC to seventh century AD. After the Arab conquest and the introduction of Islam in the seventh century AD, sculpture was little practised but architecture flourished. Painting became a major art in the period from the thirteenth to the seventeenth century. In the twentieth century these ancient arts have been revived, and traditional forms were combined with Western technology and contemporary materials.

Among the earliest examples of Persian architecture are a number of small houses of packed mud and mudbrick found at several Neolithic sites in western Iran: Tepe Ali Kosh, Tepe Guran, Ganj Dareh Tepe, and Hajji Firuz Tepe. These sites show that small villages made up of one-room houses and storage structures were already established along the western border of the country by 6000 BC. Excavations at Tal-i Bakun, near Persepolis, and Tal-i Iblis and Tepe Yahya, near Kerman, show that by 4000 BC buildings with a number of rooms were being erected and grouped into villages or small towns. All these structures indicate that the traditional building techniques, in which packed mud and sun-dried mudbrick are used, were already developed. At Shahr-i Sokhta, in Seistan, an elaborate Bronze Age palace was excavated. The plans of these remains show a steady growth in complexity ending with the establishment of important commercial centres on the plateau.

At the end of the second millennium BC, Iranian tribal groups, including the Medes and Persians, spread over the plateau and displaced or absorbed the indigenous inhabitants. The architecture and crafts of this Iron Age period, which immediately preceded the founding of the Persian Empire by Cyrus the Great, have been brought to light by excavations near Kangavar (Godin Tepe and Babajan Tepe), near Hamadan (Nush-i Jan Tepe), and at Zendan-i Suleiman and Tepe Hasanlu in north-western Iran. These sites revealed the earliest known tradition of building in Persia in which large columnar halls are used as a central feature. The columns were of wood set on stone slabs, while the buildings themselves were of uncut stone and mudbrick construction. Stairways and terraces, along with other features, formed the prototypes for later developments in the imperial architecture of Pasargadae and Persepolis. If, as is thought, the buildings at Nush-i Jan Tepe and Godin Tepe are Median in origin, they are the first structures built by the Medes to be excavated. These discoveries confirm the generalized descriptions of battlements and palaces found in the literary sources, especially the writings of the Greek historian Herodotus.

ARCHITECTURE

The first great development of ancient Persian architecture took place under the Persian Empire of the Achaemenid dynasty, which ruled from about 550 to 331 BC. Remains of Achaemenian architecture are numerous, the earliest being ruins at Pasargadae, the capital city of Cyrus the Great. These ruins include two palaces, a sacred precinct, a citadel, a tower, and the tomb of Cyrus. The palaces were set in walled gardens and contained central columnar halls, the largest of which was thirty-seven meter. The principal rooms were either square or rectangular and all were lit by a clerestory. Walls were constructed of mud brick; foundations, doorways, columns, and dados along the walls were of stone. Columns were capped with stone blocks carved to represent the forequarters of horses or lions with horns, placed back to back. The roof was flat and was probably made of wood. The sacred precinct consisted of a walled court containing two altars and a rectangular stepped platform. The tower was a tall rectangular structure built of yellow limestone; a contrasting black limestone was used for the doorway and two tiers of blind windows. The tomb of Cyrus was a small gabled stone building placed on a stepped platform. The columns surrounding the tomb were erected in recent Islamic times.

Darius I built a new capital at Persepolis, to which additions were made by Xerxes I and Artaxerxes I. Three vast terraces were hewn and levelled out of the rocky site, and on them mudbrick and stone buildings, similar to those at Pasargadae, were erected. The buildings at Persepolis differed from those at Pasargadae in a number of ways. The columnar halls were square, walls were broken by windows and window-like niches of stone, and the stone dado was not applied. Doorways bore a quarter-round cornice ornamented with a petal motif, probably of Egyptian origin. Column shafts were fluted rather than plain, the bases and caps were ornamented with floral decorations, and the termination of the column, called the impost block, took the form of naturalistically rendered forequarters of bulls or bulls with wings. These buildings had ceilings of cedar, carried on heavy balks or beams that rested on the stone impost blocks at the tops of the columns.

Other remains of Achaemenian architecture exist at Susa, where Darius I built a large palace, which was subsequently rebuilt by Artaxerxes II. Royal architecture under the Achaemenids also included tombs cut in solid rock, of which the best-known examples are those at Naqshah Rostam, near Persepolis. Little is known of the popular building practices of the period, but archaeologists believe that the ordinary dwelling was made of mudbrick.

After the conquest of Persia by Alexander the Great in 331 BC, and the assumption of power by the Seleucid dynasty, Persian architecture followed the styles common to the Greek world. The great Greek-style Temple of Anahita at Kangavar was excavated by the Archaeological Service of Iran with a view to eventual restoration. The temple had been destroyed by a severe earthquake in antiquity. Subsequently, under the Parthian Arsacid dynasty, which was in existence from about 250 BC to AD 226, a small number of buildings were constructed in native Persian style. The most notable monument of this period is a palace at Hatra, dating from the first or second century AD and exemplifying the use of the barrel vault on a grand scale. The vaults, heavy walls, and small rooms of this palace indicate a continuation of earlier Assyrian and Babylonian tradition.

A great renaissance in architecture took place under the Sasanian dynasty, which ruled Persia from 226 until the Islamic conquest in 641. Construction was radically different from that of the Achaemenian period. Walls were built of burnt brick or small stones bound with mortar; barrel vaults of brick were used to span rooms and corridors; and domes were erected over the large halls. The principal features of the plan of the palaces at Persepolis were adopted, but the various rooms were enclosed within a single building. Thus, the same building incorporated a public audience hall, a smaller private audience hall, and a complex of lesser rooms. Remains of the major monuments of Sasanian architecture include the ruins of domed palaces at Firuzabad, Girra, and Sarvestan, and the vast vaulted hall at Ctesiphon. The large site of Bishapur was systematically excavated in the mid-twentieth century by the Archaeological Service of Iran. Palace sites have also been excavated at Qais, Hira, and Damghan. Other ruins include bridges at Dezful and Shushtar and a number of small temples built at various locales for the worship of fire that formed part of Zoroastrianism.

The mosque became the major type of building in Iranian architecture. The established style of vaulted construction continued; common features were the pointed arch, the ogee arch, and the dome on a circular drum. Outstanding examples of early Islamic Iranian architecture include the Mosque of Baghdad, built in 764; the Great Mosque at Samarra, erected in 847; and the early tenth-century mosque at Nayin. Under the expansion of the Mongol Empire, much of early Islamic architecture was in Iran, but after the Mongols' conquest of Baghdad in 1258, building was resumed according to Iranian traditions. Subsequently, a number of the most notable buildings in the history of Iranian architecture were erected. They include the Great Mosque at Veramin, built in 1322; the Mosque of the Imam Reza at Meshad-i-Murghab, erected in 1418; and the Blue Mosque at Tabrîz. Other major structures include the mausoleums of the Mongol conqueror Tamerlane and his family at Samarqand, the Royal Mosque at Meshad-i-Murghab, and the vast madresahs, or mosque schools, at Samarqand, all of them erected during the fifteenth century.

Under the Safavid dynasty, a vast number of mosques, palaces, tombs, and other structures were built. Common features in the mosques were onion-shaped domes on drums, barrel-vaulted porches, and pairs of towering minarets. A striking decoration was the corbel, a projection of stone or wood from the face of a wall, used in rows and tiers. These corbels, arranged to appear as series of intersecting miniature arches, are usually called stalactite corbels. Colour was an important part of the architecture of this period, and the surfaces of the buildings were covered with ceramic tiles in glowing blue, green, yellow, and red. The most notable Safavid buildings were constructed at Esfahan, the capital at that period. The city, laid out in broad avenues, gardens, and canals, contained palaces, mosques, baths, bazaars, and caravanserai.

Since the eighteenth century, the architectural styles of western Europe have been adopted to an increasing degree in Iran. At the same time, traditional forms have remained vital, and native and imported elements have often been combined in the same building. Recently, unadorned steel and concrete structures, similar to those seen in other parts of the modern world, have been built as dwellings, public buildings, and factories.

There are about 50 fire-temples in Iran, associated with the fire-worshipping Zoroastrian religion. Generally square on plan, they consist of four massive piers carrying an arch on each side (so called *chahar taq*, meaning 'four-arched"), the whole composition roofed over with a dome supported on squinches. They are likely to be of the Sassanian period. After the Muslim invasion, many fire-temples were destroyed, but some were converted into mosques, and indeed some may have been the prototypes of prayer-halls.

At the city of Baku in former Iranian province of Arran, today known as the republic of Azerbaijan, on the shore of the Caspian Sea, there was for a long time a very old fire-temple; this particular fire-temple was probably older than recorded history.

Atish-gah or Atish-jah—that is, the Place of Fire; in Persian, 'fire-temple' is atash kuda—had been recently rebuilt: the holy flame issued from a central opening and also from four hollow pillars in the temple, which was a building of triangular form, about one hundred and ninety paces to the side, constructed by a Hindu merchant in the eighteen hundreds. He described the flame as about four feet high, bright, and a wondrous sight as it waved heavily to and fro against a dark sky - ie, the temple was unroofed.

In 1876, the English traveler James Bryce also visited the fire-temple, and remarks that its maintenance and the upkeep of the one attendant priest was paid for by the Parsee community of Bombay, whose members also visited Baku on pilgrimage.

And in 1784, by the account of George Forster of the Bengal Civil Service, the Atish-gah was a square structure about 30 yards across, surrounded by a low wall and containing many apartments, in each of which was a small jet of sulphurous fire issuing from a funnel "constructed in the shape of a Hindu altar." The fire was used for worship, cookery and warmth. On closing the funnel the fire was extinguished, at which time a hollow sound was heard accompanied by a strong and cold current of air. Exclusive of these, there was a large jet from a natural cleft, and many small jets outside the wall, one of which was used by the Hindus for burning their dead.

SCULPTURES

Persian sculpture flourished little over a century, consequently it has but little history and varies only slightly during the course of its development. We notice toward the close the increased influence of Greek artists from Thessaly or from Asia Minor. The earliest sculpture known is that of the winged figure of King Cyrus, standing in an attitude of adoration, carved over a door jamb at Pasargadea, and dating probably from the first years of Darius. The largest series of sculptures thus far discovered is that of the palace of Darius at Persepolis. The subject of these sculptures is the glorification of the king. All the figures are rep resented as directing their steps toward a central point. A double procession, on either side of the stairway, mounts the steps, and there is another procession higher up on the inner faces of the door frames. These are the subject-peoples bringing to the king their gifts and tributes—horses, wild asses, camels, rich stuffs, rare products, objects in precious metals; and these figures are passing through the long array of life guards, officers, and courtiers, the Medes in flowing garments and the Persians in tight-fitting dress. Further on we see the king, either enthroned on his high platform supported by caryatid-like figures of the conquered nations, or walking under a sunshade, or plunging a dagger into some wild beast who represents the foes of his majesty.

The range of Persian sculpture was the glorification of the king in one great composition. In the rock-cut relief of the royal tombs the same subject was repeated in a simplified form. There was no variety, as in Assyrian art, either in subject or in treatment. As no distinct event, but only a symbolic representation, was given, the scene had an air of unreality. At the same time, it had distinct merits. For the first time Oriental sculpture attempted to give the soft texture of drapery and imitated its natural folds, and here we trace distinctly the influence of archaic Ionic Greek sculpture. There was also a distinct advance in the ability to bring sculpture into its proper relationship to architecture. Instead of scattering scenes broadcast over the surface, as in Egypt, in fine disregard of any distinctive grouping or subordination; instead of using sculpture as an art connected with architectural structure, as in Assyria, the Persians showed some of the Greek conception of the harmonious relationship possible between the two arts. Thus, the processions carved on the sides of the staircases followed the natural architectural outlines, as was the case later with the stairway at Pergamon, and the faces of the limestone portals were used for reliefs, like the inner sides of the Roman triumphal arches. But this peculiar merit was shown especially in the use of sculpture for distinctly architectural decoration. The colossal bull-capitals at Persepolis and Susa were masterpieces. The treatment of the bulls in these works was the greatest triumph of Persian sculpture, for naturalism, technique, and spirit.

In the first great period of Persian art, during the reign of the Achaemenids, sculpture was created on a monumental scale. In about 515 BC, Darius I ordered an enormous relief and inscription to be carved on a cliff in the Zagros Mountains. It is known today as the Behistun Inscription from its location near the village of that name. While the inscription records the genealogy of Darius and recounts his conquests, the relief shows him triumphing over his enemies as Ahura Mazda, the chief Zoroastrian deity, looks on. In plan and detail the carving is derived from Assyrian models, but the naturalistic treatment of the figures' eyes and clothing is original.

At Persepolis, sculpture was an important adjunct to architecture. In addition to the sculptured animal capitals on the columns, which were a dominant feature of the interiors of the buildings, friezes representing lions were set on the exterior cornices. Doorways were carved with reliefs of the king, and staircases were decorated with friezes of royal guards and tribute-bearers carved in low relief. The main gateway to the city was flanked by a pair of huge bulls with human heads, carved in high relief.

The decoration of the palace at Susa consisted of stone reliefs in the style of those at Persepolis, and panels of bricks glazed in blue, green, white, and yellow. The use of glazed bricks continued a tradition that was first established in Assyria and Babylonia. The glazed-brick panels at Susa portrayed soldiers, winged bulls, sphinxes, and griffins. The best known of these panels make up the Frieze of Archers. Further examples of Achaemenian sculpture in relief is known from Naqshah Rostam, where four royal tombs were hewn out of the rock. At each tomb the face of the cliff was carved to represent the façade of a palace; above the palace, figures support a dais on which the king stands worshipping the gods.

After the conquest of Persia by Alexander the Great, Greek influence, in its late, Hellenistic phase, was predominant in the arts of Persia. Examples from this period include fragments of bronze sculpture found at Shami, and the Parthian sculptural reliefs at Behistun. The second great period of Persian art began, as already noted, with the reign of the Sasanian dynasty in AD 226. A single example of sculpture in the round, a colossal standing figure of a king near Bishapur, has survived from this period. A few statuettes have also survived, but the characteristic sculptural work, as in Achaemenian times, was the relief cut in rock. The best-known examples are colossal reliefs at Naqshah Rostam portraying the Persian kings Ardashir I and Shapur I mounted on horses. A similar equestrian relief at Taq-i-Bustan represents another Persian king of this dynasty, Khosrau II. Following the Sasanian period, sculpture ceased to exist as a major art.

CALLIGRAPHY

The history of calligraphy in Iran dates back to the pre Islam era. In Zoroastrianism beautiful and clear writings were always praised. Around one thousand years ago, Ebne Moghleh Beyzavi Shirazi and his brother created six genres of Iranian calligraphy namely "Tahqiq", "Reyhan", "Sols", "Naskh" and "Toqih" and "Reqah". These genres were common for four centuries in Persia. In seventh century, a new genre of Persian calligraphy was invented and named "Ta'liq". Morteza Gholi Khan Shamlou and Mohammad Shafi Heravi created a new genre called "Shekasteh Nastaliq". Abdol-Majid Taleqani brought this genre to its highest level. In the ancient Persia and in the different historic eras, languages such as "Ilami", "Avestaaee", "Pahlavi", and "Farsi-e-Mianeh" were spoken. It is believed that ancient Persian script was invented by about 500-600 BC to provide monument inscriptions for the Achaemenid kings. These scripts consisted of horizontal, vertical, and diagonal nail-shape letters and that is the reason in Farsi it is called "Script of Nails" or "Khat-e-Mikhi".

Centuries later, other scripts" scrip such as "Avestaee" and "Pahlavits were created. The Avestan alphabet or "Avestaaee" was created in the third century CE for writing the hymns of Zarathustra. Avestan is an extinct Indo-Iranian language related to Old Persian and Sanskrit. Avestaaee script was related to the religious scripts of Zoroastrians' holy book called "Avestaa" and unlike the nail script -that was carved on flat stones- Avestaaee script was written with a feather pen, usually on animal-skin pages. It is surprising that this script has similarities with Arabic scripts such as "Sols" and "Naskh" that centuries later were invented. However, unlike these scripts, letters in Avestaaee were not connected to each other to form a word but they just were written separately next to each other. However it wrote from right to left.

After initiation of Islam in the seventh century, Persians adapted Arabic alphabet to Farsi language and developed contemporary Farsi alphabet. Arabic alphabet has twenty-eight characters and Iranians added another four letters in it to arrive at existing thirty-two Persian letters.

"Nas'taliq" is the most popular contemporary style among classical Persian calligraphy scripts. It is known as "Bride of the Calligraphy Scripts". As a matter of fact, this calligraphy style has been based on such a strong structure that it has changed very little since that time. It is as if "Mir Ali Tabrizi" has found the optimum composition of the letters and graphical rules so it has just been fine-tuned during the passed seven centuries. Nas'taliq is the most beautiful Persian Calligraphy style and also technically the most complicated. It has strict rules for graphical shape of the letters and for combination of the letters, words, and composition of the whole calligraphy piece as a whole. Even the second popular Persian calligraphy style i.e. "Cursive Nas'taliq" or "Shekasteh Nas'taliq" noticeably follows the same rules as Nas'taliq, with more flexibility of course.

It was about tenth century that "Ebn-e-Moqlah Beyzavi Shirazi" conducted a research and studied six major calligraphy styles and categorized them. These styles were "Mohaqqaq", "Reyhan", "Sols", "Naskh", "Reqaa", and "Towqee". All of these calligraphy styles followed twelve major principles. After "Ebn-e-Moqlah" another calligraphy master named "Hassan Farsi Kateb" combined "Naskh" and "Reqaa" styles and invented a new style, called "Taliq". Eventually in the fourteenth century, "Mir Ali Heravi Tabrizi" combined two major scripts of his time i.e. Naskh and Taliq and created the most attractive Persian Calligraphy style, "Nas'taliq".

PRESENT DAY EXAMPLES

- Inside Iran:
  - — Arg-é Bam Cultural Landscape, Kerman
  - — Naghsh-i Jahan Square, Isfahan
  - — Pasargadae, Fars
  - — Persepolis, Fars
  - — Tchogha Zanbil, Khuzestan
  - — Takht-e Soleyman, West Azerbaijan
  - — Dome of Soltaniyeh, Zanjan
  - — Behistun Inscription
- Outside Iran:
  - — Minaret of Jam, Afghanistan
  - — Mausoleum of Khoja Ahmed Yasavi, Kazakhstan
  - — Historic Centre of Bukhara
  - — Historic Centre of Shahrisabz
  - — Samarkand - Crossroads of Cultures
  - — Citadel, Ancient City and Fortress Buildings of Darband, Daghestan

REFERENCES

Avesta: Translated into English by James Darmesteter and L. H. Mills. In Sacred Books of the East, vols, 4, 23, 31.

Avesta: Pahlavi, and Ancient Persian Studies in Honour of the late Shams-ul Ulama Dastur Peshotanji Behramji Sanjana. Strassburg, 1904.

Bahman Yasht: Translated from the Pahlavi text by E. W. West. In Sacred Books of the East, vol. 5.

Benveniste, Emile: *The Persian Religion according to the chief Greek Texts.* Paris, 1929.

Bundahishn: An Untranslated Chapter of the Bundehesh. Edited and translated by Jivanji Jamshedji Modi, in Journal of the Bombay Branch of the Royal Asiatic Society. Bombay, 1902.

Bundahishn: Edited by T. D. and B. T. Anklesaria. Bombay, 1908.

Cama Memorial Volume: Edited by J. J. Modi. Bombay, 1900.

Carter, G. W.: *Zoroastrianism and Judaism.* Boston, 1918.

Firdausi: Translated into English by A. G. Warner and E. Warner. vols. 1-9. London, 1905-1925.

Fluegel, M: *The Zend-Avesta and Eastern Religions.* Baltimore, 1898.

ovindacharya, A.: *Mazdaism in the Light of Vishnuism.* Mysore, 1913.

Gray, L. H.: *The Foundations of the Iranian Religions.* Bombay, 1929.

Hadokht Nask: The Pahlavi text, edited and translated by Hoshangji Jamaspji Asa, Martin Haug, and E. W. West. Bombay, 1872.

Hoshang Memorial Volume: Bombay, 1918.

Kohut, Alexander: *The Jewish Angelology and Demonology based upon Parsism.* Translated from the German by K. R. Cama. Bombay, 1883.

Lazarus, M. E.: *The Zend-Avesta and Solar Religions.* New York, 1852.

Lehmann, Edvard: *Zarathushtra.* Kobenhavn, 1899.

Nirangastan: Translated from the Avesta-Pahlavi text by S. J. Bulsara. Bombay, 1915.

Oriental Studies in honour of Cursetji Erachji Pavri: London, 1933.

Pahlavi Zend-i Vohuman Yasht: Edited by Kaikobad A. Nosherwan. Poona, 1899.

Rezwi, T.: Parsis: *A People of the Book.* Calcutta, 1928.

Sad Dar: Translated from the Pahlavi-Pazand text by E. W. West. In Sacred Books of the East, vol. 24.

Sad Dar: Edited by B. N. Dhabhar. Bombay, 1909.

Taraporewala, Irach, J. S: *Some Aspects of the History of Zoroastrianism.* Bombay, 1928.

19

Zoroastrianism in Modern World

Zoroastrianism in modern times has undergone tremendous reformist changes and has tended to focus on peace rather than war. Though there has not been any scriptural development in Zoroastrianism. In modern times, India was under British imperialism from 1757 to 1947. As part of this interaction, Zoroastrianism was invoked on certain occasions of conflict.

In modern times many texts have been written relating to Zoroastrianism, nothing emerged in modern times as part of cultural or political development that has been accepted as part of Zoroastrianism scripture.

DIASPORA

The followers of Zarathustra, the Zoroastrians, are members of one of the world's smallest religions, numbering approximately 160,000 to 200,000 individuals worldwide. Zoroastrians have a strong conception of Iran as an ancestral homeland. Bombay became the major center and headquarters of the Zoroastrians of India, known as Parsis, from the eighteenth century. Bombay remains the largest and most historically significant diaspora community, which still influences other Zoroastrian communities in the world. Indeed, it is debatable whether Bombay is the actual 'homeland' of the Parsis. The history of the community is of considerable accomplishment in pre- and post-Independence India, in the fields of education, politics, culture, and social advancement, including female rights; yet, the demographic data are grim with a steady decline in the number of Indian Zoroastrians from 114,490 in 1941 to 76,382 in 1991, as recorded in the Indian Censuses. The demographic decline is attributable to various factors, not least of all Parsi social progress that has led to small families and late marriages. The bugbear of the community remains the Zoroastrians' endogamous nature and refusal to admit "converts" to the Parsi fold.

The real consequences of the demographic decline include a large aging population and the loss of material and social infrastructure, from decaying community buildings to the diminishing numbers of priests. Significantly, Parsis are painfully familiar with their grave predicament and essentially have sought to "cope with the situation" with vigorous debate, social welfare proposals, and resolve. In particular, debate encompasses the three core areas: the preservation of traditions, such as the future of the dokhma or tower of silence as a funerary rite, community boundaries, of which the most important are intermarriage and conversion, and the demographic problem. The debates are often acrimonious, yet a dialogue continues and reflects how the Zoroastrians of Bombay refuse to see themselves as a dying community.

The diaspora communities in the non-western world are the result of the Parsis' commercial expansion and migration during the colonial period. The Zoroastrian communities in Hong Kong, Canton, and the China Seas took shape from the Parsis' China trade in commodities such as cotton and opium during the eighteenth and nineteenth centuries. Substantial Parsi fortunes were made that benefited the Parsis of India. New traditions also took shape in the Zoroastrian out-ports, as, for example, the Zoroastrians of Canton established the first Zoroastrian cemetery or aramgah outside British India in 1847.

The Zoroastrian community of Karachi dates from the middle of the nineteenth century. Before the creation of Pakistan, Karachi had the fourth largest Zoroastrian population in the subcontinent, and it continued to have regular contact with the other Indian communities, while also developing its own religious, educational, and social infrastructure. Karachi was the home of one of Zoroastrianism's great religious thinkers, Dastur M. N. Dhalla. With the creation of Pakistan in 1947 and the rise of the first Islamic republic, the Zoroastrians of Karachi and Pakistan faced similar challenges as those of the Iranian Zoroastrians living under an Islamic regime. The Zoroastrians' good will during partition, their existing small numbers, and their sense of Pakistani identity and contribution to the nation have made the Zoroastrians valuable citizens in Pakistan under modernizing and orthodox regimes.

The Zoroastrians of East Africa encompass communities in Zanzibar, Tanzania, Kenya, and Uganda. Their presence in East Africa is part of the spread of Parsi influence around the Indian Ocean Basin from the Persian

Gulf and Arabian Peninsula to East and Southern Africa. In the colonial period, economic opportunity propelled migration, and the Zoroastrians controlled many large and small business interests throughout the region. Hinnells' examination of the influence and power of the Zoroastrians of Zanzibar is noteworthy. The Zoroastrians of both the China Seas and East Africa are part of the larger South Asian diaspora in the region, and specifically the Gujarati-speaking community. At the same time, Zoroastrians maintained a strong sense of their religious identity and cultural difference from the locals, other Indians, and British. All of the diaspora communities examined thus far reflect how the sojourn and settlement of Zoroastrians outside India and away from the regular traditions of community life entailed the beginnings of accommodations with the social milieu and adaptation of tradition for the Zoroastrians.

The Zoroastrians of Britain formed the first Zoroastrian diaspora in the western world. The first Zoroastrian went to Britain in 1724. By the nineteenth century, a small permanent Zoroastrian community had taken shape. In 1861, the Zoroastrian Trust Funds of Europe (ZTFE) began as the first Zoroastrian community institutional body and Asian association in the western world. The first Indians elected members of parliament at Westminster were Zoroastrians, including Dadabhai Naoroji who was known as the "Grand Old Man of India".

While the youngest of the diaspora communities, the Zoroastrians of the USA, Canada, and Australia are experiencing some of the most dynamic changes. These communities largely took shape post-1965. New York City boasted the first Zoroastrian association in North America, although it was initially short lived. From the 1960s, one Zoroastrian organization of some nature was started in a North American city virtually every year. The North American communities also hold regular gatherings or Congresses of Zoroastrians since the first Congress in Toronto in 1975. Indeed it is in the new world centres that change is most profound, with issues relating to Zoroastrian and non-Zoroastrian intermarriage, religious confirmation of children born of intermarriage, and conversion to Zoroastrianism being addressed and in many respects have become non-issues.

MODERN RELIGIOUS MOVEMENTS

It was once custom to keep a ritual flame burning in the home of a pregnant woman, though in the present day the more common practice is to light a lamp after the fifth and seventh weeks of pregnancy. The purity rules of most importance are those pertaining to the birth itself and the confinement of the mother afterward. The delivery room should be consecrated, and a light should burn for three or more days in the confinement room as protection from evil forces. The mother should stay isolated in the confinement room for forty days, unable to contaminate others through contact with the regular living quarters. The confinement is concluded with a ritual bath for which a priest and consecrated water are required. In modern day, however, the strict observances of practices such as these has grown somewhat lax.

Though the Navjote remains the most important rite of passage, marriage holds an almost equally special place. Endogamy in marriage among Zoroastrians in the modern day is strongly encouraged and expected due to the waning numbers of the religion and the sheer focus on survival. In Iran, endogamy became the simple consequence of minority status among a Muslim majority. In India, endogamy became expected to discourage the possible disloyalty to the faith which is often produced by a mixed marriage. But the issue of endogamy versus exogamy is hotly debated among modern Zoroastrians. While endogamy remains the fundamental belief of orthodox traditionalists believing in genetic superiority, the main argument in defence of endogamy is that identity in Zoroastrianism is patrilineal.

Therefore, the Zoroastrian Parsis in India regard children of non-Zoroastrian fathers as ineligible for Navjote - and thereby ineligible for membership in the community. But even the marriage of a Zoroastrian man to a non-Zoroastrian woman is frowned upon, as religious instruction is generally received more from the mother. On the other side, however, young advocates for reform maintain that due to the small numbers of Zoroastrians worldwide, exogamy would actually be beneficial to survival. There would be fewer restrictions on who is "marriageable", and therefore there would presumably be more marriages. Another argument for exogamy holds that many young Zoroastrians leave the faith if they fall in love with a non-Zoroastrian, as they do not want to have such restrictions placed upon them. In addition, economic well-being has been on the decline, especially among the Parsis; as poverty leads to slow marriage and birth rate, many Zoroastrians seek to better themselves and their community by marrying outside that community. Parsis therefore display a higher rate of exogamy than do Zoroastrians in Iran, but a lower rate than that "overseas".

Today, engagement is more a consequence of the couple's personal choice rather than parental arrangement. The day of the wedding is determined based on the concept of auspicious days and times. The home of the bride is the setting. Following the Nahn, the groom is seen, wearing a stiff hat, a robe over pants, and a shawl in his hand. He sits opposite the bride, who is gowned in white. Initially, a cloth curtain separates the two, but after symbolic acts that culminate in the tying of their right hands together, the cloth is removed. This is a symbol of the fact that their union has ended their separateness. Blessings for long life and prosperity are given, and the will to marry is affirmed both by the couple and their families. Particularly unique about the Zoroastrian wedding, however, is that the most liturgical portion of the wedding rite is largely incomprehensible. This is due to the use of a language that has passed from common practice - but more importantly, to the fact that the meaning of the texts is never supplied to anyone.

But an enormous issue in current Zoroastrianism is the debate over conversion - should converts to Zoroastrianism be permitted? Orthodox Zoroastrians, standing in staunch opposition to the idea that converts should be considered "true Zoroastrians", do so largely because Zarathustra was not a convert to Mazdayasnianism before reforming it into Zoroastrianism. Rather, he was from birth a member of the Mazdayasnian faith (worship of Ahura Mazda), and reformed what he saw to be its errors at a later date. Therefore, there is the issue of genetics to be dealt with. Traditionalists, also in strict favour of endogamy, espouse the idea of genetic superiority - or at least the need to preserve the genetics of their waning race rather than see it mixed with others. Many modern day Armenians are of the same mindset, seeking to preserve their ethnicity in the face of their small numbers. Also a matter of concern is the fear that people would convert to exploit funds and charities meant for Zoroastrians. Eventually, however, sanction was granted to conversion by marriage and extended to the children of the mixed marriage in a 1977 decision of the Federation of Parsi Zoroastrian Anjumans of India. But even with the few converts who are given permission, no one seems to be able to decide how religious benefits for them should be divided from benefits available only to bloodline Zoroastrians.

Yet in the West, as is the case in other aspects of the religion such as marriage issues, tradition has been more likely to bend in the interests of survival, with "membership" becoming increasingly defined by belief rather than genetics. Traditionalists, however, continue to argue that while the name of Zoroastrianism may be preserved this way, the "substance" will be lost.

Modernity holds seemingly innumerable persisting concerns for Zoroastrianism, the above being merely a taste. Cultic (ritualistic) issues are a matter of debate. Remaining the same over the years has been the retention of artifacts, the litugical use of archaic language, the kindling and nourishing of fires, priestly purity, and the hereditary nature of the priesthood. Some modern Zoroastrians, however, have found themselves of the belief that the priesthood should not be restricted to heredity, as the numbers of priests have fallen drastically due to low income and waning religiosity. Zoroastrians themselves have largely exchanged agrarianism for urbanization, and increased priestly poverty exemplifies the laity's thinning excitement in donations and ceremonies. Nor have there been very many new fire temples.

Orthodox traditionalists see the solution to this not in radical reconstruction, but in reaffirmation and fidelity to the traditional religion. They want to retain all Avestan prayers in the original language, whereas reformist Parsis desire to replace it with modern language, seeing the practice of the traditional "cultus" as irrelevant. The tradition of disposing of the dead in dakhmas has virtually disappeared, replaced by burial or cremation.

The main problem persists that in modern Zoroastrianism, there is a glaring lack of a central representative; therefore, too much debate on single issues is always produced. As a result, nothing seems to ever be firmly resolved. Zoroastrianism has borne and overcome cloudy times in the past - yet it seems that these ostensibly small, detailed issues threaten to severely weaken this ancient religion.

SPIRITUAL REVOLUTION

During the period of classical Persia a religion began that was different than religions of its time. In a polytheistic world, Zoroastrianism taught of one true god who spoke to his people thru his prophet, Zoroaster. This religion played an important role in world history by greatly influencing major religions of our day. Christianity owes a great deal to the influence of Zoroastrianism. Many major doctrines of the Christian religion most likely began from Zoroastrian influence. Zoroastrianism began in ancient Persia in the region of modern-day Iraq. It began with a man named Zarathustra, known as Zoroaster in Greek and Roman writings.

Zoroaster lived sometime during the seventh to sixth centuries BC. He was born in Azerbaijan, north-west of Media. At twenty years old, he left home in search of wisdom. Allegedly, ten years later he received a vision. While attending a spring festival, he went to draw water from a river. There an archangel appeared to him and led him to the presence of Ahura Mazda, convincing him that he was chosen as a prophet to spread the truths revealed to him. He taught that Ahura Mazda was a supreme deity, creator of all good things, and supreme judge of the actions of men. This was a radical concept for the time, since he lived in a polytheistic world. The Zoroastrian scriptures were known as the Avesta, with the earliest section, the Gathas, thought to be the words of Zoroaster himself. The religion successfully spread and became the official religion of the Achaemenid kingdom, and it continued under the succession of the Parthians and Sassanians. There is no doubt that early Jews and Christians were in close contact with Zoroastrians in ancient Persia.

When the Persian king Cyrus allowed the Jews to return to their homeland to rebuild their temple, many Jews stayed in Persia where they interacted with Iranians for several centuries. During that time Jewish religion developed teachings about heaven and hell, angelic beings, and afterlife that were not in earlier texts and were likely developed from Zoroastrian influence. While it is possible for similar ideas to develop independently under similar circumstances, "it does not seem at all likely that so many similarities could have been formed in parallel independently, and in most of the parallel points one may feel quite confident that the ideas were indigenous to Iran." The concept of dualism, or good versus evil, is one teaching that likely came from Zoroastrian origins. Zoroaster taught of two dominating spirits: spenta mainyu and angra mainyu. The Avesta speaks of Ahura Mazda and Spenta Mainyu, his "good spirit."

The concept is very similar to and just as elusive as the Christian teachings of the Holy Spirit. In contrast to the forces of good, the Avesta teaches of Ahriman, the "foe of the Supreme God…and the origin of all suffering, affliction, bodily deformities, evil, and demise," and his force of evil, angra mainyu. He originally existed in a pit of endless darkness, but during the creation of earth he surfaced to try to bring about destruction and evil. The Christian concepts of good versus evil and God versus Satan are quite similar. Christianity teaches of Satan trying to turn humans to evil right from the beginning, appearing to Eve as a snake in the Garden of Eden. Also, in both Zoroastrianism and Christianity each side has an array of warriors, angels and demons. Zoroaster also taught that creation would become a battleground.

The most important part of this battle is the "spiritual self of man." This may very well have been the root of the Christian concept of the soul. Zoroaster taught that humans were divided into two groups, the righteous and the evil-doers. A choice had to be made. In fact, in the Avesta, the spiritual part of man is called "urvan", which literally translates to "chooser", implying that man has to choose for itself which of the two paths it will follow. The Avesta also contains the idea of "the worst existence" which was where those who chose the course of evil would go when they died, like the Christian teaching of hell. Therefore, both religions teach the responsibility of each person to choose between good and evil, and that with this free will we each decide our own destiny. This concept of choice leads to another Christian doctrine that is very likely rooted in Zoroastrianism: judgment day. In Zoroastrianism it is taught that Ahura Mazda is the final judge of the actions of men.

After demise the soul journeys to a place of judgment called the "Chinvat Bridge" that leads to paradise by crossing over the abyss of hell. If one led a good life, they cross without difficulty. If one did not, the bridge turns on its side and sends them into hell. Judgment day became a key doctrine in the Christian religion as well. In the book of Matthew it says, "Every idle word that men shall speak, they shall give account thereof in the day of judgment." Another scripture says, "For the Son of man shall come in the glory of his Father with his angels; and then he shall reward every man according to his works." In both faiths judgment day is used to encourage followers to use their free will wisely.

Interestingly, both faiths also include a millennia timeline for the final judgment of all humankind. In Zoroastrianism it is believed that the evil spirit will be banished for one thousand years, during which there is to be a resurrection and restoration of the earth. At the end of this thousand years the evil spirit is let loose for one final judgment. After that evil is defeated and good will sovereignty forever.

The Zoroastrian concept of a Messiah was another influence on religions, including Christianity. The Christian idea that a messiah will return to rid the world of evil was most likely derived from the teaching of Saoshyant, "one who will bring benefit." Zoroastrian doctrine teaches that there will be three Saoshyants, and that each one would be miraculously born from a virgin. The Bible teaches that the Christian messiah was also born from a virgin: And she shall bring forth a son, and thou shalt call his name Jesus: for he shall save his people from their sins.

Now all this was done, that it might be fulfilled which was spoken of the Lord by the prophet, saying, 'Behold, a virgin shall be with child, and shall bring forth a son.In addition to the influence of major doctrine, Zoroastrian influence can be seen in early Christian artwork and stories.

For example, in nativity scenes the three wise men who followed the star and visited the newborn Jesus were very likely Zoroastrian priests, known as magi.26 These priests were known to be skilled in astrology, and they were the major religious leaders of the Persian kingdom in those times. Many versions of the story today call them the magi. Christianity owes much credit to ancient Iran. Doctrines such as god and the devil, free will and judgment of all humans, the soul, heaven and hell, the Messiah, and the millennia of the last judgment all show major similarities to the teachings of the Avesta. During a time of expansion, with the spread of cultures and faiths, Zoroastrianism had a large impact on the development of early Christianity. These influences were so profound that we still see their effects in the modern day world.

FUTURE

Better than anybody else before or after him, Zarathushtra understood the timeless mechanisms that define the human condition. But he also understood the mechanisms by which the whole universe operates and considered the two systems, both the spiritual and the physical, to be one and the same force. Zarathushtra called this system of laws Asha.

The amazing thing is that modern science has reached exactly the same conclusions that Zarathushtra put forward some 3,700 years ago. Namely, that the universe operates, although also incorporating the element of chance, within definite laws of physics that are timeless and ever existent and that these laws have a specific purpose, namely the upholding and expansion of the universe.

Zarathushtra based his spiritual laws on his perfect understanding of the human condition. Interestingly, Zarathushtra's concept of Asha and the newly discovered laws of physics are, as we shall see, one and the same. Zarathushtra's 3,700 year-old religion is therefore not only correct in its observations of the human condition, but also in 100% agreement with the achievements of modern science. No other religion can make a similar claim.

Zarathushtra studied the human condition and reached his existentialist conclusions, which he characterized as Asha. Modern science has studied the universe both from its macro and micro perspectives and reached similar conclusions. It is therefore safe to say that the validity of Asha is reinforced on both fronts. Asha is the law according to which the universe operates but it is also the law according to which we should live our lives to be constructive and harmonious.

The fact is that if we were to invent an entirely new world religion based on modern science and in accordance with what we now know about the world, we would end up inventing something that already exists, namely Zoroastrianism. There is therefore no need to invent a New World religion. Our mission is instead to raise Zoroastrianism to its proper status as the world's dominant faith and the way forward is to go back to its roots, the message of Zarathushtra, and show the world the genius at work in The Gathas.

So what then is all the fuzz about in modern science? Which are these massive breakthroughs we hear about and what effects will they have on our worldview, on the way we think? We shall not only look at that but we shall also study the consequences the new scientific paradigm will have on the different systems of thought competing within the areas of religion and philosophy today.

We have chosen to divide current thinking into nine different alternatives and we shall look at the effects of the upcoming paradigm shift on each of these systems. We will study these effects from four different scientific perspectives, three of them discoveries within physics and cosmology and one within sociology, namely the arrival of the network society.

The new worldview taking shape within science will have a dramatic effect on the status of religion and philosophy. We are about to experience some dramatic changes that will shake the established faiths and ideological systems at their very foundations. And we are in for some surprising consequences.

New age is essentially the western adoptions of Eastern thinking in all their variety. Since Rousseau in 18th century France, Nature as God, and the pantheistic approach towards existence, has had a great attraction on Westerners as an alternative to the collapsed Christian hegemony of the middle ages. Its modern-day equivalent is the crystals and pyramids crowd of environmentalist fundamentalists appearing everywhere from California to Germany.

Any serious religious or philosophical alternative set to attract attention in the next 50 to 100 years can easily be referred to at least one of these nine alternatives. So we should be fairly well covered within this framework.

Cosmology was long based on the assumption that time was somehow an illusion and that there was therefore no physical limits to the concepts of time and space. The universe had neither beginning nor end but had always existed and would always exist keeping basically the same characteristics. The same would be true about space, which was assumed to be endless. Even Albert Einstein subscribed mainly to this worldview.

In the 1920s, scientists began to challenge this paradigm. If the universe had always existed and had always had the same properties, should it not then be full of light and radiation, as these are the by-products of stellar explosions? How come the universe contained so much dark, empty space? Perhaps instead the galaxies moved away from each other and the universe was expanding rather than standing still?

If the universe were expanding, it would have had to progress from a smaller, more concentrated form to its current status. In the early 1950s, a Russian-Jewish woman named Vera Rubin was the first to see the full consequences of an expanding universe. The universe was indeed a prisoner of time. It had to have a beginning, a big bang, in which both the universe and the dimensions of time and space were born, and the whole thing has expanded at a rapid pace ever since.

Applied to religion, there is no room for polytheism. Hinduism is based on polytheism and consequently does not survive this scientific finding. Neither does New Age which is based on and thrives on the notion of parallel truths. The reality is that two assumptions that contradict each other can not both be true.

Let us now move on from macro to microphysics. Quantum mechanics is a concept we have all heard about but few of us understand. Basically, quantum physics deals with the atomic and subatomic particles, their properties and how they interact. Quantum mechanics has been studied since the beginning of this century but has only recently begun to be applied to technology and influence our view of the world.

One of the most interesting phenomena in quantum physics is that when we observe and register the movement of a particle as small as an electron, we find that we can not determine the position of the particle and its movement simultaneously. This has a dramatic consequence, namely that the activity of the very foundations of our universe can not be predicted even when we have perfect access to information.

The world is therefore indeterministic rather than deterministic. We can never with certainty predict what will happen, only make more or less accurate speculations or design fields of likely outcomes. If God exists, not even God can know, in advance, exactly what will happen.

The Ibrahimic faiths are all four based on the concept that God knows everything, including what will occur in the future. Nothing can be hidden from God, not even the future. When Judas kissed Christ, he did so because this had already been determined. It was Judas' fate to kiss and betray Christ. There was nothing Judas could do to change or alter his fate. Neither could Christ avoid his crucifixion. It was determined.

The same goes for Judaism, Islam and Bahai, in which telling the future is an integral part of religious beliefs and without which the very foundations of the religions collapse. Modern science, especially quantum physics, has proved this assumption to be incorrect.

If we can not predict with certainty the movements and positions of the smallest particles in the universe, there is no way we can predict anything bigger with certainty either. Of all the five monotheist religions founded in the Middle East only one, Zoroastrianism, is indeterministic and therefore compatible with the consequences of quantum physics.

If we can not predict even the very next second with certainty, we certainly can not predict that the current universe will return to the same position as its current status somewhere in the future. Therefore, the circular time universe dependent systems of thought also have a major obstacle to overcome staying credible following the breakthroughs of quantum physics.

We live in a rapidly changing world where the effects of technological invention are dramatic. The world is becoming one global village. Through new fast and cheap electronic media we can all have constant access to perfect information. The network society evolving can not be controlled by any individual or organization and staying out of the network revolution means total exclusion from every aspect of modern society, including trade and economic and technological development.

The revolution that overthrew the Communist dictatorships in Eastern Europe became a possibility through the widespread use of fax machines in those countries. The Rodney King trial in Los Angeles would never have caused so much controversy were it not for the videotapes authentically showing the behavior of the LAPD. New network media are popping up everywhere, registering everything that happens or is said, and the world can study just about everything that happens in detail. We move into a transparent society. Nothing important can be hidden from the masses any longer.

Every aspect of social behavior, from family life to corporate structures, will be affected. Your boss can no longer close the door to hold secret meetings. Information will be out and for all to know within minutes anyway. Hierarchies will have to go and freedom of information and freedom of choice will sovereignty. Even dictatorships like those in Communist China or the Iran of the mullahs must change due to technological change. 50 years from now, there will be no more dictatorships in the world.

How do these changes affect our nine alternatives? Well, belief systems that require obedience to a specified divine truth, no matter what, can not survive. A belief system has to be able to handle constant questioning, analysis and the freedom of choice. The very foundations of a faith have to be credible intellectually with every follower to be an alternative. Which of our nine alternatives survive this upcoming test?

Islam states that Allah rules and that there is no other god than Allah and Allah must be feared by everybody although often not understood. In Bahaiism, the House of Justice decides the rules and regulations for every aspect of life for all Bahai followers without allowing being questioned. Christianity and Judaism have similar concepts of God and with The Pope in charge of all Catholics in the world, giving them orders what to think and how to act, their pattern is similar although possibly not as strict as that of Islam and Bahai.

Among religions, only Zoroastrianism, Buddhism and Hinduism allow for individuals to find out and understand for themselves how things work. Naturally, Western Humanism and New Age are also tolerant enough towards individual thinking to be able to survive the test of the network revolution. But the Ibrahimic religions will not be able to keep their foundations and survive the open society revolution simultaneously.

If we look at all the nine alternatives from the four perspectives I have discussed above, we will soon find that Zoroastrianism, as presented by Zarathushtra in The Gathas, is the only alternative which survives all four tests and therefore has a future to prosper in.

We believe that question is up to the Zoroastrians themselves to answer. But nothing can be more important within the Zoroastrian community today than living up to the fact that we and we alone, carry the eternal truth from pre-historic times to the modern age. It is an enormous responsibility.

ZOROASTRIANISM AS A GLOBAL RELIGION

As a minority community in various parts of the world, especially in India and Iran, whose total population may not exceed a few hundred thousand, the Zoroastrians today face many challenges that threaten to destroy their identity and survival as a religious community. The Zoroastrians who live in India have many questions and concerns, especially in a community whose younger generation does not view the problems of duality between God and evil as seriously as the religion emphasizes. The major challenges faced by them today are:

Modern life presents its own challenges to maintain the purity and sanctity of our lives amidst the people we meet, places we visit and live.

Unfamiliarity with the tradition often results in the misinterpretation of the Zoroastrian beliefs and practices by people who are brought up with a different set of values. One glaring example is the way the Zoroastrian practice of the disposal of the dead is dramatized and presented to the general public for the shocking effect it produces.

Difficulties in disposing off the dead. The method and the manner in which the dead bodies are disposed of poses its own challenges for the community in the modern world.

Difficulties in enforcing the code of conduct and religious observance due to lack of enforcing authority, which used to be the state backed priestly community in ancient times.

Difficulties in practicing good thought, good words and good actions due to the invasion of TV, radio and other communication channels, which keep transmitting negative content day and day out. From a Zoroastrian perspective, these communication tools project evil, glorify evil and transmit evil.

The latest craze amongst Parsi youngsters and the self proclaimed intellectual reformists is modernization. With the latest swing to modernize everything and anything they come across in their daily lives, they want to modernize their age old invaluable heritage, viz. their simple, elegant, pure and perfect Zoroastrian religion.

Modernization, according to their definition, seems wholesale imitation of the worst in the Western Culture and in the prevalent Western customs and habits. This modernization is unfortunately not only reflected in their outward dress but what is worse, in an accompanying mentality itself. They abandon their excellent religion and its rich heritage, sacrificing it at the altars of fashion and unreason.

It refers to something that is used in the present day, something that is recent, something that is new and up-to-date. Yet, let us keep in mind that what is modern today and up-to-date, becomes obsolete and outworn tomorrow. Only the eternal Truth is everlasting, complete and perfect. The Law of Asha laid down by our dear Dadar Ahura Mazda is the ultimate and it requires no change or modernization, ever.

Change or modernization is required only for something that is not yet perfect, which is still in an incomplete imperfect stage, but no change is required for something that is already perfect and complete and eternal. The Zoroastrian Religion is truly mazistacha, vahishtacha, sraeshtacha meaning it is the greatest, the best and the most exalted. This quixotic approach of modernizing our noble Zoroastrian religion and its most scientific practices (Tarikats) is the direct consequence of the ignorance of these self-styled intellectuals regarding modern science.

Fact after fact and observation after observation of modern science reveal that the explanations of Nature given by science are just surface explanations; today, science is just a grand collection of unsolved mysteries. The condition of observation is very important for arriving at scientific truth and without a proper frame of reference, 3 different observers will give 3 different scientific truths! But truth cannot have 3 different answers! However, that is science with its limitations. As religion is eternal truth, it has only one answer. Religion is inner, absolute wisdom while science remains formulated knowledge and there is a vast difference between knowledge and wisdom.

Today, Extra Sensory Perception has been an extraordinary problem for the modern scientists, as it defies our limited senses and description. Telepathy and the sixth sense are known to science. All that they have to say is that people do receive accurate knowledge through sources other than the physical senses. All that they know and accept is that these things exist but the exact nature by which people gain accurate knowledge through sources other than the physical sense is unknown, and keep the modern scientists on a wild goose chase.

It is rather difficult to define faith ; for those who do not have faith, no explanation is possible and for those who have faith, no explanation is necessary. Yet it is the force of life and the head chemist of our mind. It is a luminous opening on another world, and wisdom and human life cannot survive without faith. Faith is as essential in science as in religion.

Science is partitive. It is channeled down to a number of its branches. Scientists are scholars only in their own branches. There has not been a single scientist with simultaneous discoveries in the various branches of science. Except one scientist and that is our Zarathushtra. Prophet is not only the greatest Ecologist but also the greatest Microbiologist, Atomic and Nuclear Physicist and Health Physicist. He is the only scientists with simultaneous discoveries in each and every existing branch of science.

Today, there is a growing concern in various countries for prevention of pollution of air, water and land. This has led to, tremendous development in the field of Ecology, yet the proponents of ecology have a lot to learn from our supremely scientific religion. No ecologist has preached with the same degree of rigidity and strictness as is done in our religion in keeping the environment pure and clean. The Holy Vendidad will act as an encyclopaedia for the modern ecologist.

No ecologist has yet bothered to go beyond the pollution of the physical environment but our tarikats are meant to prevent pollution of not only the physical environment but of the total environment including the mental and spiritual.

While the modern ecologist may just be beginning to concern himself with the physical purity and cleanliness which, as yet, are highly primitive by the standards prescribed in our religion, modern medicine in the last few decades has become increasingly conscious of psychosomatic diseases.

It is the purpose of Religion that while binding the spiritual nature of man to supreme intellectual and primordial thinker the Creator, it offers him the best way of life and conduct, helps him to establish and accommodate himself in his environment and urges him to use his God-given faculty to think and reason, thereby advancing himself and the society to the noblest and happiest existence. And no life ever grows great until it is focused, dedicated and disciplined by one's religion.

REFERENCES

Cheyne, T. K.: Book of Psalms, its origin, and its relation to Zoroastrianism. In Semitic Studies in Memory of Rev. Dr. A. Kohut. Berlin, 1897.

Dinkard: Books 7-9. Translated from the Pahlavi text by E. W. West. In *Sacred Books of the East*, vols. 37, 47.

Dinkard [Denkard]: The Complete Text. Edited by D. M. Madan. 2 vols. Bombay, 1911.

Geiger, Wilhelm: Civilization of the Eastern Iranians in Ancient Times. Translated from the German by Darab Dastur Peshutan Sanjana. 2 vols. London, 1885, 1886.

Geiger, W., and Windischmann, Fr.: Zarathushtra in the Gathas and in the Greek and Roman Classics. Translated by Darab P. Sanjana. Leipzig, 1897.

Inostranzev, M.: Iranian Influence on Moslem Literature. Translated by G. K. Nariman with Supplementary Appendices from Arabic Sources. Bombay, 1918.

Jackson, A. V. Williams: Zoroaster, the Prophet of Ancient Iran. New York, 1899.

Jackson, A. V, Williams: Die Iranische Religion. In *Grundriss der Iranischen Philologie, vol. 2, p. 612-708. Strassburg, 1896-1904.*

Jackson, A. V. Williams: Zoroastrian Studies. New York, 1928.

Mills, L. H.: Zarathushtra and the Greeks. Leipzig. 1903. 1904.

Mills, L. H.: Zarathushtra, Philo, the Achaemenids and Israel. Leipzip, 1905, 1906.

Mills, L. H.: Avesta Eschatology compared with the Books of Daniel and Revelations. Chicago, 1908.

Spiegel Memorial Volume: Edited by Jivanji Jamshedji Modi. Bombay, 1908.

Bibliography

Aerpatastan: Translated from the Avesta-Pahlavi texts by S.J. Bulsara. Bombay, 1915.

Andarz-i Atarpat-i Maraspand: The Pahlavi text, edited and translated by Peshutan Dastur Behramji Sanjana. Bombay, 1885.

Andarz-i-Khusro-i-Kavatan: The Pahlavi text, edited and translated by Peshutan Dastur Behramji Sanjana; Bombay, 1885.

Aogemadaecha: The Pazand and Sanskrit texts, edited and translated into German by Wilhelm Geiger. Erlangen, 1878.

Aogemadaecha: Translated into English by James Darmesteter. In Sacred Books of the East, Vol. 4, second edition.

Aogemadaecha: The Pahlavi Texts of, Edited by B. N. Dhabhar in Indo-Iranian Studies in honour of Dastur D. P. Sanjana, London, 1925.

Arda Viraf: The Pahlavi text, edited and translated by Hoshangji Jamaspji Asa, Martin Hang, and E. W. West. Bombay, 1872.

Arda Viraf Nameh: The Original Pahlavi Text with Persian version of Zartosht Behrain in verse, edited by Kaikhusru J. Jamasp Asa. Bombay, 1902.

Avesta: The Sacred Books of thë Parsis. Edited by Karl F. Geldner. Stuttgart, 1885-1896. (For Yt. 22-24 and the Avestan Fragments see N. L. Westergaard's Zendavesta, Copenhagen, 1852-1854.).

Avesta: Translated into English by James Darmesteter and L. H. Mills. In Sacred Books of the East, vols, 4, 23, 31.

Avesta: Pahlavi, and Ancient Persian Studies in Honour of the late Shams-ul Ulama Dastur Peshotanji Behramji Sanjana. Strassburg, 1904.

Bahman Yasht: Translated from the Pahlavi text by E. W. West. In Sacred Books of the East, vol. 5.

Balsara, P. P.: *Ancient Iran. Its contribution to Human progress.* Bombay, 1936.

Benveniste, Emile: *The Persian Religion according to the chief Greek Texts.* Paris, 1929.

Bharucha, Sheriarji D: *A Brief Sketch of the Zoroastrian Religion and Customs.* Bombay, 1893.

Bilimoria, N. F.: *Zoroastrianism in the Light of Theosophy.* Bombay, 1896.

Bradke, P. von: *Dyaus, Asura, Ahura Mazda.* Halle, 1885.

Brodbeck, A.: *Zoroaster.* Leipzig, 1893.

Buch, M. A.: *Zoroastrian Ethics.* Baroda, 1919.

Bundahishn: Translated from the Pahlavi text by E. W. West. In Sacred Books of the East, vol. 5.

Bundahishn: An Untranslated Chapter of the Bundehesh. Edited and translated by Jivanji Jamshedji Modi, in Journal of the Bombay Branch of the Royal Asiatic Society. Bombay, 1902.

Bundahishn: Edited by T. D. and B. T. Anklesaria. Bombay, 1908.

Cama Memorial Volume: Edited by J. J. Modi. Bombay, 1900.

Carter, G. W.: *Zoroastrianism and Judaism.* Boston, 1918.

Casartelli, L. C.: *The Philosophy of the Mazdayasnian Religion under the Sassanids.* Translated from the French by Firoz Jamaspji Jamasp Asa. Bombay, 1889.

Chatterjee, J. M.: *The Ethical Conceptions of the Gatha.* Navsari, 1932.

Cheyne, T. K.: *Book of Psalms, its origin, and its relation to Zoroastrianism.* In Semitic Studies in Memory of Rev. Dr. A. Kohut. Berlin, 1897.

Collected Sanskrit Writings of the Parsis: Part 1. Khorda-Avesta. Part 2. Ijisni. Part 3. Mainyoi Khard. Part 4. Skanda Gumani Gujara. Edited by Sheriarji D. Bharucha. Bombay, 1906-1913.

Cumont, Franz: *The Mysteries of Mithra.* Translated from the French by T. J. McCormack. Chicago, 1903.

Dabistan: Translated from the original Persian by Shea and Troyer. 3 vols. Paris, 1843.

Dadachanji, F. K.: *Light of the Avesta and the Gathas.* Bombay, 1913.

Dadistan-i Dinik: Translated from the Pahlavi text by E. W. West. In Sacred Books of the East, vol. 18.

Dastur, M. N.: *The Moral and Ethical Teachings of Zarathushtra.* Bombay, 1928.

Dawson, M. M.: *The Ethical Religion of Zoroaster.* New York, 1931

Desatir: Published by Mulla Firuz Bin Kaus. Persian and English. 2 vols. Bombay, 1818.

Dhalla, M. N.: *Zoroastrian Theology.* New York, 1914.

Dina i Mainu i Khrat: Edited by Darab P. Sanjana. Bombay, 1895.

Dinkard: Books 3-9. Edited and translated from the Pahlavi text by Peshutan and Darab Sanjana. Vols. 1-19. Bombay. 1874-1919.

Dinkard: Books 7-9. Translated from the Pahlavi text by E. W. West. In Sacred Books of the East, vols. 37, 47.

Dinkard: The Complete Text. Edited by D. M. Madan. 2 vols. Bombay, 1911.

Dinshaw, V.: The Date and Country of Zarathushtra. Hyderabad (Deccan), 1912.

Encyclopaedia of Religion and Ethics: Edited by James Hastings. 12 vols. Edinburgh, 1908-1921.

Epistles of Manushchihar: Translated from the Pahlavi text by E. W. West. In Sacred Books of the East, vol. 18.

Firdausi: Translated into Engiish by A. G. Warner and E. Warner. vols. 1-9. London, 1905-1925.

Fluegel, M: *The Zend-Avesta and Eastern Religions.* Baltimore, 1898.

Fox, W. S., and Pemberton, R. E. K.: *Passages in Greek and Latin Literature relating to Zoroaster and Zoroastrianism* ,translated into English in the Journal of the K. R. Cama Oriental Institute, No.14. Bombay, 1929.

Ganj-i Shayigan: The Pahlavi text, edited and translated by Peshutan Dastur Behramji Sanjana, Bombay, 1885.

Gatha: Translated into English by J. M. Chatterjee. Navsari, 1933.

Gathas: Translated into English by K. E. Punegar. In the Journal of the K. R. Cama Oriental Institute, No. 12. Bombay, 1928.

Geiger, Wilhelm: *Civilization of the Eastern Iranians in Ancient Times.* Translated from the German by Darab Dastur Peshutan Sanjana. 2 vols. London, 1885, 1886.

Geiger, W., and Windischmann, Fr.: *Zarathushtra in the Gathas and in the Greek and Roman Classics.* Translated by Darab P. Sanjana. Leipzig, 1897.

Gottheil, R. J. H.: *References to Zoroaster in Syriac and Arabic Literature.* In Classical Studies in Honour of Henry Drisler. New York, 1894.

Govindacharya, A.: *Mazdaism in the Light of Vishnuism.* Mysore, 1913.

Gray, L. H.: *The Foundations of the Iranian Religions.* Bombay, 1929.

Hadokht Nask: The Pahlavi text, edited and translated by Hoshangji Jamaspji Asa, Martin Haug, and E. W. West. Bombay, 1872.

Haug, Martin: *Essays On the Sacred Language, Writings, and Religion of the Parsis.* 3d ed. Edited and enlarged by E. W. West. London, 1884.

Henry, Victor: Le Parsisme. Paris, 1905.

Hodivala, S. K.: *Zarathushtra and His Contemporaries in the Rig Veda.* Bombay, 1913.

Hodivala, S. K.: *Parsis of Ancient India.* Bombay, 1920.

Hodivala, S. K.: *Indo-Iranian Religion with parallelisms in the Hindu and Zoroastrian Scriptures.* Bombay, 1925.

Hoshang Memorial Volume: Bombay, 1918.

Indo-Iranian Studies: Being Commemorative Papers contributed by European, American and Indian Scholars in honor of Dastur Darab P. Sanjana. London, 1925.

Inostranzev, M.: *Iranian Influence on Moslem Literature.* Translated by G. K. Nariman with Supplementary Appendices from Arabic Sources. Bombay, 1918.

Jackson, A. V. Williams: *Zoroaster, the Prophet of Ancient Iran.* New York, 1899.

Jackson, A. V. Williams: *Zoroastrian Studies.* New York, 1928.

Jackson, A. V. Williams: *Researches in Manichaeism.* New York, 1932.

Jamaspi: Edited and translated from the Pahlavi-Pazand iexts by Jivanji Jamshedji Modi. Bombay, 1903.

Jamsetjee Jejeebhoy Madressa Jubilee Volume: Bombay, 1914.

Kapadia, S. A.: *The Teachings of Zoroaster and the Philosophy of the Parsi Religion.* London, 1905.

Karaka, Dosabhai F.: *History of the Parsis.* 2 vols. London, 1884.

King, L. W., and Thompson, R. C.: T*he Sculptures and Inscriptions of Darius the Great on the Rock of Behistun in Persia:* a new Collation of the Persian, Susian, and Babylonian Texts. London, 1907.

Kohut, Alexander: *The Jewish Angelology and Demonology based upon Parsism.* Translated from the German by K. R. Cama. Bombay, 1883.

Lazarus, M. E.: *The Zend-Avesta and Solar Religions.* New York, 1852.

Lehmann, Edvard: *Zarathushtra.* Kobenhavn, 1899.

Lord, Henry: *The Religion of the Parsees.* London, 1630.

Madan, D. M.: *Discourses on Iranian Literature.* Bombay. 1909.

McNeile, H.: *The Avesta and the Bible.* Bombay, 1905.

Mills, L. H.: *Zarathushtra and the Greeks*. Leipzig. 1903. 1904.

Mills, L. H.: *Zarathushtra, Philo, the Achaemenids and Israel*. Leipzip, 1905, 1906.

Mills, L. H.: *Avesta Eschatology compared with the Books of Daniel and Revelations.* Chicago, 1908.

Mills, L. H.: *Our Own Religion in Ancient Persia.* 1913.

Minu-i Khrat: Translated from the Pahlavi text by E. W. West. In Sacred Books of the East, vol. 24.

Mistri, R. H.: *Zoroaster and Zoroastrianism.* Bombay, 1906.

Modi, Jivanji J.: *The Religious System of the Parsees.* Bombay, 1885.

Modi, Jivanji J.: *The Parsis at the court of Akbat and Dastur Meherjee Rana.* Bombay, 1903.

Modi, Jivanji J.: *A few events in the early history of the Parsis and their dates.* Bombay, 1905.

Modi, J. J.: *The Religious Ceremonies and Customs of the Parsees*. Bombay, 1922.

Modi Memorial Volume: Bombay, 1930.

Moffatt, J.: *Zoroastrianism and Primitive Christianity.* In Hibbert Journal, 1903.

Moulton, James H.: *Early Religious Poetry of Persia.* Cambridge, 1911.

Moulton, James H.: *Early Zoroastrianism.* London, 1913.

Moulton, James H.: *The Teachings of Zarathushtra.* Bombay, 1916.

Moulton, James H.: *The Treasure of the Magi.* Oxford, 1917.

Namakiha-i Manushchihar: *The Epistles of Manushchihar.* Edited by B. N. Dhabhar. Bombay, 1912.

Nirangastan: Translated from the Avesta-Pahlavi text by S. J. Bulsara. Bombay, 1915.

Oriental Studies in honour of Cursetji Erachji Pavri: London, 1933.

Pahlavi Zend-i Vohuman Yasht: Edited by Kaikobad A. Nosherwan. Poona, 1899.

Pavri, Jal C.: *The Zoroastrian Doctrine of a Future Life.* New York, 1926.

Pazend Texts: Collected and Collated by E. K. Antia. Bombay, 1909. Two Afrins, three Patits tr. into Eng. from Spiegel's German translation by A. H. Bleeck in Khordah Avesta Hertford, 1864. Seven Afrins, Sitayishes, and other Pazend prayers tr. into Gujarati by Phiroze E. Masani in Pazend Prayers Series Nos. 1, 2, 3. Bombay, 1916, 1920, 1931.

Rapp, A.: *The Religion and Customs of the Persians and other Iranians as described by the Grecian and Roman Authors.* Translated from the German by K. R. Cama. Bombay, 1876-1879.

Rawlinson, George: *The Five Great Monarchies of the Ancient Eastern World, Chaldea, Assyria, Babylon, Media, and Persia.* 4 vols. London, 1862-1867.

Rawlinson, George: *The Sixth Great Oriental Monarchy.* London, 1813.

Rawlinson, George: *The Seventh Great Oriental Monarchy.* London, 1816.

Rezwi, T.: Parsis: *A People of the Book.* Calcutta, 1928.

Sad Dar: Translated from the Pahlavi-Pazand text by E. W. West. In Sacred Books of the East, vol. 24.

Sad Dar: Edited by B. N. Dhabhar. Bombay, 1909.

Sanjana, Darab P: *Zarathushtra in the Gathas and the Greek and Roman Classics.* Translated from the German of Geiger and Windischmann. Leipzig, 1897.

Sanjana, Rastamji E.: *Zarathushtra and Zarathushtrianism in the Avesta.* Leipzig, 1906.

Sanjana, Rastamji E.: *The Parsi Book of Books, the Zend-Avesta.* Bombay, 1924.

Sanjana, Rastamji E.: *Spiritualism through Zoroastrian Eyes.* Bombay, 1929.

Shatroiha-i Airan: Translated from the Pahlavi text by Jivanji Jamshedji Modi. Bombay, 1899.

Shayast la-Shayast: Translated from the Pahlavi text by E. W. West. In Sacred Books of the East, vol. 5.

Shayast-ne-Shayast: Edited, transliterated, and translated by Jehangir C. Tavadia. Hamburg, 1930.

Shikand Gumanik Vijar: Translated from the Pahlavi-Pazand text by E. W. West. In Sacred Books of the East, vol. 24.

Spiegel Memorial Volume: Edited by Jivanji Jamshedji Modi. Bombay, 1908.

Taraporewala, Irach, J. S: *Some Aspects of the History of Zoroastrianism.* Bombay, 1928.

Index

A

B

C

D

E

F

G

H

I

J

K

S

T

V

W

X

Y

Z